The
Criminal Justice
NETWORK

SECOND EDITION

■

An Introduction

STEVEN M. COX / JOHN E. WADE

Western Illinois University

wcb

Wm. C. Brown Publishers
Dubuque, Iowa

Cover design by Laurie Entringer.

Copyright © 1985, 1989 by Wm. C. Brown Publishers. All rights
reserved

Library of Congress Catalog Card Number: 88–71924

ISBN 0–697–03177–2

Printed in the United States of America by Wm. C. Brown Publishers
2460 Kerper Boulevard, Dubuque, IA 52001

10 9 8 7 6 5 4 3 2 1

Contents

3 Politics and the Criminal Justice Network   35

4 Discretionary Justice   49

5 Types of Crime: I   61

6   Types of Crime: II   81

7   The Police: History and Development   93

15 Prisoners' Rights and Alternatives to Incarceration   239

16 Juvenile Justice   249

Preface

In this text, we have attempted to provide a comprehensive, practical view of criminal justice in the United States. We believe the criminal justice network can best be understood by comparing the day-to-day, practical aspects of the network with the theoretical model upon which the network is based. In our view, this approach involves a thorough examination of the role of the public, the uses and abuses of discretion throughout the system, and the effects of political considerations on the day-to-day operations of the criminal justice network. For example, we feel it is important to recognize the public as the most crucial (and most often neglected) component of the criminal justice network. Without public cooperation, the police would be severely hampered, the courts would not be properly utilized, probation and parole would be totally unworkable, and the entire system could not be financed. Similarly, the importance of discretion in the criminal justice network cannot be underestimated. Discretion plays an important role at all levels of the network from the use of discretion by citizens in calling the police, to the use of discretion by police officers and departments in determining how to handle calls from the public, to the use of discretion by the prosecutor in deciding whether a particular case should be prosecuted, to judicial discretion in sentencing.

Superimposed on the criminal justice network is the political structure of the society in which the network exists, and the influence of political decisions and considerations cannot be overlooked.

In the following pages, we have tried to take these practical aspects of criminal justice into consideration as we discuss the various components, procedures, and bases of criminal justice in the United States. We have attempted to define technical terms clearly when they are presented, and we have included personal experiences and practical examples in an attempt to present the introductory student with a basic understanding of both the theoretical and practical aspects of the criminal justice network.

In chapter 1, the issue of whether or not we have a criminal justice "system" in the United States is raised, as is the issue of "justice." Also in this chapter, we take a close look at the role of the public in criminal justice and at some of the underlying assumptions of the criminal justice network.

The relationships among law, criminal law, and justice are explored in chapter 2. The origins, nature, and functions of law are discussed, and law is examined as one type of social control.

Chapter 3 stresses the importance of political considerations in the day-to-day operations of the criminal justice network. The pervasive influence of politics, from the selection of local fire and police commissioners, prosecutors, and judges to the appointments made by the president of the United States to fill Supreme Court vacancies, is considered. Relationships among power, authority, and political position are examined in order to better understand why some segments of the public feel powerless and perceive the criminal justice process in the United States as basically "unjust." We point out that politics play a major role in criminal justice by changing many of the ideals of the "system" into practical realities. The chapter concludes with a discussion of some of the positive and negative consequences of political considerations for the criminal justice network.

Chapter 4 deals with discretionary justice. The major premise of this chapter is that discretion is a normal, and desirable, part of the criminal justice network. The exercise of discretion by the public, police, prosecutors and defense counselors, judges, and correctional officials is discussed in terms of such everyday occurrences as testifying in court, setting bail, sentencing, and granting parole or probation.

In chapters 5 and 6, we discuss various types of crime, beginning with the distinction between felonies and misdemeanors. The chapters deal with white-collar crimes and crimes without victims, or as we prefer to call them, "crimes without complainants." The feasibility of enforcing laws dealing with these types of offenses is discussed in terms of public perceptions; the exercise of discretion; and the influence of politics, power, and status.

The police are the topic of chapters 7 and 8. We begin with a brief historical overview of the police and go on to discuss the various functions and responsibilities of the police in contemporary society. Positive and negative aspects of the traditional police organization are discussed and some recent organizational innovations are introduced. Procedures employed by the police in processing offenders are described in the overall context of the criminal justice network. Legal requirements related to arrest, search, and seizure are analyzed in terms of both theory and practice. Selection and training requirements are also discussed.

An overview of the courts is provided in chapter 9. The dual court system employed in the United States is discussed, and both state and federal systems are explained. The role of the grand jury, the use of the information, and the importance of jury trials are discussed, and the chapter concludes with the presentation and analysis of some pressing problems of contemporary courts.

In chapter 10, court personnel, including the prosecutor, defense counsel, and judge, are considered. The functions and responsibilities of these officials are discussed, as are methods of selection, the exercise of discretion, and the importance to each of plea bargaining.

Chapter 11 deals with pretrial procedures from initial appearance and the setting of bail through the preliminary hearing. Different types of pleas, the arraignment process, the rules of discovery and disclosure, and other pretrial options are considered.

The criminal trial itself is the subject of chapter 12. The chapter begins with a comparison of jury and bench trials, and includes an analysis of reasons why the defendant might choose one instead of the other. Moving through the trial sequentially, we explain both the theoretical and practical significance of opening statements, rules of evidence, and various motions and objections that may be encountered. Closing arguments, instructions, jury deliberations and verdicts, and sentencing and appeals processes are also discussed.

In chapter 13, the roles of victims and witnesses in the criminal justice network are discussed. The fact that victims and friends of victims help shape public perceptions of the network is stressed, as are the rights of the victim—until recently a largely forgotten person in the criminal justice network. Victim compensation and restitution programs are also described.

Jails and prisons are the topics of chapters 14 and 15. These chapters focus on the purposes and uses of correctional facilities, both in theory and practice. Problems with incarceration are discussed as are prisoners' rights, capital punishment, and alternatives to incarceration.

Chapter 16 deals with the juvenile justice network. A brief historical overview is presented, followed by a discussion of juvenile justice procedures. The chapter concludes with a look at some of the problems faced by contemporary juvenile justice practitioners.

Chapter 17 focuses on careers in criminal justice.

Acknowledgments

A number of people have helped in the preparation of this book. For their encouragement and assistance we would like to thank Professor Donald J. Adamchak, Professor John J. Conrad, Dr. Rodney Fink, Dr. Robert Fischer, Dr. Giri Raj Gupta, William C. Flint, Glenn Hedenberg, and Professor Robert W. Whittenbarger.

For substantive contributions we would like to thank Professor Dennis C. Bliss, Professor Stan Cunningham, Professor G. E. Davila, Professor Gary S. Foster, the late Professor Robert Jaquith, Professor William E. Johnson, Ray Kasak, the late Jerri Pecharich, and Professor Richard Brede.

Special thanks to Joyce Becker, and Sheila, Matthew, and Melissa Cox for their patience, support, and understanding. Thanks also to Bud and Freda Wade.

Criminal Justice in the U.S.: A Network of Interaction

1

Key Terms

criminal justice network	public
territorial jealousy	unofficial probation
crime control model	presumption of innocence
due process model	justice

The **criminal justice network** in the United States has been greatly discussed, maligned, and misunderstood. The discrepancies between the "ideal" network and the "real" network are perhaps more numerous than the similarities. What are the assumptions upon which the network is based and what are the day-to-day realities by which the network operates?

The criminal justice network is often illustrated through the use of a flowchart that shows each component of the system receiving cases from, and passing cases on to, other components (figure 1.1). The chart indicates that the police process some alleged offenders and send them on to the prosecutor, who passes some on to court officials, who pass some on to correctional officials, who eventually return some to the society from which they originally came. While the flowchart approach is not totally inaccurate, it is somewhat misleading in that it fails to indicate:

1. the routine pursuit of different, sometimes incompatible, goals by various network components;
2. the effects of feedback based upon personal relationships inside and outside the criminal justice network;
3. the importance of political considerations;
4. the widespread, routine use of discretion at all levels of the network;
5. the centrality of the role the public has in criminal justice.

This chart seeks to present a simple, yet comprehensive view of the movement of cases through the criminal justice system. Procedures in individual jurisdictions may vary from the pattern shown here. The differing line weights indicate the relative volumes of cases disposed of at various points in the system, but this is only suggestive since no nationwide data of this sort exists.

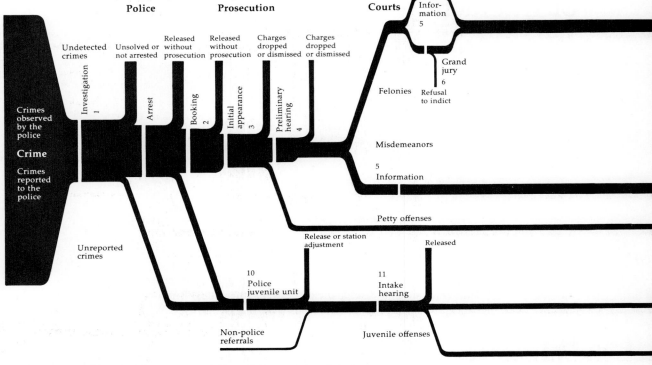

1. May continue until trial.
2. Administrative record of arrest. First step at which temporary release on bail may be available.
3. Before magistrate, commissioner, or justice of peace. Formal notice of charge, advice of rights. Bail set. Summary trials for petty offenses usually conducted here without further processing.
4. Preliminary testing of evidence against defendant. Charge may be reduced. No separate preliminary hearing for misdemeanors in some systems.

5. Charge filed by prosecutor on basis of information submitted by police or citizens. Alternative to grand jury indictment, often used in felonies, almost always in misdemeanors.
6. Reviews whether government evidence sufficient to justify trial. Some states have no grand jury system, others seldom use it.
7. Appearance for plea; defendant elects trial by judge or jury (if available); counsel for indigent usually appointed here in felonies. Often not at all in other cases.

Figure 1.1 A general view of the criminal justice system. *The President's Commission on Law Enforcement and the Administration of Justice.* The Challenge of Crime in a Free Society *(1967), 72, 73.*

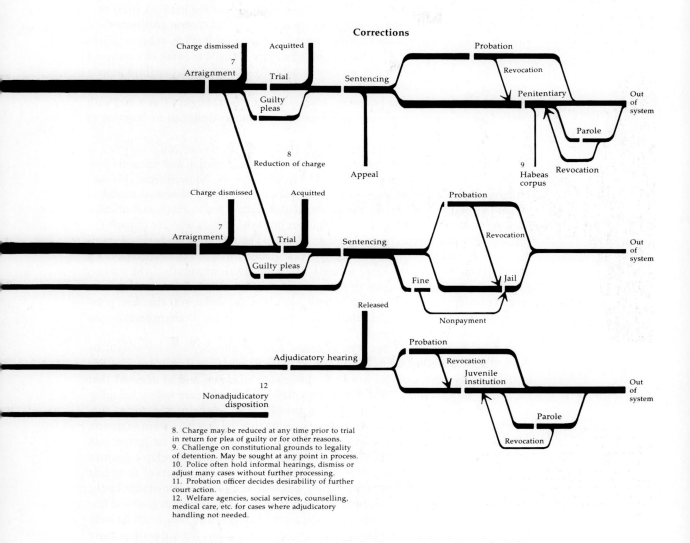

Corrections

Charge dismissed   Acquitted

7

Arraignment   Trial   Sentencing   Probation

Revocation

Guilty pleas   Penitentiary   Out of system

8   Parole

Reduction of charge   Appeal

9   Revocation

Habeas corpus

Charge dismissed   Acquitted

7

Arraignment   Trial   Sentencing   Probation

Revocation

Guilty pleas   Out of system

Fine   Jail

Nonpayment

Released

Adjudicatory hearing   Probation

Revocation

Juvenile institution   Out of system

12

Nonadjudicatory disposition   Parole

Revocation

8. Charge may be reduced at any time prior to trial in return for plea of guilty or for other reasons.
9. Challenge on constitutional grounds to legality of detention. May be sought at any point in process.
10. Police often hold informal hearings, dismiss or adjust many cases without further processing.
11. Probation officer decides desirability of further court action.
12. Welfare agencies, social services, counselling, medical care, etc. for cases where adjudicatory handling not needed.

The flowchart approach often leads to statements about what the network does or does not *do,* leading us to overlook the fact that it is not the network itself that acts or fails to act, but individuals who interact or fail to interact (subject, to be sure, to some structural constraints—again, of human origin) to achieve differentially perceived goals. Therefore, it may be more realistic to think of a criminal justice "network" consisting of a web of constantly changing relationships among individuals, some of whom are directly involved in criminal justice pursuits, others of whom are not. For our purposes, a network may be thought of as a net with intersecting lines of communication among components designed to function in a specific manner.

Perhaps the most familiar example of a network is the tv or radio network in which stations share many programs, but in which each station also presents programs that are not aired by other stations in the network. Viewed from this perspective, the criminal justice network appears as a three-dimensional model in which the public, legislators, police, prosecutor, judge, and correctional officials are involved in interactions with one another and with others who are outside the traditionally conceived criminal justice system. The everyday business of criminal justice is accomplished, according to this model, through negotiations among any or all involved parties[1] (see figure 1.2). In any given negotiation, the various parties may pursue the same or different goals. Thus, interaction among concerned parties may be influenced by both overt (visible) and covert (hidden) pressures and considerations, which the flowchart fails to indicate. Perhaps an example will help clarify this approach.

Suppose a small child has been molested and the offender is being sought by the police. Certain segments of the public (parents with small children who live in the locality, for example) are likely to become alarmed and to demand that the police "do something." The mass media may publicize the case widely, bringing additional pressure on the police to find the offender, on the prosecutor to successfully prosecute the guilty party, on the judge to hand down a severe sentence, and, eventually, on parole board members not to grant parole. The police may want very badly to catch the offender in order to maintain or develop a positive public image. The prosecutor, who may be thinking about the effects of favorable or unfavorable publicity on an upcoming election, may want a conviction badly. Thus, both the police and the prosecutor are pursuing a common goal—crime control—but either or both may be pursuing additional, different goals as well. The police chief, for example, may use this case as a basis for requesting more resources, the public may demand more patrols, and political officials may call for the chief's dismissal for failing to prevent such incidents.

Let us suppose that the police arrest a person they think may have committed the crime discussed above, but that they do not have what they consider to be a strong case. They need, they believe, a confession before they can present a reasonable case to the prosecutor. In order to obtain such a confession, they may pressure the alleged offender to talk to them so that they can clear the crime by arrest and relieve public pressure. At this point, the prosecutor may step in and tell the police not to use undue pressure, to see that the alleged offender clearly understands his or her rights, and to make certain that the arrestee has access to a lawyer if he or she wants one. These statements by the prosecutor may make it more difficult for the police to obtain their confession and may cause conflict between the police and the prosecutor. Still, both are pursuing the same goal—crime control. In our hypothetical case, the police are primarily concerned with obtaining the facts to control crime, while the prosecutor is also concerned with due process, which may at times make crime control more difficult.[2]

To take our example one step further, we might ask why the prosecutor would caution the police as indicated above. Using the network approach to criminal justice, it becomes clear that the prosecutor is bringing the courts, political considerations, and public opinion into the interactive network. The United States Supreme Court Justices have ruled that due process must be followed by all criminal justice network personnel, and their decisions have limited police practices concerning search, seizure, and interrogation.[3]

Further, these rulings are supposed to represent the will of the people as expressed in the First, Fifth, and Fourteenth Amendments to the Constitution (see appendix). Of course, the manner in which the Constitution is interpreted at any given point in time depends, to some extent, upon the composition of the Supreme Court, which depends upon political appointments made by the president, who depends upon votes from the public for obtaining office. Thus, it can be clearly seen that decisions in cases in other locales made by criminal justice personnel who have no knowledge of or concern with this particular case affect this case. To be sure, any case dealt with by the criminal justice network can be analyzed in this fashion, and a great many activities and decisions that otherwise appear to make little or no sense can be understood. So, we believe the best way to view the criminal justice system is as a network of interrelated, but independent individuals who are subject to many internal and external pressures, and who work under (and are at the same time developing) a set of operating procedures in pursuit of similar, but not always identical, goals. While public and political influence, legal requirements, and discretionary justice pervade the entire network, each party in the network has goals and problems not shared by other parties. For example, the police are concerned with making arrests, the prosecutor with obtaining convictions, the judge with providing impartial trials, and correctional officials with custody and/or rehabilitation. While the judge may also be concerned with rehabilitation and custody (in terms of sentencing), she or he is not directly concerned with the physical act of making an arrest, prosecutors are not directly concerned with keeping people in custody, and correctional officials are not directly concerned with obtaining convictions. Each party, however, is indirectly concerned with what all of the other parties do. Criminal justice, then, is not a one-way street with cases and information flowing only in one direction. It

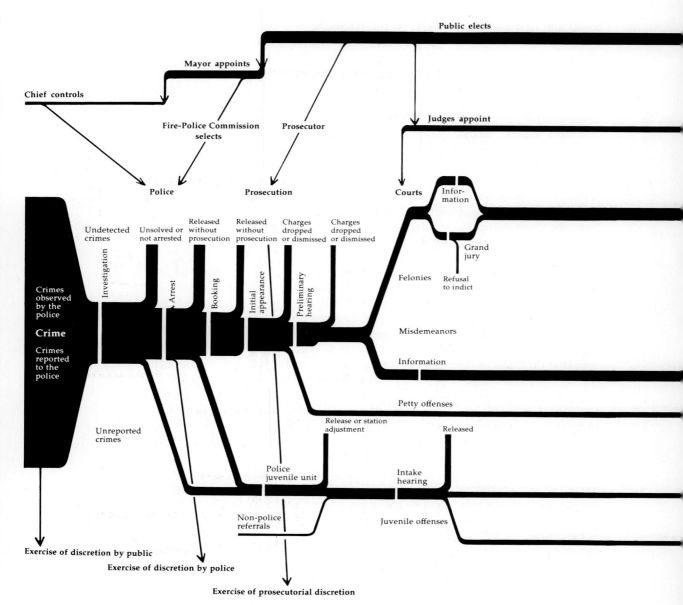

Figure 1.2 A network view of criminal justice. *Modified from The President's Commission on Law Enforcement and the Administration of Justice.* The Challenge of Crime in a Free Society *(1967), 72, 73.*

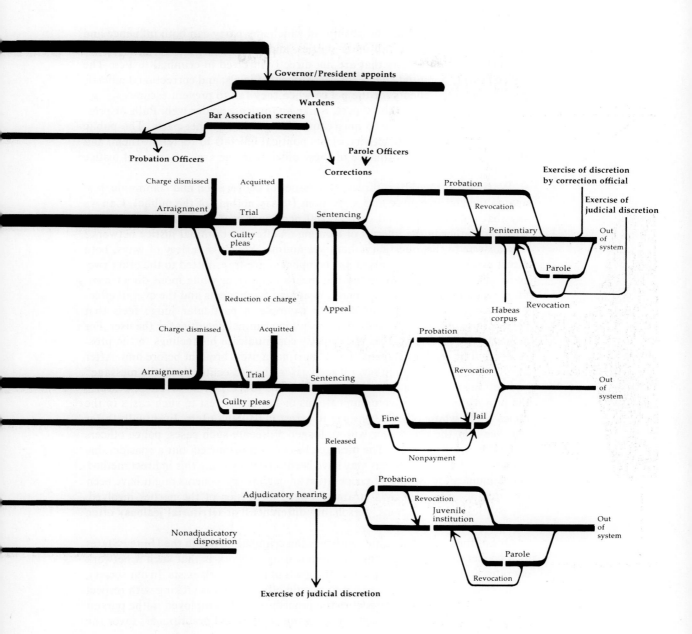

Governor/President appoints

Wardens

Bar Association screens

Probation Officers

Parole Officers

Corrections

Charge dismissed   Acquitted   Probation   Exercise of discretion
by correction official

Arraignment   Trial   Sentencing   Revocation   Exercise of
judicial discretion

Guilty
pleas   Penitentiary   Out
of
system

Reduction of charge   Parole

Appeal   Revocation

Habeas
corpus

Charge dismissed   Acquitted   Probation

Arraignment   Trial   Sentencing   Revocation   Out
of
system

Guilty pleas   Fine   Jail

Released   Nonpayment

Probation

Adjudicatory hearing   Revocation
Juvenile
institution   Out
of
system

Nonadjudicatory
disposition   Parole

Revocation

Exercise of judicial discretion

consists of a network of relationships in which any party can both influence and be influenced by any or all other parties, and all may be influenced by public opinion and other factors that are not directly involved in criminal justice. The police provide potential clients for correctional officials, and correctional officials provide potential clients for the police when they fail to prevent escape.

Criminal justice, in this respect, is like an intricate spider web. Pulls or pressures on one part of the web may cause changes in all other parts. The public defines socially harmful activity, elects political officials to represent them, and then evaluates the performance of these officials in the area of criminal justice as well as in other areas.

We have yet to address directly the issues of cooperation and communication among the police, courts, and corrections (to say nothing of the public). Can we say that police, court, and correctional personnel cooperate and communicate with each other in the interest of forming an effective criminal justice network? The answer to this question is both yes and no. Yes, in a variety of ways, both direct and indirect, the goals of one component are transmitted to the other two. Indirect communication is often the means employed, while more direct communication might improve cooperation among components and the overall effectiveness of the network. Suppose, for example, a particular judge feels that personal use of marijuana should not result in criminal penalties for the user. For a variety of reasons, he does not directly communicate his feelings to the prosecutor, but he imposes no penalties on marijuana users brought before him. After unsuccessfully prosecuting several such cases, the prosecutor "gets the message" and refuses to prosecute such cases before this judge. For a variety of reasons, the prosecutor may not communicate his or her disinterest in such cases to the police chief, whose officers continue to arrest marijuana users. Eventually, after they see that the prosecutor will no longer prosecute such cases, police officers stop making such arrests. The message has been transmitted, but a considerable amount of time and resources may have been wasted by using this indirect method of communication. Similarly, cooperation among the components might have been considerably improved by a straightforward discussion of the parties involved, but political considerations, personality differences, or **territorial jealousy** often hamper such discussion.

One of the major difficulties with viewing criminal justice in the United States as a cooperating, goal-sharing, communicating network is that such a network operates best when consensus about the goals of the network exists. In our society, such consensus exists with respect to certain offenses, but is lacking with respect to many others and with respect to the procedures to be employed in the pursuit of alleged offenders. On the one hand, many citizens and practitioners favor the

Traffic Control—One Police Function.
Bob Eckert, EKM-Nepenthe

Political Campaigning.
James L. Ballard

Probation Officer—Friend or Foe?
John R. Maher, EKM-Nepenthe

Typical Courtroom Scene.
James L. Shaffer

Publics—Critical Components of Criminal Justice.
Richard L. Good

crime control model, which allows for the arrest and prosecution of individuals who are known to be factually guilty of committing a crime. On the other hand, many prefer the **due process model,** which requires that evidence of guilt presented in court be obtained according to legal guidelines. For instance, the police might receive a tip from an anonymous caller who states that a specific individual living in a specific hotel room has a kilo of cocaine in his possession. Using the crime control model, the police break down the door to the room, find the cocaine, arrest and charge the offender, and use the cocaine as evidence in the ensuing trial. Under the due process model, the police must demonstrate that the tip came from a reliable informant, obtain a proper search warrant, and maintain a proper chain of evidence, or the cocaine will be inadmissable as evidence in court and the defendant will be acquitted. That is, even though he was factually guilty of possessing the cocaine, he is not legally guilty because the procedures established to safeguard the rights of citizens were violated in this case. The emphasis on crime control versus due process shifts with changes in political administrations, public opinion, and changes in the judiciary, demonstrating the importance of understanding criminal justice as a network and the lack of consensus as to how best to proceed in dealing with crime and criminals.

Similarly, when the public is uncertain about the desirability of rehabilitation, the enforcement of morality, or the best way to punish offenders, it is difficult for practitioners to cooperate and share goals, and the use of discretion is widespread. The exercise of discretion may further confuse both the public and other practitioners. For example, in an attempt to avoid the problems of indirect communication mentioned above, a prosecutor recently announced at a news conference that he would no longer prosecute individuals charged with possessing small amounts of marijuana for personal use. Within a week, several citizens' groups announced that they would try to oust the prosecutor. In addition, several judges commented privately that the prosecutor was overstepping his authority, and some local police officials indicated that it was decisions such as this that made their job difficult. The important point to note is this: the prosecutor was simply making a formal announcement of a policy that had been in existence for some time, and with which none of the above-mentioned parties disagreed until it was formally announced. Viewing criminal justice as a web of interacting parties, each with a set of goals that may or may not all be compatible with those of others, makes it easier to understand how such events can occur. This view is especially important when we realize that we are not dealing with a small number of criminal justice agencies, but with thousands of agencies—each with its own regional variations and each with its own personnel. In addition, we have said very little up to this point about perhaps the most important party to any criminal justice network, the public.

The Forgotten Component: The Public's Role in the Criminal Justice Network

The **public** is the most important part of the criminal justice network for a variety of reasons. Before discussing these reasons, it should be pointed out that the term *public* is somewhat misleading. Actually, we are not dealing with one large homogeneous group called a public, but with thousands of different publics. These publics are divided by factors such as geographical area, race, sex, age, social class, and degree of adherence to law, to mention just a few. Many of these publics have unique interests and concerns that separate them on most issues from other publics. In short, there is no one, united, consensual group of citizens who make up a single public. Citizens comprise a variety of different publics. As we shall see, this heterogeneity is extremely important for criminal justice. At least as important, however, is the fact that, with respect to any given issue, many of these publics are apathetic (unconcerned) about the criminal justice network. A great deal of what happens in the name of criminal justice goes largely unnoticed by most citizens, and pressures to modify the network or the activities that occur within it are often brought to bear by small, vocal groups who have an interest in a particular issue, but who become apathetic again once this issue is resolved.

Regardless of which of the many publics we are talking about, it is important to recognize the role that each may play in the criminal justice network. First, the vast majority of social control in any society is performed not by the police and courts, but by various segments of the public (families and peer groups, for example). Second, these publics provide resources for and evaluations of the entire network. Without public support, police, court, and correctional officials would be helpless to achieve their goals. If citizens refuse to provide information to the police, the police (a largely reactive body) cannot perform their duties. Successful prosecution (or defense) is impossible if members of the public refuse to testify. Ex-convicts cannot be reintegrated into society without the cooperation of the citizenry. Without financial resources provided by the public, none of the criminal justice agencies could hire new personnel, develop new programs, or improve efficiency. From beginning to end, then, there is no doubt that the public (all of the many publics or segments) plays a major role in criminal justice and should not be overlooked when we discuss the criminal justice network, since each segment wants and expects something from representatives of that network. Some want specific types of laws enforced (e.g., liquor violations) and specific types of offenders taken into custody (troublesome youth), some want their property returned, and some want a police report so that insurance claims for lost or stolen property can be settled. When a prisoner on prison furlough commits a crime, the public often demands either a cutback or the elimination of such programs. Most generally stated, the public wants their real or imagined problems to be dealt with and resolved officially. In short, "publics" are involved in the criminal justice network in a variety of ways, and this involvement (or lack of involvement) is crucial to the functioning of the network.[4]

Church robbery attempt ends in death

FORT LAUDERDALE, Fla. (AP)—A gunman who was jumped by worshipers after he tried to hold up a congregation during an evening church service collapsed and died less than two hours later, officials said.

"Naturally I hated to hear that," said the Rev. Leroy London, Sr. of the Bible Church of God near Fort Lauderdale, where the robbery attempt occurred.

Vincent Keith Smith, 21, collapsed in the substation of the Broward County sheriff's department Sunday after being seized in a struggle that left a church-goer wounded in the ankle. Smith was taken to Plantation Hospital where he died shortly after 9:30 P.M. Broward sheriff's department spokesman George Crolius said Smith died of an apparent heart attack.

After the robber took the cash from the collection plate, worshipers told him to take the money and go. But then he decided to take money from everyone in the church, said the minister's son, Leroy London, Jr.

Smith, carrying a .38-caliber handgun and wearing a ski mask, walked into the church about 8 P.M. Sunday, witnesses told police.

"I grabbed his hand and the gun," said 51-year-old Willie Mayhue.

The pastor and several other worshipers joined the struggle. The gun went off, hitting Janie Patten, 36, in the ankle, Broward sheriff's communications supervisor Mary Frazier said Monday. Patten was listed in good condition Monday at Plantation General Hospital.

Smith was wrestled to the back of the church and held until sheriff's deputies and paramedics arrived several minutes later.

Reprinted by Permission of Associated Press.

Some Key Assumptions

In the chapters that follow, we will take a close look at the criminal justice network in the United States. In order to understand how that network actually functions (as compared to how it functions in theory), we need to look at some of the assumptions upon which the network is said to be based. These assumptions include, among others, the following:

1. The components of the network cooperate and share similar goals.
2. The network operates according to a set of formal procedural rules to insure uniform treatment of individuals.
3. Each person accused of a crime receives due process and is presumed innocent until proven guilty.
4. Each accused person receives a speedy, public trial before an impartial jury of his or her peers.
5. Each accused person is represented by competent legal counsel, as is the state.
6. Innocence or guilt is determined on the basis of "the facts."
7. The outcome of criminal justice procedures is "justice."

We have already dealt with the first assumption, the cooperative, goal-sharing network. We will simply add that each component in the network is continually competing with all other components for budgetary dollars.

The second assumption is that the criminal justice network operates according to a set of formal procedural rules to insure uniform treatment of individuals. To the extent that this assumption is true, race, social class, or sex should have no bearing on the manner in which cases are handled. Similarly, each individual being processed should go through the same clearly delineated steps. There is, however, considerable evidence to indicate that blacks and whites, males and females, and middle-class citizens and lower-class citizens receive differential treatment in the criminal justice network. According to Reid,

> Minorities face discrimination in the system of criminal justice beginning with arrest and following through all of the stages. They are more likely to be arrested and to be victims of police brutality; less likely to have an attorney immediately; more likely to have appointed rather than retained counsel; and less likely to make bail.[5]

Similarly, it is clear that not all defendants go through the same procedural steps when they enter the system. Some are handled by administrative review boards rather than criminal courts (e.g., white-collar offenders). Some are prosecuted, others are not. Some are involved in plea bargaining, others are not. Some are convicted and sentenced to prison, while others who are convicted of the same type of offense are not. As we shall see, public opinion, political power, and the exercise of discretion may affect what happens at all levels of the criminal justice network. Assumption number two, then, is at least questionable.

Assumption number three concerns due process and the **presumption of innocence.** No doubt due process applies in theory to all accused individuals, but what is to guarantee that due process is observed in a practice, for example, like plea bargaining? While several formal procedures have been developed to help insure that due process is observed in plea negotiations, a great deal of the negotiating remains largely invisible. For example, in some jurisdictions, juveniles receive **unofficial probation** from juvenile probation officers as part of a negotiated settlement. The juvenile is told she or he must meet certain requirements for a specified period of time "or else." "Or else" means the juvenile will be processed through the juvenile court if she or he does not agree to the unofficial probation. Note that the juveniles involved have not been adjudicated delinquent, the facts of the case have not been heard by the court, and the evidence possessed by the juvenile probation officer is sometimes contested. Where, we might ask, does due process fit into such an arrangement? Nonetheless, such programs exist and are encouraged in many jurisdictions.

With respect to the presumption of innocence, we might simply note that, in general, the police do not believe they arrest innocent people and prosecutors do not believe they prosecute innocent people. There is also evidence to indicate that public defenders do not assume their clients to be innocent.[6] It may be that judges and juries presume the defendant to be innocent, but it certainly appears that others in the network assume the defendant is guilty.

Assumption number four, dealing with speedy, public trial before a jury of peers, is clearly questionable. A tremendous backlog of cases insures that a speedy trial is more an ideal than the reality in many jurisdictions. Since the vast majority of trials involve a guilty plea before a judge, the notions of *public* trial and *jury of peers* are called into question. Even when jury trials do occur, the issue of whether the jury consists of peers remains unresolved due to the routine exclusion or excusal of certain types of jurors.

With respect to the assumption that the accused and the state are competently represented, many lawyers and judges, including a U.S. Supreme Court Justice, have indicated that a significant proportion of lawyers practicing in criminal courts are not competent to do so.

Assumption number six states that the facts of each case will be used to determine innocence or guilt, yet some claim that *actual* guilt or innocence is the least important factor in determining legal innocence or guilt.[7] Instead, they claim, the resources of the state and defense counsel; the style, presentation, and knowledge of the attorneys involved; and various public and political pressures often determine guilt or innocence.

Finally, assumption number seven concerns the notion of **justice.** If the network or the product of the network is perceived as just by most citizens, we can expect considerable public support for the network. If, however, some groups believe that justice is not uniformly, fairly, or equally applied, we can expect opposition to the network.

In a society such as ours, where citizens are free to voice their dissent and dissatisfaction (within broad limits), it is easy to see that justice is differentially perceived. Those who have little (power, money, status, etc.) often perceive less justice than those who have a great deal. Minority groups, who have been treated as second-class citizens (officially or unofficially), tend to view the network as less just than do members of the dominant group. Victims of crimes and their relatives and loved ones often see little justice in plea bargaining or probation. Offenders seldom see justice in the balance of power between themselves and the state.

Justice is often exemplified by the courtroom scene in which the champion of the state (the prosecutor) and the champion of the defense do battle before a jury of twelve (today, perhaps fewer) "tried and true" persons who decide innocence or guilt based upon a presentation of facts with the aid of an impartial mediator (the judge). Today, such scenes are rare, occurring in less than ten percent of all criminal trials.[8] The reality of the criminal "trial" today involves no jury, but a plea negotiated between the prosecutor and defense counsel with the consent of the accused and, sometimes, the judge. In those cases involving jury trials today, the prosecution and defense would each like the jury to believe that he or she is *just* presenting the facts. In reality, both the prosecution and the defense present the "facts" in such a way as to make their own case look better and to sway the jury. And we are all aware that jurors are not simply chosen on the basis of their good intentions (see chapter 7). Whether or not one believes justice is done also depends upon the role one plays in the system (e.g., victim, witness, or offender).

Justice, then, appears to be largely in the eyes of the beholder. Whether or not a particular network for dealing with criminals is seen as just depends, in part at least, upon the extent to which the network operates according to the assumptions upon which it is based. If these assumptions are not followed in practice, a discrepancy is soon observed between the real and the ideal. As a result, citizens may not know what to expect from the network, may view it as operating on other than an equitable basis, and may believe that justice depends more upon access to knowledge and resources required to beat the system than upon actual guilt or innocence. Another possible conclusion is that the network simply does not work at all and is not worth supporting.[9]

In taking a critical look at some of the key assumptions concerning criminal justice in the United States, our intent has not been to convince you that the network does not work. Rather, it has been to point out that the network often does not work in the fashion we say it does or should. As we proceed through this book, we hope you will continue to question the workings of the criminal justice network, and we hope you will continually compare what you know about the network with the material presented.

In the chapters which follow, it will be helpful to keep in mind some guidelines that will help us comprehend both the ideal and the reality the criminal justice network. Unquestionably, one of the most important factors to keep in mind is the set of legal statutes and court and administrative decisions that spell out the formal procedures that guide the system. At the same time, in order to analyze activities within the criminal justice network, we feel it is important to examine the influence of public opinion, political factors, and discretionary justice. Unless we focus on these areas, much of what happens in the criminal justice network will be difficult to comprehend. Why, for example, do we characterize Supreme Courts (generally thought to be the most impartial, scholarly courts in the United States) as liberal or conservative? Are political considerations important in this highest of courts? If so, in what ways? And what are some of the effects of such considerations?

Similarly, we might ask why white-collar offenders (who, by most estimates, cost the United States public more in terms of dollars annually than robbers, burglars, and other thieves) are infrequently handled by criminal courts?[10] Do the various publics view white-collar offenders as criminals? If not, why not? And what are the implications for offenders and society?

To what extent are the police accountable for "adjusting" cases on the street or in the station? To whom are prosecutors accountable for their decisions concerning prosecution? Why do great inequities in sentencing occur among judges? Is discretion a normal and/or necessary part of criminal justice?

Satisfying answers to these and other questions can seldom be found simply by referring to formal procedures, laws, or regulations. References to these formalized procedures need to be supplemented by looking behind the scenes in order to determine how specific decisions are made within the broad framework of criminal justice. We believe this can best be accomplished by using the network approach discussed in the first section of this chapter. The usefulness of this approach is illustrated by a recent operation conducted by the FBI in Cook County, Illinois. Operation Greylord involved the investigation of corruption among judges, lawyers, bailiffs, court clerks, and at least one police officer allegedly involved in accepting or offering bribes to influence the outcomes of court cases. The impact of such action on defendants, victims, and the public is obvious. In response to this investigation, one police officer committed suicide and a number of interest groups have called for a change in the method by which judges are placed in office, from popular elections to appointment of Supreme Court and appeals judges by the governor.[11] Such a change would require that legislators change the Illinois Constitution, and this would lead legislators to poll their constituents to determine whether or not such a change would receive voter support. Political groups in favor of both approaches are waging campaigns to arouse public support (and, therefore, legislative approval) of their plans.

Summary

In this chapter, we have attempted to contrast the real and the ideal of some aspects of criminal justice in the United States. Some assumptions concerning criminal justice have been discussed. As we have pointed out, it may be that we have assumed the existence of a network that is more orderly and coordinated than the reality, which is characterized by diversity—of goals, personnel, and geography. Still, as we have shown, there is little doubt that the components form a loose network, since changes in one component have clear implications for other components.

We have stressed the importance of viewing the public as an important, perhaps the most important, component of the criminal justice network, and we have indicated that what we generally think of as the public really consists of many different publics with varied interests and concerns, or with no interests or concerns at all, with respect to criminal justice. It is the combination of these publics that supports and evaluates (or fails to support and evaluate) criminal justice agencies and programs.

We discussed the concept of justice and concluded that justice means different things to different people. Whether or not justice is done in a particular case depends upon whether we take the perspective of the defendant, the victim, or the police officer. Justice in the ideal sense—as the outcome of a battle by two champions before a mediator and jury—is the exception rather than the rule in criminal cases in the United States.

Finally, we pointed out some of the important factors involved in understanding the criminal justice network and its operations. Public opinion, political considerations, feedback, and the exercise of discretion are important factors in the day-to-day operations of the criminal justice network and should be recognized as such.

Key Terms Defined

criminal justice network a web of constantly changing relationships among individuals involved more or less directly in the pursuit of criminal justice.

territorial jealousy a concern with protecting the turf of one's own agency, which sometimes makes cooperation among agencies difficult or impossible.

crime control model the model for procedures to be employed in the pursuit of alleged offenders which is based on factual guilt.

due process model the model for procedures to be employed in the pursuit of alleged offenders which is based on establishing factual guilt while adhering to legal guidelines.

public thousands of different groups divided by characteristics such as age, race, sex, adherence to law, social class, and geographical area, which are often mistakenly regarded as a cohesive whole—"the public."

unofficial probation probation imposed prior to a determination of guilt or innocence.

presumption of innocence the belief that an accused is innocent until proven guilty, which is often lacking among the police, prosecutors, and defense counselors.

justice the belief that the various parties involved in a dispute get more or less what they deserve. To some extent, this belief depends upon the role of the person doing the perceiving, (e.g., is he or she the victim, the offender, or a witness).

Discussion Questions

1. What are the advantages in viewing criminal justice as a network, as opposed to using the more traditional flowchart?

2. Do all of the various components of the criminal justice network have identical goals? Similar goals? Overlapping goals? Explain your answer.

3. Why are politics, discretion, and the public important components of the criminal justice network?

4. Practically speaking, do we operate under the presumption of innocence or guilt in our current criminal justice system? Support your answer.

Notes

1. Abraham S. Blumberg, *Criminal Justice* (Chicago: Quadrangle, 1967); or Steven M. Cox, "Ideology, Negotiation, and Emergent Organizations" (Ph.D. diss., University of Illinois, Urbana, 1971).

2. Jerome H. Skolnick, *Justice Without Trial* (New York: Wiley, 1975).

3. See decisions such as *Mapp v. Ohio, Miranda v. Arizona, Escobedo v. Illinois.*

4. Thanks to Richard M. Brede for this conceptualization of different expectations of the police.

5. Sue Titus Reid, *Crime and Criminology* (Hinsdale, Ill.: Dryden Press, 1976), 300.

6. Jonathan Casper, *American Criminal Justice: The Defendant's Perspective* (Englewood Cliffs, N.J.: Prentice-Hall, 1972).

7. F. Lee Bailey, *The Defense Never Rests* (New York: Stein and Day, 1971).

8. Henry W. Ehrmann, *Comparative Legal Cultures* (Englewood Cliffs, N.J.: Prentice-Hall, 1976), 94.

9. Philip H. Ennis, "Crime, Victims, and the Police," *Trans-action* 4 (June 1967): 36–44.

10. Gilbert Geis, *White-Collar Criminal: The Offender in Business and the Professions* (New York: Atherton, 1968); Daniel Glaser, *Crime in Our Changing Society* (New York: Holt, Rinehart and Winston, 1978), 421; or Edwin H. Sutherland, *White-Collar Crime* (New York: Dryden, 1949).

11. " 'Greylords' Ask Deals," *Chicago Tribune,* 11 Dec. 1983, 1; and "New Drive Planned for Merit Selection," *Peoria Journal Star,* 19 Dec. 1983, A9.

Suggested Readings

Beckman, Erik. "Criminal Justice and Politics in America: From the Sedition Act to Watergate and Beyond." *Journal of Police Science and Administration* 5, no. 3 (September 1977): 285–89.

Clark, Robert S. *The Criminal Justice System: An Analytical Approach.* Boston: Allyn and Bacon, 1982.

Cohn, Alvin W. "Training in the Criminal Justice Nonsystem." *Federal Probation* (June 1974): 32–37.

Fairchild, Erika S. "Interest Groups in the Criminal Justice Process." *Journal of Criminal Justice* 9, no. 2 (1981): 181–94.

Formby, William A., and Smykla, John O. "Citizen Awareness in Crime Prevention: Do They Really Get Involved?" *Journal of Police Science and Administration* 9, no. 4 (December 1981): 398–403.

Skolnick, Jerome, and Bayley, David, *The New Blue Line: Police Innovation in Six American Cities.* New York: The Free Press, 1986.

Criminal Law as One Category of Law

2

Key Terms

law	case law
sanctions	precedent
mores	civil law
folkways	criminal law
functions of law	crime
conflict model	*mens rea*
substantive law	canon law
procedural law	common law
statutory law	courts of equity

We all are born and we live, work, play, and die within the parameters of complex cultural systems. From the moment of birth, and even before birth, until the administration of last rites, we are affected directly and indirectly by a seemingly infinite number of rules and regulations. For example, there are rules and regulations governing the hospitals in which we are born, and the physicians and nurses who assist at birth. Other rules and regulations govern the schools we attend, the leisure time activities in which we engage, our rights as employers and employees, and even our funeral procedures.

Among these rules and regulations are some that we come to regard as laws. The ways in which such distinctions are made are discussed in the following section. For now, it is sufficient to recognize that these laws touch everyone—they regulate virtually every aspect of human behavior in modern societies. Try to imagine American life without laws. Something as simple as driving to the corner grocery would be extremely risky without laws. One could drive at any speed, on either side of the street (or down the middle), pass through intersections without

Rules, Regulations, and
Laws Govern Us All.
James L. Shaffer

Rules, Regulations, and
Laws Govern Us All.
James L. Shaffer

regard for others, and park anywhere and in any fashion he or she chose. Further, without laws, a company manufacturing cars could build unsafe vehicles that could result in the deaths of innocent people and have no fear of being held liable. This simple example is indicative of the extent to which we rely upon laws in day-to-day living. Laws help create stability and change, protect private and public interests, provide for the orderly resolution of conflict, and uphold certain traditions and institutions or bring about change in these traditions and institutions.

The purpose of this chapter is to explain what law is, how it is created, the forms it takes, and the functions it serves.

What is law? This question may be approached from a number of different perspectives. Putting the question to a number of citizens might lead to responses such as "the cops are the law," "the judge is the law," "law consists of the rules we play by," and so forth. While each of these responses is partially accurate, none will suffice to explain in meaningful form what the law is.

Law is a complex, dynamic, social phenomenon. It is more than the sum total of persons who actively participate in the administration of rules. It consists of rules administered, decisions rendered, legislation passed, and interpretations handed down by specially designated individuals who have been given the authority to impose sanctions of specified types on those who violate these rules, decisions, and interpretations (see chapter 3). Law is a formal means of social control involving the use of rules that are created, interpreted, and enforceable by specially designated persons in a particular political community.[1]

> Sources of law are the materials out of which legal rules are fashioned once distinctively legal obligations have emerged in society. Customs based here on religions, there on secular traditions, decisions by judicial bodies or other notables, written rules, standards of justice, and, possibly, authoritative writings about law furnish these materials. Singly, or more frequently in combination, these are the sources common to all legal orders. . . .[2]

How do these "distinctively legal obligations" emerge in a society? How do certain rules and regulations become recognized as less formal customs or mores, and how are they enforced in different ways?

We might speculate that the following developments occurred in the evolution of law.[3] Humans interacting with each other over time developed expectations concerning proper and improper (normal and abnormal) behavior of individuals in certain positions. Chiefs, priests, hunters, wives, warriors, and cooks were all expected to perform in certain ways. This role-associated behavior might vary to some extent as different individuals filled the role of chief or priest, for example, but certain expectations of the position and not the individual occupying the position remained. Behavior that met these expectations was considered normal, that which failed to meet the expectations was considered abnormal or "deviant." That is, it became customary for individuals occupying certain roles (positions) to behave in certain ways. It is not a big step from saying that chiefs behave in a particular way to saying that chiefs *should* behave in a particular way, *ought* to behave in a particular way, or *must* behave in a particular way.[4] Initially, those who violated the expectations of others could be sanctioned through applying group pressure. Violations of these expectations may be considered violations of **folkways** (customs) or **mores** (religious or ethical standards), and **sanctions** (punishments) for violating folkways and mores include gossip, ostracism, and, in some cases, excommunication.[5]

As communities grew in numbers, specialization became necessary. The once homogeneous community became diversified. Conceptions of normal and abnormal behavior were no longer consensual. Behavior accepted as normal among warriors might be defined as deviant by farmers, yet each specialized group needed the others to survive. That is, each group had to be able to depend upon the performance of certain tasks by other groups. Failure to perform needed tasks could have dire consequences. Insuring performance (contracts) became too important to leave solely to informal or group pressure. Some tasks had to be performed. To insure their performance, certain individuals were appointed to look for behavior that violated expectations. These specially designated individuals were given the power to use certain types of sanctions (arrest, fines, and even death) to insure compliance with expectations or to punish those who failed to comply. The legal rights and obligations of all parties in the community had been specified, and formal institutions for insuring that rights were protected and obligations were fulfilled emerged. Law became important as one form of social control.

While the concept of law has probably existed in all societies, law, in the sense of formal or written rules enforceable by specially designated persons, has evolved over time and is particularly characteristic of complex societies. While custom, tradition, and religion could once be used to handle most disputes, modern industrial societies rely more heavily upon legislative and administrative law to deal with rapidly changing social conditions.[6] These laws are based, of course, to a great extent upon custom, tradition, and precedent.

In attempting to understand the origins, nature, and **functions of law,** it is important to recognize that the formulation of law does not occur in a vacuum. Law is the result of political action.[7] One school of thought says that in a democracy, law represents the views or values of the majority of citizens and results from consensus.[8] Another widely accepted model is the **conflict model,** which indicates that it is conflict between interest groups with varying degrees of power that leads to the formation of law.[9] According to proponents of this model, coalitions among the many groups existing in society form with respect to specific issues. The more powerful the coalition (in terms of money, prestige, political skills), the more likely they are to create or pass the laws they desire. Since the interests of these groups vary over time, the coalitions formed are temporary and constant change characterizes the society. There is no one stable, identifiable majority on all issues. Glaser has combined the two approaches by demonstrating that in the initial stages of the development of law the conflict model clearly applies, but that with time and practice consensus develops.[10]

The discussion above indicates another important characteristic of law—its dynamic nature. That is, the law is constantly changing as the interests of groups and individuals change, leading to the election of new political figures, the appointment of new judicial officials, the passing of new legislation, and the handing down of new court decisions. While it is easy to talk about the law as if it were something real and concrete, numerous scholars have pointed out the difficulties in saying exactly what the law is at any given point in time. Thus, Ehrlich speaks of the "living law," Holmes discusses law as what the courts are likely to do in a given place at a given time, and Weber emphasizes the difference between the normative aspects of a legal proposition and what actually happens in a given time as a result of these normative aspects.[11]

Regardless of time and place, there are certain functions that law helps to perform. Law defines relationships among individuals and groups by specifying rights and obligations, it may be used to help tame the use of naked force, it may be used to assist in the orderly resolution of conflict, it is used to dispose of problem or "trouble" cases (those that arise repeatedly) as they arise, and it may be used to help society adapt to changing conditions.[12] Perhaps the way in which the law may be used to perform these functions will become more clear if we take a look at several different ways of classifying law.

Substantive law is the "body of law that creates, discovers, and defines the rights and obligations of each person in society."[13] The two key elements of substantive law are specificity and penalty. That is, substantive law specifically defines proscribed (prohibited) behaviors and specifies the penalties that may be administered to those who commit such acts. Laws concerning rape, medical malpractice, income tax evasion, and so forth are substantive in that they specifically define the acts constituting rape, malpractice, and evasion.

Procedural law is the body of law that specifies the manner in which substantive laws will be applied. If the law is to be used in the orderly resolution of conflict, specific, predictable procedural steps must be followed. Thus, we have developed rules concerning the seizure and admissibility of evidence, the circumstances under which a confession may be legally obtained and admitted in court, the use of informants, and so forth.

The law may also be analyzed in terms of **statutory** versus **case law.** Statutory law consists of those laws passed by a legislative body, and is typically codified and published as revised at the federal, state, and local levels. Case law is derived from court decisions. These decisions are sometimes based upon statutory law and sometimes arrived at in the absence of statutes. The deciding judge usually takes into account past case decisions in cases involving similar conditions or **precedent** in handing down case law. In either case, the ultimate sources of law are the federal and state constitutions.

Finally, for our purposes, law may be divided into **civil** and **criminal** categories.

> The 'civil law' is the portion of the law that defines and determines the rights of the individual in protecting his person and his property. The 'criminal law' is that body specifically established to maintain peace and order. Its purpose is to protect society and the community from the injurious acts of individuals. The same act causing injury to person or property, a civil wrong called a 'tort,' may also be a breach of the peace, a 'crime.' The wrongdoer may then be subject to both civil and criminal proceedings.[14]

These differences are apparent in the manner in which cases are filed in court and cited in the legal literature. If, for example, in our reading we note a case cited *United States v. Smith,* we can tell that Smith has been charged with a crime by the federal government. In such citations, the plaintiff, or person initiating the action, is always listed first. The plaintiff in all criminal cases will be a governmental entity—federal, state, or local, since the state is considered to be an "injured party" in such cases. In civil cases, the plaintiff will normally be a private party. So, if in our reading we find a citation *Jones v. Smith,* we can be reasonably certain the case involves a civil matter. It is possible for a governmental entity to be a plaintiff in a civil matter; but as a rule of thumb, the distinction outlined above holds. Another difference between civil and criminal law concerns the nature of the sanctions involved. Sanctions in criminal cases are said to be punitive, while those in civil matters are generally compensatory (although they may also be punitive or exemplary). In the former, the intent is to punish for wrongs done to society (the state); in the latter, to award compensation for harm, damages, or suffering to the individual.

In addition to the differences listed above, there are important procedural distinctions between civil and criminal law. The most basic of these is in the standard of proof required to establish guilt. In civil proceedings, a "preponderance of evidence" must exist to support a guilty verdict, whereas in criminal proceedings guilt must be established "beyond reasonable doubt."

Since this book deals with the *criminal* justice network, most of our attention will be devoted to criminal law. It should be noted, however, that there are numerous, complex relationships between civil and criminal law. Thus, a finding of guilt or innocence in criminal court may be used in civil proceedings resulting from the same case.

Criminal Law

In this section, we will examine the characteristics of criminal law. In order to do this, it will be helpful if we first define **crime**. According to Paul Tappan, "Crime is an intentional act or omission in violation of criminal law, committed without defense or justification, and sanctioned by the state as a felony or misdemeanor."[15] Included in Tappan's definition are five specific elements that, taken together, establish the criteria necessary for the violation of criminal law. The five elements are (1) an unjustifiable act or omission, (2) intent, (3) a union of intent and action, (4) the existence of a statute prohibiting the act, and (5) the existence of a prescribed penalty.

The act or omission considered criminal must be defined by law. For example, under common law (still followed in some states), the crime of rape occurs only when there is penetration of the sexual organ of the victim by the alleged offender. In a battery, physical contact must occur; in criminal homicide, one person's life must be taken by another person without justification; and so forth.

Notice that thoughts of committing a crime do not, in and of themselves, violate criminal law. (Many of us have probably secretly planned the "perfect crime"!) There must be some action in furtherance of these thoughts for a crime to occur. Failure to act constitutes one type of action. Therefore, failing to file an income tax report and failure to register for the draft are criminal acts, since there are legal requirements that both be performed by certain categories of individuals. In some cases, an individual may feel a moral obligation to act, while not legally required to do so. Thus, a passerby seeing a drowning person may feel morally obligated to help, but will not be guilty of a crime if he or she fails to do so since there is no legal requirement that he or she act.[16]

Criminal law recognizes that some acts which are generally considered criminal are justifiable under specific circumstances. In such cases, the actor must prove that she or he committed the act with justification. Thus, a police officer in the line of duty may intentionally take the life of another citizen (homicide) without committing a crime if he or she sees the person kill while committing a serious felony and has reason to believe that his or her own life, or the life of others, is in immediate danger from the felon. Such action is termed "justifiable homicide." Criminal acts committed under duress (at gunpoint, for example) may also fall into this category.

Intent *(mens rea)* is another important element of criminal law. An act alone is not enough for the commission of a crime.* Thus, one who kills another by accident (without intent) does not commit criminal homicide. For some crimes, specific actions are required to prove intent. For example, laws concerning shoplifting may require that the shoplifter leave the store in which he or she has shoplifted before a charge of shoplifting can be sustained. These laws are based on the premise that as long as the shoplifter stays in the store he or she can argue that he or she intended to pay before leaving (even though he or she has hidden several items on his or her person). For other crimes, most felonies, for example, general intent is all that is required. The intent to commit a felonious act makes the perpetrator responsible for all consequences following from the commission of the felony, even though such consequences are unforeseen.

In our society, there are several categories of persons who cannot be convicted of crimes because they are said to be incapable of forming criminal intent. Among these groups are juveniles under thirteen or fourteen years of age, those who have been declared insane, and the severely retarded. These persons may be dealt with through legal means (commitment hearings, for example) other than criminal proceedings. Some of these categories of individuals who are exempt from criminal prosecution have caused considerable controversy, particularly following the attempted assassination of former president Ronald Reagan.

As we have noted above, neither an act alone nor an intention alone is sufficient for the commission of a crime. Intent and act must come together for a crime to be committed. Further, the act considered criminal must be prohibited by law at the time it is committed or no crime has occurred. Finally, criminal codes must specify the punishments that may be administered for particular crimes in order

---

*An exception to the strict interpretation of intent is the felony murder rule, which, under certain circumstances, makes offenders committing dangerous felonies liable for the consequences of their acts regardless of their intention to produce such consequences. The offender must still, however, have had the intent to commit the dangerous felony that led to the unintended consequences.

John Hinckley, Jr., was Judged to be Incapable of Forming Criminal Intent When He Shot Former President Ronald Reagan. *AP/Wide World Photos*

to avoid capricious punishment. We know of a community in which parking meters were installed and tickets issued for failure to put money in the meters. However, the local government failed to enact laws requiring citizens to put money in the meters and, thus, failed to specify the amount of the fine to be paid for violation. Needless to say, the city council soon corrected the situation, but those who initially received tickets did not have to pay fines.

There are many other aspects of criminal law and numerous exceptions to the general rules stated here. Some of these will be discussed in later chapters, particularly in chapters 5 and 10. The overview presented in this chapter should enable you to better understand the general nature and functions of law. Perhaps a brief review of some of the historical sources of American law would be useful at this point.

Although there is evidence that laws were codified as early as the twenty-fifth century B.C., the first complete surviving code, the Code of Hammurabi, originated in the eighteenth century B.C. This code deals with subjects ranging from specific punishments for specific crimes to medical malpractice. Five hundred to one thousand years later, the Mosaic Code, including the Ten Commandments, was developed. The impact of the Ten Commandments, prohibiting behaviors such as murder, adultery, and perjury, is well established. Roman law was codified about 450 B.C. and became the basis for **canon law** or the law of the Roman Catholic church.[17] These various codes were tied together in the Napoleonic Code in 1804.

In Britain, the kings traditionally dispensed law throughout the country by traveling around and establishing "court" at various locations. The same laws were, in general, applied throughout the country; thus, the law came to be referred to as **common law.** When canon law came to England, **courts of equity** (in which decisions were based more upon conscience than upon strict interpretation of common law) were also established and the two systems coexisted for a number of years. In 1215, the Magna Carta, the basis for British civil liberties, became the law and, over the following years, British common law continued to develop—based upon customs, tradition, and precedent. This common law became the most important single aspect of the legal system in the new country—America.

When the colonial period ended in 1776, a new governmental system had to be developed. The Federal Constitution, written in 1787, established the executive, legislative, and judicial branches of government; and included a system of checks and balances among the branches, and between state and federal governments. The Constitution became the law of the land in 1789 and, with twenty-six amendments, remains so today. The twenty-six amendments insure freedom of worship and speech, insure trial by jury, abolish slavery, extend voting rights to all citizens, protect privileges and immunities of citizens, and guarantee a variety of other civil rights.

Of the twenty-six amendments, five are particularly important for the criminal justice network. These amendments establish, clarify, and regulate many elements of procedural law.

The Fourth Amendment regulates arrests and searches by prohibiting "unreasonable" searches and seizures. The Fifth Amendment affects grand jury proceedings, self-incrimination, and double jeopardy. The Sixth Amendment regulates interrogation and criminal prosecution by establishing the right to counsel, trial by jury, and the speedy trial doctrine. It also establishes the rules of venue, the right to confront witnesses, and the right to call one's own witnesses.

The Eighth Amendment prohibits excessive bail and cruel and unusual punishment. The Fourteenth Amendment applies all basic constitutional privileges at the state level. Although many of these amendments have been interpreted and refined through court decisions, they remain the fundamental source of procedural law.[18]

Summary

Law is a complex and extensive phenomenon. Among the multitude of rules and regulations developed by societies over time, some come to be designated as laws. These laws help us resolve conflict in orderly fashion by establishing rights and obligations of individuals, and by defining relationships among individuals and groups. Law is dynamic, or constantly changing, and is one form of social control that helps societies adapt to changing conditions.

Law is the result of political action and results from conflicts of interest among individuals and groups, rather than the will of the majority, at least in most cases.

Criminal law is only one type of law and is characterized by requiring higher standards of proof than, for example, civil law. A crime is an unjustifiable act that is accompanied by intent. The combination of act and intent that violates a specific statute prohibiting the act in the presence of a specified punishment constitutes a violation of criminal law. The body of criminal law may be analyzed in a variety of ways using categories such as substantive v. procedural law, case v. statutory law, and so forth.

Key Terms Defined

law a complex, dynamic, social phenomenon consisting of legislative rules and court decisions as they are administered and interpreted by specifically designated individuals in a political community.

sanctions rewards or punishments.

mores ethical or religious standards.

folkways customs or traditions.

functions of law law defines relationships among individuals and groups, helps regulate the use of force, may assist in the orderly resolution of conflicts, helps dispose of "trouble cases," and may help society adapt to changing conditions.

conflict model a model that views law as emerging from conflict between interest groups with varying degrees of power.

substantive law law that creates, discovers, and defines the rights and obligations of each person in a society. Key elements are specificity and penalty.

procedural law rules specifying the manner in which substantive law is to be applied.

statutory law law passed by a legislative body.

case law law derived from court decisions.

precedent a court decision that provides guidance as to how future similar cases are to be decided.

civil law the portion of law that defines and determines the rights of individuals in protecting person and property.

criminal law law established to maintain peace and order by protecting society from the injurious acts of individuals.

crime an intentional act or omission in violation of criminal law.

mens rea a guilty mind, criminal intent.

canon law church or religious law.

common law law based upon judges' decisions that become widely accepted.

courts of equity courts in which decisions are based more upon conscience than strict interpretation of law.

Discussion Questions

1. Discuss how law develops and how it differs from folkways and mores. What or who determines which norm will become law?

2. What are some of the basic functions of law? What legal machinery and societal actions are necessary if these functions are to be successfully performed?

3. Discuss some of the ways in which law can be classified. In what ways does criminal law differ from civil law?

4. What are the basic requirements for a violation of criminal law? What are some of the exceptions to these requirements?

Notes

1. For the bases of this definition, see F. James Davis, E. Eugene Davis, and Henry H. Foster, Jr., *Society and the Law: New Meanings for an Old Profession* (New York: Free Press, 1962), 41; and E. Adamson Hoebel, *The Law of Primitive Man* (Cambridge, Mass.: Harvard University Press, 1954), 22, 24, 27.

2. Henry W. Ehrmann, *Comparative Legal Cultures* (Englewood Cliffs, N.J.: Prentice-Hall, 1976), 21.

3. Emile Durkheim, *The Rules of Sociological Method* (Chicago: University of Chicago Press, 1938), 65–75; Herbert Blumer, *Symbolic Interaction: Perspective and Method* (Englewood Cliffs, N.J.: Prentice-Hall, 1969); or Steven M. Cox and Jack D. Fitzgerald, *Police in Community Relations: Critical Issues* (Dubuque, Ia.: Wm. C. Brown Publishers, 1983), ch. 3.

4. For thorough discussions of the way in which law develops and emerges in society, see Emile Durkheim, *The Division of Labor in Society* (New York: Free Press, 1947); Bronislaw Malinowski, *Crime and Custom in Savage Society* (London: Routledge and Kegan Paul, Ltd., 1926); Howard S. Becker, *The Outsiders: Studies in the Sociology of Deviance* (New York: Free Press, 1963), chs. 1, 7, 8; and Kurt H. Wolff, trans., *The Sociology of George Simmel* (New York: Free Press, 1950), 99–104.

5. For a more complete discussion of folkways and mores, see William Graham Sumner, *Folkways* (Boston: Ginn and Co., 1906).

6. Ehrmann, *Comparative Legal Cultures,* 24.

7. Ralph Baker and Fred A. Meyer, Jr., *The Criminal Justice Game: Politics and Players* (North Scituate, Mass.: Duxbury Press, 1980).

8. Ralph Dahrendorf, *Class and Class Conflict in Industrial Society* (Stanford, Calif.: Stanford University Press, 1959), 161–62.

9. Becker, *The Outsiders,* chs. 1, 7, 8; or Richard Quinney, *Criminology: Analysis and Critique of Crime in America* (Boston: Little, Brown and Co., 1975), ch. 11.

10. Daniel Glaser, *Crime in Our Changing Society* (New York: Holt, Rinehart and Winston, 1978), 15–16.

11. Eugene Ehrlich, *Fundamental Principles of the Sociology of Law,* trans. Walter L. Moll, (Cambridge, Mass.: Harvard University Press, 1936), 486–93; Oliver Wendell Holmes, "The Path of Law," in *The Sociology of Law: Interdisciplinary Readings,* ed. Rita James Simon (San Francisco: Chandler Publishing Co., 1968), 19–28; and Max Rheinstein, ed., *Max Weber Law and Economy in Society* (Cambridge, Mass.: Harvard University Press, 1956), 11–20.

12. Hoebel, *The Law of Primitive Man,* 275–76.

13. Hoebel, *The Law of Primitive Man,* 275.

14. Martin J. Ross, *Handbook of Everyday Law* (Greenwich, Conn.: Fawcett, 1967), 14.

15. Paul Tappan, *Crime, Justice and Correction* (New York: McGraw-Hill, 1960), 10.

16. For another example of this type, see *Jones v. State,* 43 X. 3. 2d. 1017, (1942).

17. Graham Berry, "With Justice for All," in *Annual Editions: Criminal Justice 83/84,* ed. John L. Sullivan and Joseph L. Victor (Guilford, Conn.: Dushkin, 1983), 119–21.

18. Rolando V. del Carmen, *Criminal Procedure for Law Enforcement Personnel* (Monterey, Calif.: Brooks/Cole, 1987).

Suggested Readings

Becker, Howard S. *The Outsiders: Studies in the Sociology of Deviance.* New York: Free Press, 1963, chs. 1, 2, 7, 8.

Chambliss, William J., and Seidman, Robert B. *Law, Order, and Society.* New Haven, Conn.: Yale University Press, 1971.

Ehrmann, Henry W. *Comparative Legal Cultures.* Englewood Cliffs, N.J.: Prentice-Hall, 1976.

Schwartz, Richard D., and Skolnick, Jerome H. *Society and the Legal Order.* New York: Basic Books, 1970, parts I, II.

Wolfe, Nancy Travis, "*Mala in Se:* A Disappearing Doctrine?" *Criminology* 19, no. 1 (May 1981): 131–43.

Politics and the Criminal Justice Network

3

Key Terms

politics
power
authority

The relationship between law and politics has been recognized since ancient times.[1] As Allen points out, "The present century has given no cause to dispute Aristotle's description of man as 'by nature a political animal'."[2] Allen continues by indicating that the twentieth century has been a period in which "politics has gained ascendancy in the thoughts and lives of men to an extraordinary degree."[3] The social conflicts of the 1960s and 1970s and the development and spread of "critical" or "radical" criminology have alerted us to the fact that "criminal justice is allocated in ways that reflect the values of those individuals and groups holding power in the political system."[4] Allen agrees, indicating that, "among the institutions that lend themselves most readily to political interpretation are the agencies of criminal justice."[5]

There is a tendency when discussing the relationships between politics and criminal justice to focus on the negative aspects of those relationships. This is perhaps true because cases involving political corruption or manipulation of the criminal justice network for personal gain receive a great deal more attention in our society than the day-to-day influence of politics on the network. A moment's reflection, however, is all that is required to note that political input into the criminal justice network is both necessary and desirable in a democratic society.

Bent points out that "the injection of outside interests reflecting the social values of the community" is crucial to the criminal justice network because it helps lead network practitioners "to a more realistic awareness and observance of these values."[6] The intermingling of politics and criminal justice is characteristic of all known societies and so may be considered perfectly normal. In fact, a crucial distinction between totalitarian and free nations is that while both develop criminal justice networks controlled by government, governments in totalitarian societies often acknowledge no accountability, while in a free society, criminal justice practitioners are answerable to a democratically elected political body.[7]

The Pervasive Influence of Politics: From the Police and Courts to Corrections

As Baker and Meyer point out, the law is not written in a vacuum, but results from a political act.[8] **Politics** may be defined as the process by which tangible (material) and symbolic rewards or resources are differentially distributed or allocated.[9] "Politics is who gets what, when, and how."[10]

As we point out throughout this book, criminal justice practitioners work in a network of reciprocal relationships, many of which are shaped by political considerations or are directly political. Cole indicates that "the confluence of law, administration, and politics results in a system in which officials who are sensitive to the political process make decisions at various points concerning the arrest, charges, conviction, and sentences of defendants."[11] At one level, we are all aware of the importance of political parties in determining who the prosecutors, judges, police chiefs, and wardens will be, who staff our criminal justice network. But, just how important are political considerations in the day-to-day functioning of the network, and in what ways?

In his study of the relationship between politics and the police, James Q. Wilson found that there was little direct day-to-day political influence on the police in the communities he examined.[12] However, he did find that what he calls the "political culture" of the communities was very important in determining the style of law enforcement employed, the type of chief selected, and the nature of departmental policy.[13]

Observations indicate that the political form of city government (commissioner, mayor/council, city manager) makes a great deal of difference in the extent to which politics permeates police departments (figure 3.1). On the one hand, the commissioner form of government places a political figure, who may or may not be acquainted with the complexities of police operations, at the top of the police administrative hierarchy. On the other hand, a professional city manager may make political intervention into police operations less likely. Regardless of the form of government involved, however, police administrators are dependent upon the political figures mentioned for resources. Personnel, equipment, salaries, and benefits are all negotiated through the political representatives of local citizens. At the same time, of course, the police themselves as voters and citizens can influence the outcome of elections and, thereby, have a voice in selecting the political figures with whom they will negotiate.

We are all familiar with the misuses of political power in relation to police departments. Politicians who use, or attempt to use, the prestige of office to place themselves above the law have become infamous, particularly in recent decades. There are also able politicians who seek office in order to attempt to correct some of the wrongs that have been uncovered in police departments, courts, or correctional facilities.

The police are influenced by political considerations in yet another way. The cases that they prepare must eventually be transferred to the prosecutor for further processing; thus, the policies and desires of the prosecutor influence the kinds of cases sent forward by the police, as well as the manner in which such cases are prepared.

Figure 3.1 The police and three types of city government.

Mayor/Council Government

Mayor hires/fires and controls Police Chief with City Council approval.

Mayor/Commissioner Government

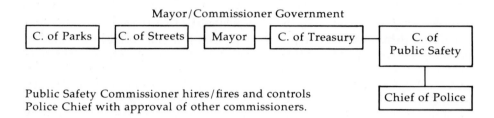

Public Safety Commissioner hires/fires and controls Police Chief with approval of other commissioners.

City Manager Government

Mayor hires/fires City Manager with City Council approval; City Manager hires/fires and controls Police Chief.

Note: C.C. is City Council Person

The prosecutor is first and foremost a political figure. In most cases, she or he runs for election with the support of one of the major political parties. As Cole points out, prosecutors are "political actors of consequence" because they are generally elected with party support, they have patronage jobs at their disposal, and they exercise considerable discretion. Prosecutors are tied both to the internal politics of the criminal justice network and to local, state, or national political organizations.[14] Since the discretionary powers of the prosecutor are considerable, he or she may be persuaded to take political advantage of the criminal justice position. So, charges may be dropped to avoid the possibility of losing difficult cases (and, thereby, political support), disclosures of wrongdoing by political opponents may be made at opportune moments, and decisions about the types of crimes to be prosecuted may be made for strictly political reasons.[15] The prosecutor, of course, does not have total freedom to exercise his or her discretion, since the police, the publics, and the judges all have vested interests of their own to protect, and they exert varying degrees of pressure on the prosecutor. Some prosecutors are more concerned about advancing their own political careers than providing the legal expertise required by some other components of the criminal justice network. Others, elected to office soon after graduation from law school, may have promising political skills, but little or no competence or experience in the courtroom. Still others are basically concerned about providing the services required by the public in a competent, professional manner. In any case, the public has the opportunity to indicate satisfaction or dissatisfaction with the prosecutor every two or four years. The prosecutor who wishes to continue in office or to advance in the political arena is constrained, to some extent, by the conflicting interests of those who surround him or her, as well as by financial obstacles.[16]

The next step in the career ladder of many prosecutors is that of judge, and deeds performed for a political party are often invaluable in obtaining a judgeship.[17]

In a number of states, county and circuit court judges are elected directly by the voters. In other states, judges are appointed by the governor from a list prepared by a more or less nonpartisan committee. In either case, the appointments are clearly political, and most judges have records as active political campaigners.

As Baker and Meyers point out, "Federal judges are appointed to the bench by the president with confirmation by the Senate in a highly politicized process."[18] When federal judges are appointed, partisan politics are clearly not set aside, since 90 percent of all federal judges ever appointed have been members of the same political party as the president who appointed them.[19] In addition, at least one study shows clearly that party affiliation of judges makes a difference in the way they decide on issues presented to them.[20]

That the United States Supreme Court is not exempt from party politics is demonstrated clearly by Woodward and Armstrong in *The Brethren: Inside the Supreme Court*.[21] From consideration of nominees by the president, through Senate approval or disapproval of such nominees, the appointment process is clearly political. The Court's decision to hear or not hear a case and the decision concerning who will write which opinion are also clearly made in a political context.[22] Finally, we should all be aware of the ramifications of changes resulting when the political ideology of the Supreme Court changes as a result of retirements and new appointments. Over the last two decades such changes have occurred, for example, with respect to defendants' rights as the Court has changed from the liberal Warren Court to the more conservative Burger Court, and there is currently a fear that erosion of defendants' rights might well continue under the even more conservative Rehnquist Court.

Before leaving our discussion of politics and lawyers, we would like to note the importance of the many local and state bar associations, as well as the American Bar Association, to the criminal justice network. These associations commonly screen and recommend candidates for positions in the network, and, thereby, play a key role in determining the level of competence and the extent of partisan politics in the network, demonstrating the manner in which organizations not included in the traditional systems model influence the criminal justice network.

In the field of corrections, once again, the impact of political decisions on the criminal justice network can be clearly seen. As Fox indicates, "The political appointment of wardens has been a significant handicap in developing good correctional programs."[23] He continues, however, by pointing out that as the network currently operates, the warden "had better know the politics and the political system with which he is dealing or he will be ineffectual in dealing with the legislature on whom he is dependent for appropriations."[24]

In addition to playing a key role in determining the type of custody or treatment an individual receives while in prison, political considerations are generally involved in determining the makeup of the parole board who decide if and when an individual will be released from prison. In all fifty states and in the federal prison system, a parole board decides whether or not to release an inmate. In the majority of jurisdictions, parole board members are appointed by the governor with legislative confirmation.[25]

Probation officers are generally appointed by the chief judge of a circuit, or by a panel of judges. In locally administered probation offices, political considerations play an important role in determining who will be appointed to the probation officer's job.[26] In state-administered probation departments, the influence of political considerations may be less apparent. Today, the majority of states have eliminated local administration in favor of statewide administration of probation.[27] However, there is little doubt that local interests still play a part in the selection and retention of probation personnel in indirect ways.

Power, Authority, and Politics

We can define **power** as the net ability of persons or groups to recurrently impose their will on others despite resistance.[28] The exercise of power depends upon the ability to supply rewards and/or punishment, and to withhold rewards and/or punishment.[29] As you will recall from an earlier section in this chapter, politics may be defined as the process by which rewards are differentially allocated. Power and politics, then, are inextricably interwoven.

The legitimate use of power by persons in specially designated positions may be termed **authority**.[30] In other words, we agree to grant people in certain positions the right to use certain types of power. The granting of this right is a political process that involves elections or appointments by others in positions of authority. Thus, we elect an individual to the office of president and this individual consequently has the right to exercise certain types of power based upon the authority of the office. Similarly, the president may appoint federal judges who then have certain powers as a result of their offices. The municipal fire and police commissions around the country are appointed by mayors/councils and then appoint individuals to the position of police officer. The police officer may then use certain types of power that go with the position.

Appointment or election to office does not give the appointee the right to use all forms of power or to exercise power indiscriminately. To the extent that an officeholder uses power in accordance with the rules of appointment or election, we consider his or her behavior to be legitimate. The use of powers other than those prescribed or the use of power in situations other than those specified as appropriate for the office involved is considered illegitimate. For example, the police officer who uses deadly force in self-defense while on duty is exercising legitimate power. The same officer who uses deadly force against a fleeing adolescent who has committed a minor misdemeanor is overstepping the boundaries of his or her authority and using power illegitimately.

The exercise of power from positions of authority requires that the person occupying the position of authority be *granted* the right to hold the position by those over whom authority is to be exercised. In a democratic society, this "granting" normally involves an election process or an appointment process. In a totalitarian society, the "granting" may be passive, as when citizens fail to resist by revolution or *coup*. Nonetheless, power and authority are not unilateral. They involve the consent (either passive or active) of those governed. A major difference between democratic and totalitarian societies is the procedure by which those exercising illegitimate power from positions of authority may be removed from office. In our society, for example, illegitimate use of the powers of office led a president to resign from office. Had he not done so, impeachment proceedings might have removed him. Citizen dissatisfaction with the performance of a public official may lead to a turnover in the presidency every four years, the recall of a judge, or the suspension of a police officer. In totalitarian societies, these peaceful means of addressing wrongs involving politics, power, and authority may be of little value, and revolution may be the only alternative available.

In the pages that follow, try to keep in mind the nature and extent of the relationships among politics, power, and authority. In doing so, you may find it easier to understand the ins and outs of the criminal justice network and the practitioners who operate within and upon that network.

Recognizing the Consequences of Politics in the Criminal Justice Network

Based upon our discussion of politics and the criminal justice network in this chapter, it should be clear that political considerations are a necessary, normal, and desirable part of the network. The most certain way for us to maintain control of the network and direct its practitioners to serve societal goals is the political process. When we elect and remove from office the individuals who control key resources in the criminal justice network, we determine the direction and practices adhered to by those who exercise varying degrees of authority over us. We control the criminal justice network to the extent that we select officials who operate openly and to the extent that we take the time to exert our political influence by monitoring the conduct of these officials and removing from office those who fail to meet our expectations.

There are, however, some very real dangers in the politics of criminal justice. There are those who argue that criminal justice is a game played by those who have wealth and political power against those who have neither.[31] To the extent that these charges are true, we might expect to find resentment and hostility toward the criminal justice network among those who have little or no political power. That such resentment and hostility exist is clear. Studies have shown that upper income groups hold more favorable attitudes toward the police than lower income groups, that blacks at all levels of income have negative attitudes toward the police, and that more blacks than whites feel the police are disrespectful to them.[32] Other evidence indicates that Puerto Ricans share these negative attitudes toward the police.[33] In 1980, the National Minority Advisory Council on

Criminal Justice indicated that minorities are treated by the criminal justice network in ways that stigmatize, brutalize, and reinforce minority oppression in our society.[34] The council went on to say that America is a "classic example of the heavy-handed use of state and private power to control minorities and suppress their continuing opposition to the hegemony of white racist ideology."[35] Further, there are charges that contemporary research in criminal justice, by its very nature, "is contributing to established racially discriminatory criminal justice policies."[36] Last, but not least, a recent study indicates that although legal counsel for the accused in criminal and juvenile cases is a constitutional right, ". . . meaningful compliance with the Constitution is often absent due to inadequate funding. Indeed, public defender and assigned counsel programs experience virtually every imaginable kind of financial deficiency. There are neither enough lawyers to represent the poor, nor are all the available attorneys trained, assisted by ample support staffs, or sufficiently compensated."[37]

Finally, we have to assess carefully the demands from criminal justice practitioners that certain portions of their operations remain covert. The exercise of discretion is another necessary, normal, and desirable part of criminal justice; but the invisibility of practitioners involved in plea bargaining and the political considerations involved in decisions to prosecute a case, hear a case, or grant parole often lead to suspicion and distrust. As we will see in chapter 4, serious problems for citizens and the criminal justice network may result from this invisibility.

Summary

The relationship between law and politics has long been recognized, but events of the past two decades have indicated just how important that relationship can be. While cases involving the negative impact of politics on criminal justice receive a great deal of attention, we need to be aware of the many positive contributions of political considerations to the criminal justice network. Societal values are transmitted to the network through the political process. Law, itself, is a political act, since politics involves the distribution of rewards and punishments.

From the police to prosecutors, judges, and correctional officials, the political culture helps shape policies and practices. The police chief is a political appointee, prosecutors and judges are politicians, and wardens, and parole and probation officers are political appointees. It makes little sense, therefore, to think of the criminal justice network as outside the realm of politics.

Power, or the ability to influence others, and authority, the right to use certain forms of power in certain circumstances, are critical components of the criminal justice/political network. Authority does not allow individuals to use power indiscriminately, and the exercise of authority requires either the active or passive consent of the governed.

Political considerations are a necessary, normal, and desirable part of the criminal justice network. They provide a way for concerned citizens to influence the scope and direction of the network. However, if political access is not uniformly available to all citizens, resentment and hostility among those denied such access may be expected.

Key Terms Defined

politics the process by which rewards/resources are differentially distributed or allocated.

power the ability of persons or groups to impose their will upon others despite resistance.

authority the right of specially designated persons to use power in legitimate fashion.

Discussion Questions

1. Discuss the complex relationships among law, politics, and the criminal justice network.

2. Do the positive effects of political considerations outweigh the negative effects with respect to criminal justice? Why or why not?

3. What are the relationships among power, authority, and politics? How do these relationships affect the criminal justice network?

4. To what extent can you identify and analyze the political culture in which the criminal justice network in your hometown operates? Be specific.

Notes

1. George F. Cole, *Criminal Justice: Law and Politics,* 3d ed. (North Scituate, Mass.: Duxbury Press, 1980), 1.

2. Francis A. Allen, *The Crimes of Politics: Political Dimensions of Criminal Justice* (Cambridge, Mass.: Harvard University Press, 1974), 1.

3. Allen, *The Crimes of Politics*, 1.

4. Cole, *Criminal Justice*, 1.

5. Allen, *The Crimes of Politics*, 1.

6. Alan E. Bent, *The Politics of Law Enforcement: Conflict and Power in Urban Communities* (Lexington, Mass.: D. C. Heath and Co., 1974), 7.

7. Bent, *The Politics of Law Enforcement*, 7.

8. Ralph Baker and Fred A. Meyer, Jr., *The Criminal Justice Game: Politics and Players* (North Scituate, Mass.: Duxbury Press, 1980), 5.

9. Baker and Meyer, *The Criminal Justice Game*, 3–11; and Cole, *Criminal Justice*, 2.

10. Harold Lasswell, *Politics: Who Gets What, When, and How?* (New York: Meridian, 1958).

11. Cole, *Criminal Justice*, 4.

12. James Q. Wilson, *Varieties of Police Behavior* (Cambridge, Mass.: Harvard University Press, 1968).

13. Wilson, *Varieties of Police Behavior*.

14. Cole, *Criminal Justice*, 3.

15. Cole, *Criminal Justice*, 147–48.

16. Baker and Meyer, *The Criminal Justice Game*, 115.

17. Cole, *Criminal Justice*, 3.

18. Baker and Meyer, *The Criminal Justice Game*, 145.

19. Baker and Meyer, *The Criminal Justice Game*, 146.

20. Stuart S. Nagel, "Political Party Affiliation and Judges' Decisions," *American Political Science Review* 55 (1961): 844–50.

21. Bob Woodward and Scott Armstrong, *The Brethren: Inside the Supreme Court* (New York: Simon and Schuster, 1979).

22. Woodward and Armstrong, *The Brethren*.

23. Vernon Fox, *Introduction to Corrections*, 2d ed., (Englewood Cliffs, N.J.: Prentice-Hall, 1977), 163.

24. Fox, *Introduction to Corrections*, 163.

25. Leonard Orland, *Justice, Punishment, Treatment: The Correctional Process* (New York: Free Press, 1973), 425; George C. Killinger, Hazel B. Kerper, and Paul F. Cromwell, Jr., *Probation and Parole in the Criminal Justice System* (St. Paul, Minn.: West Publishing Co., 1976), ch. 12.

26. Killinger, Kerper, and Cromwell, *Probation and Parole in the Criminal Justice System,* 96–97.

27. Killinger, Kerper, and Cromwell, *Probation and Parole in the Criminal Justice System,* 96–97.

28. This is essentially the definition given by Peter M. Blau, *Exchange and Power in Social Life* (New York: John Wiley and Sons, 1964), 116–17.

29. Blau, *Exchange and Power in Social Life,* 116–17.

30. Blau, *Exchange and Power in Social Life,* 199–200; Max Weber, *The Theory of Social and Economic Organization* (New York: Oxford University Press, 1947), 324.

31. Baker and Meyer, *The Criminal Justice Game;* Jeffrey H. Reiman, *The Rich Get Richer and the Poor Get Prison: Ideology, Class, and Criminal Justice* (New York: John Wiley and Sons, 1979); Richard Quinney, *Critique of Legal Order: Crime Control in Capitalist Society* (Boston: Little, Brown and Co., 1973); or Larry Tifft and Dennis Sullivan, *The Struggle to be Human: Crime, Criminology and Anarchism,* Sanday, Orkney, U.K.: Cienfuegos Press, 1980).

32. Philip H. Ennis, "Crime, Victims, and the Police," *Trans-action,* 4 (June 1967): 36–44.

33. Wayne L. Cotton, "Perceptions of Police Practices in New York's 'el barrio'," in *Police Community Relations: Images, Roles, Realities,* ed. A. W. Cohen and E. C. Viano (New York: J. B. Lippincott, 1976), 342–50.

34. *Criminal Justice Newsletter* 11, no. 21 (27 Oct. 1980): 1.

35. *Law Enforcement News* 6, no. 19 (10 November 1980): 1.

36. Paul Takagi, "Race, Crime, and Social Policy: A Minority Perspective," *Crime and Delinquency* 27, no. 1 (January 1981): 48–63.

37. Norman Lefstein, *Criminal Defense Services for the Poor: Methods and Programs for Providing Legal Representation and the Need for Adequate Financing* (The American Bar Association Standing Committee on Legal Aid and Indigent Defendants, May 1982), 56.

Suggested Readings

Allen, Francis A. *The Crimes of Politics: Political Dimensions of Criminal Justice.* Cambridge, Mass.: Harvard University Press, 1974.

Baker, Ralph, and Meyer, Fred A., Jr. *The Criminal Justice Game.* North Scituate, Mass.: Duxbury Press, 1980.

Chambliss, William J. "Vice, Corruption, Bureaucracy, and Power." *Wisconsin Law Review* 4 (1971): 1150–1173.

Cole, George F. *Criminal Justice: Law and Politics,* 3d ed. North Scituate, Mass.: Duxbury Press, 1980.

Hagan, John. *Crime, Criminal Behavior, and Its Control.* New York: McGraw-Hill, 1985.

Discretionary Justice 4

Key Terms

discretion   selective enforcement
full enforcement   plea bargaining

The exercise of discretion by practitioners in the criminal justice network has been a controversial issue for a number of years. Many students of criminal justice are concerned about the largely invisible and, therefore, uncontrollable nature of discretionary justice. Kenneth Culp Davis puts his concerns in these terms:

> I think the greatest and most frequent injustice occurs at the discretion end of the scale, where rules and principles provide little or no guidance, where emotions of deciding officers may affect what they do, where political or other favoritism may influence decisions, and where the imperfections of human nature are often reflected in the choices made.[1]

There is little doubt that, if we define **discretion** as the exercise of individual choice or judgment concerning possible courses of action, discretion is a normal, necessary, and even desirable part of the criminal justice network. As More indicates, ". . . discretion exists at the inception of a criminal matter and persists to the end."[2] Davis cites a variety of examples that support this assessment:

> Through plea bargaining a prosecutor agrees with one defendant to reduce a felony charge to a misdemeanor, but refuses to do so with another defendant. . . . A traffic policeman warns a violator instead of writing a ticket because the violator is a lawyer and the police of the city (Chicago) have a long-standing custom of favoring lawyers. . . . A judge who has power to sentence a convicted felon to five years in the penitentiary imposes a sentence of one year and suspends it, even though he knows one of his colleagues would impose a five-year sentence.[3]

Atkins and Pogrebin state,

> Discretion is exercised in the police officer's decision to apprehend a suspect, the prosecutor's decision to file, dismiss, or reduce formal charges, the judge's decision to admit a defendant to bail, release on recognizance, grant or deny trial motions, suspend sentence, release on probation, impose severe or minimal sentence in prison, and the parole board's decision whether or not to release a prisoner from incarceration.[4]

Obviously, the exercise of discretion in the criminal justice network is extensive. In what ways do individuals in various components of the network exercise such discretion? What are the consequences of the exercise of discretion for the network, for practitioners, and for those being processed? Is it possible to control discretion "so as to avoid the unequal, the arbitrary, the discriminatory, and the oppressive"?[5]

Public Discretion

One of the reasons we feel so strongly that the public must not be overlooked or underestimated as a component of the criminal justice network is that members of the public have discretionary powers of considerable magnitude. With respect to observed criminal or suspicious acts, each citizen may exercise discretion in terms of reporting or not reporting, testifying or not testifying, telling the truth or not telling the truth, and so forth. Evidence indicates that over 50 percent of the crimes occurring in the United States go unreported as the result of this exercise of discretion.[6] As a consequence, the police do not investigate a large proportion of all crimes committed since they do not know (except in the relatively rare case of on-view or proactive police work) that they exist. Similarly, the prosecutor is helpless to prosecute offenders in cases where testimony on the part of witnesses is required to substantiate charges if citizens refuse to come forth to testify or testify falsely. Among the reasons for failure of citizens to cooperate are the beliefs that the police are ineffective in arresting offenders, that prosecutors give away too much in plea bargaining, that judges hand out sentences that are too lenient, and that the entire criminal justice network is too time-consuming and uncertain.

The exercise of discretion with respect to specific criminal activities, however, constitutes a relatively small part of the wide range of discretionary activities available to the public. Voting for politicians who campaign for or against stricter law enforcement, supporting or failing to support bond issues intended to improve police services, aiding or failing to aid in the social integration of ex-convicts, and obeying or failing to obey laws are all within the scope of public discretionary activities. At the most basic level, then, members of the public serve as "gate-keepers" for the criminal justice network as they exercise discretion.

Police Discretion

The police serve as the second level of gatekeepers for the criminal justice network. Among their discretionary powers are arrest or nonarrest, life or death, citation or verbal reprimand, investigation or lack of investigation, and many more. Just as the police may be unable to arrest an offender without citizen cooperation, the prosecutor may be unable to prosecute if the police fail to make a legal arrest.

For a variety of reasons, a police officer may decide not to enforce the law. He or she may consider enforcement of certain laws a waste of police resources. The personal characteristics of the offender, departmental regulations, the time of day, the place in which an encounter occurs, public expectations, and previous court decisions may all influence the officer's decision. The realizations that **full enforcement** is seldom possible or desirable, that **selective enforcement** can be an effective technique, or a personal belief that the law is inappropriate may also affect an officer's actions.

In addition, the police sometimes take less than proper action to avoid due process of law. Observers of police departments have found that police may fabricate charges or details of incidents to benefit themselves in court proceedings. This option is open to police as a discretionary aspect of their work. Harassment, either mental or physical, can be viewed as a discretionary measure.

> Harassment is the imposition by the police, acting under cover of law, of sanctions prior to conviction as a means of ultimate punishment, rather than as a device for the invocation of criminal proceedings. Characteristic of harassment are efforts to annoy certain "offenders" both by temporarily detaining or arresting them without intention to seek prosecution and by destroying or illegally seizing their property without any intention to use it as evidence. Like other police decisions not to invoke the criminal process, harassment is generally of extremely low visibility, probably because the police ordinarily restrict such activity to persons who are unable to afford the costs of litigation, who would, or think they would, command little respect even if they were to complain, or wish to keep themselves out of public view in order to continue their illicit activities.[7]

If laws were written in perfectly clear language, if they contained no contradictions or ambiguities, if there was no difficulty in applying the principles stated in laws to particular situations, and if all officers were thoroughly familiar with all laws, deciding whether or not a particular law has been violated would be a simple and straightforward task for the officer. Unfortunately, these conditions, taken either singly or in combination, are seldom met.

The law in the United States, as we have seen, is a huge, complex, sometimes contradictory, and constantly changing collection of prescriptive and proscriptive rules. The large number of professionally trained legal experts, lawyers and judiciary officials who make their living arguing over different interpretations of the law, gives some indication of the ambiguities and complexities involved in applying the law. A police officer is not and, for that matter, does not need to be a lawyer, but familiarity with the basics of law is required if the officer is to discharge her or his responsibilities appropriately. Even the best police training programs provide little formal training in the law, however, and many officers receive no formal training whatsoever. Consequently, most of the police officer's understanding of the law is achieved indirectly.

Through the informal instruction and advice offered by colleagues and supervisors, through in-service training programs, cramming for promotional exams, self-initiated reading, day-to-day work experiences, and through experiences in the courtroom, however, police officers quickly acquire what might be called a working knowledge of the law. For all practical purposes, this working knowledge acquired through these channels *is* the law as it functions in the day-to-day activities of police officers. It is this work-generated interpretation of the law, which may or may not correspond with the interpretations made by lawyers and judiciary officials, that guides the officers as they carry out their law enforcement duties.

The law explicitly grants some discretionary powers to police officers and creates a framework within which other discretionary judgments may legitimately be made. It is one measure of the importance of discretion in police work that these are among the first items that become incorporated into the officer's working knowledge of the law. The officer understands, for example, that certain leeway is permitted in determining whether or not probable cause for a search is present (though recent legislation and court rulings have increased the confusion surrounding the legal latitude granted the officer in these matters). It is also common knowledge among officers that the overlap that frequently exists among laws gives the officer the opportunity to pick and choose which laws, if any, will be cited once a suspect is apprehended; thus, the officer can choose to "throw the book" at a person, by citing violations of several laws, or charge a person with a more, or less, serious offense than circumstances and evidence might warrant. In a variety of ways, then, the law, as interpreted and understood by the officer, creates the framework within which, and sometimes around which, police discretion is exercised.

Deciding whether or not a violation of the law has taken place is perhaps the most basic, though perhaps not the most consequential, discretionary judgment a police officer makes. If the officer decides that no violation has taken place, there are usually no further formal consequences for anyone involved. If the decision is that an offense has occurred, the officer has the power to set in motion a highly complex, very expensive, and extremely inconvenient set of procedures that may end with the deprivation of a citizen's liberty. To be sure, the officer's judgment that a violation of the law has occurred is by no means the last word on the subject. Prosecutors and judges may eventually reverse the officer's decision, but it is typically the first judgment made by an official of the criminal justice network and, as such, must be considered a basic discretionary power. For example, in one community, we learned that certain police officers were issuing traffic citations for "careless driving." Several offenders were so charged, found guilty in court, and fined. Eventually a discussion between two patrolmen of the differences between "careless driving" and "reckless driving" occurred, leading to a search of traffic statutes and to the discovery that there was no statute dealing with careless driving. The police had been enforcing a nonexisting statute, defendants had pled guilty to violating a nonexisting statute, and had paid fines for violating a nonexisting statute. The exercise of police discretion had, in essence, led to the creation of a new traffic law.

While determining whether or not an offense has been committed is a basic discretionary decision, it is probably not the most consequential so far as the exercise of police discretion is concerned. In essence, it is a technical judgment, dependent upon the officer's knowledge of the law and capacity to apply the general principles embodied in the law to the particular events that have occurred. However difficult this judgment may be (and it *is* difficult in many instances), it is a decision that merely sets the stage for a far more consequential one—deciding whether or not to take official action. If the police officer decides not to arrest, the remainder of the legal machinery in the criminal justice network does not normally come into play. Once an officer decides to take official action in a criminal matter, he or she again exercises discretion with respect to the number and type of charges to be brought against the defendant.[8] The case is then turned over to the prosecutor who makes a number of discretionary decisions.[9]

Prosecutorial and Defense Discretion

"Viewed in broad perspective, the American legal system seems to be shot through with many excessive and uncontrolled discretionary powers, but the one that stands out above all others is the power to prosecute or not to prosecute."[10] Discretionary activities on behalf of the prosecutor include deciding whether or not to prosecute a given individual, what charges to file, whether or not to plea bargain, how much time and money are to be devoted to a particular case, what type and how much evidence is to be shared (under discovery motions) with the defense, and, in some cases, what type of sentence or punishment to recommend if the defendant is found guilty. Like the police officer, the prosecutor operates within a network that places limits on the amount of discretion he or she may exercise. Economic considerations, political considerations, public opinion, the law, and expectations of other network practitioners all influence the decisions made. A list of possible reasons for failing to file a felony complaint follows.

I. Departmental policy
II. No corpus delecti (facts that prove a crime was commited)
    A. No specific intent
    B. No criminal act
III. No connecting evidence
    A. Statement problem
    B. Witness problem
    C. Physical evidence problem
IV. Insufficient evidence
    A. Facts weak
    B. Evidence not available
    C. Incomplete investigation
    D. Witnesses not available
    E. Evidence inadmissible
        1. Illegal detention
        2. Fruit of poisoned tree
        3. Search warrant problem
        4. Search and seizures
        5. Warrant of arrest
        6. Miranda plus (see the appendix)
V. Lack of jurisdiction
VI. Statute of limitation
VII. Offense-misdemeanor
    A. Filed
    B. Referred
VIII. Interest of justice[11]

Defense counsel, in conjunction with the defendant, has discretionary powers as well. He or she must decide whether to plea bargain, what plea to enter, what motions to file, how much time and effort to devote to a given case, whether or not to accept any given case (at least when private counsel is involved), and so forth. In addition, the attitude of defense counsel toward plea bargaining (demanding or reasonable, for example) appears to be related to the likelihood of success in reaching a compromise.[12] Again, these are constraints that shape the decisions made to some extent, but the exercise of discretion by counsel obviously occurs frequently and has important consequences.

Judicial Discretion

Judges decide whether objections that attorneys make to the questions asked of witnesses by other attorneys should be sustained or overruled. They decide whether evidence may be admitted or must be excluded, whether there is sufficient evidence to let the case go to the jury for a decision on the factual

question of guilt, or whether a mistrial must be declared as a result of some serious error that would prejudice the case. . . . They may have great influence over the jury through their attitudes, their rulings, and their charges. They will also have an impact on those who testify and those who are parties in the trial.[13]

Judges, too, are in positions that permit considerable discretionary activity. Some are more lenient than others in admitting certain types of evidence. Some have reputations for being "maximum sentence" judges, while others may be regarded as "bleeding heart liberals." Some are more trusting of police testimony and less inclined to pay strict attention to "technicalities" than others. Disparities in sentencing individuals who have committed similar crimes are yet another example of judicial discretion. At the level of the United States Supreme Court, judicial discretion is even involved in deciding whether or not to hear a particular case.[14] The discretion exercised by judges may not have the immediate life or death impact that sometimes characterizes police discretion, but the long-term effects of sentencing decisions may have the same impact.

Plea Bargaining as a Form of Discretion

Plea bargaining is a form of discretion that involves at least the defendant, the defense counsel, and the prosecutor. It may also involve the police and the judge, in some cases. Since bargained or negotiated pleas account for 90 to 95 percent of guilty pleas in the United States, plea bargaining is a key part of the criminal justice process. The parties involved all exercise discretion in bargaining over the charges to be filed and the sentence to be imposed. The defendant may exercise her or his discretion in deciding whether or not to enter into plea negotiations. The same is true of defense counsel and the prosecutor. Once they agree to negotiate, the opposing parties attempt to gain concessions from each other. The extent to which the parties are willing to grant such concessions depends upon their individual judgments (discretion) as to what may be gained in return. The judge, in some jurisdictions, exercises his or her discretion in determining whether or not to accept a negotiated guilty plea along with the attendant conditions. In some cases, the prosecutor may talk to the police officers involved in the arrest or investigation before deciding what concessions, if any, to grant in the negotiations.

As we have repeatedly pointed out, none of the discretionary powers exercised is without limits. Each participant in plea bargaining is constrained by the facts of the case, resources available, and the goals of other participants. Again, the network model allows us to analyze the workings of criminal justice practitioners as they go about their day-to-day duties.

Correctional Discretion

The exercise of discretion also occurs frequently and regularly among correctional officials. As Gifis indicates, the differential treatment accorded convicted criminals lodges enormous discretionary power in the hands of correctional officials.[15] Probation and parole officers decide what conditions to impose upon their charges and how strictly to enforce such conditions. In juvenile cases, for example, the judgment of a probation officer may determine whether a probationer can marry, move out of state, or join the armed forces.

Although parole boards operate according to specific regulations, discretion plays an important part in determining when and if parole or early release will occur. The discretionary powers of prison wardens to make inmate assignments and to allow minor infractions of prison rules to go unpunished by instructing guards as to the type of conduct they consider worthy of note is considerable. Similarly, prison staff members exercise their discretion in determining what to overlook and what to report to the warden.

While we have not attempted to discuss all the types of discretion in the day-to-day operations of the criminal justice network (for example, the discretion exercised by political figures in determining whether to try to influence the decisions of the police or prosecutor, or the discretion exercised by offenders in deciding when and how to commit a crime), it should be clear that discretion plays an important role at all levels of the network. Network participants, of course, are limited as to the amount and type of discretion they may employ by the factors we have discussed above. Still, the range of alternatives available at any given place in the network is sufficient to make it difficult to predict with certainty exactly what actions, if any, will be taken except, perhaps, in cases involving serious predatory crimes (and even these are sometimes not predictable). Selective reporting of crimes, selective enforcement of laws, and selective processing of those against whom the law is enforced are necessary and normal activities in the criminal justice network. Criminal justice, as we know it, could not exist without discretion. We should not, however, lose sight of the fact that the exercise of discretion sometimes confuses those who participate in or observe the network. When the exercise of discretion becomes whimsical or haphazard, predictability is lost and, for those in a democratic society, the network may cease to be perceived as one dispensing justice.

Summary

Discretion, or the exercise of individual choice or judgment, is an important part of the criminal justice process. While choices and judgments made by participants in the criminal justice network are limited by the resources available, the expectations of other participants, the law, and other factors, there is still considerable latitude in the decision-making process. Discretion is a normal, necessary part of criminal justice, but discretion can also be misused. The American Friends Service Committee has documented the following types of misuses of discretion: to increase managerial efficiency (as in plea bargaining), for political expediency (passing a law which is unenforceable, but which pacifies some pressure group), to do the publicly unmentionable (to control certain groups of people while giving the appearance of fairness, as in vagrancy laws), to protect one's own kind (to grant informal immunity to others in the same class or category), and to increase the sense of adequacy (to give the appearance of getting tough with criminals by passing harsh laws, even though these laws are seldom used).[16] When the exercise of discretion leads to unpredictability or predictable favoritism in the criminal justice network, it is likely that the network will be characterized as unjust.

Key Terms Defined

discretion the exercise of individual choice or judgment concerning possible courses of action. A normal and necessary part of the criminal justice network.

full enforcement enforcing all the laws all of the time.

selective enforcement enforcing some laws at one time and place, and others at other times and places.

plea bargaining a form of discretionary activity in which the charges to be filed and/or the sentence to be recommended are negotiated by at least the defendant and his or her counsel, and the prosecutor.

Discussion Questions

1. What does the term *discretion* mean and what are some of the factors that limit its use in the criminal justice network?

2. Why is the exercise of discretion by members of the public so crucial for all components of the criminal justice network?

3. Give specific examples illustrating the exercise of discretion by each of the following: police officers, prosecutors, and judges.

4. What are some of the dangers involved in the exercise of discretion by participants in the criminal justice network?

Notes

1. Kenneth Culp Davis, *Discretionary Justice: A Preliminary Report* (Chicago: University of Illinois Press, 1971), p. *v;* for further evidence of the concern over discretionary justice, see Jerome H. Skolnick, *Justice Without Trial* (New York: Wiley, 1975); Joseph Goldstein, "Police Discretion Not to Invoke the Criminal Process: Low-Visibility Decisions in the Administration of Justice," *The Yale Law Journal* 69 (Mar. 1960): 543–94.

2. Harry W. More, Jr., *Critical Issues in Law Enforcement* (Cincinnati, Ohio: Anderson, 1972), 151.

3. Davis, *Discretionary Justice,* 9–10.

4. Burton Atkins and Mark Pogrebin, "Introduction: Discretionary Decision-Making in the Administration of Justice," in *The Invisible Justice System: Discretion and the Law,* ed. Burton Atkins and Mark Pogrebin, (Cincinnati, Ohio: Anderson, 1978), 1.

5. Charles Breitel, "Controls in Criminal Law Enforcement," *University of Chicago Law Review* 27 (Spring 1960): 427.

6. Philip H. Ennis, "Crime, Victims, and the Police," *Trans-action* 4 (June 1967): 36–44.

7. Goldstein, "Police Discretion Not to Invoke the Criminal Process," 543–94.

8. Paul Chevigny, *Police Power: Police Abuses in New York City* (New York: Vintage Books, 1969).

9. George F. Cole, "The Decision to Prosecute," *Law and Society Review* 4 (February 1970): 313–43.

10. Davis, *Discretionary Justice,* 188.

11. *Southern California Law Review* 42 (1969), cited in Atkins and Pogrebin, *The Invisible Justice System: Discretion and the Law,* 141.

12. Juanita Jones, "Prosecutors and Public Defenders: Cooperative Relationships and Non-Negotiable Cases," in *The Invisible Justice System: Discretion and the Law,* ed. Burton Atkins and Mark Pogrebin (Cincinnati, Ohio: Anderson, 1978), 201.

13. Sue Titus Reid, *Crime and Criminology* (Hinsdale, Ill.: Dryden Press, 1976), 300.

14. Bob Woodward and Scott Armstrong, *The Brethren: Inside the Supreme Court* (New York: Simon and Schuster, 1979).

15. Steven Gifis, "Decision-making in a Prison Community," in *The Invisible Justice System: Discretion and the Law,* ed. Burton Atkins and Mark Pogrebin (Cincinnati, Ohio: Anderson, 1978), 317.

16. American Friends Service Committee, *The Struggle for Justice* (New York: Hill and Wang, 1971), ch. 8.

Suggested Readings

Aaronson, David A., Dienes, C. Thomas, and Musheno, Michael C. *Public Policy and Police Discretion: Processes of Decriminalization.* New York: Clark Boardman, 1984.

Atkins, Burton, and Pogrebin, Mark. *The Invisible Justice System: Discretion and the Law.* Cincinnati, Ohio: Anderson, 1978.

Cole, George F. *Criminal Justice: Law and Politics.* 3d ed. North Scituate, Mass.: Duxbury Press, 1980.

Curran, Debra, A. "Judicial Discretion and Defendant's Sex," *Criminology* 21, no. 1 (Feb. 1983): 41–58.

Davis, Kenneth C. *Discretionary Justice: A Preliminary Report.* Chicago: University of Illinois Press, 1971.

———— *Police Discretion.* St. Paul, Minn.: West Publishing Co., 1975.

James, Howard. *Crisis in the Courts.* New York: David McKay, 1977.

Kerstetter, Wayne A. "Police Participation in Structured Plea Negotiations," *Journal of Criminal Justice* 9, no. 2 (1981): 151–64.

Powell, Dennis D. "Race, Rank, and Police Discretion." *Journal of Police Science and Administration* 9, no. 4 (Dec. 1981): 383–89.

Roberg, Roy R., and Webb, Vincent J. *Critical Issues in Corrections: Problems, Trends and Prospects.* St. Paul, Minn.: West Publishing Co., 1981, ch. 10.

Visher, Christy A. "Gender, Police Arrest Decisions, and Notions of Chivalry," *Criminology* 21, no. 1 (Feb. 1983): 5–28.

Types of Crime: I   5

In chapter 2, we noted differences between substantive and procedural law, and differences between civil and criminal law. In this chapter, we will discuss several types of crime in order to familiarize the reader with some important elements of such crimes. A comprehensive examination of criminal law is beyond the scope of this text, but an overview of some types of crime should help the reader to examine, analyze, and interpret in general fashion any given criminal code. Since each state enacts its own criminal code, there is considerable variation among the states in the definitions of specific crimes. We recommend that each reader familiarize himself or herself with relevant state statutes to gain detailed understanding of the various offenses discussed therein.

Criminal law is enacted by legislative (state and federal) bodies (**statutory law**), and interpreted and/or modified by court decisions (**case law**). Criminal law, then, represents some of society's values (that a specific act is wrong) and, since these values are subject to change, criminal codes undergo periodic revisions. It is important, therefore, that both students and practitioners keep abreast of changes in relevant codes. This can be done by reviewing the revised statutes published by the various states periodically.

The laws discussed below have been developed over time (many originate in British common law) with numerous revisions. These laws are not necessarily the ones most frequently violated, but they do cover violations that are considered to be serious by most, if not all, states.

Some Important Distinctions

The offenses discussed below may be divided into two categories, crimes against the person and crimes against property. Crimes without complainants and white-collar/corporate offenses will be discussed in the next chapter. Before proceeding to our discussion of these offenses, we should distinguish between offenses known as felonies and those considered misdemeanors. **Felonies** are usually offenses punishable by sentences of more than one year in state or federal prisons. **Misdemeanors** are offenses punishable by sentences up to one year, usually in a county or local jail (although some states maintain institutions specifically for misdemeanants). Offenses of either type may also be punishable by fines.

In addition to the distinction between felonies and misdemeanors, we may categorize crimes as *malum in se*—acts which are wrong in and of themselves, or *malum prohibitum*—acts which are wrong because they are prohibited. Examples of the former include most crimes against the person (murder, rape, battery) and some property crimes (burglary, for example). Examples of the latter include the use of marijuana, tax evasion, and disorderly conduct.

A word should also be said about attempts to commit offenses. Generally, a person commits an attempt when she or he intentionally commits an act that constitutes a substantial step toward committing that offense. Thus, an individual who intentionally fires a pistol at another person without legal justification and with the intent to kill has attempted murder.

Crimes against the Person

Homicide

Homicide is generally considered to be the most serious felony. The term refers to the killing of a human being and it is often thought to be synonymous with murder, but murder is only one category of homicide.

Homicide Scene.
James L. Shaffer

Each time one human being kills another, a homicide occurs. However, it does not necessarily follow that a crime has been committed, since the law distinguishes between justifiable homicides, a legal execution or the use of deadly force in self-defense that is authorized or commanded by the law; criminal homicides, murder and manslaughter (voluntary, involuntary, and negligent); and excusable homicides, certain self-defense killings and killings resulting from accidents not involving negligence or unlawful acts.[1]

Historically, for a homicide to occur, the death of the victim had to occur within a given time period—usually a year and a day—after the attempted killing. This time requirement has now been deleted by some states and California has increased the length of the period to three years and one day.[2] For a homicide to occur, it must also be shown that the alleged victim was alive at the time of the offense and that death was not a result of the actions of an intermediate party (for example, a nurse who fails to give an available life-saving injection), but the consequence of the offense itself.

As we turn our attention to criminal homicides, keep in mind that the types are differentiated on the basis of the intent of the perpetrator. Murder and voluntary manslaughter generally require proof of a specific intent to kill or cause great bodily harm. Involuntary manslaughter normally requires only general criminal intent. In either case, the key elements of criminal homicide include the killing of one human being by another without justification.

Murder occurs when one human being is killed by another without lawful justification and with malice aforethought. A detailed examination of this definition tells us exactly what murder is and is not. First, we note that murder involves the "killing of one human being by another." This tells us that killing oneself is not murder (referred to instead as **suicide**), that the killing of some other animal is not murder, and that the killing of a human by an animal other than another human (or at the direction of another human) is not murder. Second, we note the words "without lawful justification." These words indicate that the killing of one human being by another is not murder if lawful justification can be proved. Finally, we note that **"malice aforethought"** is required for murder to exist. This phrase means simply that an intention to seriously harm someone or to commit a serious crime must exist for murder to occur, and that the killing of one human by another which results from an accident is not murder since no such intention exists. It is this phrase that distinguishes murder from other types of criminal homicide, as we shall see below.

While we will not analyze each definition of an offense in the step-by-step manner we have used for murder, we encourage the reader to use this technique to better comprehend the nature of any given statute. Exact comprehension of any statute is difficult even using this technique since some of the words used to define a criminal act are vague, ambiguous, or both. In the case of murder, the terms killing, human being, and lawful justification have empirical referents and are relatively easy to comprehend. Malice aforethought, however, refers to a state of mind and there is confusion concerning what the term means. At common law and in the minds of many today, malice involves ill will or hatred, while aforethought requires premeditation; but as we have indicated above, this is no longer true.

Actually, malice may be categorized as either expressed or implied. An example of expressed malice might involve a person "lying in wait" holding a pistol in another person's garage and firing the pistol at the garage owner when he or she enters the premises. Implied malice is involved in cases in which there was no actual intent to kill. Deaths resulting during the commission of a felony other than murder and deaths resulting from a total disregard for a substantial and foreseeable risk often involve implied malice.[3] In cases such as this, the action (or failure to take action) of the offender is considered so serious that he or she may be held responsible for the consequences of his or her actions even though he or she did not specifically intend these consequences (see felony murder rule below).

Some states distinguish between first- and second-degree murder. Such a distinction is generally based upon the presence of expressed malice aforethought in first-degree murder. Evidence of lying in wait, the use of poisons or intoxicants, and the brutal nature of a killing may all be used to demonstrate expressed malice aforethought in order to obtain a conviction for first-degree murder. The final decision, however, usually rests with a jury, which may or may not follow the letter of the law in reaching a verdict.[4]

Another form of murder is covered by what is referred to as the **felony murder doctrine**. This doctrine states that deaths resulting from the commission of a felony are the responsibility of the felon and, in some jurisdictions, his or her accomplices. Today, the felony murder rule is generally applied only when a dangerous or forcible felony (such as robbery, kidnapping, rape, or arson) is involved, although historically it has been applied in other types of cases.[5] Generally speaking, homicides that involve malice aforethought but do not meet the requirements of first-degree murder are murder in the second degree in those jurisdictions making such distinctions. Thus, second-degree murder may result from the commission of less dangerous felonies, from the commission of an act intended to cause great bodily harm, or from other actions that imply a disregard for human life (such as firing a weapon at a car on the freeway).

Manslaughter is unlawful homicide committed without malice aforethought and is a distinct crime rather than a degree of murder.[6] There are two categories of manslaughter—voluntary and involuntary or negligent. Voluntary manslaughter involves an intent to kill and may be distinguished from murder by the circumstances existing prior to the commission of the act. If great provocation exists, if the offender is in the "heat of passion," or if the offender is acting in a "blind rage," these factors may be taken as mitigating in the formulation of malice and the offender may be charged with voluntary manslaughter rather than murder. In determining whether an act is murder or manslaughter, a jury faces the difficult task of determining the degree of provocation, passion, or rage involved and the extent of provocation required to transform murder into manslaughter. In attempting to resolve such dilemmas, the courts have developed some general guidelines. For example, it is generally agreed that words alone are not sufficient provocation to transform a murder into manslaughter.[7] Some action such as a battery, mutual combat, the commission of adultery,[8] or resistance to an unlawful arrest is required. The courts have also consistently held that the provocation must be immediately related to the killing. That is, the killing must occur while the offender is in a provoked or passionate state. As the court stated *In re Fraley,* "the law will not permit a defendant to deliberate his wrong, and, avenging it by killing the wrongdoer, set up the plea that his act was committed in the heat of passion."[9]

The distinguishing feature of involuntary manslaughter is its unintentional nature. (This is the reason for the frequent reference to negligent manslaughter). Gross negligence or recklessness is a key element in this offense. Since many of us have committed reckless or negligent acts at one time or another, some standard was required to establish gross negligence. The established standard requires a definite disregard for the safety of others in the conduct leading to a death. Examples include unsafe operation of a motor vehicle,[10] failure to employ reasonable care in hunting game, and failure to provide proper exits in buildings. Some states have developed misdemeanor manslaughter laws that are similar to the felony murder doctrine. The basis for these laws is the belief that the commission of some misdemeanors (generally, *malum in se* offenses) implies negligence and, therefore, the offender is responsible for any deaths resulting from the commission of these offenses.

Punishment for homicide varies according to the category of homicide involved. The most severe punishment may be handed down for first-degree murder (including the death penalty in certain circumstances) and the least severe for involuntary manslaughter, with degrees of punishment in between. In Illinois, for example, murder is a Class X felony (death or up to 30 years in prison), voluntary manslaughter is a Class Two felony (not more than seven years in prison), and involuntary manslaughter is a Class Four felony (not more than three years in prison).[11]

Assault and Battery

All crimes against the person do not, obviously, result in the victim's death. The unlawful application of force by one individual against another may constitute a **battery,** and the attempt or threat to commit a battery may constitute an **assault.** Some jurisdictions combine the two offenses while others treat each separately. Contrary to popular misconceptions, an injury need not result for a battery to occur. It is the unlawful application of force, not the result of the application that constitutes the battery. Such actions as pushing a chair into another, pushing another, or patting another on the buttocks may constitute battery even if no injury occurs.[12] Further, spitting on another or striking another with a thrown projectile has been considered battery, even if the person spit upon or hit by the projectile was not the intended target. Batteries can also include administering poison, communicating a disease, and even exposing a person to inclement weather.[13] Of course, not all contact, or even all violent contact, constitutes battery. Contact sports such as boxing, wrestling, and football are generally exempt from battery rules so long as the contact is within the rules of the game. Similarly, the parent who physically disciplines his or her child does not commit a battery unless such discipline is excessive. The reasonable use of physical force against another in self-defense may also be justified.

Actions that place one person in reasonable apprehension of being battered (threat) or an attempt to batter may constitute assault; thus, the unlawful attempt to strike another constitutes an assault and if the attempt is consumated (successful) a battery has occurred. Some interpretations of assault statutes seem to require an awareness on behalf of the victim that he or she is in danger of being battered, while others simply require a criminal state of mind on the part of the offender. Interpretations also vary with respect to whether the offender has the ability to commit a battery or only the apparent ability. Threatening another person with a soft rubber knife might be an assault under the latter interpretation, but not under the former.

The key issue in determining whether or not an assault has occurred is whether or not reasonable apprehension exists on behalf of the victim. Generally, words alone do not appear to be sufficient to generate such apprehension, but must be accompanied by some threatening act on behalf of the offender.

Some jurisdictions include aggravated assault and aggravated battery in their criminal codes. **Aggravated** assault occurs when one conceals his or her identity, employs a deadly weapon, or assaults a member of a special class of people—teacher, firefighter, or police officer, for example—while they are performing their duties.[14] Aggravated batteries are those batteries involving the conditions just mentioned, or batteries that are likely to cause great bodily harm.

In some jurisdictions, no battery can occur without an assault (the consummated battery includes the threat or attempt to batter) and the two offenses are combined into one statute.

Forcible Rape

Traditional definitions of **rape** generally involve the following elements: (1) sexual intercourse; (2) by a male with a female other than his wife; (3) against her will and without consent; and (4) by force or threat of force, or while she is unconscious. Again, the definition may be broken down into its component parts to better enable us to comprehend the nature of the offense.

Traditionally, sexual intercourse requires penetration of the female sex organ by the male sex organ. Lewd fondling or caressing, and oral or anal sexual contact may constitute batteries, indecent liberties, deviate sexual conduct, or **sodomy;** but they do not traditionally constitute rape.

Historically, the courts have adhered to a principle of spousal immunity and have excepted forced intercourse by a husband with his wife from the category of forcible rape. The underlying assumption seems to have been that marriage is a permanent consent to sexual intercourse. Some states—Iowa, Oregon, Illinois, and Delaware among others—have eliminated this exemption, however, and it is now possible in these states for a husband to be convicted of rape if the wife can prove that she did not consent to sexual intercourse. Another modification being witnessed involves the gender (sex) of the offender and victim. Under the

4 men sentenced for barroom rape

FALL RIVER, Mass. (AP)—Four men convicted of gang-raping a woman on a barroom pool table were sentenced to prison terms ranging from 6 to 12 years Monday by a judge who said they "brutalized a defenseless young woman and sought to degrade and destroy her human, individual dignity."

The lawyer for the victim said afterward that the 22-year-old mother of two feared for her safety and had moved permanently from the area.

As friends and family wept, Superior Court Judge William Young imposed terms of 9 to 12 years upon Daniel Silva, 27, Victor Raposo, 23, and John Cordeiro, 24.

Young also sentenced Joseph Vieira, 28, to a term of 6 to 8 years. Bristol County District Attorney Ronald Pina asked for a more lenient sentence for Vieira, noting that he had no prior record. Also, the woman's testimony that he was directly involved in the rape was not corroborated by other witnesses.

The maximum penalty for aggravated rape is life imprisonment.

A crowd of several hundred stood quietly outside the century-old courthouse while the sentences were read. But the silence erupted into shouts of "Let them go!"

The defendants, all Portuguese immigrants, have drawn support from many in their community who feel they were treated unfairly because of their national origin.

All the sentences will be served at Walpole State Prison, a maximum-security facility. Under state law Vieira must serve at least four years of his sentence. The others face a minimum of six years behind bars before being eligible for parole.

Reprinted by permission of Associated Press.

traditional definition of rape, it was virtually an all male offense and virtually all victims were female. Today, however, the word *person,* in some jurisdictions, has been substituted for the words *male* and *female,* making it legally possible for a male to rape another male or for a female to rape a male.[15] Some states also specify a minimum age for the offender.

There is considerable controversy regarding what constitutes "consent" on behalf of a rape victim. In general, a victim who is incapacitated by use of alcohol or other drugs, who is unconscious, who is mentally ill or severely retarded, or who is a victim of deception or fraud is incapable of giving consent. However, some courts have held that the victim must resist to the utmost and that any form of submission, prior to forced penetration, constitutes consent. For example, an alleged offender was acquitted of rape when it was disclosed during cross-examination that the victim had a knife in her possession at the time of the incident, but made no attempt to use it to defend herself.[16] Opinions such as this are rare, however, and most cases today hinge upon factors such as the number of assailants, the presence of a weapon, etc. Further, there is a trend toward limiting the introduction of evidence concerning the victim's previous sexual experiences in rape trials.[17]

The element of force or threat of force in rape is somewhat ambiguous. Cases in which a battery occurs are relatively clear-cut. It is equally clear that the presence or use of a deadly weapon is not required to prove that force was used. Torn clothing, cuts, bruises, or teethmarks are frequently used as indicators that force accompanied sexual intercourse. Generally speaking, courts have held that coercion sufficient to accomplish the intended result—sexual intercourse—fulfills the force or threat of force requirement for rape.

Other Sex Offenses

Although forcible rape is considered the most serious of the sex offenses, there are a number of other such offenses that should be mentioned. Some jurisdictions hold that a female under a given age (usually sixteen to eighteen) cannot legally consent to sexual intercourse. If such intercourse occurs, the male involved may be charged with statutory rape. Other states categorize such acts as indecent liberties with a minor or contributing to the sexual delinquency of a minor, and these categories may include sexual contact other than intercourse.[18]

One of the recent trends in criminal law is to reduce the number of sex crimes by incorporating all forms of sexual penetration (vaginal, oral, and anal) into the crime of sexual assault or sexual abuse. Cases involving force, minors, or weapons are then termed aggravated sexual assault or aggravated sexual abuse and carry a stiffer penalty.[19]

Traditionally, a number of sexual acts, including oral/genital and anal/genital contact were prohibited under the general heading of **sodomy.** The trend today is toward accepting these acts as legal if they occur in private between consenting adults. In a number of states, **deviate sexual assault** statutes may be used to prosecute perpetrators who use force in the commission of such acts.

There are numerous other sex offenses, but space does not permit a detailed discussion of all such offenses. Analysis of your own state's criminal code under headings such as adultery, fornication, prostitution, incest, and indecent exposure will familiarize you with such offenses.

Robbery

Robbery is unique in that it may be characterized as both a crime against the person and a crime against property. In addition, unlike homicide and aggravated assault, the majority of robberies involve victims and offenders who are strangers. **Robbery** involves taking property (theft) from another person by force or threat of force (assault, battery, or murder). Such theft must occur in the presence of the victim, but need not involve taking the property from the person of the victim.

As long as the property is within the general proximity of the victim and under the victim's control (cash stolen from a teller at a bank), and as long as force or threat of force is used (the presence of a gun pointed at the teller) with the intent to permanently deprive the victim of the property, a robbery has occurred. Threat of deadly force is not required—pushing, jostling, or striking with a fist are sufficient to substantiate the force element in robbery. So, the pickpocket who is caught trying to remove the victim's wallet and who struggles with the victim to pull the wallet away has crossed the line between theft and robbery. Similarly, threats to destroy valuable property or to inflict bodily injury have consistently been found sufficient to substantiate a charge of robbery.

Gradations of robbery are fairly common, with armed or aggravated robbery being the most serious form of the crime and subject to the most severe punishment.

Crimes against Property

The law protects the property of citizens as well as their persons. The list of crimes against property is extensive, and we shall illustrate the nature of these crimes by focusing on three of them: theft, burglary, and arson.

Theft or Larceny

Theft occurs when one obtains unauthorized control over the property of another with the intent to permanently deprive the rightful possessor of the property. Many statutes include receiving stolen property and obtaining property through deception (embezzlement, for example) or under false pretenses under the general heading of theft. Theft is a crime against the right of possession, not necessarily ownership, and statutes usually protect both actual and constructive possession. Actual possession involves physical control of property. For example, Jones is walking down the street carrying some packages. Smith takes one of the packages, runs away, and sells the contents of the package. Smith has committed a theft involving actual possession. Constructive possession occurs when the property involved is outside of the owner's control, but the right of ownership has not been relinquished. Jones drives his car to Brown's house and leaves it there. While Brown is not looking, Smith steals the car. Neither Jones nor Brown had actual possession of the car, but Jones retained constructive possession and is the victim of a theft.

Since theft is a crime against possession, it is possible for a person to be charged with stealing his or her own property. An apartment owner who signs a legally binding contract to rent an apartment complete with stereo, refrigerator, and television relinquishes ownership to the renter for the duration of the lease. If the apartment owner enters the apartment without the renter's knowledge and removes the stereo with the intent to keep it permanently, she or he may be charged with theft even though the stereo belongs to her or him. One, then, does not have to own the property stolen in order to be the victim of a theft; he or she must simply have legal possession of the property. The property involved may be either real property (land, buildings, etc.) or personal property (all other property).

The issue of intent to permanently deprive an individual of his or her property is frequently the key to theft cases. If you borrow a rake from your neighbor's garage to use for an afternoon, you have not committed theft since you did not intend to permanently deprive your neighbor of the rake. If, however, you pick a watermelon from the neighbor's garden and eat it, you could be prosecuted for theft since you have unquestionably deprived your neighbor permanently of the use of the watermelon.

The issue of intent to permanently deprive arises frequently in shoplifting cases. When a person conceals stolen merchandise and passes the checkout lanes in a store or leaves the premises with the stolen property, such intent is easy to demonstrate. If, however, a security officer confronts the person concealing the merchandise at the time the merchandise is concealed, intent to permanently deprive is considerably more difficult to prove, since the shoplifter can claim that he or she intended to pay for the items at the checkout lanes.

Automobile theft presents some of the same problems. Does the teenager who takes an auto without permission to go to a dance across town and then leaves the auto unharmed intend to permanently deprive the owner of the use of the vehicle? A number of states have created "joyriding" or "unauthorized use of a vehicle" statutes to deal with such cases. The intent to permanently deprive is not an element of these statutes.

In most instances, theft is divided into two categories based upon the dollar value of the items involved. The dividing line varies (in some states it is three hundred dollars), but the lesser dollar amounts are categorized as petty theft while the more substantial sums constitute grand theft.

Burglary

"I've been robbed!" is a common cry among property owners who return from a weekend away to find their television or stereo gone. Actually, these individuals have been burglarized, not robbed.

Traditionally, **burglary** involves breaking into and entering the dwelling of another, at night, with the intent to commit a felony. The use of force to enter such a dwelling constitutes "breaking into." Courts have held that the amount of force required may be exceedingly little, such as turning a door knob[20] or raising an unlocked window.[21]

A Man Peeking through a Porch Window— Voyeurism. *James L. Shaffer*

Some jurisdictions hold that one who enters a building lawfully but remains within without authorization after the building is closed commits "breaking in." This type of action may be referred to as "constructive breaking" and applies to acts of deception used to gain entry.

Unlawful entry must also occur for a burglary to transpire. The entry may be very slight: reaching inside to extract some article is sufficient. Constructive entry, involving the use of a trained animal, rope, or other device, may also occur.

Burglary statutes today cover not only the dwellings of others, but also telephone booths, unoccupied buildings, automobiles, aircraft, watercraft, and railroad cars. Similarly, modern burglary statutes have dropped the requirement that the breaking and entering occur at night. Some jurisdictions do maintain a distinction between day and night burglaries with stiffer penalties for the latter.

With burglary again, the intent element is often the most difficult to prove. The prosecution must prove both the intent to enter and the intent to commit a felony. One who falls asleep in a library and awakens after the building is closed has not committed a burglary, nor has the individual who enters the wrong apartment reasonably believing it to be his or her own. This sometimes happens when an intoxicated individual breaks into an apartment near and similar to his own, believing that his spouse has locked him out. In this case, there is no intent to enter unlawfully and even though a breakin occurs, the individual is not committing a burglary (although he may be liable for any damages occurring).

With respect to the second form of intent, the intent to commit a felony, there is some disagreement. Some courts hold that intent to commit any felony will suffice, others that only dangerous felonies will suffice. In some jurisdictions, any type of theft, including misdemeanor theft, is taken as evidence of this type of intent. Intent is easy enough to prove when the burglar is caught with stolen property on his or her person, or when the burglar uses a knife or gun to threaten others at the scene. The intent to commit a felony may be more difficult to prove when the burglar is caught making his or her entry. The presence of a torch, burglary tools, dynamite, or a weapon may be sufficient to indicate such intent. It need not be shown that the accused did, in fact, commit a felony, only that he or she intended to do so.

Arson

Arson poses a serious threat to both human life and property. **Arson** involves the willful and unlawful burning of a building or structure. At one time arson was limited to burning dwellings belonging to another, but today statutes include all buildings and structures, including those belonging to the culprit.

A general criminal state of mind, rather than a specific intent to commit arson, is all that is required by most arson statutes. An act intended as vandalism or an act of extortion that leads to the unlawful burning of a structure may constitute arson as well. In some cases, gross negligence may also result in prosecution for arson.

Total destruction of the property involved is not required to prove arson. Similarly, the arsonist need not be physically present to ignite the fire. A time bomb or other device causing fire that detonates after the offender has left the premises is sufficient to establish arson. Motor vehicles, watercraft, and aircraft are also covered by arson statutes.

Arson for profit has become a major problem in the United States. Burning one's own property in order to collect insurance has become almost fashionable among property owners experiencing financial difficulties. The property owner who engages in such actions hopes that evidence of arson will be destroyed by the fire, making the disaster look like an accident.

Measuring Crime

Official crime statistics are available at the national level in the **Uniform Crime Reports** (UCR) prepared by the Federal Bureau of Investigation. The FBI claims that the UCR cover about 99 percent of the total national population with the most complete reporting from urban areas (99 percent) and the least complete reporting from rural areas (93 percent). Although the FBI statistics are the most comprehensive available at the national level, they are subject to a number of sources of error. First, reporting is voluntary and not all agencies report. Second, the UCR are based upon reports prepared and submitted by individual police agencies, and reporting errors made by each agency are added to those made by all other agencies in the final report. Such errors include mistakes in calculations and mistakes in placing offenses in appropriate categories. Third, statistics in the UCR say nothing about whether the alleged offender was actually convicted of the offense for which he or she was arrested. If we are interested in the number of offenders arrested for certain types of crime in a certain time period, UCR data are useful, but if we want to know something about the actual extent and nature of criminal behavior, these data are considerably less valuable. It should be noted that the weaknesses we have pointed out are also noted by the FBI in their annual publication, *Crime in the United States.*

There are a variety of official statistics available at the local and state levels. Most police departments have statistics on **offenses known to the police** (those offenses observed by or reported to the police) and **offenses cleared by arrest.** Of all official statistics, offenses known to the police probably provide the most complete picture of the nature and extent of certain types of illegal activities (not including white-collar, organized, corporate, or political crime). Even when we consider the "Index Offenses"—criminal homicide, aggravated assault, forcible rape, robbery, burglary, theft (over three hundred dollars), auto theft, and arson—there is considerable evidence to indicate that less than 50 percent of these crimes are reported to the police.[22]

If estimates are reasonably accurate, the police are able to arrest a suspect for only about one out of five Index Offenses reported, which means that about 80 percent of these offenses reported to the police are not included in statistics based upon crimes cleared by arrest.

Official statistics may be collected at a number of levels in the criminal justice network. However, each level includes some possible sources of error. Table 5.1 indicates some sources of error that may affect official statistics collected at each level in the network. Each official source of statistics has appropriate uses, but generally speaking, the sources of error increase as we move through each level in the network.

Finally, there are two additional sources of error that may affect official statistics. First, in our current criminal justice network, there is a strong tendency for those who are least able to afford the luxury of private counsel and middle-class standards of living to be overrepresented at all levels. Whether official statistics represent actual differences in the nature and extent of crime by social class or whether they reflect the inability of members of the lower social class to avoid official labeling as readily as their middle-class counterparts is not entirely clear, although there is considerable support for the latter explanation. Second,

Table 5.1 Some Sources of Measurement Error at Specified Levels in the Criminal Justice Network

Levels at Which Data May Be Collected		Sources of Error in Official Statistics
Police	1. Offenses known to police	All offenses not detected
		All offenses not reported to or recorded by the police
	2. Offenses cleared by arrest	Errors from level 1
		All offenses reported which do not lead to arrest
Prosecutor	3. Offenses leading to prosecution	Errors from levels 1 and 2
		All offenses which resulted in arrest but which did not lead to prosecution
Courts	4. Offenses leading to a conviction	Errors from levels 1, 2, 3
		All offenses prosecuted which do not lead to conviction
Detention Facilities	5. Offenses leading to incarceration	Errors from levels 1, 2, 3, 4
		All offenses leading to adjudication but not to incarceration

Source: Used by permission of Cox/Conrad, *Juvenile Justice,* p. 18.

it is important to remember that agencies collect and publish official statistics for a variety of purposes (such as justifying next year's budget request). This does not mean that all or even most agency personnel deliberately manipulate statistics for their own purposes, but all statistics are open to interpretation and may be presented in a variety of ways to suit the purposes of the presenters.

It is apparent that using official statistics to assess the extent and nature of crime is like looking at the tip of an iceberg; that is, a substantial proportion of crime remains hidden beneath the surface. While much crime occurs that is not reported to or recorded by officials, there is no precise way of determining just how much remains hidden. Attempts to assess the extent and nature of criminal activity have involved victim survey research and self-report studies.

Our knowledge of "hidden crime" has been improved considerably over the past several years by **victim survey research.** Random samples of citizens are taken in specified cities or on a nationwide basis, and these citizens are asked to indicate whether or not (and how often) they have been the victims of crime in a specified time period. Respondents who indicate they have been victims, unlike respondents in self-report studies, are not generally admitting illegal behavior and may, therefore, be more honest than self-report respondents. Victim survey research indicates that somewhere between 50 and 66 percent of all serious crime in the United States is not reported to the police and that the reporting rate varies for different types of crime. Most homicides and auto thefts are reported, most rapes, aggravated assaults, robberies, burglaries, and thefts are not.

Although victim survey research has expanded our knowledge of the crime picture considerably, it too has limitations. For obvious reasons, we cannot collect data on homicidal victimizations from victims; we generally do not ask about white-collar, corporate, or political crime or drug-related crime; and victims of some types of crimes (rape, for instance) may be hesitant to report. Undoubtedly some under- and over-reporting occur as the result of misinterpretation of the questions asked, and memory also plays a role in victim reports.

Self-Report Studies

Recognizing that official statistics provide a "false dichotomy" between criminals (those officially labeled) and noncriminals (those who may commit crimes, but are not labeled), Short, Nye, and others decided to use self-reports from juveniles to compare the extent and nature of delinquent activity on the part of institutionalized (labeled) and noninstitutionalized (nonlabeled) juveniles.[23] **Self-reports** of delinquent behavior were obtained by distributing questionnaires to both labeled and nonlabeled juveniles. These questionnaires allowed respondents to indicate what types of delinquent acts they had committed and the frequency with which the acts had been committed. Short and Nye conclude that delinquency among noninstitutionalized juveniles is extensive and that there is little difference in the extent and nature of delinquent acts committed by noninstitutionalized and institutionalized juveniles. In addition, Short and Nye indicate that official statistics lead us to misbelieve that delinquency is largely a lower-class phenomenon, since few differences in the self-reported incidence of delinquency exist among lower, middle, and upper social class juveniles. The conclusions reached in similar studies by Porterfield, Voss, and Akers generally agree with those of Short and Nye.[24]

Self-report studies are subject to criticism on the grounds that those who serve as respondents may under- or over-report their illegal activities. Some researchers have included questions designed to detect deception. Clark and Tifft used follow-up interviews and the polygraph to assess the extent to which deception occurred in their self-report study and found that all respondents made corrections on their original questionnaires when given the opportunity. Three-fourths of all the changes increased the frequency of admitted deviancy, all respondents under-reported their misconduct on at least one item, and one-half over-reported on at least one item. Clark and Tifft conclude that "those items most frequently used on delinquency scales were found to be rather inaccurate."[25]

In conclusion, the use of self-report scales as the only means of determining the extent and nature of crime is risky. However, these scales provide information which can be cross-checked in a variety of ways (e.g., through police records) and they allow comparisons between official and unofficial estimates of crime.

Summary

In this chapter we have examined selected criminal laws in some detail to familiarize the reader with the important aspects of such laws. By analyzing the definitions of the various crimes step-by-step, we can better understand the exact nature and requirements of these crimes.

The general distinction between felonies and misdemeanors has been discussed, along with differences between offenses which are *malum in se* and *malum prohibitum.*

Criminal homicides, rape, and robbery are among the most serious of the crimes against the person. The elements of these offenses, as well as those of the property crimes of theft, burglary, and arson, have been briefly analyzed in this chapter.

There are a variety of ways of collecting information concerning crime. The Uniform Crime Reports are the most widely used source of official crime statistics, but they considerably underestimate the extent of crime if we can believe information collected through victim survey research and self-report studies.

Key Terms Defined

statutory law law enacted by legislative bodies.
case law law based on court decisions.
felony an offense punishable by a sentence of more than one year in prison.
misdemeanor an offense punishable by up to one year in jail.
acts *malum in se* acts that are wrong in and of themselves.
acts *malum prohibitum* acts that are wrong because they are prohibited.
homicide the killing of another person.
murder the premeditated and unlawful killing of another person.
suicide killing oneself.

malice aforethought the intention to seriously harm someone or commit a serious crime.

felony murder rule the rule stating that an accidental killing that occurs during the commission of felony may be a murder.

manslaughter an unlawful homicide committed without malice aforethought.

assault an act that creates in one person the reasonable fear of being battered by another by reason of threat or attempt to batter.

battery an intentional, unprovoked harmful physical contact by one person (or an object controlled by that person) with another.

aggravation an act that increases the seriousness of the crime in question.

rape sexual intercourse by force or threat of force without lawful consent.

sodomy (deviate sexual assault) sexual contact between the sex organs of, or an object controlled by, one person and the mouth or anus of another.

robbery the illegal taking of property from another by force or threat of force.

theft (larceny) taking unauthorized control over the property of another with the intent to permanently deprive the rightful possessor of the property.

burglary generally, breaking into and entering the dwelling of another with the intent to commit a felony.

arson the willful and unlawful burning of a building or structure.

Uniform Crime Reports reports prepared by the Federal Bureau of Investigation concerning reported crimes in the United States.

offenses known to the police offenses reported to, or observed by, the police.

offenses cleared by arrest offenses in which an individual has been made available for prosecution.

victim survey research research that requests a sample of the population to report their experiences as crime victims over a given period of time.

self-report studies studies asking respondents to report their criminal activities over a period of time.

Discussion Questions

1. Why is it important to have a framework for analyzing current criminal codes?

2. What is the significance of the "mental state" of the offender in homicide and burglary cases?

3. What factors differentiate between robbery, theft, and burglary?

4. What sources of information would you use to obtain the most accurate possible picture of crime in the United States? Why?

Notes

1. Rollin M. Perkins, *Perkins on Criminal Law* (Mineola, N.Y.: Foundation Press, 1969), 33.

2. Allen L. Gamage and Charles F. Hemphill, *Basic Criminal Law* (New York: McGraw-Hill, 1979), 5.

3. Hazel B. Kerper and Jerold H. Israel, *Introduction to the Criminal Justice System* (St. Paul, Minn.: West Publishing Co., 1979), 136.

4. Joel Samaha, *Criminal Law* (St. Paul, Minn.: West Publishing Co., 1983), 86–90.

5. Perkins, *Perkins on Criminal Law*, 45.

6. Perkins, *Perkins on Criminal Law*, 81.

7. *Mullaney v. Wilbur*, 421 U.S. 684 (1974).

8. *Dabney v. State*, 21 So. 211, 113 Ala. 38 (1897).

9. *In re Fraley* 109 P. 295, 3 Okla. Crim. 719 (1910).

10. *Commonwealth v. Welansky*, 316 Mass. 383, 53 NE 2nd 902 (1944).

11. *Illinois Criminal Procedure for 1986*, ch. 38, art. 8–4, p. 47.

12. Perkins, *Perkins on Criminal Law*, 107–8.

13. *Woodward v. State*, 144 So. 895 (1932); *State v. Lankford*, 12 A. 13 (1917); and *Pallis v. State*, 26 So. 339 (1899).

14. *Moreland v. State*, 188 SWI, 125, Ark. 24 (1916).

15. *State v. Flaherty*, 146 A. 7 (1929).

16. "Man, 22, Acquitted of Rape, to Face Parole, Pardon Board," *Peoria Journal Star*, Friday, 7 Jan. 1977, C-14.

17. Sandy Hotchkiss, "The Realities of Rape," *Human Behavior* (December 1978): 20.

18. "Legal Developments," *Concern* 2, no. 1 (January 1980): 6.

19. *Illinois Criminal Procedure for 1986*, ch. 38, sec. 12:13–12:16.

20. *State v. Perry*, 145 N.W. 56 (1914); *State v. Rosencrans*, 24 Wash. 2d. 775 (1946).

21. *State v. McAfee*, 100 S.E. 2d. 249 (1957).

22. Philip H. Ennis, "Crime, Victims, and the Police," *Transaction* (June 1967): 36–44; Department of Justice, *Criminal Victimization Surveys in 13 American Cities*, June 1975.

23. James F. Short, Jr. and F. Ivan Nye, "Extent of Unrecorded Juvenile Delinquency: Some Tentative Conclusions," *Journal of Criminal Law, Criminology, and Police Science* 49, no. 4 (July-August 1958): 296–302.

24. Austin L. Porterfield, *Youth in Trouble* (Fort Worth, Ind.: Potisham Foundation, 1946); Harwin L. Voss, "Socioeconomic Status and Reported Delinquent Behavior," *Social Problems* 13, (Winter 1966): 314–24; Akers, R. L., "Socioeconomic Status and Delinquent Behavior: A Retest," *Journal of Research on Crime and Delinquency* 1 (1964): 38–46.

25. John P. Clark and Larry L. Tifft, "Polygraph and Interview Validation of Self-Reported Deviant Behavior," *American Sociological Review* 31, no. 4 (August 1966): 516–23.

Suggested Readings

Brumbaugh, John M. *Criminal Law and Approaches to the Study of Law: Cases and Materials.* Mineola, N.Y.: Foundation Press, 1986.

Gamage, Allen L., and Hemphill, Charles F. *Basic Criminal Law.* 2d ed. New York: McGraw-Hill, 1979.

Glaser, Daniel. *Crime in Our Changing Society.* New York: Holt, Rinehart and Winston, 1978.

Inbau, Fred E., Moenssens, Andre A., and Thompson, James R. *Criminal Law: Cases and Comments.* 4th ed. Mineola, N.Y.: Foundation Press, 1987, ch. 4–6.

LaFave, Wayne R. *Principles of Criminal Law: Cases, Comments, and Questions.* St. Paul, Minn.: West Publishing Co., 1978.

Perkins, Rollin M. *Perkins on Criminal Law.* 2d ed. Mineola, N.Y.: Foundation Press, 1969.

Samaha, Joel. *Criminal Law.* St. Paul, Minn.: West Publishing Co., 1983.

Types of Crime: II   6

Key Terms

crimes without complainants
prostitution

white-collar crime
fraud
organized crime

In this chapter, we will discuss two categories of crime that have been surrounded for some time by controversy—**crimes without complainants** and **white-collar crimes**. The former, often called crimes without victims,[1] involve the provision of goods and services that are in demand, but illegal. The latter are crimes committed by persons who occupy positions of trust in business, medicine, law, and other areas.[2] As we analyze these crimes, we will indicate why they remain controversial, the procedures involved in dealing with individuals involved in such crimes, and the consequences of these crimes for our society.

Crimes without Complainants

Schur's discussion of "crimes without victims," published in 1965, led to considerable controversy. His initial analysis focused on abortion, homosexuality, and drug addiction as crimes without victims in the sense that they all involve "the willing exchange, among adults, of strongly demanded, but legally proscribed, goods or services."[3] In the years following the publication of Schur's book, both abortion and homosexuality have been largely decriminalized. Others, following Schur's lead, began to include in the general category of crimes without victims—prostitution, gambling, and pornography/obscenity.[4] The debate concerning whether or not these activities involve victims has raged for some time.

Pornography Shops—
Legal or Illegal?
Images of Life
1984, Howard A.
Patenaude, Jr.

We prefer to use the term "crimes without complainants," since it accurately describes the majority of such activities in the sense that the supposed victims of these acts seldom file complaints. Whether they see themselves as victims and whether society should consider them victims are issues that are indeed difficult to resolve. It is clear, however, that attempts to legislate morality and to enforce such legislation produce serious consequences for those involved in the criminal justice network.[5] Among these consequences are the necessity for the police themselves to serve as complainants with respect to such activities and tremendous costs in police resources (time, money to pay informants and to make drug buys, place bets, etc.), prosecutorial resources, court time, and rehabilitation programs. Most importantly, there is general consensus among those who study crimes without complainants that there is seldom any "payoff" or return for the investment made in attempting to enforce laws regulating these activities. It is common knowledge that the street-level drug pusher is replaced within hours (perhaps minutes) of his arrest, that the prostitute is often back working the streets before the arresting officer has finished the arrest reports, and that gamblers and addicts return to their habits more often than not regardless of the punishment/rehabilitation programs prescribed.

Prostitutes protest

BERKELEY, Calif. (AP)—Prostitutes chased out of a neighborhood by a citizens' patrol have gone to City Hall to protest what they call a "witch hunt" that creates an atmosphere ripe for violence against them.

Since Feb. 10, a half-dozen residents have patroled the West Berkeley stretch of University Avenue nightly, talking to hookers and following them until they leave the area.

Members of the neighborhood patrol say they want to clean up the streets. The hookers say they are poverty victims forced into prostitution to feed their children.

"Hounding one woman out of one neighborhood and into another does not solve the problem," Rachel West, spokeswoman for the U.S. Prostitutes Collective, said Wednesday. "They harass the women. They follow them around. They want to take away their economic livelihood."

Tuesday night, supporters of the prostitutes asked the Berkeley City Council to condemn the patrol's actions and support abolition of prostitution laws.

Reprinted by permission of Associated Press.

Prostitution and Related Offenses

Prostitution involves agreeing to, or engaging in, sexual acts for compensation. While it has traditionally been treated as an offense committed by women, today many jurisdictions recognize that the offender may be of either sex. The offense is generally a misdemeanor and the most common punishment upon conviction is a fine. Patronizing a prostitute, allowing a house to be used for purposes of prostitution, soliciting (arranging or offering to arrange) for a prostitute, pandering (compelling or arranging for a person to commit prostitution), and pimping (making money from the prostitution of another) are also generally prohibited by law. In spite of the numerous laws prohibiting prostitution and related activities, however, these activities continue to flourish more or less openly throughout the world and certainly in every major city in the United States.[6] Law enforcement efforts to reduce the incidence of these activities sometimes succeed in forcing participants to move from one location to another, but the elimination of such activities seems highly unlikely. The demand and willingness to pay for sexual services virtually insures the supply, as is characteristic of all the activities covered by the umbrella term crimes without complainants. Recognition of this fact has led a number of countries to legalize prostitution and at least some jurisdictions in the United States (some counties in Nevada, for example) to follow suit.[7]

Drug Offenses

The sale, manufacture, distribution, and possession/use of all narcotic (opium-based) drugs, alcohol, most hallucinogenic drugs, cocaine, and certain other stimulant (amphetamine) drugs, barbiturates, and marijuana are regulated by both federal and state laws. Our society, however, can be characterized as a drug-using or abusing society, and attempts to regulate the use and traffic of some drugs while allowing others to be used without such regulations have been highly unsuccessful. For example, we allow adults to use tobacco and alcohol quite freely even though tobacco has been determined by the Surgeon General of the United States to be harmful to the health of the user and alcohol has been shown to be among the most frequently abused and dangerous of all drugs. At the same time, we prohibit marijuana use among the general population even though test results concerning its effects are contradictory, and we prohibit the use of heroin even though there is no evidence that, when taken in regulated doses under sanitary conditions, such use would be harmful.[8]

Further confusion in the attempt to regulate drugs results from the fact that while sale, use, possession, or manufacture of certain substances is illegal, addiction itself is not a crime. The addict is not a criminal unless he or she is engaged in one of the prohibited activities.

The same rules of supply and demand, and the same outcomes of enforcement attempts discussed earlier with respect to prostitution, apply to drug-related offenses. Further, the fact that many drugs of choice are illegal results in a black market characterized by relatively high prices for such drugs. In order to obtain money to purchase these drugs, users may turn to burglary, theft, robbery, or prostitution. The incidence of these crimes then increases, placing further demands upon the resources of the criminal justice network. This cycle is perpetuated when attempts to rehabilitate users fail and they return to society unemployed to take up their old habits.

Gambling

Another common, though often illegal, practice in our society involves placing a bet or wager on the outcome of some event. As Gardiner noted some time ago, public attitudes toward gambling are often more permissive than the statutes that are common to the United States—"gambling is either positively desired or else not regarded as particularly reprehensible by a substantial proportion of the population."[9] In 1976, the Commission on the Review of the National Policy Toward Gambling made the following observation: "Gambling is inevitable. No matter what is said or done by advocates or opponents of gambling in all its various forms, it is an activity that is practiced, or tacitly endorsed, by a substantial majority of Americans. That is the simple, overriding premise behind all the work of this Commission."[10] That this remains true is illustrated by the fact that in some states and countries, gambling is legal (although presumably subject to licensing and regulation by the state)—Atlantic City, New Jersey and some counties in Nevada, for example—and some types of gambling are legal in many states (for example, state-operated lotteries and on-track horse race betting).

The major objection to gambling appears to be its relationship to organized crime. The President's Commission determined that "there is no uniformity of organized crime control of gambling throughout the country; in some cities such control exists; in others, not. The Commission regrets the notion that organized crime controls all illegal gambling or that all illegal gambling provides revenues for other illegal activities."[11] The Commission's report, however, indicates that some proceeds of some illegal gambling do go to organized crime, and many law enforcement officials continue to believe gambling is a major source of income for organized crime and, therefore, should be eliminated or strictly controlled. The enforcement of gambling laws is extremely difficult, however, due to the many forms that exist and the demand for gambling activities. While most local law enforcement officials are willing to concede that control of social gambling— such as a card game at an individual's home or the weekend office football, basketball, or baseball pool—is impossible, these same officials may, from time-to-time, make serious attempts to curtail more organized forms of gambling (bookmaking, punchboards, for example). State and federal officials are also concerned about illegal gambling, since winners are not inclined to declare their winnings at income tax time. In spite of selective local, state, and federal law enforcement attempts to control organized gambling, it is unlikely that such attempts will be successful so long as there is a public demand for such activities. As is often the case with the other crimes without complainants, the "payoff" for criminal justice personnel is often minimal in terms of the resources expended.

White-Collar Crime

The term "white-collar crime" was coined in 1939 by Edwin H. Sutherland, although the concept itself was not new at that time. The term, as used by Sutherland, referred to crimes "committed by a person of respectability and high social status in the course of his occupation."[12] There have been many attempts to refine and particularize this definition, and it is probably safe to conclude that today the term white-collar crime is used as an umbrella to cover most crimes committed by guile, deceit, and concealment, whether or not they are committed by persons of "respectability and high social status."[13] Used in this sense, the term might include such disparate crimes as corporate crime, credit card fraud, computer fraud, medical/health fraud, false advertising, insurance fraud, false weights and measures, and tax fraud.[14]

Ex-congressman gets 6 to 18 months on Abscam charge

WASHINGTON (AP)—Former Rep. Richard B. Kelly, R-Fla., was sentenced to six to 18 months in prison Thursday on his Abscam bribery conviction nearly three years ago.

Before imposing sentence, U.S. District Judge William B. Bryant said he was "very reluctantly" not throwing out Kelly's convictions for a second time. A higher court reversed Bryant's earlier decision throwing out Kelly's conviction on grounds he was entrapped.

Kelly, 59, also received three years probation on his other two convictions, conspiracy and interstate travel in aid of bribery.

Unlike the six other members of Congress convicted in the Abscam case, Kelly was not fined. The others received prison terms of one to three years and fines of up to $50,000.

Kelly, the last to be sentenced, could have received 15 years in prison and been fined $30,000. He was allowed to remain free on bond pending an appeal, which his lawyers filed immediately.

In his trial three years ago jurors saw Kelly, on an FBI videotape, stuffing into his coat pocket $100 bills from a $25,000 bribe that came from an undercover FBI agent posing as an Arab sheik seeking help with an immigration problem.

Kelly mounted two defenses: that he took the money to further his own investigation of "shady characters" close to his staff, and that he was enticed impermissibly into committing a crime.

The overall costs of white-collar crime are difficult to measure accurately, but speaking strictly in economic terms it is likely that the annual cost to Americans is in the billions of dollars. More difficult to measure are costs that result from loss of public confidence in business and the professions. Unnecessary surgery, ghost surgery, reports issued by nonexistent or nonfunctioning medical laboratories, and intentional release of hazardous waste materials, for example, erode public trust in the medical profession and industry, and cause health-related problems and deaths, the costs of which are incalculable. Bribery of public officials, illegal campaign contributions, and tax evasion by high-placed political officials in recent years have made many Americans highly skeptical about honesty in politics.

One of the reasons for public anxiety and cynicism concerning white-collar crime is the manner in which it is handled upon discovery. Although all states and the federal government have statutes designed to regulate the activities discussed above, the actual response to most white-collar crime has traditionally been a slap on the wrist, often prescribed by an administrative agency rather than the courts. Penalties assessed often appear trivial in comparison to the profits realized by white-collar offenders. Although white-collar crime is clearly widespread, the frequency with which it occurs cannot be determined by looking at police records or the Uniform Crime Reports. The extent of white-collar crime remains largely unknown, and perhaps partly because of the nebulous nature of these offenses, public reaction to the offenders remains largely unorganized. Because this is the case, legislators remain relatively unconcerned about passing statutes designed to reduce the incidence of white-collar crime, municipal police continue to have few if any personnel who are properly trained to investigate such crimes, prosecutions remain few, and criminal court action is infrequent.

Since those who commit white-collar offenses are not particularly likely to be treated as criminals, they often do not view themselves as criminals and, except for periods of anger and frustration, the public does not view these offenders with the same distaste as other criminals. Coupled with the fact that white-collar crimes are often undetected and are difficult to prosecute because of their complexity, these attitudes do little to help reduce the likelihood of such offenses. Perhaps looking at fraud as an example of white-collar crime will illustrate some of the difficulties associated with prosecution.

Fraud

Fraud involves obtaining the property of another by misrepresenting a material fact. The accused must also intend to permanently deprive the owner of the use of that property. In this offense, the property is relinquished willfully by the owner and the illegal act centers on the misrepresentation that induces the relinquishing.

The misrepresentation must be of a material fact and not an opinion or prediction. For example, if a car salesman claims a car will be the "fastest, hottest car in town," he is not misrepresenting a material fact, only giving an opinion or possibly a prediction. On the other hand, if he alleges the car has only accumulated ten thousand miles, while actually the odometer was turned back and the car has been driven fifty thousand miles, he has misrepresented a material fact.

The misrepresentation must be known by the offender and must be one that a "reasonable person" would not be aware of. Referring back to the previous example, if a second party purchases the auto thinking it to have been driven only ten thousand miles and, without detecting the misrepresentation, sells it to a third party, then no fraud has occurred. A person who purchases the Brooklyn Bridge or the Eiffel Tower has gone beyond the standards of reasonableness to claim fraud.

As with theft and embezzlement, the accused must intend to permanently deprive the owner of the use of the property. Courts generally hold that once ownership has passed, the fraud has transpired.

Some of the more commonly known frauds involve the work of "con men" who play on people's greed or willingness to "get rich quick."

Fraud among retailers and wholesalers is common as well. Such practices as false advertising, violations of truth in labeling, and employing false weights and measures are detected frequently enough to suggest that they commonly occur. Like other types of white-collar crime, these offenses are often difficult to detect, but are very rewarding to their perpetrators. Consider, for example, a super-market chain that has one hundred stores. If the chain were to misrepresent the weight of every package of steak sold by adding only one ounce to the real weight of the meat, if the cost per ounce for steak was twenty cents, and if each store in the chain sold one hundred packages of steak in a day; the additional profit to the chain would be twenty cents times one hundred times one hundred equals two thousand dollars per day, or fourteen thousand dollars per week, or over seven hundred thousand dollars year! Still, each customer would be paying only an additional twenty cents. And, the risk involved is minimal compared to the potential return because few customers take their steak home and weigh it, and even those who did so might believe their own scales to be in error; those who were suspicious would be unlikely to take much definite action to recoup only twenty cents; and even if the violation was somehow detected, most customers would not become overly irate at the loss of a few dollars over the period of a year or so. The risk involved is minimal compared to the potential return.

There are some organized attempts to prevent or reduce the incidence of white-collar crime. The National District Attorneys' Association in conjunction with the Chamber of Commerce of the United States has distributed a handbook that includes sections on combating bribery, kickbacks, and payoffs; countering computer-related crime; combating fraud; preventing embezzlement; and a section on collective action as a means of combating white-collar crime. Specific tactics for dealing with white-collar crime are discussed and available sources of assistance are listed.[15] In addition, there are now numerous community-based groups across the country oriented toward publicizing and confronting a variety of white-collar offenses and offenders.[16] As Geis and Meier point out, "No consideration of white-collar crime would be complete without reference to the work of Ralph Nader and his associates."[17] Nader is convinced that illegitimate practices are an integral part of American industry and "that there ought to be more, and more severe, criminal penalties for white-collar criminals."[18] Nader and his group combat white-collar crime primarily through publicity and recourse to legal processes. He appears to remain convinced that the American public will rise up and take action against white-collar offenders if they are made aware of the extent and seriousness of the problem and if they can be organized. There is, however, a great deal of evidence to indicate that while some segments of the public do become concerned about some types of white-collar crime, the concern is short-lived. In addition, most citizens appear to be apathetic about this type of crime most of the time.

Organized Crime

The longstanding prevalence of prostitution, gambling, drug use, and other crimes without complainants has made them attractive "business" ventures for criminal syndicates. Business enterprises organized for the purpose of economic gain through illegal means constitute **organized crime.**[19]

Although they may employ illegal means, organized criminal syndicates often operate under rational business principles. Maximum profit is predicated upon public demand for goods and services and efficient delivery of "products" through a formally organized system. In addition, payments for political protection are not uncommon.[20]

While the most celebrated organized crime unit is the Mafia or la Cosa Nostra, as defined here organized crime includes street gang activities, drug distribution networks, and racially or ethnically based criminal syndicates. We should note that all organized crime activites are not criminal. In an attempt to fend off the Internal Revenue Service (the common prosecutor of organized criminals), many criminal syndicates engage in legal business activities, often entered through illegal means, in an attempt to launder their illegally obtained profits.

Summary

Crimes without complainants involve the provision of goods and services that are in demand, but illegal. These offenses include illegal drug manufacture, sales, and distribution; prostitution; gambling; and obscenity/pornography, among others. Since complainants rarely come forth voluntarily with respect to these offenses, the police themselves often serve as complainants. The costs involved in developing these cases are high and the payoff is minimal. Attempts to legislate morality generally lead to these results. Nonetheless, a considerable proportion of the resources of various components of the criminal justice network is expended on crimes without complainants.

White-collar crime involves offenses committed by people in the course of their occupations or professions. Tax evasion, embezzling, consumer frauds, and medical malpractice are examples of white-collar crime. The costs of white-collar crime are high, both in terms of economic considerations, and in terms of loss of confidence and trust in government, industry, and the professions. Still, in spite of numerous crusades to arouse the public, white-collar offenders are seldom treated as or thought of as criminals. Only organized, sustained action on behalf of a concerned public is likely to reduce the incidence of white-collar crime, and such action appears unlikely at this time.

Key Terms Defined

crimes without complainants crimes that provide goods and/or services that are in demand, but illegal; in which the police themselves typically serve as complainants since citizens are usually not willing to accept this role.

prostitution engaging in or agreeing to engage in sexual acts for compensation.

white-collar crime crime committed by guile, deceit, or concealment, typically by people in positions of trust.

fraud an act that involves obtaining the property of another, with the intent to permanently deprive the owner of the use of that property, by misrepresenting a material fact.

organized crime criminal conspiracies leading to personal economic gain for those involved.

Discussion Questions

1. What is the importance of the distinction between crimes without complainants and crimes without victims? In your opinion, are crimes without complainants crimes without victims?

2. What similarities and differences do you see between crimes without complainants and white-collar crimes?

3. Should white-collar offenses and offenses without complainants be classified as criminal? Why or why not?

4. Suggest what you would consider to be effective means for attempting to combat white-collar crime and crimes without complainants. Indicate the likelihood that your suggestions would be effective in our current society.

Notes

1. Edwin M. Schur, *Crimes Without Victims: Deviant Behavior and Public Policy* (Englewood Cliffs, N.J.: Prentice-Hall, 1965).

2. Edwin H. Sutherland, *White Collar Crime* (New York: Holt, Rinehart, and Winston, 1959).

3. Schur, *Crimes Without Victims,* 169.

4. Alexander B. Smith and Harriet Pollock, *Some Sins are Not Crimes: A Plea for Reform of the Criminal Law* (New York: New Viewpoints, 1975).

5. Troy Duster, *The Legislation of Morality: Law, Drugs, and Moral Judgment* (New York: Free Press, 1970).

6. Charles Winick and Paul M. Kinsie, *The Lively Commerce: Prostitution in the United States* (Chicago: Quadrangle Books, 1971).

7. Robert M. Castle, "Ash Meadows: A Fly-In Brothel," in *Deviance: Field Studies and Self-Disclosures,* ed. Jerry Jacobs (Palo Alto, Calif.: National Press Books, 1974), 41–51. For a good discussion of some of the career and economic aspects of prostitution see James H. Bryan, "Apprenticeships in Prostitution," *Social Problems* 12, no. 3 (Winter 1965): 278–97.

8. Frank Gannon, *Drugs: What They Are, How They Look, What They Do* (New York: Third Press, 1971); Lester Grinspoon, *Marihuana Reconsidered* (Cambridge, Mass.: Harvard University Press, 1971).

9. John A. Gardiner, "Public Attitudes Toward Gambling and Corruption," *Annals of the American Academy of Political and Social Science* 374 (November 1967): 134.

10. Commission on the Review of the National Policy Toward Gambling, *Gambling in America* (Washington, D.C.: U.S. Government Printing Office, 1976), 1.

11. Commission on the Review of the National Policy Toward Gambling, *Gambling in America,* 4.

12. Sutherland, *White Collar Crime.*

13. Gilbert Geis, "Toward a Delineation of White-Collar Offenses," *Sociological Inquiry* 32 (Spring 1962), 160–71; Marshall B. Clinard and Richard Quinney, eds., *Criminal Behavior Systems: A Typology,* 2d ed. (New York: Holt, Rinehart and Winston, 1973), 206–23.

14. Herbert Edelhertz, *The Nature, Impact, and Prosecution of White-Collar Crime,* National Institute of Law Enforcement and Criminal Justice (Washington, D.C.: U.S. Government Printing Office, 1970).

15. Chamber of Commerce of the United States, *A Handbook on White Collar Crime: Everyone's Problem, Everyone's Loss* (Washington, D.C.: Chamber of Commerce of the United States, 1974).

16. For a list of some of these groups see Janice E. Pearlman, "Grassrooting the System," *Social Policy* 2 (September/October 1976), 13–17.

17. Gilbert Geis and Robert F. Meier, *White-Collar Crime: Offenses in Business, Politics, and the Professions* (New York: Free Press, 1976), 12.

18. Ralph Nader, "Business Crime," in *Hot War on the Consumer*, ed. David Sanford (New York: Pitman, 1969), 138–40.

19. F.A.J. Ianni and F. Ianni, eds. *The Crime Society: Organized Crime and Corruption in America* (New York: New American Library, 1976), xvi.

20. Clinard and Quinney, *Criminal Behavior Systems: A Typology.*

Suggested Readings

Abadinsky, Howard. *Organized Crime*. 2d ed. Chicago: Nelson-Hall, 1985.

Bequai, August. *White-Collar Crime: A 20th Century Crisis*. Lexington, Mass.: Lexington Books, 1978.

Duster, Troy. *The Legislation of Morality: Law, Drugs, and Moral Judgment*. New York: Free Press, 1970.

Geis, Gilbert, and Meier, Robert F. *White-Collar Crime: Offenses in Business, Politics, and the Professions*. New York: Free Press, 1976.

Herman, Robert D., ed. *Gambling*. New York: Harper and Row, 1967.

Schur, Edwin. *Crimes Without Victims*. Englewood Cliffs, N.J.: Prentice-Hall, 1965.

Simon, David R., and Eitzen, D. Stanley. *Elite Deviance*. Boston: Allyn and Bacon, 1982.

Smith, Alexander B., and Pollack, Harriet. *Some Sins are Not Crimes: A Plea for Reform of the Criminal Law*. New York: New Viewpoints, 1975.

Swartz, Joel. "Silent Killers at Work." *Crime and Social Justice* (Spring-Summer 1975): 15–20.

The Police: History and Development

7

Key Terms

social control
due process model of justice
crime control model of justice

arrest
booking
chain of evidence

As the official agency most accessible to and most frequently used by the public, the police play a crucial role in the criminal justice network. As "gatekeepers" for the other official criminal justice agencies, some 460,000 police officers in more than 12,000 police agencies are a vital link between the public (who are also gatekeepers in terms of reporting or not reporting crimes) and the remainder of the network. In this chapter we will discuss the historical development of the police and some of their current functions and responsibilities. First, however, it is important to note the position of the police in the social control network.

The Role of the Police in Social Control

In all societies, there are at least two distinct means of attempting to persuade people to adhere to group expectations or norms. The first involves the use of informal or group pressure that influences, for example, what we eat, what we wear, and how we speak. The second involves the use of formal pressure or legal coercion. Both are clearly important to **social control,** which may be defined as "the process of attempting to influence persons or groups to conform to group expectations."[1] Important factors in the attempt to produce such conformity include rates of detection and apprehension.[2] The ratio of police officers to other citizens in the United States (roughly 500,000 to 235,000,000 or 1 to 400) should be enough to convince us that the likelihood of detection and apprehension for those who violate norms (in this case, laws) is quite low if we rely totally upon the police for such detection and apprehension. Police activities in the form of legal coercion, then, are likely to be unsuccessful in preventing violations of legal norms (laws) unless they are supplemented by informal, group, or social pressure to conform.[3] The various groups that comprise the public (families, peers, religious groups, for example) must also take an active part in social control if conformity to norms is to occur and if those who violate norms are to be detected and apprehended. It is important, therefore, to realize that the police are only one of many groups involved in the social control process and that their efforts are sure to fail unless they receive cooperation from these other groups.

From "Watch and Ward" to "Protect and Serve"

Perhaps nowhere is the importance of the public to the criminal justice network clearer than in a historical discussion of the development of the police. In the western world, citizens have been formally responsible for assisting in the maintenance of public order and the enforcement of law for centuries. In both England and colonial America, citizens were called upon to serve terms as watchmen who were responsible for protecting their cities and towns from invasion from the outside, and fire and criminals from the inside. In addition, these watchmen were given the added responsibilities of containing those afflicted with plague, preventing commercial fraud, enforcing licensing regulations, and so forth.[4] These watchmen were paid little, held in low esteem by the public, and subject to considerable manipulation by the wealthy who wished to use the law for their own benefit.

Over time, as crime became an increasingly complex problem, watchmen were recognized as inadequate for the protection of other citizens from criminals. The watchmen were unorganized, untrained, and undependable. In addition, they were operating under a system of laws that many people considered barbaric, so citizen support was often lacking. Reformers such as Jeremy Bentham, Edward Chadwick, and Patrick Colquhoun, who recognized the importance of public support for successful law enforcement and believed prevention to be an important part of such law enforcement, called for drastic changes in the law.[5] Along with others, they also called for the development of a centralized, organized, mobile, preventive force to deal with the crime problem. In both England and America, there were strong objections to the creation of such a force because many citizens were afraid it might be used as an instrument of government oppression. However, by the 1850s, an increasing demand for public order led to a growing consensus about the need for an organized police force.[6] Although there were several localized police forces operating in England in the early 1800s, the first municipal force was the London police force organized in 1829 under the direction of Sir Robert Peel. This force, referred to as the Metropolitan Police, was organized to help allay public fears arising from an increasing number of crimes being committed with impunity in and about the city of London. Peel believed that the police could only be effective if they were centrally organized, had the support of the public (i.e., enforced laws which received wide public support), exhibited a restrained demeanor, and understood the norms of the community in which they policed. The London police were organized according to territories or "beats" which they patrolled in such fashion that they could be fairly easily located by those desiring their assistance. The beat patrol concept was soon adopted in cities and towns throughout Europe and the United States.

While Peel's principles of organization solved many of the problems of the watch and ward system, other problems remained unsolved. In the United States, the police were in frequent conflict with some segments of the public as a result of their attempt to enforce vice laws, which did not have widespread public support.[7] In addition, hiring and promotion were based upon political patronage systems in many American cities, which made the impartial administration of justice by competent police officers highly suspect. Despite attempts beginning in the 1870s to introduce reforms in order to reduce direct political influence, the political image remained.[8] In the first part of the twentieth century, the introduction of the automobile led to further police community relations problems since many middle- and upper-class citizens who had previously supported crime control efforts by the police were now, themselves, subject to the actions of traffic officers.[9]

Another major problem involved communication, and this problem, to a great extent, negated the advantages of an organized, mobile police force, since the police could not be summoned, and could not summon other police assistance themselves, without the use of messengers or face-to-face contact. The invention and use of the telegraph, telephone, two-way radio, and patrol car made rapid, relatively certain communication possible by the 1930s in many police departments. Now many police administrators felt that crime (in the urban areas, at least) could be greatly reduced, if not eliminated. Public expectations concerning police performance were raised, and the public responded by dramatically increasing requests for services to the police who were the only public service agency (other than the fire department) available twenty-four hours a day, every day. The police soon found themselves unable to respond adequately to all these service requests, found little time available for crime-related activities, and found public dissatisfaction growing. At the same time, police administrators began to realize that they had underestimated the ingenuity of law violators who rapidly achieved the same level of communication and mobility attained by the police. In short, by the middle of the twentieth century, the police (particularly those in large urban centers) were having difficulty "protecting and serving" and the public knew it. In attempting to be all things to all people, the police found themselves unable to perform all the services requested, capable of solving only about one in five reported major crimes, and unable to find ways out of these dilemmas. The issues of political corruption, lack of professionalism, and public distrust, which shaped police public relations historically, had been complicated by increasing demands for services based on unrealistic expectations. Today these dilemmas remain unsolved. To understand why this is so, let us look at the functions the police are currently expected to fulfill.

Current Police Functions

Before discussing specific police procedures, we should note that full enforcement of the laws is not possible. While the police may be technically responsible for full enforcement of a variety of statutes, in reality they selectively enforce most laws. To be sure, they make every attempt to enforce laws prohibiting predatory crimes, but even these are subject to selective enforcement based upon whether or not violations are observed and reported, whether or not the victim is willing to serve as a witness/complainant, the seriousness of the offense, and numerous other factors. With respect to less serious but more common offenses, the police often tailor their efforts to specific geographic locations and/or times. For example, the police cannot fully enforce traffic laws prohibiting speeding. While an officer is writing a citation to one speeding offender, several other speeders may escape his or her attention. Further, as members of the criminal justice network, police officers often tailor their activities based upon decisions of prosecutors and judges. The police officer who sees violations relating to use of marijuana, for instance, many initially arrest violators, but if the prosecutor or judge routinely dismisses such cases, the officer will in all likelihood alter his or her enforcement patterns so that his or her behavior conforms to the expectations of others (including the public) in the network.

The police are visible representatives of authority whose decisions, to a great extent, determine whether or not other components of the official criminal justice network will take official action.[10] They are largely a reactive agency, dependent upon public cooperation and information. As Ed Davis, former Los Angeles Chief of Police indicates, the police are ". . . members of the public who are paid to give full-time attention to duties which are incumbent on every citizen, in the interests of community welfare and existence."[11] Davis goes on to make the point that we have repeatedly emphasized in this book: public cooperation is necessary if the police are to effectively perform their functions.[12] Yet, there is little doubt that public cooperation with the police leaves a great deal to be desired. Many segments of the public are uncooperative with the police and some are openly hostile a good deal of the time. Other segments criticize the police for being unable to do anything about the crime problem or appear largely apathetic regardless of police action or inaction. The police are equally critical of and hostile toward some segments of the public. What are the major functions that the public expects the police to perform? Why are the police often judged ineffective? What do the police expect from the public?

The police in the United States are primarily providers of services. Among the services they provide are law enforcement and order maintenance. Successful performance of either of these functions, of course, requires public cooperation.[13] When members of the public take their responsibilities seriously, a high level of police performance is possible. When members of the public fail to accept responsibilities, the police are not likely to be highly effective. Currently, large segments of the American public appear to be willing to leave law enforcement largely to the police. Failure to report crimes, failure to assist victims of crimes in progress, a desire "not to get involved," and failure to assist police officers upon request, have become commonplace. The prevailing attitude seems to be "it's not my job" or "it's none of my business." Thus, the police are left to handle the tasks of law enforcement themselves. As we shall see later in this chapter, these tasks include prevention, detection, apprehension, arrest, etc. Interestingly enough, however, the vast majority of police work involves providing services that have little to do with criminal conduct.[14] Most patrol officers in American cities spend their working hours responding to one service request after another. Normally, some time is spent on routine patrol, even though the value of such patrol is seriously in doubt.[15] Only about 5 to 10 percent of the typical officer's time is spent handling criminal matters, contrary to the image presented by the media in the United States. Other services commonly provided by the police include, but are not limited to, the following:

security checks of buildings
traffic regulation
accident investigation
transportation of prisoners and the emotionally disturbed
providing information
escorting funeral processions and parades
finding lost children
providing first aid
making public speeches
handling animal calls
handling domestic disputes
enforcing licensing regulations
fingerprinting
administering breathalyser tests
staffing and managing jails
typing reports.

Police Procedures and the Criminal Justice Network

There are certain crime-related tasks that the police are expected to perform, although, as we have seen, they perform numerous additional tasks as well.

Generally speaking, the police are held responsible for the following crime-related tasks: (1) prevention; (2) recording; (3) investigation; (4) apprehension; (5) arrest; (6) interviewing and interrogation; (7) booking; (8) acceptance of certain types of bail or temporary detention; (9) collection and preservation of evidence; (10) recovery of stolen property; (11) transmission of reports to the prosecutor in useable form; and (12) testifying in court.

As we discuss each of these areas, recall our previous discussions (chapters 3 and 4) of the exercise of discretion and the influence of politics at all levels in the criminal justice network.

With respect to crime prevention, the police are generally expected to provide programs to educate the public, to provide deterrent patrol, to make house and building checks, and to use informants and intelligence sources to stop criminal acts from occurring. In some societies, the task of prevention is made easier by legislation that allows the police to stop, search, inventory, and detain any suspicious person. In our own society, such tactics are severely limited in the interest of preserving **due process** and individual rights. For example, in our society, a police officer may "know" (in a factual sense) that a person is in possession of dangerous drugs and intends to sell those drugs illegally in his home. If the "tip" that provided the officer with this information did not come from a source known to be reliable, however, the officer may be unable to obtain a warrant to search the home and is prohibited from entering the home without the resident's permission unless he can establish probable cause to do so.[16] In short, the officer may be unable to prevent a crime that he personally "feels" is about to occur. We, the citizens, have decided, in order to maintain a relatively free society, that due process is at least as important as **crime control.** While this may hamper police efforts to prevent and solve crimes, few of us would be willing to sacrifice the right to due process to make the work of the police easier.

While crime prevention programs developed by the police may deter some crimes, it is clear that prevention is one area in which public cooperation is critical (in terms of following police guidelines for security, reporting suspicious persons, and other activities). Prevention is made even more difficult by the fact that there is no visible end-product to prevention programs and so it is difficult to justify resources to support such programs.

A second crime-related duty of the police is to record crimes reported by the public or observed by police officers. Such recording is important, since both our local and national official statistics on the incidence of different types of crime depend upon accurate recording. Once a citizen exercises his or her discretion to report an offense to the police, the police exercise their discretion as to whether the report should become part of the official record. When the report is accepted as worthy of attention, it becomes a "crime known to the police."

Having accepted and recorded a crime report, the police are expected to investigate the crime in question. A great deal of discretion is used by the police in deciding whether or not to expend police resources on an investigation, and if an investigation is to be conducted, how extensive it should be. Investigations range from simply making a preliminary report describing stolen property (used largely for insurance purposes) with little or no follow-up, to investigations of homicide that require that the crime scene be sealed off, that complete inventories of evidence be made, and that many persons be located and interviewed. Investigations such as the former are often conducted over the phone in a matter of minutes, while the latter may take months or years.

The use of informants is common in most police departments. Informants can often provide information that cannot be obtained in any other way and, where they have been shown to be reliable, may be important in helping to prevent crime and/or apprehending offenders. Perhaps nowhere is the use of discretion by the police more clearly illustrated than in dealing with informants. In order to obtain valuable information, the police frequently overlook minor (and occasionally even fairly serious) violations by informants. It is not uncommon, for example, for the police to be aware of the fact that an informant is in possession of illegal drugs and, in fact, to provide the informant with funds that they know will be used to purchase such drugs. The discretion not to arrest is exercised in the hopes of obtaining information about more serious offenses committed by others.

When an investigation turns up a likely suspect, the police are expected to apprehend that suspect and, where appropriate, to make an arrest. Here, at the point of arrest, the police officer possesses considerable discretionary power. It is true that she or he is influenced by the law, departmental policy, and other network constraints. Still, there is often no one physically present to supervise her or his actions and she or he may respond to a variety of cues other than legal ones. The age, sex, race, dress, prior history, or location of a suspect may all influence her or his decision, which is crucial because if the police officer decides not to arrest, the matter is, practically speaking, closed. It is the exercise of discretion by individual police officers in thousands of police-citizen encounters every day that helps shape public attitudes toward the police (and, we might add, the exercise of discretion by members of the various publics that help shape police attitudes toward them). If the officer arrests one person for a particular offense, but allows another who has committed the same offense to go free, the arrested party (when he or she knows about the discrepancy) can hardly be expected to feel the criminal justice network is just. When one officer ignores a particular offense, but another arrests everyone who commits that offense, the public is confused. The way in which police officers exercise discretion, therefore, plays an important part in shaping relations between the police and the public.[17]

The process of **arrest** itself is quite complicated. Generally speaking, however, a police officer is empowered to make an arrest when he or she has a warrant or signed complaint, sees someone commit a felony or misdemeanor, or has reason to suspect that someone has committed a felony. The actual point at which an arrest occurs depends upon the officer's intent to arrest and the citizen's understanding that intent.[18] When the officer says, "You are under arrest!" his or her intent is quite clear provided he or she is speaking the same language as the arrestee. It is less clear when the officer says, "You, stay here. I want to talk to you." Further, a police officer exercising his or her discretion may try to use this ambiguity to give him or her time to decide whether or not to make an arrest. For example, for the most part, arrests based solely on "suspicion" are illegal. But, at what point does "suspicion" become "probable cause" or a "reasonable belief"? You can see, then, that even arrest, a function that all of us would agree is important to the police, is not as simple as it first appears.

When a suspect has been arrested and made available for prosecution, the police say the crime has been "cleared by arrest." Note that a crime listed as cleared by arrest may involve a police suspect who is never prosecuted for the crime or who is eventually determined to be not guilty. With respect to the crimes

Fingerprinting—Both a Public Service and a Crime-Related Function. *Tom Moore*

classified by the FBI as Index Offenses (criminal homicide, forcible rape, aggravated assault, robbery, burglary, grand theft, arson, and auto theft), the police are successful in clearing by arrest about 20 to 25 percent.[19] In other words, about four out of five Index Offenses are not cleared by arrest. This inability of the police to clear crimes by arrest is both caused by, and causes, public belief that the police are ineffective.[20] This belief creates a vicious circle that needs to be broken if the police are to clear more crimes by arrest.

Once an arrest is made, the police are responsible for informing the suspect of the charges against him or her, for **booking,** and interviewing or interrogating the suspect. The booking process involves taking an inventory of the suspect's property, fingerprinting, and photographing. It is at this stage, during or just after the arrest, but before booking, that the suspect is informed of his or her rights and allowed to contact a lawyer.[21] Based upon the suspect's desires or the suspect's lawyer's advice, interviewing and/or interrogation may occur.

Also at this stage, the police may inform the suspect that he or she is eligible for bail and, under certain circumstances (generally in the case of misdemeanors), may accept bail and release the suspect from custody. If bail is not allowable, or if the suspect cannot make bail, the police may detain him or her in a holding cell, or, in the case of a county sheriff, in a jail until the suspect makes bail or goes to trial.

From the time of the initial investigation through arrest, interviews, and interrogations, the police are responsible for collecting evidence (physical and testimonial) concerning the crime in question. The collection of evidence depends upon the skill of the investigator and available clues. The preservation of evidence to be presented in court requires that a **chain of evidence** begin when the evidence is first collected and continue until the evidence is presented in court or determined to be of no value. The chain of evidence must be fashioned in such a way that location and control of the evidence can be documented at every point in time from discovery to presentation. The chain normally begins when an investigator initially finds what he or she considers to be evidence, collects and tags or identifies clearly the evidence (use of photos may be of great value), turns it over to an evidence custodian or technician who gives the investigator receipts for the evidence, and concludes with the presentation of the evidence in court by the original investigator (who signs a receipt for the evidence custodian when he or she removes the evidence from the evidence locker or room).

During the investigation and collection of evidence, the police officers involved are also interested in recovering stolen property that will eventually be returned to its rightful owner. Similarly, the officers involved in the arrest and investigation are aware that they must proceed in such a way that they can establish both a factual and legal (following due process) case against the suspect that the prosecutor may use in court. Police reports form the starting point for the prosecutor's case, and inadequate performance in any of the areas we have just discussed may make prosecution either impossible or unsuccessful. The same is true of the last requirement of the police—testifying in court. Inaccurate or perjured testimony can lead not only to the release of guilty persons or the conviction of innocent persons, but can have serious repercussions for the officer personally and the police image in general.[22] It is important, therefore, that police officers take and retain complete, accurate notes during the investigation; that they be honest; and that they be unafraid to admit they don't know when, in fact, they don't know. Only when police testimony meets these standards can we expect public cooperation with, and support of, the police.

Summary

The evolution from the "watch and ward" system to the notion of "protect and serve" occurred over several centuries in both England and America. Increasing public concern over crime, rapidly growing population, urbanization, and industrialization led to the development of the Metropolitan Police in London in 1829. The territorial strategy of the London Police was adopted by most European and American cities, and by the mid-twentieth century technological advances led to increasingly optimistic assessments by some police administrators. However, calls for services from the public and adaptability of offenders placed serious strains on police resources. Additionally, the tremendous variety of services demanded by the public made it increasingly difficult for police performance to meet public expectations. The duties that the police are expected to perform are numerous and complicated—from the point of arrest through the collection and presentation of evidence.

Key Terms Defined

social control the process of influencing, or attempting to influence, persons or groups to conform to expectations.

due process model of justice a model designed to insure that the rights of individuals as guaranteed by the constitution and various court decisions are protected.

crime control model of justice a model emphasizing the importance of factual guilt and minimizing the importance of legal guilt or due process.

arrest the process of taking an individual into official custody.

booking the recording of facts about a person's arrest, including fingerprinting, inventorying personal property, and photographing.

chain of evidence refers to preserving evidence in such a way that it can be accurately accounted for from the time it is seized until the time its usefulness has been finally determined (generally in court).

Discussion Questions

1. It has been said that the police and the public are, or should be, one. What basis for this statement can you find in the history of the police in England and the United States?

2. Discuss the duties that the police are expected to perform with respect to criminal cases. In your opinion, how effective are the police in performing these duties? How could their effectiveness be improved?

3. What are the proper roles of the police and the public in law enforcement? In social control? In the criminal justice network?

4. What is the nature of the relationship between the police and the public in your community? How could the relationship be improved?

Notes

1. F. James Davis, "The Law as a Type of Social Control," in *Society and the Law: New Meanings for an Old Profession,* ed. F. James Davis, Henry H. Foster, C. Ray Jeffries, and E. Eugene Davis (New York: Free Press, 1962), 39–61.

2. Franklin Zimring and Gordon Hawkins, "The Legal Threat as an Instrument of Social Change," *Journal of Social Issues* 27, no. 2 (1971): 33–48.

3. Zimring and Hawkins, "The Legal Threat as an Instrument of Social Change," 33–48.

4. Jonathan Rubinstein, *City Police* (New York: Farrar, Straus, and Giroux, 1973); James F. Richardson, *Urban Police in the United States* (Port Washington, New York: Kennikat Press, 1974).

5. T. A. Critchley, "The New Police in London, 1750–1830," in *Police in America,* ed. Jerome H. Skolnick and Thomas C. Gray (Boston: Little, Brown and Co., 1975), 6–15.

6. Richardson, *Urban Police in the United States,* 3–34.

7. Richardson, *Urban Police in the United States,* 29–30.

8. Richardson, *Urban Police in the United States,* 63.

9. Richardson, *Urban Police in the United States,* 110–11.

10. Jerome H. Skolnick, *Justice Without Trial* (New York: Wiley, 1975).

11. Edward M. Davis, *Staff One: A Perspective on Effective Police Management* (Englewood Cliffs, N.J.: Prentice-Hall, 1978), 7.

12. Davis, *Staff One,* 218, 229–238.

13. Albert J. Reiss, Jr., *The Police and the Public* (New Haven, Conn.: Yale University Press, 1971).

14. James Q. Wilson, *Varieties of Police Behavior* (New York: Atheneum, 1971), 17–19; Elaine Cumming, Ian Cumming, and Laura Edell, "Policeman as Philosopher, Guide, and Friend," *Social Problems* 12 (Winter 1965): 276–86.

15. George L. Kelling, Tony Pate, Duane Dieckman, and Charles E. Brown, *The Kansas City Preventive Patrol Experiment: A Summary Report* (Washington, D.C.: The Police Foundation, 1974).

16. *Draper v. United States,* 358 U.S. 397 (1950); *Jones v. United States,* 362 U.S. 257 (1960).

17. Kenneth Culp Davis, *Police Discretion* (St. Paul, Minn.: West Publishing Co., 1978).

18. Paul B. Weston and Kenneth M. Wells, *Criminal Evidence for Police* (Englewood Cliffs, N.J.: Prentice-Hall, 1971), 181–88; Yale Kamisar, Wayne R. La Fave, and Jerold H. Israel, *Basic Criminal Procedure,* 4th ed., (St. Paul, Minn.: West Publishing Co., 1974), 172–412.

19. F.B.I., *Uniform Crime Reports for the U.S.,* Washington, D.C., 1986.

20. Phillip H. Ennis, "Crime, Victims, and the Police," *Trans-action* 4 (June 1967): 36–44.

21. *Escobedo v. Illinois,* 378 U.S. 478 (1964); *Miranda v. Arizona,* 384 U.S. 436 (1966).

22. Paul Chevigny, *Police Power* (New York: Pantheon Books, 1969).

Suggested Readings

Amidon, Harold T. "Law Enforcement: From the 'Beginning' to the English Bobby," *Journal of Police Science and Administration* 5, no. 3 (September 1977): 355–67.

Broderick, John J. *Police in a Time of Change.* 2d ed. Prospect Heights, Il: Waveland Press, 1987.

Cox, Steven M., and Fitzgerald, Jack D. *Police in Community Relations: Critical Issues.* Dubuque, Iowa: Wm. C. Brown, 1983.

Kirkham, George. *Signal Zero.* New York: Ballantine Books, 1976.

Richardson, James F. *Urban Police in the United States.* Port Washington, N.Y.: Kennikat Press, 1974.

Rubinstein, Jonathan. *City Police.* New York: Farrar, Straus, and Giroux, 1973.

Skolnick, Jerome H. *Justice Without Trial.* New York: Wiley, 1966.

Skolnick, Jerome H., and Gray, Thomas C. *Police in America.* Boston: Little, Brown and Co., 1975.

Wilson, James Q. *Varieties of Police Behavior: The Management of Law and Order in Eight Communities.* Cambridge, Mass.: Harvard University Press, 1969.

The Police: Organization, Selection, and Training   8

Key Terms

neighborhood (team) policing
dual career ladder system
community service officer
targeted patrol

split patrol
Police Officer Standards and Training
    Board (P.O.S.T.)
probationary officer
accreditation
community-oriented policing

In order to achieve the goals of providing service by maintaining order and enforcing the law, many police agencies have developed organizational structures similar to the one depicted in figure 8.1. Note that there are many variations on this formal organizational structure (for example, the use of an assistant chief) and also note that this chart concerns the police department only and does not show that the chief is accountable to a mayor, city manager, or commissioner and the public.

The patrol division is normally the largest division in terms of personnel and other resources, and the duties of the patrol officer have been outlined previously. The investigative division normally handles most of the serious criminal cases and is staffed by investigators who have had (or should have had) either specialized training in crime scene investigation and preservation, or an affinity for investigation. In larger departments, there may be criminalistic specialists, fingerprinting experts, polygraph operators, and juvenile officers in the investigative

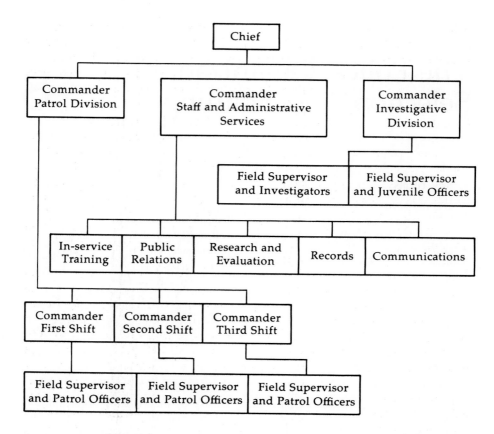

Figure 8.1 Typical police organizational chart.

division. Members of this division do little in the way of order maintenance, responding to service requests, or routine patrol. Instead, they conduct surveillances, follow-up leads, collect and preserve evidence, interrogate, and so forth. They do not, for the most part, wear uniforms, and they do most of the undercover work of the police organization.

A third division commonly found in police departments may be variously identified as staff services, operations, records and communication, or training and evaluations. Primary functions of this division are record keeping, communications, research and planning, training and education, and sometimes logistics. In some departments, most of these functions are performed by sworn officers, but there is a clearcut trend toward hiring civilian employees to perform the majority of these tasks.

While some departments have divided the tasks mentioned above differently, most follow this division of activity. There is normally a division commander in charge of each division who reports to the chief of police or a deputy chief of police. These division commanders have shift commanders, field supervisors, and staff personnel under their control as well as line officers and/or civilians. In metropolitan departments, several precinct headquarters are established throughout the city, and each precinct may be organized as indicated above or various types of services may remain centralized to be called in when the need arises.

In most instances, police departments have maintained a paramilitary structure that stresses use of the chain-of-command in issuing orders and directives and solving problems. While this structure has some advantages in terms of discipline and control, it is resistant to change. In addition, it fails to promote communication and interaction among members of different divisions and, in fact, often promotes a sense of competition among departmental personnel, which may not always have beneficial consequences.[1] In some departments, patrol officers and investigators seldom interact because of rivalry between division commanders, physical separation of facilities, and aloof attitudes on the part of the investigators. In addition, patrol officers tend to view investigators as "glory seekers." As a consequence, investigators who are actively looking for a wanted felon are not always provided with available information as to his or her whereabouts. Several patrol officers might see the individual in question, but be unaware that investigators are looking for him or her due to the lack of communication. Such occurrences are not rare, as is indicated in *Helter Skelter,* an account of the development of the case against Charles Manson and his "family."[2]

Many students of the police believe that one reason the police have not kept pace with private industry in adapting to changing conditions is the paramilitary structure typical of many police agencies. When followed to the letter, such formal organizational structure is often quite cumbersome. Partially as a response to the inflexibility of the formal organizational structure, informal arrangements often arise among various divisions and individuals that may speed up organizational procedures or impede such procedures. Thus, a police lieutenant who wants to change the activities of his shift personnel may not go to the patrol commander, who would then have to go to the assistant chief, who would then have to seek the chief's approval. Instead, he may see the chief after hours, or he may discuss his idea with an alderman or the mayor over drinks, to gain support. Similarly, individual patrol officers and investigators may meet informally to discuss a case and share information which their immediate supervisors may not wish to share as a result of divisional rivalries. In considering organizational structures, then, it is important to consider both the formal and informal arrangements which characterize the agency in question.[3]

As a result of some of these problems with traditional police organizations and as a result of ongoing research, some police departments have started to make changes in their organizational structures. Let us now turn our attention to some of these changes.

Some Variations on the Traditional Police Organization—Research and Change

A number of attempts have been made in recent years to make police departments more flexible and responsive to the needs of both the public and other criminal justice agencies. Many of these attempts are still in the experimental stage, but let us take a brief look at some of the more promising innovations.

To solve the problems of territorial jealousy between investigators and patrol officers, and to improve the morale of patrol officers, some departments have done away with distinctions between the two groups. Instead, all personnel are referred to as police officers, and all are expected to both initiate and follow through their own cases. Skills of both investigators and patrol officers are developed and used by each police officer. Departments that have tried this approach often find that investigators initially dislike this program, but the morale of patrol officers does improve. Whether or not the quality of services provided improves remains to be seen, but it is worth noting that enough problems exist to lead some chiefs of police to consider returning to the more traditional organizational structure.

Another strategy employed by some departments to improve services and efficiency is **neighborhood policing** or **team policing.** Here a number of officers, each having some special training, are assigned as a team to serve a particular geographic area. The team is responsible for providing services to area residents twenty-four hours a day and operates under the direction of a field supervisor who coordinates his or her team's efforts with those of the larger department. The rationale for neighborhood policing is the belief that such teams will be more familiar with, and more familiar to, area residents, patterns, and problems. Further, decentralized control should result in greater flexibility and responsiveness to the varying needs and desires of different neighborhoods. Once again, the effectiveness of such programs remains to be determined.[4]

Yet another attempt to change traditional police structure involves instituting a **dual career ladder system** that provides for more than one promotional channel. In most police departments, chances for promotion are tied to a military rank/ supervisory structure (patrol officer to corporal, to sergeant, to lieutenant, and so on). Promotional opportunities depend, then, upon vacancies at each supervisory level and upon the ability and desire to supervise personnel. Obviously, in any given department there is only one chief, a limited number of assistant chiefs, or division commanders, so possibilities for upward mobility are rather limited. In addition, many patrol officers and investigators who possess high levels of skills in the field have little desire or ability to supervise others. Traditionally, these individuals have remained in a single status with pay increases based upon longevity and cost of living. A dual career system, such as the one proposed by Chief Jerry Bratcher of Palatine, Illinois, would allow those patrol officers who are skilled, but who wish to remain on the streets, to advance from junior through senior patrol ranks with attendant pay increases and recognition.[5] The outcome of such a program would presumably be higher morale among patrol officers and better services for the public. Traditional promotional opportunities through supervisory positions would, of course, remain open.

In an attempt to encourage more public involvement with the police and to relieve sworn officers from duties that do not require their expertise, some departments are developing **Community Service Officer (CSO) programs.**[6] CSOs handle calls involving nonemergencies, make home security checks, assist stranded motorists, attend community functions, and serve as liaison between the police and the community. CSOs are hired at lower salaries than sworn officers, are generally unarmed, and provide many of the social services often requested by the public, thereby improving the cost effectiveness of the department. Research conducted in the Addison, Illinois, Police Department indicates considerable satisfaction with the CSO program on the part of community residents and sworn officers.[7]

Also, in an attempt to improve community relations and provide better services (to say nothing of complying with affirmative action guidelines), many police departments are beginning to employ women and minorities as patrol officers. This invasion of a predominantly male world has come about slowly and with considerable resistance. Nonetheless, the evidence is quite clear: Women and minorities perform patrol duties as well as white males.[8] As time passes, these newcomers to patrol operations will gain supervisory positions and, if they can avoid being co-opted by the police hierarchy, further structural changes in police departments may be expected.

No discussion of changes in police organization and practices would be complete without a brief mention of computer usage. Installation of computer facilities has made possible virtually instant analysis of crime and accident trends, recall of information on suspects, and analysis of the amount and type of activities engaged in by departmental personnel. This rapid analysis capability, coupled with greater willingness to experiment on behalf of many police administrators, has enabled the police to become more responsive to changing conditions and requirements.

As a result of research conducted in Kansas City and elsewhere, the effectiveness of patrol officers on routine patrol has been questioned.[9] This cornerstone of good police work is currently being defended by many police administrators, but evidence indicates, in some cities at least, that routine patrol does not prevent crime, improve citizen satisfaction, or cut down response time. If these findings are supported by further research, a large amount of police resources have been, and are currently being, wasted. If this is so, a thorough rethinking of police operations is required. Such rethinking has already occurred in many progressive departments that now employ **targeted patrol** or **split patrol** strategies to improve

Police Staff Meeting.
James L. Shaffer

their efficiency. In the former, certain areas are designated as high-risk areas and are patrolled quite thoroughly. In the latter, specially designated patrol teams are formed to respond to specific types of calls in an attempt to insure that the right services are available in the right place at the right time.[10]

One change in police operations that is occurring in some states now, and may soon be occurring in others, involves police accreditation programs. The objectives of these programs include developing standards against which agency performance may be measured and developing accreditation procedures that facilitate objective assessment of police performance.[11]

> Given the strong American tradition that police power should be decentralized, it has been nearly impossible to establish generally accepted standards of quality in law enforcement. There are almost as many points of view concerning how different police functions ought to be performed as there are police departments.[12]

Nonetheless, a number of national police organizations are involved in attempting to develop standards for police departments. Minnesota, for example has created a **Peace Officer Standards and Training (P.O.S.T.) Board,** which is a licensing board for police officers in that state. This board licenses police officers who meet predetermined standards of training and education, and who pass a standardized written examination. The license to be a police officer is intended to insure a minimum level of knowledge among police officers throughout the state and is seen as an important step toward professionalization.[13]

The Commission on Accreditation for Law Enforcement Agencies was established in 1979 and administers a voluntary **accreditation** program aimed at achieving excellence, efficiency, and professionalism among police agencies. The commission has established some 944 standards by which to evaluate police agencies. These standards are devised to fit agencies of various sizes and to help police agencies evaluate themselves. If an agency desires to be evaluated by a team of assessors working for the commission, they submit an application. The agency is then sent a questionnaire which is used to determine the standards which apply to that particular agency. A self-assessment is then conducted by agency personnel and, if the agency desires, an on-site assessment by a team of assessors follows. The on-site assessment is then reviewed by the commission to determine whether the agency will be accredited. As of 1988, 69 agencies had been accredited and some 500 were involved in the process.[14]

The implications of police licensing and accreditation are far-reaching. Transfer between departments and lateral entry would be facilitated among licensed officers. The overall level of training among rural law enforcement personnel should improve. Finally, the overall level of service provided to the public should improve.

Still another approach being tested in a number of American police departments has been called **community-oriented policing.** This approach is based upon the same assumption Robert Peel utilized in developing the New Police in London in 1829, that "police must involve the community in a practical way in the police mission." Community-oriented policing is based on police-community reciprocity (police and public must cooperate in order to prevent and solve crimes); decentralization of command (substations to heighten police-community interaction); reorientation of patrol (basically a return to proactive foot patrol); and civilianization (addition of civilian employees to police departments). The goals of community-oriented policing are to eliminate the "we-they" dichotomy which often exists in American communities and to strenghten the notion that all citizens have some responsibility for order maintenance and law enforcement.[15]

These and numerous other adaptations being made in police agencies throughout the United States indicate that the organizational structure of police departments can take a variety of forms and still permit the police to play their role in the criminal justice network. Let us now turn our attention to a discussion of the procedures used by the police to fill that role.

Selection, Training, and Education of the Police

It is clear that adequate police performance in all of the areas mentioned above requires specially selected, specially trained, and perhaps specially educated personnel. How are such personnel selected? What type, and how much training and education do these personnel require?

Standards for police officers vary across the United States, but certain considerations appear to be important in most jurisdictions. Generally speaking, potential police officers must meet some or all of the following criteria:

1. Age—range currently appears to be from about nineteen to thirty-six years of age for initial employment without prior service;
2. Height-weight in proportion;
3. Education—generally a high school diploma or G.E.D., but many departments now require some college;
4. Agility Test—test of physical capabilities required by the job;
5. Written Test—to measure aptitude and/or intelligence;
6. Psychological Exam—to determine mental fitness for the job;
7. Medical Exam—to insure that no debilitating conditions exist at the time of initial employment;
8. Polygraph Exam—to determine honesty;
9. Background Investigation—to insure character of applicants;
10. Oral Interview—to determine applicant's reactions to job-related issues.[16]

Many, if not all, of these requirements have come under attack in recent years. Realistically, a number of these requirements have been applied subjectively with the effect (if not the intent) of excluding females and minorities from police work. We know of several division commanders in different police departments who have advanced through the ranks from patrol officer to lieutenant or captain who could not have met existing height requirements at the time of their initial employment, yet, they were hired and others who met these requirements were not. One police captain told us that he was measured with his boots on, while others were measured in bare feet. In short, height might exclude certain applicants, but if those responsible for hiring felt a certain individual would make a good police officer, the height requirement could be manipulated. As another example of subjectivity, agility tests at one time were set up in such fashion as to routinely exclude women, but these tests have since been shown to have little or no relationship to activities performed by police officers.

Psychological exams are generally considered to be unreliable (scores for the same individual are subject to considerable variation over time). In addition, analyzing scores of potential police officers often involves comparing the scores they obtain with an "ideal" profile. Since no one knows what the characteristics of an ideal police officer are, such analysis seems nonsensical.

Written tests vary tremendously in content and form. Some are job related or situation specific, others are general aptitude or intelligence tests. The validity of most of these tests in terms of predicting successful performance as a police officer is yet to be established.

Similarly, the oral board interview is extremely subjective. While race, sex, dress, etc. are formally excluded from the criteria to be considered by the board in most jurisdictions, one of the authors who has repeatedly served on such boards notes that these variables are frequently subjects of discussion among board members and undoubtedly influence the ratings received by applicants. Affirmative action programs have, in many locales, improved the chances that applicants will be selected without regard to race or sex, although informal pressures clearly counteract such programs in some areas.

As Gray aptly points out, all of these selection procedures may be used for covert as well as overt purposes.[17] Overtly, the procedures are designed to fulfill the requirements of the formal police organization. Covertly, they may be used to satisfy the requirements of the police subculture. This subculture, or police fraternity, has developed over the years as the police and other citizens have increasingly come to view each other as "we" and "they."[18] To the police, "we" consists of other police officers (members in the fraternity). These members are expected to be loyal to the police subculture, trustworthy, willing and able to use force, authoritarian, and so forth. "They" consists of everyone who is not a police officer, who cannot be regarded as loyal to the subculture, trustworthy, etc. To some other citizens (members of racial minorities, for example) the police constitute the "they" group. This relationship between the police and other citizens is both caused by, and helps to maintain, a gap in communication.

At any rate, the requirements of the police subculture are often made known to police selection boards. As a result, most new recruits, though certainly not all, meet both formal and informal requirements for the job. Using the network approach, let us examine how these informal or subcultural requirements can influence hiring procedures even though the law may prohibit their consideration.

The authors are aware of several cases in which police chiefs, mayors, city managers, or council members have contacted selection board members informally to express their feelings concerning who should be hired to fill a police vacancy. In one case, a police chief indicated to the president of a selection board that he wanted no more college graduates hired because they were too intellectual. In another, a chief of police informed two of the three board members that the department really needed a minority officer.

Informal suggestions or pressures such as these may, of course, be ignored by board members. Theoretically, they must be ignored, since the applicant is to be rated on the formal qualifications discussed above, and there is no formal mechanism for adding or detracting rating points for reasons involving race, sex, or creed. Practically speaking, however, members of selection boards are often political appointees, appointed precisely because they are willing to listen to the desires of the police chief or police commissioner. Thus, we know of a case in which a liberal college professor was appointed to a board of fire and police commissioners. His idea of the selection process was that applicants should be rated strictly on the basis of their qualifications, regardless of race, sex, or creed. He

Table 8.1 Requirements for police entry-level training programs. By type of competency area and state, as of December 1985 (In hours)

State	Total number of hours required	Human relations	Force and weaponry	Communications	Legal	Patrol and criminal investigations	Criminal justice systems	Administration
Hawaii	954	17	153	65	133	444	29	113
Rhode Island	661	42	65	0	48	480	0	26
Vermont	553	4	80	30	74	330	3	32
Maine	504	27	62	17	73	277	21	27
West Virginia	495	14	98	20	120	195	36	12
Pennsylvania	480	76	88	10	94	196	16	0
Maryland	471	0	0	0	73	366	0	32
Massachusetts	460	35	132	28	90	167	8	0
Utah	450	19	73	27	49	247	15	20
Connecticut	443	23	48	8	64	284	11	5
Indiana	440	21	73	4	83	192	32	35
Michigan	440	9	105	8	48	244	0	26
Washington	440	34	152	24	85	145	0	0
New Hampshire	426	20	75	8	60	205	8	50
New Mexico	421	30	69.5	18	56	238.5	9	0
Arizona	400	24	110	16	78	135	12	25
California	400	15	80	15	60	185	10	35
Iowa	400	33	75	12	44	175	13	48
Kentucky	400	6.5	84.5	3.5	75.5	182.5	6	41.5
South Carolina	382	18	77	12	72	178	2	23
Texas	381	14	48	18	68	233	0	0
North Carolina	369	28	64	20	72	170	0	15
Delaware	362	12	64	17	87	174	6	2
Montana	346	22	77.5	14	19.5	183.5	15	14.5
Nebraska	341	36	58	10	62	158	2	15
Colorado	334	19	55	22	79	141	18	0

State								
Florida	320	24	39	18	54	158	9	18
Kansas	320	34	42	20	45	170	1	8
Mississippi	320	8	70	20	50	153	7	12
Wyoming	320	10	71	14	53	119	33	20
North Dakota	313	10	23	20	84	139	16	21
Idaho	310	0	47	9	51	169	16	18
New Jersey	310	26	40	13	49	116	17	49
Arkansas	304	14	60	6	19	190	0	15
New York	285	9	38	7	44	169	10	8
Alabama	280	14	49	8	48	138	3	20
Ohio	280	16	42	10	76	111	20	5
Oregon	280	14	64	12	62	104	8	16
Alaska	276	1	20	7	74	139	13	22
Georgia	240	18	45	5	47	110	2	13
Louisiana	240	16	57	8	36	78	5	40
Tennessee	240	2	50	7	31	136	8	6
Wisconsin	240	18	30	9	16	121	10	36
Nevada	200	8	28	11	46	96	2	9
South Dakota	200	17	32	8	22	109	6	6
Missouri	120	3	23	10	28	55	1	0

Note: These data were obtained through a mail survey of law enforcement training directors. Oklahoma, Illinois, Virginia, and Minnesota were omitted from the study due to incomplete data regarding their curriculum content. Each state mandates the minimum hourly requirements reported above, but police agencies within each state may establish entry-level training in addition to state requirements.

"Human relations" training stresses the development of the whole person in dealing with the problems of society. Training involves subjects such as human relations, crisis intervention, and stress awareness. "Force and weaponry" involves the development of skills in the use of firearms, chemical agents, hand-to-hand combat, and other measures of physical force. "Communications" is the development of interpersonal skills for conducting interviews and interrogations; included in this category are report writing, basic training in grammar, spelling, and body language. "Legal" training encompasses criminal law, rules of evidence, basic Constitutional law, laws of arrest, search and seizure, civil rights, and liability. "Patrol and criminal investigation" training focuses on patrol techniques and procedures, defensive driving, basic criminal investigation, emergency medical aid, traffic control, physical fitness, accident investigation, jail-custody procedures, and other technical competencies. "Criminal justice systems" training stresses the knowledge needed for understanding the criminal justice system; included in this area are corrections and courts, and professional conduct and ethics. "Administration" covers training matters related to the use of equipment, basic orientation to the training program, and diagnostic testing and/or examination time. (Source, pp. 8–10.)

Source: Robert J. Meadows, "An Assessment of Police Entry Level Training in the United States: Comformity or Conflict with the Police Role?" Boone, NC: Appalachian State University, 1985. (Mimeographed.) Table II. Table adapted by SOURCEBOOK staff.

felt informal pressures should be prohibited or ignored, and refused to listen to those not on the board who tried to influence him. He was a rather persuasive fellow and was able to convince one or both of the two more conservative board members to rate with him on some occasions. When he resigned from the board, several police officials confided they were not disappointed. Now, they said, someone who "understood the requirements of police work" would be appointed and things would run more smoothly. Clearly, the influence of court decisions and executive orders (Equal Employment Opportunity Act, for example), the influence of political ties, and the influence of the police subculture are all at work in the selection of police officers.

Applicants who successfully meet the requirements outlined above and are selected for police work generally go to a training institute or academy where they receive training in a variety of police subjects ranging from self-defense and weapons through first aid to criminal law and human relations (see table 8.1). Successful completion of a training program leads to the status of **probationary officer,** a status that normally lasts from six months to a year. During the probationary period, the new officer receives on-the-job training from senior officers and supervisors. If the recruit successfully completes the probationary period, he or she becomes a full-fledged police officer.

As we indicated above, many of the criteria involved in the selection of police officers have been questioned. One area of controversy worthy of mention here is that of education. Do college educated people make better police officers than noncollege educated individuals? Are certain types of college programs preferable to other types? Is level of education an important variable to consider when selecting police officers? In the last fifty years, there has been a hue and cry for professional police. While training may help make the police more technically proficient, many believe the real hope for professionalization rests with education, since educational requirements are a basis for most highly regarded professions in our society (e.g., medicine, law, teaching, and so forth). The issue of education is complicated by financial considerations. In an era of increasing concern over cost effectiveness, are the higher salaries required to hire and retain college educated police officers justifiable? Currently, there is some evidence to indicate that college educated officers are likely to have less absenteeism and fewer citizen complaints filed against them than noncollege educated officers.[19] Whether or not these differences are worth higher salaries, and whether or not other differences, which have not yet been detected, exist are still areas of controversy. In addition, the issue of whether criminal justice or law enforcement college programs are more or less desirable than liberal arts programs remains unresolved. These ambiguities were reflected by changes in LEAA programming, which originally gave financial aid to police officers interested in furthering their education, but which later placed less emphasis on this area. The debate continues, with an emphasis on empirical research to help provide answers to questions concerning the necessity or desirability of advanced education for police officers.[20]

Summary

In an attempt to meet public expectations, police selection and training procedures were developed and modified. Recruits are expected to be mentally and physically fit, of reasonably good character, and able to fit into the police subculture. Formal training is now required in most jurisdictions and may be quite comprehensive in nature. Once training at an academy or institute has been completed, the new officer goes through a probationary period and she or he is regularly evaluated during this period by senior and supervisory officers.

The need for education, once assumed to be a prerequisite for professionalization, is currently being reevaluated and further research is needed in this area.

In this chapter, we have discussed both traditional, paramilitary police organizations and some of the more recent changes in these organizations. Attempts are being made to solve problems caused by centralization, rigidity, single promotional channels, and the chain of command by decentralizing (neighborhood policing), dual career programs, and less emphasis on authoritarianism. Additionally, programs (such as CSO) to improve cooperation and communication between the police and the public are being developed. The effectiveness of routine patrol is being rethought and more realistic alternatives (such as split patrol and targeted or directed patrol) are being tried. Increasing numbers of women and minorities are being employed as police officers, and the once clear-cut lines between investigators and patrol officers are being blurred in some departments.

Key Terms Defined

neighborhood (team) policing assigning a team of police officers to police a specific geographic area on a 24-hour-a-day basis.

dual career ladder system a system for recognizing and promoting through a number of patrol ranks officers who do not wish to be supervisors, but who are able to meet certain objective performance standards.

community service officer a nonsworn officer who handles nonemergency situations for the police department.

targeted patrol patrol that focuses on specific areas as opposed to routine, nonspecific patrol.

split patrol patrol based upon crime-specific assignments (some units respond to traffic calls, others to burglaries, and so forth).

Police Officer Standards and Training Board (P.O.S.T.) a licensing board for police officers.

probationary officer a person who has successfully completed all the requirements for being a police officer and is obtaining on-the-job training (generally for the period of one year) while being evaluated in terms of potential for becoming a full-fledged police officer.

accreditation acknowledgement of compliance by a police agency with a set of nationally recognized standards established and evaluated by professional police organizations.

community-oriented policing an approach to policing based upon the principle that effective policing depends upon community-police reciprocity which recognizes the need for decentralization and flexibility.

Discussion Questions

1. Describe the traditional police organization and some of the changes that are occurring in it today. Are there other changes that need to be made? If so, what are they and why do they need to be made?

2. Discuss the criteria currently used to select police officers. Do all of these criteria make sense to you? If not, which ones would you change and why?

3. Discuss the pros and cons of college education for police officers. In your opinion, should such education be a prerequisite for selection as a police officer?

4. Discuss the topics you believe should be covered in all police training academies and institutes. Which of these topics do you regard as most important? Why?

Notes

1. Egon Bittner, *The Functions of the Police in Modern Society* (NIMH, 1970).

2. Bugliosi, Vincent, *Helter Skelter* (New York: Bantam Books, 1976).

3. Peter K. Manning, "Rules, Colleagues, and Situationally Justified Actions," in *Policing: A View from the Street*, ed. Peter K. Manning and John Van Maanen (Santa Monica, Calif.: Goodyear Publishing Company, 1978), 71–90; Larry Tifft, "Control System, Social Bases of Power and Power Exercise in Police Organizations," *Journal of Police Science and Administration* 3, no. 1 (1975): 66–76.

4. Lawrence W. Sherman, Catherine A. Milton, and Thomas V. Kelly, *Team Policing: Seven Case Studies* (Washington, D.C.: Police Foundation, 1973).

5. Personal interview with Chief Jerry Bratcher in Palatine, Ill. in January 1983.

6. John Blockmore, "CSOs: Tedious Work, But Good Training," *Police Magazine* (May 1979): 50–54.

7. Emile Novotony, "Community Service Programs: An Assessment," (M. A. thesis, Western Illinois University, 1979).

8. Peter B. Bloch and Deborah Anderson, *Policewomen on Patrol: Final Report* (Washington, D.C.: Police Foundation, 1974).

9. George Kelling, Tony Pate, Duane Dieckman, and Charles E. Brown, *The Kansas City Preventive Patrol Experiment: A Summary Report* (Washington, D.C.: The Police Foundation, 1974).

10. "Split-Force Patrols Boost Efficiency," *L.E.A.A. Newsletter* 6, no. 16 (December 1977): 10, 11, 14.

11. Roy C. McLaren, "The Impact of Law Enforcement Agency Accreditation on Police Performance Measurement," (Paper presented at the National Conference of the American Society for Public Administration, Detroit, April 1981).

12. Richard S. Allison, "Police Accreditation: A New Effort to Set Standards," *Police Magazine* (January 1980): 52.

13. "Facts About the Minnesota Peace Officer Standards and Training Board," Minnesota P.O.S.T. Board, St. Paul, Minn., 1980.

14. "Cheers for 13 more agencies: State and Local Records set," *Commission Update,* (Fairfax, Va. Commission on Accreditation for Law Enforcement Agencies, Summer 1988): 1.

15. Jerome H. Skolnick and David H. Bayley, *The New Blue Line: Police Innovation in Six American Cities* (New York: The Free Press, 1986).

16. Leonard Territo, C. R. Swanson, Jr., and Neil C. Chamelin, *The Police Personnel Selection Process* (Indianapolis, Ind.: Bobbs-Merrill, 1977).

17. Thomas C. Gray, "Selecting for a Police Subculture," in *Police in America,* ed. Jerome H. Skolnick and Thomas C. Gray (Boston: Little, Brown and Co., 1975), 46–54; Jerome H. Skolnick, "Why Police Behave the Way They Do," *New York/World Journal Tribune* 23 October 1966, pp. 12–14.

18. Gordon W. Allport, *The Nature of Prejudice* (Boston: Beacon Press, 1954), chs. 3 and 4.

19. Leonard W. Sherman and the National Advisory Commission on Higher Education for Police Officers, *The Quality of Police Education* (San Francisco: Jossey-Bass, 1978).

20. Kathryn Golden, "Students in Law Enforcement: Occupational Interests and Attitudes Toward Women as Patrol Officers" (M. A. thesis, Western Illinois University, 1979).

Suggested Readings

Hoover, Larry T. *Police Educational Characteristics and Curricula.* Washington, D.C.: U.S. Department of Justice, Law Enforcement Assistance Administration, 1975.

Sherman, Lawrence W., and Bemis, Warren. "Higher Education for Police Officers: The Central Issue." *The Police Chief* 44, no. 8 (August 1977): 32–34.

Souryal, Sam S. *Police Organization and Administration.* Cincinnati, Ohio: Pilgrimage, 1985.

Territo, Leonard; Swanson, C. R., Jr.; and Chamelin, Neil C. *The Police Personnel Selection Process.* Indianapolis, Ind.: Bobbs-Merrill, 1977.

Weston, Paul B., and Fraley, Philip K. *Police Personnel Management.* Englewood Cliffs, N.J.: Prentice-Hall, 1980.

Whisenand, Paul M., and Ferguson, R. Fred. *The Managing of Police Organizations.* 2d ed. Englewood Cliffs, N.J.: Prentice-Hall, 1978.

The Courts: An Overview

9

Key Terms

jurisdiction	*de novo*
venue	circuit courts
stare decisis	appellate courts
precedent	supreme court
lower courts	district courts
magistrate	writ of certiorari
trial courts	speedy trial

In the previous chapter, we discussed the front line of the criminal justice network, the police. In this chapter, we will focus our attention on another component, the court system. The basic function of the court is to determine the legal outcome of a dispute. In the criminal justice network, this process usually involves the determination of guilt or innocence of one accused of a criminal violation. Disputes in civil matters often concern the determination of monetary damages, custody of children, and injunctions against certain business practices, to name only a few.

Although the determination of guilt or innocence is central to the function of the criminal court, it is by no means the only function. The court is also responsible for determining bail, conducting preliminary hearings, ruling on the admissibility of evidence, and determining the appropriate sentence when a finding of guilty has been reached.

One of the major responsibilities of the court is to provide impartiality to the criminal justice network. This goal is to be achieved by using neutral bodies as decision makers (judges and juries) and by allowing both parties, the prosecution and the defense, to present their arguments in open court. The court operates under formal rules of procedure to guarantee objectivity. For example, there are

A Metropolitan
Courthouse.
James L. Schaffer

limitations as to how evidence may be introduced, what types of evidence may be admitted, and what types of questions may be asked. Questions that are clearly leading are generally not allowed, evidence that was obtained illegally is inadmissible, and evidence admitted must be material (relate to a relevant issue in the case in terms of the charges against the accused).

The court system is not a new phenomenon, although the method of trial has varied greatly throughout history. Techniques, such as trial by ordeal (in which the accused had to withstand some physical ordeal, such as walking through heated plow shears blindfolded) and trial by battle (in which the defendant challenged his or her accuser to combat and the outcome determined the outcome of the case) have been employed.

Today, we employ a more formalized system of presenting evidence, both physical and testimonial, in a court following a strict procedural format. Although historically the courts and court personnel have been held in high esteem, criticism and scrutiny of this branch of the criminal justice network have increased considerably in recent years. Many blame the courts for allowing too many defendants to go free or for issuing sentences that appear exceptionally lenient. Others blame the courts for overcrowding the prisons by sentencing too many defendants to incarceration. One of the major complaints is that the court process is very slow and many trials are frequently delayed for long periods of time for various reasons. In this chapter we will provide a general overview of the court systems, both federal and state, in the United States. We will begin by looking at some basic concepts.

Basic Concepts

One of the most fundamental concepts concerning the court system is that of **jurisdiction.** Quite simply, it is the authority or power to hear a case. No court in the land has unlimited jurisdiction. Even the United States Supreme Court is restricted to hearing specific kinds of cases (discussed later in this chapter).

As a general rule, a distinction is made between courts possessing general jurisdiction and those with specific or limited jurisdiction. A court of general jurisdiction generally has the power to hear a variety of cases. For example, many county or district courts hear both criminal and civil cases involving such issues as murder, probate, divorce, and suits for monetary damages. Courts with special or limited jurisdiction can hear only a narrow range of cases. The juvenile court can hear only cases involving youth in a specific age group; thus, it has a fairly limited jurisdiction. Also, some states maintain magistrate and/or police courts that are restricted to hearing cases carrying a narrowly defined punishment, usually petty offenses and some misdemeanors.

A distinction is also made between courts of original jurisdiction and those with appellate jurisdiction. Original jurisdiction means the court is empowered to hear the case initially. Appellate jurisdiction means that a specific court can hear a defendant's appeal of conviction from the court of original jurisdiction. The power to hear cases is defined through statute, the Constitution, or previous court decisions.

A key, related concept is that of **venue.** Venue is commonly referred to as the place of trial. Under normal conditions the trial will take place within the legally defined geographical area in which the alleged offense was committed. This may be on a municipal, county, or regional basis. Obviously, if you are charged with committing an offense in Los Angeles, California, you would be tried in that vicinity rather than in Dallas, Texas. It should be noted that the possibility to have a change of venue, or location of the trial, does exist. If the defendant can show that he or she cannot obtain a fair trial in the geographical jurisdiction of trial, a petition may be filed with the court to have the location (venue) changed to a neutral jurisdiction. This is not a matter of right, but of privilege. Generally, reasonable grounds for the requested change must accompany the petition. One of the more common grounds is that pretrial publicity has biased potential jurors.

There are situations in which more than one court has jurisdiction. For example, when a federally insured bank is robbed, both the state in which the bank is located and the federal court system would have jurisdiction. These situations are often referred to as cases involving concurrent jurisdiction. As a practical matter, usually one court will *waive* (give up) jurisdiction and the defendant will be tried in only one court. Cases in which only one court has jurisdiction are referred to as involving exclusive jurisdiction.

The terms *stare decisis* and **precedent** are also important in the understanding of the court system. *Stare decisis* means "let the decision stand." When a court issues a ruling on a matter of law, future cases should abide by or adhere to the precedent or legal rule set forth by the earlier case. For example, if a court rules that a defendant charged with a capital offense must be represented by counsel, then as a rule of law all future defendants in capital cases must also be represented by counsel. Such decisions may be applied prospectively, only in subsequent cases, or retrospectively, to past cases as well. Most decisions are applied prospectively.

As you can see, the concepts defined here are important in determining how and where the law will be enforced. A system without such formalized concepts and subsequent rules enforcing them would be chaotic and inconsistent.

The Court Systems

The United States has what is commonly called a dual court system. In 1985, this system employed 172,000 judges, clerks, bailiffs, and other court personnel at an annual cost to taxpayers of about 5.8 billion dollars.[1] There is a federal court system that hears cases involving violations of acts of Congress and a state court system that hears cases concerning violations of state statutes. This dual system is a by-product of the separation of powers clause of the United States Constitution. As we previously stated, there are circumstances in which a single act can violate both an act of Congress and a state statute—concurrent jurisdiction. It is generally estimated that 80 to 90 percent of all criminal cases will be heard in the state courts.

State Court Systems

If one were asked to describe the state court system of the United States, the most definitive term used would have to be variation. The states have considerable latitude in the organization of their court systems. As with the chapters explaining criminal offenses (i.e., chapters 5 and 6), we encourage each student to examine his or her own state's statutes to obtain a better understanding of how the state court system is structured. What follows is a general overview of state court systems.

State court systems are divided into three or four levels depending upon state constitutions or statutes. These levels are usually arranged in a hierarchical fashion.

Lower courts are usually courts of limited jurisdiction. They are empowered to hear only cases of a minor nature (e.g., traffic cases and misdemeanors) with lower levels of punishment. The lower court system is probably one of the most neglected areas of study in the criminal justice network, even though most of the public's experience with the court system is at this level. Attitudes about the courts and the criminal justice network in general are often based upon experiences and impressions gained from lower courts.

The lower court system has been severely criticized for the way in which it processes cases.[2] Most lower courts are characterized by an emphasis on speed and routinization. They are basically courts where one can answer a charge with a guilty plea and pay a standardized fine within a matter of minutes or even seconds. The lower courts have also been criticized for neglecting constitutional procedures. Most defendants enter the court without counsel and may or may not be made aware of this and other constitutional rights. Despite these criticisms, the lower court system fulfills an important function. Most of the court cases are heard in the lower courts (estimates of up to 90 percent). If they were abolished, other courts would have to handle the cases now heard by the lower courts. Presently many of the other courts have such overloaded dockets that there is a backlog of cases, and a considerable time gap exists between the act in question and the decision of the court. If we did not have a lower court system, the lag would increase, defendants would spend more time in jail, other criminal justice personnel would be overworked, and important cases might be overlooked or slighted in an effort to lessen the backlog. Despite the many criticisms of the lower court system, it fulfills a necessary function, and its abolition without provisions for some alternative would result in grave consequences for the entire criminal justice network.

There have been many attempts to upgrade the lower court systems. Historically, the lower court system was often staffed by justices of the peace. These justices were often lay persons possessing little or no legal training, who were almost totally ignorant of proper judicial decorum and procedures. Records were often ill kept, if they were kept at all, and facilities depended upon whatever the justice could afford. Justice of the peace courts have been held in living rooms, on front porches, and in the backs of stores. The trend has been to abolish justice of the peace courts and replace them with other, more formalized courts.

Currently, one of the more common lower-level court systems is the magistrate system. **Magistrates** are members of the bar who are either elected or appointed (depending upon the jurisdiction). They are limited to hearing specific types of cases, but they are generally better qualified than their predecessors; they are familiar with constitutional guarantees and court procedures; and they can, and in some states are empowered to, perform other functions such as issuing warrants and conducting bail hearings.

Some jurisdictions also have police courts, traffic courts, and/or municipal courts. These, too, are considered lower courts and are limited in their jurisdiction. Some of the problems commonly associated with justice of the peace courts continue to plague these lower courts.

The second level of the state court system consists of the **trial courts.** These courts have general jurisdiction and hear both civil and criminal cases as well as appeals, in some jurisdictions, from lower courts.

The stereotyped image of the court often produced by the media characterized by proper decorum, flowing orations, and extreme formality is based primarily upon the trial courts. Unlike the limited courts, where trials generally last a few minutes, cases heard in trial courts may run for days or, in some instances, weeks and months. Unlike the lower courts, trial courts are characterized by full-time court personnel, sophisticated methods of record keeping, the use of juries, more emphasis on formality, and the protection of constitutional guarantees. There is also a lesser degree of routinization in sentencing in the trial courts than in the lower courts.

Although the trial courts are courts of general jurisdiction, the majority of their cases are civil in nature, rather than criminal. Some jurisdictions maintain separate specialized trial courts to hear each type of case. In general, trial court judges hear felony or serious misdemeanor cases, although in many areas they hold concurrent jurisdiction with lower courts over minor offenses. In some jurisdictions, trial courts hear appeals from the lower courts; but as a practical matter, this occurs infrequently (less than ten percent of the time) and does not generally tax the resources of the trial courts. If an appeal is heard from a lower court it may be heard *de novo* (trial anew), since many lower courts do not keep adequate records of their proceedings.

Trial courts are often organized on a county or regional (multicounty) basis. Historically, trial courts were county courts. The county court system was to some extent impractical because many small counties could not afford to maintain their own courts and, before transportation was modernized, county inhabitants often encountered difficulty in traveling to the county seat. As a result of these and other factors (including greater emphasis on governmental efficiency), **circuit** or **regional courts** appeared. These courts may cover considerable geographical area and are characterized by the use of judges who move from courthouse to courthouse on either a scheduled or "as needed" basis.

The third level of state court systems consists of intermediate **appellate courts.** The presence of intermediate appellate courts is characteristic of the more largely populated states as a method of relieving the case load of the state supreme court. It should be noted that approximately half of the states maintain intermediate appellate courts. Where such courts exist, they consist of three to nine judges or justices, and are usually organized on a regional or multicounty basis (one intermediate appellate court for a specific number of county or district courts). These courts are normally restricted to appellate jurisdiction; that is, they can only review cases on their record. In some jurisdictions, they are limited by law to hearing cases arising from specific lower courts or cases involving less than a specified dollar value. Again, as is the case with courts of general jurisdiction, the majority of cases heard at this level are civil rather than criminal. In states that employ intermediate appellate courts, decisions are largely finalized at this level, since very few cases are heard by the highest court.

At the top of the state court hierarchy we find the state **supreme court** or, as it is referred to in some jurisdictions, the state judicial court or the supreme court of appeals. It is, in many cases, the court of last resort, since very few state cases are heard by the United States Supreme Court.

In cases requiring an interpretation of state statutes or the state constitution, the state supreme court has the final decision unless that statute or portion of the state constitution is inconsistent with the United States Constitution.

State supreme courts are composed of three to nine judges who primarily hear civil cases and who review cases on their record (by reviewing the transcripts). Additional powers they may possess include issuing judicial assignments, confirming the nomination of judges, and reviewing cases of alleged judicial misconduct.

The Federal Court System

The other branch of the dual court system is made up of the federal courts. These courts are empowered to hear both civil and criminal cases. The federal system consists of United States District Courts, United States Courts of Appeal, and the United States Supreme Court.

The United States **District Courts** were created by Congress in the Judicial Act of 1789. These courts are the trial courts of the federal system. Each state will have from one to four federal district courts and from one to twenty-four judges. The District of Columbia and United States territories maintain federal district courts as well. Judges in federal district courts are appointed by the president of the United States, with Senate confirmation, for life terms. Federal magistrates are appointed by the district court judges and serve an eight-year appointment. The federal magistrates relieve pressure from the federal district judges by performing limited functions such as issuing warrants, conducting preliminary hearings, determining bail, and so on.

The federal district courts were created to lessen the demands on the United States Supreme Court. As we shall see, the United States Supreme Court hears only a small portion of the cases it is asked to hear. By establishing the district courts to hear the "actual cases," Congress has provided an alternative to the Supreme Court.

The criminal jurisdiction of the United States District Courts includes all cases where a federal criminal statute has been violated. Examples include kidnapping, the assassination or attempted assassination of the president, postal violations, violations of federal fish and game laws, and cases involving interstate transportation of stolen goods as well as interstate flight to avoid prosecution. Again, we should note that in some instances concurrent jurisdiction may exist with a state court. The civil jurisdiction of the United States District Courts is limited to suits exceeding $10,000 in which (1) a federal question is raised, (2) the suit involves citizens of two or more separate states, or (3) when a citizen of one state sues another state.

Within the federal court system there exists intermediate appellate courts—the United States Courts of Appeal. Created in 1891, these courts were established to reduce the number of appeals made to the United States Supreme Court.

Defendants have a right to appeal the decision from the federal district courts. Most, but not all, appeals from the federal trial courts will be heard at this level, and for most the final decision will be rendered at this level.

Prior to 1949, these intermediate appellate courts were referred to as circuit courts of appeals. Today, the geographical division of circuits is maintained, but judges are not required to travel to various locations to hear cases as they did in the past. Within the United States, there are eleven circuits composed of three to nine states or territories except for Washington, D.C., which has its own court. Except for Washington, D.C., each circuit is identified by a number. Circuit court offices are generally located in the larger metropolitan areas, and the appellant must travel to the location of the office to have his or her case heard.

Each court of appeals has three to nine permanent judgeships. Judges are appointed by the president for life or good behavior. The most experienced judge who has not reached his or her seventieth birthday will serve as chief judge of the circuit. In most instances, cases will be heard by three-judge panels with two considered a quorum. In certain circumstances all judges will hear a case, a process called sitting *en banc*.

The United States Courts of Appeals maintain appellate jurisdiction and only review records of lower courts rather than retrying cases. These appellate courts review the records for interpretation of law, both statutory and constitutional, and not issues of fact (i.e., whether or not a defendant was provided with counsel at required times, or whether or not there was an error in admitting evidence or instructing the jury). The United States Courts of Appeals also review and enforce the decisions of nineteen quasi-judicial tribunals, including the Food and Drug Administration and the National Labor Relations Board.

The court of last resort for both the federal and state systems is the United States Supreme Court. This Court is composed of nine judges appointed by the president and confirmed by the Senate who sit for life or good behavior. They may be removed by impeachment or voluntary retirement. The president also appoints one of the judges as chief justice. The chief justice assumes administrative duties, such as assigning one of the judges to write the Court's decision, but has no greater authority than the other judges in the determination of each case.

By statuatory provision the Court convenes the first Monday each October and sits until mid-June unless all cases have been decided prior to that time. Many of us have heard someone proclaim, "I will take this case all the way to the Supreme Court." Realistically this is very unlikely. In most instances, an appellant must petition the Court to hear his or her case. The Court hears approximately 5 percent of all petitions. If the Court decides to hear the case, they issue a **writ of certiorari,** a demand for the transcripts of the proceedings to be sent to the Court for review. In special circumstances, arguments may be presented, as in the decision of the constitutionality of the death penalty; but arguments are limited to a specific time frame. The Court operates on the basis of majority opinion with six members constituting a quorum. One judge, who voted with the majority, is assigned by the chief justice to write the Court's opinion or often the chief justice personally writes it. In addition, other members may write a concurring opinion (if they are in the majority) or a dissenting opinion (if in the minority). Neither opinion has an impact on the case, but in the future it may be a basis for changing the precedent set in the present case.

The Court was established by the United States Constitution; however, its status as the supreme determinant of legal issues was not conferred at its inception. One of the important factors in the development of the Supreme Court's authority was the case of *Marbury v. Madison*.[3] This decision gave the Court the "power of judicial review." In essence, it held that the authority of the United States Constitution shall supercede acts of Congress and that the Constitution should be interpreted by the Court.

The Supreme Court is somewhat unique in that it maintains both original and appellate jurisdiction. The Court has limited original jurisdiction in cases involving treaties made by the federal government, controversies in which the United States government is a party, and disputes between two states, to name only a few areas.[4]

The Court also has been granted appellate jurisdiction by Congress, and the majority of its work involves this responsibility (cases of original jurisdiction account for less than one percent of the Court's activities). We previously noted that the Court has considerable discretion in determining which cases it hears. While this is basically true, the Court is required to grant jurisdiction when (1) a federal court holds an act of Congress to be unconstitutional; (2) a United States Court of Appeals finds a state statute unconstitutional; (3) a state's highest court holds a federal law to be invalid; and (4) an individual's challenge to a state statute is upheld by a state supreme court.

We should note the different decisions the Court can reach. If they affirm the decision, the lower court decision is held to be correct and the case is finalized. They may also reverse the lower court decision, in part or in total. Many times a petition will include more than one point of contention. If the court reverses in part, the case is usually remanded (sent back to the court of original jurisdiction) and retried with modifications made as designated by the Court. In some instances, there are such serious constitutional errors that the original decision is completely overturned.[5]

"In all criminal prosecutions, the accused shall enjoy the right to a **speedy** . . . **trial**."[6] As we noted in the introduction to this chapter, courts are the targets of considerable criticism. Failure to provide speedy trials is one of the leading areas of concern. In reality, most of the people who do obtain a speedy trial only do so by pleading guilty in a lower court. At the trial level, it is not uncommon for the trial to commence at least a year after arrest in felony cases, and the delay in civil cases is often much greater (sometimes more than five years). Delays also plague the appellate courts, and appeals are often not finalized until years after a decision was reached at the trial level.

A major question surrounding this problem is the definition of speedy trial. The President's Crime Commission recommended a maximum of eighty-one days between arrest and trial for those defendants not detained in jail and seventy-one days for those who are detained.[7] This was only a recommendation and no jurisdiction is bound by it. In fact, few cases at the trial court level are processed within this time frame. At the federal level, Congress has applied the Speedy Trial Act of 1974[8] to the federal system. The act holds that only sixty days may elapse between arraignment and trial. Although such efforts are commendable, few defendants, at either the trial or appellate levels, actually receive speedy trials.

Why the concern over court delay or backlog? First, it has tainted the image of the justice network in the eyes of the public who have little respect for a network that moves so slowly. Second and closely related, it has necessitated the practice of plea bargaining—pleading guilty for consideration. Roughly ninety percent of all felonies are processed by negotiation rather than by trial. Victims, the public, and the police are frequently unhappy about this practice; but if it were to be discontinued now, the delays would be unconscionable. Third, delay can cause undue financial and/or emotional hardship on those defendants who remain in jail and on their families, particularly if the defendants are eventually found innocent. Guilty defendants who are released on bail may commit additional illegal acts while awaiting trial. Repeated delays also cause hardships for victims and witnesses who must appear in court on numerous occasions.

Why, with such negative effects, does the problem persist? There are several reasons for court delay. Some of the reasons more commonly stated are: a shortage of judges and courtrooms, the use or abuse of continuances by attorneys, the filing of too many petty cases, and inefficient methods of court administration.[9] Neither the number of courtrooms nor the number of judges have kept pace with population increases, or with increases in criminal prosecutions or civil cases. Legislatures have been hesitant or unwilling to appropriate adequate funds for judicial budgets.

Additionally, lawyers sometimes waive defendants' right to a speedy trial by asking for continuances. Undeniably, the continuance may be necessary to uncover evidence or aid in the development of the case for the defense, but, as Blumburg has argued,[10] it is also used as a method to collect fees. The continuance may be a part of the defense strategy. Banfield and Anderson[11] found that the longer a case was continued the more likely it is that the defendant would not be found guilty. As the time between the crime and trial increases, witnesses are more difficult to locate and cannot always testify accurately to what has transpired months or years ago.

As we previously noted, most court cases are civil rather than criminal. Our citizens are quite willing to file suit with respect to almost any issue. The result is court congestion. One recommendation to remedy this situation is to use quasi-judicial tribunals to arbitrate claims involving less than a specified dollar amount. This would relieve judges to handle more trials; however, the problem of court delay is very complex and will not be resolved simply. An effort involving the court system, the government, and the public is needed if change is to occur.

In the previous section, we identified inefficient court administration as a contributing factor to court delay. Traditionally the chief judge is primarily responsible for the administrative duties of the court as well as for hearing cases. These duties include, but are not limited to, (1) preparing the budget, (2) scheduling cases, (3) assigning and overseeing personnel, and (4) maintaining records. Unfortunately, many justices are not qualified to handle all these responsibilities. Law schools do not traditionally offer courses in court administration, so unless the judge has prior experience in this area, these tasks are often not effectively or efficiently performed.

There is a movement today to employ court administrators to perform these functions. The assumption is that a trained and/or experienced administrator can more effectively perform these duties, allowing the judge more time to hear cases. The federal courts, and some larger jurisdictions in the state courts, have employed court administrators with considerable success. Experimentation with court administrators and computerization have led some to believe that these changes will help to decrease the court backlog at both the trial and appellate levels because witnesses are better notified and records are better kept. Despite the common sense appeal and the success enjoyed by courts using these techniques, there have been criticisms. Some argue that the practice diminishes the authority of the chief judge—she or he becomes only another judge. It is also contended that the practice is too impersonal (too businesslike) and that the court is supposed to process cases individually, not like freight. Finally, there is the problem of expense. Federal funding has supported the hiring of many court administrators and the utilization of computer systems. Whether or not these positions can be maintained when funding expires remains to be seen, since many states find it difficult to allocate enough funds to increase the size of the judiciary, let alone to hire other personnel or enter the computer age.

Summary

There are a number of concepts common to all types of courts in the United States. These include jurisdiction (general, limited, exclusive, concurrent, original, and appellate); venue; *stare decisis;* and precedent. The court system of the United States is very complex. It consists of two more or less distinct systems—state and federal. There is considerable variation between the states, but most employ a three- or four-tiered hierarchy, while the federal system is three-tiered. Most cases heard in trial and appellate courts are civil rather than criminal, and there are serious problems of court delay at all levels. There are many identifiable causes and proposed solutions to court delay, but the problem is complex and difficult to solve satisfactorily.

Key Terms Defined

jurisdiction the authority to hear a particular case.
venue the place of trial.
stare decisis let the decision stand.
precedent decision handed down previously in a similar case.
lower courts courts with limited jurisdiction involving only specific types of cases.
magistrate a judge limited to hearing only specific types of cases, usually in a lower court.
trial courts courts with general jurisdiction (usually over both civil and criminal matters) to hear cases.
de novo trial anew.
circuit courts trial courts serving a particular geographic region or circuit.
appellate courts courts hearing appeals from lower courts.
supreme court court of last resort (highest appellate court) in a state or nation.
district courts trial courts of the federal system.
write of certiorari an order from a higher court asking a lower court for the record of a case.
speedy trial refers to insuring that the time period between arrest and trial is reasonable.

Discussion Questions

1. Distinguish between the following terms: jurisdiction - venue
general jurisdiction - limited jurisdiction
concurrent jurisdiction - exclusive jurisdiction.

2. Explain why our court system is called a dual court system. Explain, in general terms, the organization of each component.

3. Why are lower courts considered a necessity? What problems plague them and what steps may be taken to rectify those problems?

4. What is meant by court delay? What are the causes and consequences of delay and how might they be remedied?

Notes

1. *Source book of Criminal Justice Statistics—1986,* U.S. Department of Justice (Washington, D.C.: U.S. Government Printing Office, 1987), 2, 6.
2. Howard James, *Crisis in the Courts* (New York: David McKay, 1967), 20–57.
3. *Marbury v. Madison,* 1803.
4. For more detail on limitations, see United States Constitution, Article III, Section II.
5. For a detailed discussion of the Supreme Court, see Bob Woodward and Scott Armstrong, *The Brethren: Inside the Supreme Court* (New York: Simon and Schuster, 1979).
6. United States Constitution, Sixth Amendment (see appendix).
7. President's Commission on Law Enforcement and Administration of Justice, *Task Force Report: The Courts* (Washington, D.C.: U.S. Government Printing Office, 1967).
8. U.S.C.A. sec. 361 (supp. 1975).
9. Laura Banfield and C. David Anderson, "Continuances in the Cook County Criminal Courts," *University of Chicago Law Review* 35 (Winter 1968): 279–80.
10. Abraham S. Blumberg, *Criminal Justice* (Chicago: Quadrangle, 1967).
11. Laura Banfield and C. David Anderson, "Continuances in the Cook County Criminal Courts," *University of Chicago Law Review* 35 (Winter 1968): 279–80.

Suggested Readings

Abadinsky, Howard. *Law and Justice.* Chicago: Nelson-Hall, 1988.

Abraham, Henry J. *The Judicial Process.* 2d ed. New York: Oxford University Press, 1968.

Blumberg, Abraham S. *Criminal Justice.* Chicago: Quadrangle, 1967.

Downie, Leonard. *Justice Denied: The Case for Reform of the Courts.* New York: Holt, Rinehart and Winston, 1971.

Frank, Jerome. *Courts on Trial*. Princeton, N.J.: Princeton University Press, 1949.

President's Commission on Law Enforcement and Administration of Justice. *Task Force Report: The Courts*. Washington, D.C.: U.S. Government Printing Office, 1967.

Stuckey, Gilbert B. *Procedures in the Justice System*. Columbus, Ohio: Charles E. Merrill Publishing Co., 1979, ch. 2.

Waltz, Jon R. *Introduction to Criminal Evidence*. 2d ed. (Chicago: Nelson-Hall, 1983).

Court Personnel

10

Key Terms

prosecutor (state's attorney, district
attorney)
defense counsel
public defender

adversary system
judge
probation officer

In this chapter we will focus on the roles and functions of personnel who staff
the courts. In the typical course of events, an alleged offender first encounters
the police and then either a public or private defense counsel, or the prosecutor.
Since the **prosecutor** is the person to whom the police present their case with
respect to an alleged offender, let us turn our attention first to that officer.

The Prosecutor

Some eighteen thousand prosecutors are found at federal, state, and local levels
in the United States. The activities of the prosecutor involve him or her in all
aspects of the criminal justice network.

Typically, the cases processed by the prosecutor originate with a law enforcement agency, and smooth working relationships between these agencies and the
prosecutor's office are essential if the criminal justice network is to be effective
and efficient. Grand juries work under the supervision of the prosecutor and rely
upon the prosecutor for information, evidence, and advice. The role of the prosecutor in plea bargaining is detailed elsewhere in this chapter, as is his or her
role in establishing court dockets and recommending sentences to the judge. Parole
boards and probation officers also rely upon the prosecutor to provide information

relevant to their functions. In many instances, prosecutors are also involved in a variety of pretrial diversion programs (such as "unofficial probation"). Their willingness to use alternatives to incarceration determines to some extent whether such programs will survive.[1]

There are federal prosecutors' offices in each of the ninety-five U.S. judicial districts, fifty state attorney generals' offices, and about twenty-eight hundred local offices of prosecution within the states. The basic function of these prosecutors is to represent the people (the state) in criminal proceedings. This function is accomplished through the charging process and the trial process.

Charging is basically a two-step process. In step one, the prosecutor decides whether or not to file criminal charges against an individual. In step two, the prosecutor decides the nature of such charges. Any charges filed must be based upon the facts of a particular case and upon the law as it relates to that case. In order to make a charging decision, the prosecutor reviews case records, presents the case to a grand jury or files an information (a formal accusation), and the prosecutor may go through a preliminary hearing and a series of negotiations with defense counsel in determining whether to file charges and, if so, what charges are to be filed.

When a prosecutor decides to proceed to criminal trial, she or he becomes the state's "champion" who engages in courtroom combat (generally verbal) with the defense. The final decision about whether an alleged offender will be brought into court rests with the prosecutor. If the prosecutor decides not to take the case into court, no further official action is likely to be taken on the case in question.

Too broke, prosecutor drops case

PONCA CITY, Okla. (AP)—A man charged with first-degree rape has gone free because state budget cutbacks left a district attorney too broke to try the case, and the attorney general says prosecutors no longer can afford to "fight every battle."

Joe Wideman, district attorney for Kay County, said Thursday a 26 percent reduction in his office's budget last month led to the dismissal of the charge against Toby Dewayne Tomlin, 24, who was accused of raping a Ponca City woman in May.

The president of the state District Attorneys Association said the Kay County case was probably the first in which a charge involving a violent crime had been dismissed because of money problems.

Wideman said his office could not find the alleged victim, who had moved to Texas, nor could it afford to bring her to Ponca City if they had located her.

The prosecutor's office also could not pay the $250 it would cost to obtain a transcript of the victim's testimony from an earlier hearing.

"We wanted to go to trial with the transcript because we felt that would sustain our case," Wideman said. "So we zipped out and had to dismiss."

The prosecutor said if the alleged victim can be located, the state could again press charges within a seven-year statute of limitations. Conviction of a charge of first-degree rape is punishable by a jail term ranging from five years to life.

Reprinted by permission of Associated Press

The prosecutor, then, exercises an enormous amount of discretion in the criminal justice network. While the police officer may "open the gate" to the official justice system, the prosecutor may close that gate. The prosecutor may do this without accounting for his or her reasons to anyone else in the network (except, of course, to the voters who elect the prosecutor to office, and the elections often take place long after the case has been decided).

Clearly, there are some circumstances under which the prosecutor would be foolish to proceed with court action. For example, lack of evidence, lack of probable cause, or lack of due process may make it virtually impossible to prosecute a case successfully. There are, however, a number of somewhat less legitimate reasons for failure to prosecute. Evidence indicates that the prosecutor may fail to take cases to court for political reasons (as when the person in question is a powerful, local political figure) or because the case load of the prosecutor includes an "important" or "serious" case in which successful prosecution will result in favorable publicity. As a result, the prosecutor may screen out or dismiss a number of "less serious" cases, such as burglary and assault.[2] In short, the prosecutor is the key figure in the justice system and is recognized as such by both defendants and defense counsel.[3]

> A prosecutor's discretion is extensive. It encompasses the power to selectively prosecute suspected offenders; to give strength to, or emasculate, law enforcement policies by not prosecuting violations of certain laws; to drop charges once having initiated a prosecution; and, of course, to plea bargain with a defendant.[4]

A former U.S. Attorney General once made the following observations concerning the discretionary power of the prosecutor:

> The prosecutor has more control over life, liberty, and reputation than any other person in America. His discretion is tremendous. He can have citizens investigated and, if he is that kind of person, he can have this done to the tune of public statements and veiled or unveiled intimations. Or the prosecutor may choose a more subtle course and simply have a citizen's friends interviewed. . . . He may dismiss the case before trial, in which case the defense never has a chance to be heard. . . . If the prosecutor is obliged to choose his cases, it follows that he can choose his defendants. . . . [A] prosecutor stands a fair chance of finding at least a technical violation of some act on the part of almost anyone. . . . It is in this realm—in which the prosecutor picks some person whom he dislikes or desires to embarrass, or selects some group of unpopular persons and then looks for an offense, that that greatest danger of abuse of prosecuting power lies. It is here that law enforcement becomes personal. . . .[5]

Of course not all prosecutors employ the tactics and techniques discussed above, but it does happen. Sometimes prosecutorial abuse occurs as the result of a revenge motive, but perhaps more often it results from lack of adequate training on behalf of the prosecutor or his or her staff.

A brief look at the reasons for becoming a prosecutor and the process through which this occurs will help us to understand how and why such abuses occur.

The position of prosecutor may be attractive for a variety of reasons. For those attorneys who wish to become judges or state or federal legislators, it is an excellent starting point. It is, then, attractive to some individuals interested primarily in political careers rather than in prosecution.

For young attorneys just out of law school, the position of assistant prosecutor insures a steady income while it provides opportunities to make contacts upon which to build a private practice. Some of these assistants eventually become prosecutors in order to further political ambitions, to gain notoriety as criminal lawyers, or because the tremendous power and discretion accompanying the position attracts them. Finally, some attorneys become (and some remain) prosecutors because they are committed to the practice of criminal law and to representing the state in criminal cases.

There are a variety of other functions performed by most prosecutors. These include "providing legal advice to governmental bodies (especially law enforcement agencies), providing training for police on criminal law and legal processes, preparing drafts of search warrants and wiretapping applications, participating in decisions regarding court administration, and engaging in a wide variety of public information and community relations programs. The chief prosecutor must also administer his own office and engage in the political activities essential to remain in office."[6]

We should note that the prosecutor, although he or she is the state's champion, is obligated to protect the rights of the defendant as well. He or she must, for example, present evidence to show that a defendant is not guilty when it comes to his or her attention.

Since we have previously discussed the political process by which the prosecutor is selected (chapter 3), we will simply point out once again the importance of understanding political affiliations and considerations when considering the prosecutor's role.

The Defense Counsel

There are two major categories of **defense counsel**—private and public. Some seventy-five hundred lawyers are paid as **public defenders** by some governmental body (state, county, or a combination) to represent indigent clients who cannot afford to retain private counsel. For many young lawyers interested in criminal law, the position of public defender represents a stepping stone. In most jurisdictions the public defender is paid a relatively low salary, but the position guarantees a minimal income, which can be supplemented by private practice. As a rule, case loads are heavy; investigative resources are limited; and many clients are, by their own admission, guilty.[7] The public defender, therefore, spends a great deal of time negotiating pleas and often very little time with his or her clients. In fact, there are instances in which public defenders indicate to the judge that they are ready to proceed and then ask someone in the courtroom to show them which of the several defendants present is their client. As a result, public defenders often enjoy a less than favorable image among their clients.[8]

Some public defenders seem to have little interest in using every possible strategy to defend their clients. On numerous occasions, legal errors are made by prosecutors and judges, to which the public defender raises no objection. In addition, appeals are sometimes not initiated by public defenders even when chances of successful appeal seem to be good. There are also public defenders who do pursue their clients' interests with all possible vigor, even to the point of alienating the judges who initially appointed them. On the whole, defendants who retain private counsel believe they fare better than those who are represented by public defenders, and there is some evidence to support this belief.[9] Oaks and Lehman analyzed data from three categories of defense counsel and found private attorneys obtain more pretrial dismissals (29 percent) than either public defenders (8 percent), or the Chicago Bar Association's Defense of Prisoners Committee (8 percent). In addition, they found that 68 percent of private counsels' clients entered guilty pleas compared to 82 percent for public defenders' clients and overall (dismissed and not guilty categories combined), 36 percent of the clients of private attorneys were not found guilty compared to 17 percent for clients of public defenders.[10]

Nagel reports that about 90 percent of all indigents are found guilty as opposed to about 80 percent of nonindigents.

> Why these class disparities? They reflect, at least partly, inferior legal help. But even when the lawyer works hard and well, the indigent faces the handicap that he is, and looks, lower class, while those who determine his destiny—probation officer and judge—are middle class. Therefore, apart from other disabilities of the poor, class bias among judicial personnel may work against them.[11]

It is, perhaps, most interesting that while differences between private and public defense counsel do exist with respect to dismissals and not guilty verdicts, these differences do not indicate an overwhelming superiority of private attorneys over court-appointed public defenders. As Oaks and Lehman indicate, "Criminal law practice is a very chancy business. There are few private attorneys making good livings from the private practice of criminal law."[12] In fact, most good law schools offer few courses in criminal law, and most graduates of these schools have little or no interest in practicing criminal law. This is so, among other reasons, because of the type of clientele involved, difficulties in collecting fees, and the reputation generated by legal practitioners who openly solicit cases in the halls and courtrooms of courthouses, and practice law out of their briefcases. Some of the problems involved in the private practice of criminal law are discussed in the above article.

Whether defense counsel is private or public, his or her duties remain essentially the same. The duties are to see that the client is properly represented at all stages of the system, that the client's rights are not violated, and that the client's case is presented in the most favorable light possible, regardless of the client's involvement in criminal activity. In order to accomplish these goals, the defense counsel is expected to battle, at least in theory, the prosecutor in adversary proceedings. Here again, the difference between theory and practice is considerable.[14]

Lawyer closes book on criminal defense

Ronald L. Burdge, 34, is an attorney who has come to an unusual decision.

"I no longer defend criminal cases," he said the other day. "My problem is that I have found it increasingly difficult to find a defendant who is truly innocent. I have learned that a defendant is usually guilty of something related to what he is charged with. He may not be guilty of the technical charge against him. But in most cases he is guilty of something."

Burdge lives in Franklin, Ohio; he is with the law firm of Ruppert, Bronson and Chicarelli. He has told the other attorneys in the firm that they can have all the criminal cases; he wants nothing to do with them anymore.

"You might be defending a man on a drug charge," Burdge said. "Maybe it's a federal charge, and you know that it should be a state charge. So you can be a 'good lawyer' and get it thrown out of federal court, and your client walks.

"So what have you done? You have put a drug dealer on the streets again. Is that what the law is all about?"

Burdge said his personal feeling is that "over 90 percent of accused criminals who come to defense lawyers are guilty of something. I just don't feel like making my living looking for technicalities in the law so that they can go free."

He said he is well aware of the rights that accused criminals have, and of the safeguards that our system of justice provides them.

"I still believe in the technical, legal rights of the accused," he said. "I just think I'll let other lawyers defend them."

He said that most people accused of crimes, when they first visit a defense lawyer, do one of two things.

"Sometimes they simply lie to you," he said. "They tell you that they aren't guilty of anything. Only after intensive questioning do they admit the truth. You can always tell when they're playing dumb.

"A lot of the time, though, they will gladly tell you that they are guilty, and they will tell you exactly how they committed the crime. They know that you're sworn not to tell anyone else about it; they tell you everything, so you can figure out a technical way to get them free."

Burdge said he is always amazed to see the difference between an accused criminal the first time he walks into a lawyer's office and when he eventually takes the witness stand.

"At first he's stumbling, he's unsure of himself, he has his story all mixed up," Burdge said. "But after months of conferences and coaching, he gets up on that witness stand and he's as smooth as can be. The defense attorney has shown him how to present his side without actually lying—but in a way that will get him acquitted."

"If a man stabbed another man, he will be asked by his defense attorney: 'Was the other fellow making threatening gestures at you?' And the defendant will say, 'Yes, the other fellow was making threatening gestures.' The attorney is setting up a self-defense acquittal."

"But the other fellow is deceased, and what doesn't come out in court is that he was making threatening gestures because the client came in first with the knife pulled out."

Burdge said that plea-bargaining has become so widespread that a conscientious defense attorney is unlikely ever to see true justice done.

"If your client is guilty and you defend him successfully, then you have a criminal walking the streets because of your legal expertise," he said.

"But if he's not guilty, and there is all this pressure to plea-bargain, and you do it, then you're admitting that an innocent man is guilty. Nobody wants to go to trial; they just want to plea-bargain and avoid all the time that's consumed by going to trial. Who wins when you do that?"

He said that other attorneys have told him he is naive.

"They say that there are always going to be criminals out there," Burdge said. "Someone's got to defend them."

"And I suppose someone does. But not me. The underlying, fundamental purpose of the law is not to play games with technicalities. The underlying purpose of the law is to find the people who are guilty and to punish them—and I don't know

Continued

who I'm serving by helping guilty men to go free."

He said one of the reasons he decided to get out of criminal law was the people defense attorneys have to deal with every day—the people who put groceries on their tables.

"Basically it's the dregs of society," he said. "You have drug pushers, you have sex criminals, you have home invaders. Sure, they have the right to counsel. But I simply decided that I didn't want to spend the rest of my life facing them across a desk every morning."

"I have a couple of children. I just didn't like the idea of going home at night knowing that I was doing something so . . . unpalatable. I found it difficult to look at my kids, knowing that this was how I was making my living."

"I think that criminal defense attorneys these days just don't think about the moral implications of what they are doing. To keep from thinking about it, they concentrate on the technicalities of the law, and get fascinated with how they can manipulate those technicalities

so they can show their clients are technically innocent."

"But in doing that, they are helping people who are criminals. You can get a man off on a technicality, but what do you tell yourself when you know inside that he's still a criminal?"

Burdge said he is confident that there will be no shortage of attorneys to defend accused criminals. He said he is much happier, though, now that he is not one of them.

"I used to have migraine headaches," he said. "I haven't had a migraine headache in quite some time now."[13]

By Bob Greene; reprinted by permission: Tribune Co., Syndicate, Inc.

The Relationship between the Prosecutor and Defense Counsel

In theory, adversary proceedings result when the champion of the defendant (defense counsel) and the champion of the state (prosecutor) do battle in open court where the "truth" is determined and "justice" is the result. In practice, the situation is quite often different due to considerations of time and money on behalf of both the state and the defendant.

The ideal of adversary proceedings is perhaps most closely realized when a well-known private defense attorney does battle with the prosecutor. Prominent defense attorneys often have competent investigative staffs and considerable resources in terms of time and money to devote to a case. Thus, the balance of power between the state and the defendant may be almost even. This is generally not the case when defense counsel is a public defender who is often paid less than the prosecutor, often has less experience than the prosecutor, and generally has more limited access to an investigative staff than the prosecutor. For a variety of reasons then, both defense counsel and the prosecutor may find it easier to negotiate a particular case rather than to fight it out in court, since court cases are costly in both time and money.

The majority of adult criminal cases in the United States are settled by plea bargaining. In fact, it has been suggested that justice in the United States is not the result of the **adversary system,** but is the result of a cooperative network of routine interaction between defense counsel, the prosecutor, the defendant, and, in many instances, the judge.[15]

In plea bargaining, both prosecutor and defense counsel hope to gain through compromise. The prosecutor wants the defendant to plead guilty, if not to the original charges then to some less serious offense. Defense counsel seeks to get the best deal possible for his or her client, which may range from an outright dismissal to a plea of guilty to some less serious offense than the original charge. The nature of the compromise depends upon conditions such as the strength of the prosecutor's case and the seriousness of the offense. Most often, the two counselors arrive at what both consider a just compromise, which is then presented to the defendant to accept or reject. As a rule, the punishment to be recommended by the prosecutor is also negotiated; thus, the nature of the charges, the plea, and the punishment are negotiated and agreed upon before the defendant actually enters the courtroom. The adversary system, in its ideal form at least, has been circumvented.

The benefits of plea bargaining to the prosecutor, defense counsel, and the court are clear. The prosecutor is successful in prosecuting a case (she or he obtains a conviction), defense counsel has reduced the charges and penalty against his or her client, and all parties have saved time and money by not contesting the case in court. The dangers in plea bargaining, however, should not be overlooked. First, the defendant might have been found not guilty even if he or she had been tried in court. Second, since negotiations occur most often in secret, there is a danger that the constitutional rights of the defendant may not be stringently upheld. For example, the defendant will not have the chance to confront and cross-examine his or her accusers. Finally, the judge is little more than a figurehead in cases settled by plea bargaining. The judge has the responsibility to see that the trial is conducted in the best interests of both the offender and society, and has the responsibility to insure due process. Neither of these can be guaranteed in most cases involving plea bargaining.

Because of some of the difficulties characteristic of plea bargaining, some jurisdictions have taken action to greatly reduce or eliminate the practice. A ban on plea bargaining in Alaska led to a decline in charge bargaining, an increase in the work loads of both defense attorneys and prosecutors, a decrease in the time required to process felonies, an increase in trial convictions, and more severe sentences for certain types of offenses.[16]

The future of plea bargaining remains uncertain, with some groups, such as the American Bar Association (1968), recommending retention with modifications; and others, such as the National Advisory Commission on Criminal Justice Standards and Goals (1973), recommending abolition. Regardless of the outcome of such recommendations, plea bargaining currently illustrates quite clearly the value of the network approach in understanding criminal justice. Plea bargaining occurs because of a variety of factors relevant to different components of the criminal justice network. Among these are (1) a desire for convictions on behalf of prosecutors; (2) a desire for acquittals or charge reductions on behalf of defendants and defense counsel; (3) a desire on behalf of all practitioners and the public to conserve valuable resources (time and money); and (4) overcrowding of prison facilities. These and other factors impinge upon prosecutors, judges, and defense attorneys when they consider plea bargaining as an alternative.

The Judge

There are some twenty-eight thousand judges currently employed in the U.S. Of these, about fourteen hundred work in federal courts; eight thousand in state courts; and more than eighteen thousand in local courts.[17]

Theoretically, the **judge** is the most powerful figure in the justice network, although he or she often allows the prosecutor to usurp most of this power. The judge decides matters of law (is certain evidence admissible?), supervises the selection of juries, instructs jurors, presides over the trial, often does the sentencing, insures that defendants understand the consequences of different pleas and that any plea entered is voluntary, and, in bench cases, also decides matters of fact. He or she is supposed to perform these duties impartially, attending only to facts that are legally relevant to each individual case. As the following article indicates, however, political and/or financial considerations sometimes outweigh the requirement for neutrality or impartiality.

Most research indicates that the power and discretion of the judge are demonstrated most clearly in the area of sentencing.

> Judges have received more attention than other official actors. Their political party affiliation, attitudes and role orientations, group memberships, judicial experience, and prejudicial experiences as prosecutors all have been found to be related to sentencing severity.[19]

However, Frazier and Bock conclude from their own research that variations in sentence severity are not closely related to personal characteristics of judges. They argue that the recommendations of the probation officer (discussed later in this chapter) are more important than individual characteristics of judges.[20]

The judge, prosecutor, and defense counsel are (in the vast majority of cases) all members of the legal profession who have graduated from law school and who become licensed to practice law by passing a bar (law) examination. A great deal of on-the-job training characterizes individuals filling all three positions since we do not, like some other countries, require extensive training after graduation from law school and prior to employment for lawyers who occupy these positions. Individuals filling these three roles form their own more or less cooperative network as they work with one another on a regular basis. In addition, each has ties with other components in the criminal justice network.

Right price will fix cases in Cook County, judge says

CARBONDALE (AP)—A rural Illinois judge who went undercover in an FBI probe of corruption in the Chicago area says that "for the right price, you could take care of any case" in the Cook County courts.

In a copyright interview with the Southern Illinoisan, Judge Brocton Lockwood said he took part in the FBI's "Operation Greylord" probe while he was a visiting judge in the Cook County court system.

"Maybe one judge in eight is crooked," Lockwood said in the interview published Wednesday. "They don't consider a judge crooked if you do favors only for political or friendship reasons."

He also said most dishonest judges were "political hacks and about as smart as a box of rocks."

U.S. Attorney Dan K. Webb has confirmed that a federal grand jury received evidence from the probe, named Greylord after the wigs worn by British judges. Published reports have said as many as 10 Cook County judges and 25 lawyers, and a number of court officials and Chicago police officers are targets of the investigation.

Prior published reports said a Southern Illinois judge penetrated the court system as part of the inquiry but did not identify him.

Lockwood, a Williamson County associate judge, said he tucked a tape recorder into his cowboy boots and wore a microphone under his robes and draped over his shoulder while gathering evidence for the probe.

He said he used his "ignorant hillbilly" image—projected with an easy smile and a drawl—and developed a reputation as a cash-short racehorse owner to gain access to corrupt court officials.

He said he disclosed his Greylord role in the hope that it would generate interest in correcting problems in the courts. Lockwood said he was not given approval by federal officials to discuss the case.

Agent Bob Long in the FBI's Chicago office declined comment yesterday on Lockwood's statements.

Lockwood, 39, told the newspaper that normal practice in cases of court corruption is for the fix to occur early—with a judge accepting payment to rule that there is no probable cause for a suspect to be tried.

He said he was appalled not only that some judges and court officials were for sale, but that they sold themselves so cheaply.

Lockwood told the Southern Illinoisan that for the right price, cases ranging from traffic violations to divorces to murder can be fixed.

However, when asked by The Associated Press if the corruption indeed extended to murder cases, Lockwood said the statement was a "generalization."

The cost of altering the outcome of a Cook County drunken driving case could be as low as $700, including attorney's fees, Lockwood said, noting that in Southern Illinois, attorney's fees alone might be $700.

Lockwood said he approached the U.S. Justice Department during the fall of 1980 after he became aware of the extent of corruption during an obligatory stint in the Cook County system to help reduce its backlog.

He met with FBI Director William Webster in Washington in October 1981.

The judge said he believed he was Greylord's only unpaid informant and the only member of the judiciary to serve as a mole.[18]

The Probation Officer

Another officer of the court is the **probation officer.** Unlike the judge, prosecutor, and defense counsel, the probation officer is not likely to be a lawyer. Nonetheless, recent evidence suggests that probation officers have considerable impact upon judges and prosecutors, particularly with respect to sentencing.[21]

Probation officers are generally civil service employees at the state level and appointees of the courts at the county level. Although training and educational requirements vary considerably among the states, there appears to be a definite trend toward hiring college graduates as probation officers and in some states (Illinois, for example), the tendency is to appoint those with some graduate work or the master's degree.

The rationale for requiring a college education is clear when the duties of the position are analyzed. In addition to being an officer of the court and, therefore, an authority figure to probationers, the probation officer is expected to be a case-worker/therapist and, in many instances, a community liaison officer (working with local industries and businesses as well as with social agencies). Among the tasks typically performed by probation officers are (1) conducting a pre-sentence investigation, (2) making recommendations to the trial court judge on sentencing, (3) supervising probationers, (4) recommending revocation of probation when necessary, and (5) serving as a role model for probationers. As the probation officer accomplishes these tasks, he or she must attempt to maintain a reasonably close and friendly relationship with probationers in order to help change the behaviors that resulted in conflict with the criminal justice network, but the probation officer must maintain sufficient distance to take authoritative action when appropriate. Like other officials in the criminal justice network, the probation officer exercises considerable discretion in the performance of duties. The extent to which conditions of probation are enforced and the extent to which technical violations of probation (as opposed to the commission of a new crime) lead to official action are largely determined by the probation officer, who is often required to fulfill the duties outlined here while managing a relatively heavy caseload.

Given the scope and nature of probation work, it is easy to understand the trend toward hiring better-educated individuals to fill probation positions. Unfortunately, salaries in the probation field have often lagged behind those of other criminal justice employees, making it difficult to recruit and retain probation officers with such educational backgrounds.

Managing the Courts

Traditionally, American courts have been independent and self-governing because of their role as a check and balance on the other two branches of government. Historically, the concept of a judicial system has not been put into practice in the states. The trend towards unified state court systems is so recent that most state judiciaries should still be classified as nonsystems due to local jurisdictional autonomy, complexity, and lack of centralized control.

In most states, there are three distinct sets of court managers: chief judges, court clerks, and court administrators.

Chief Judges

Judges have always been responsible for the administration of their courts. Individual judicial autonomy has resulted in a variety of uncoordinated and inconsistent administrative practices. Judges are often as involved with the many aspects of management as with adjudication. Unfortunately, most judges are not trained in management. The result is that most lawyers who become judges are not adept at analyzing patterns of dispositions or at managing large dockets.

The chief judge faces the same problems. The chief judge has general administrative responsibilities in his or her jurisdiction. Since most chief judges assume their position by virtue of seniority, there is no guarantee of effective management. Election of the chief judge (by other judges) may produce a strong and effective manager or middle-of-the-road candidate.

Court Clerks

Clerks of the court play an important role in the administration of local judiciaries. They are responsible for docketing cases, collecting court fees, arranging for jury selection, and maintaining court records. Historically, they have competed with judges for control over judicial administration. Since they are elected officials in most states, they can function somewhat independently from the judge. As with judges, most clerks are not trained to manage the local courts.

Court Administrators

An innovative approach to the solution of court problems has been the creation of a professional group of trained administrators to assist judges in administrative and nonjudicial functions. Nonjudicial functions are those associated with the business management of the courts. These may include record keeping, data gathering and analysis, research and planning, budget preparation, management of physical space and supplies, management of support personnel, docketing court cases, and dispensing information to the public. Business management plays a support role to the judicial function of the courts and is essential for more effective and efficient court operations.

In 1937, Connecticut established the first centralized office of court administrator, with a number of other states following after World War II. By 1978, every state except Mississippi had established a statewide court administrator. Because the position is so new, several aspects of the court administrator's role are still being debated. Most arguments center on qualifications and administrative relations with other agencies.

Traditionally, the court administrator was a patronage position, and no set body of knowledge or skills was required. Since the creation of the Institute for Court Management in Denver, Colorado, in 1970, an increasing number of colleges and universities have been offering programs in court administration at the undergraduate and graduate levels. However, there is still no agreement as to the skills and qualifications a court administrator should possess. Many believe managerial expertise is needed and a law degree is unnecessary. Conversely, many judges believe a law degree is essential. Some contend, for example, that court administrators hired for their business background have been ineffective because they know too little about the courts and the law.

A second area of concern centers on the relationship between the court administrator and other judicial agencies. Often clerks view this position as a threat and resent the intrusion—yet, to be effective, the court administrator requires the type of data on cases that only the clerk can provide. Court clerks have played an important role in resisting the creation of court administrator positions. If the position is created, they can significantly reduce the administrators' effectiveness by not cooperating.

There can also be friction between judges and administrators. Some judges are reluctant to delegate responsibility over important aspects of the court's work—for example, case scheduling. The distinction between administration and adjudication is not entirely clear. A court administrator's proposal to streamline court procedures may be seen by judges as intruding on how they decide cases.

Despite their potential for improving the efficiency of the court, court administrators have encountered opposition from both clerks and judges. Most have not been given full responsibility over the court's nonjudicial functions. If the issues concerning qualifications and authority/accountability can be resolved, court administrators could significantly increase the efficiency of the courts.

Summary

The extent to which criminal justice practitioners use the network model in their operation is clearly illustrated by court personnel. The prosecutor, perhaps the most powerful individual in the network in terms of discretion, takes into consideration a variety of factors in deciding whether and how to prosecute cases. Among these factors are community norms, political party affiliation, his or her relationship with the police, prior court decisions, and the type of defense counsel involved. Defense counselors, judges, and probation officers also take into account these factors as well as the recommendations and desires of the prosecutor and one another in processing cases. The extent to which plea bargaining occurs and the nature of the bargains depend upon these factors and upon the extent of overcrowding in jails and prisons. Local public defenders and probation officers are often appointed to their positions by judges who consider the prosecutors' recommendations in making such appointments. And, of course, judges and prosecutors are either elected by the public or appointed by other politicians who are elected by the public.

Judges, prosecutors, public defenders, and probation officers are assisted in their functions by individuals appointed or elected to help run the courts in an orderly fashion. Controversy about the proper functions of these court administrators and court clerks characterizes the current court scene.

Key Terms Defined

prosecutor (state's attorney, district attorney) an attorney representing the people (the state).

defense counsel an attorney representing the defendant.

public defender a defense counsel paid from public funds.

adversary system theoretically, the system of law in the United States involving the opportunity of both prosecution and defense to present their cases at a trial presided over by a neutral judge.

judge an attorney elected or appointed to preside over court cases.

probation officer an individual appointed to serve as an officer of the court who supervises probationers and provides certain other services to the court.

Discussion Questions

1. Why is the prosecutor such an important and influential figure in the criminal justice network? To whom is the prosecutor accountable for his or her actions?

2. What is the proper role of defense counsel in criminal cases? How does plea bargaining fit into this role?

3. What is the relationship between judges and probation officers? Why should the recommendations of probation officers concerning sentencing have such great impact on judges?

4. Using the network approach, discuss the relationships that might exist among court administrators and other court personnel.

Notes

1. Gary Holten and Melvin E. Jones, *The System of Criminal Justice,* 2d ed. (Boston: Little, Brown and Co., 1982), 181.

2. For a more thorough discussion of prosecutorial discretion, see Sarah J. Cox, "Prosecutorial Discretion: An Overview," *The American Criminal Law Review* 13, no. 3 (Winter 1976):379–434.

3. Jonathan Caspar, *American Criminal Justice: The Defendant's Perspective* (Englewood Cliffs, N.J.: Prentice-Hall, 1972).

4. Burton Atkins and Mark Pogrebin, *The Invisible Justice System: Discretion and the Law* (Cincinnati, Ohio: Anderson Publishing Co., 1978), 4.

5. *Journal of American Judicial Society* (1940), 18–19.

6. Holten and Jones, *The System of Justice,* 185.

7. Caspar, *American Criminal Justice,* 54–65.

8. Caspar, *American Criminal Justice,* ch. 4.

9. For an example of the difference between private and public defense counsel, see John E. Conklin, *Robbery and the Criminal Justice System* (Philadelphia, PA.: J. B. Lippincott Co., 1972).

10. Dallin H. Oaks and Warren Lehman, "Lawyers for the Poor," in *The Scales of Justice,* ed. Abraham S. Blumberg (Chicago: Aldine, 1970), 91–104.

11. Stuart S. Nagel, "The Tipped Scales of American Justice," in *The Scales of Justice,* ed. Abraham S. Blumberg (Chicago: Aldine, 1970), 39.

12. Oaks and Lehman, "Lawyers for the Poor," 93.

13. Bob Greene, "Lawyer Closes Book on Criminal Defense," *Chicago Tribune* (n.d.).

14. For discussions of defense counsel's responsibility, see Charles P. Curtis, "The Ethics of Advocacy," *Stanford Law Review* 4 (December 1951): 3–23; F. Lee Bailey, *The Defense Never Rests* (New York: Signet, 1971).

15. Abraham S. Blumberg, *Criminal Justice* (Chicago: Quadrangle, 1967); David Sudnow, "Normal Crimes: Sociological Features of the Penal Code in a Public Defender's Office," *Social Problems* 12 (Winter 1965): 255–76.

16. M. L. Rubenstein and T. J. White, "Plea Bargaining—Can Alaska Live Without It?" *Judicature* 62 (December/January 1979): 266–79.

17. "The Justice System: Who Runs It, How Much It Costs," *U.S. News and World Report* (1 Nov. 1982): 36.

18. "Right price will fix cases in Cook County, judge says," *Peoria Journal Star* (12 Aug. 1983), A2.

19. Charles E. Frazier and E. Wilbur Bock, "Effects of Court Officials on Sentence Severity," *Criminology* 20, no. 2 (August 1982), 258.

20. Frazier and Bock, "Effects of Court Officials on Sentence Severity," 269. See also David J. Roberts, "Effects of Court Officials on Sentence Severity. Do Judges Make a Difference?" *Criminology* 22, no. 1 (February 1984), 135–38.

21. Ibid.

Suggested Readings

Abadinsky, Howard. *Probation and Parole.* 3d ed. Englewood Cliffs, N.J.: Prentice-Hall, 1987.

Adams, Kenneth and Cutshall, Charles R., "Refusing to Prosecute Minor Offenses: The Relative Influence of Legal and Extralegal Factors," *Justice Quarterly* 4, no. 4 (Dec. 1987), 595–609.

Allen, Harry E., Eskridge, Chris W., Latessa, Edward J., and Vito, Gennaro F. *Probation and Parole in America.* New York: Free Press, 1985.

Auerbach, Jerold S. *Unequal Justice: Lawyers and Social Change in Modern America.* New York: Oxford University Press, 1977.

Barok, Gregg. *In Defense of Whom? A Critique of Criminal Justice Reform.* Cincinnati, Ohio: Anderson Publishing Co., 1980.

Foley, Linda A., and Powell, Richard S. "The Discretion of Prosecutors, Judges, and Juries in Capital Cases." *Criminal Justice Review* 7, no. 2 (Fall 1982): 16–22.

Jacoby, Joan E. *The American Prosecutor: A Search for Identity.* Lexington, Mass.: Lexington Books, 1980.

Phillips, Charles D., and Ekland-Olson, Sheldon. " 'Repeat Players' in a Criminal Court." *Criminology* 19, no. 4 (February 1982): 530–45.

Steinberg, Allen. "From Private Prosecution to Plea Bargaining: Criminal Prosecution, the District Attorney, and American Legal History." *Crime and Delinquency* 30, no. 4, (October 1984): 568–92.

Pretrial Procedures 11

Key Terms

initial appearance
probable cause
bail
nulla poena sine crimine
bondsman
release on recognizance
grand jury
indictment

ex parte proceeding
prima facie case
information
preliminary hearing
arraignment
nola contendre
discovery
disclosure

In this chapter we will focus our attention on the various stages of the criminal justice process prior to an actual criminal trial. Although the stages in the pretrial process have not received the same attention as the trial, they are of considerable importance. We must keep in mind that our criminal justice network is supposed to be based on the principles of "innocent until proven guilty" and "due process" of law for all those accused of criminal wrongdoing. Inherent within these principles are attempts to insure that only those rightfully accused will proceed to the trial stage. Many of the pretrial processes, then, act as a sieve to filter out cases lacking necessary levels of proof for a finding of guilt. These stages are beneficial to the citizenry in that they prohibit the state from arbitrary punishment.

The pretrial stages are also beneficial to the government and the taxpayer since they help eliminate expensive and time-consuming trials when there is little probability of conviction. Because of our emphasis on due process, these stages also protect the rights of the accused specified in the United States Constitution and the Bill of Rights (the first ten amendments to the Constitution). We must keep in mind that our criminal justice network includes an adversary system consisting of two opponents—the state (prosecution) and the defense (the accused). As we have indicated elsewhere, the balance of power rests with the state. Due process serves to keep the scales of justice balanced in spite of this imbalance of power.

In this chapter, we will closely examine the six stages in the pretrial process: initial appearance, the administration of bail, the formal charging of the accused, the preliminary hearing, the arraignment, and the concepts of discovery and disclosure. Most of our attention will focus on the pretrial stages as they apply to felony cases. We will identify differences as they apply to lesser offenses. In addition, we will indicate and discuss some of the more controversial stages and practices. There is, for example, considerable debate over bail, the use of grand juries, and the plea of not guilty by reason of insanity. We will examine proposed changes in these areas and address their ramifications.

Initial Appearances

After an accused has been taken into custody by the police, he or she is to be taken without unnecessary delay before the nearest and most accessible magistrate (judge) and a charge should be filed. Most jurisdictions hold that twenty-four to forty-eight hours is not unreasonable delay. Delays caused by police procedures such as lineups, fingerprinting, and booking are usually considered reasonable. In addition, delays caused by the unavailability of the magistrate, weekends, and holidays are generally considered justifiable.

There are many responsibilities of the presiding magistrate at this stage. First, the judge is responsible for determining if **probable cause** existed for the arrest. If it is determined that probable cause did exist, the accused will be held for further criminal processing. If not, the defendant is dismissed and no formal charges are filed. This is the first stage of the filtering effect of pretrial procedures. Prior to this, both the public and the police have exercised discretion in reporting offenses or suspicious circumstances and effecting the arrest. Ideally, as the result of the **initial appearance,** only those cases in which there is a reasonable belief that a crime did occur and that the accused is the perpetrator of the act will be processed for further court action.

If probable cause is found, the accused is informed of the charges against him or her and is generally given a written copy of those charges. The magistrate will also inform the defendant of his or her right to counsel as guaranteed by the Sixth Amendment to the Constitution and interpreted by the Supreme Court. Initially the right to counsel was applied at the federal level with some controversy as to whether the doctrine applied to state proceedings. In *Gideon v. Wainwright,* 372 U.S. 335 (1963), the court held that counsel must be provided in state felony

proceedings. In *Argersinger v. Hanlin,* 407 U.S. 25 (1972), the court extended
the right to counsel to all cases where the penalty was imprisonment. If the accused is indigent (without funds), the magistrate will appoint counsel.

If the charge is a misdemeanor, the case is often heard at this time. In many
instances the defendant will plead guilty and the judge will impose a standardized
fine as sentence, although there may be circumstances that warrant incarceration. In felony cases, the judge may also inform the accused of the next stage in
the process, usually setting a date for preliminary hearing. Another function of
the judge at the initial appearance is the administration of bail. Because of the
controversy surrounding bail, we will devote the next section to its discussion.

The Administration of Bail

One of the most controversial pretrial procedures involves setting bail. Simply
stated, **bail** is the practice of releasing a defendant prior to trial with the promise
that he or she will appear before the court as directed. As we will see, the issue
of bail is extremely complex.

The practice of bail is traceable to England, as are many other facets of the
American criminal justice network. Because judges often rode circuits and court
was not held for months at a time, the English would release defendants prior to
trial upon the oath of responsible individuals insuring that the accused would be

present when the trial commenced. This practice was maintained by American settlers, but altered by requiring the posting of a bond by the accused or someone in his or her behalf. The practice was formalized by the Judiciary Act of 1789. Through this legislation, the practices of admitting defendants to bail (except in capital cases) and permitting considerable discretion in the determination of bail became routinized in the American criminal justice network.

Constitutionally, there are few guidelines regarding bail. The Eighth Amendment provides that bail shall not be excessive. There is no federal constitutional right to bail, but if bail is provided by state legislation, it cannot be excessive. This ambiguous mandate has generated conflict in several areas; e.g., does excessive pertain to the financial capabilities of the accused, the nature of the charge, or some other criterion?

Before addressing these specific questions let us first examine the practice of bail. Bail involves the posting of cash, property, or securities by the defendant or someone in his or her behalf. Originally, the manifest function of bail was to insure that the accused would be present for trial or other pretrial procedures. In most jurisdictions, bail is set by the court as a monetary sum. The defendant or another party (legally, the surety) usually posts 10 percent of that sum in cash, property, or securities, and pledges to pay the remaining 90 percent if the defendant is not present for trial—"skips or jumps bail." The amount posted and the pledge for the remainder is commonly referred to as the bail bond, and the party other than the defendant, who posts the amount and pledges for the bond, is referred to as the bail bondsman.[1] If the accused is present for trial, the amount posted or a portion of it may be returned,[2] or upon conviction it may be used to pay a fine, to pay attorneys' fees,[3] or as an appeal bond.[4] In some jurisdictions, the amount posted is not returned.

Consequences of Bail

At least in theory, then, bail is intended to insure that a defendant appears before the court and answers charges. Suffet refers to this as the "manifest" function of bail.[5] Earlier we raised several questions concerning the administration of bail. We must add to this list the question of how successfully bail realizes its intended purpose.

Under our judicial system, we adhere to a policy of *nulla poena sine crimine,* no punishment without a crime. Although bail may not have been intended to alter this legal doctrine, in practice it has, and sometimes dramatically. Some defendants spend months in jail awaiting trial simply because they cannot afford to post 10 percent of the bail bond. Bail is often attacked as discriminating against the poor. Defendants from the upper classes or those engaged in lucrative criminal ventures can make bail more readily, yet is their financial status indicative of the likelihood of appearing before the court? As a result of the inability of many accused to obtain bail money, the professional bail **bondsman** has become a central figure in the bail controversy. It is not uncommon for bondsmen to be as much, or more, of a determining factor in deciding who will, or will not, be held in confinement prior to trial, as the offense. In theory, the bondsman posts the required 10 percent and pledges to pay the remainder if the accused fails to appear. In return he charges the accused a percentage of the bond. Thus, in theory, the bondsman is risking considerable financial loss and must exercise caution in selecting clients. In practice some bondsmen simply adjust their fee according to the risk they are taking. It is sometimes argued that bondsmen generate additional crime by charging such high fees that the accused must commit another crime to pay off the bondsman. Bondsmen have also been known to engage in illegal relationships with other criminal justice personnel. Investigations have shown that bondsmen pay referral fees to police officers, and it has been alleged that judges and bondsmen split fees in some instances.[6] It is also argued that bondsmen occasionally employ unethical practices in retrieving clients who fail to appear. Unlike the police, who are regulated by the Fourth Amendment, bondsmen have often literally kidnapped defendants to insure their appearance. Bail bondsmen, then, often exercise considerable power over other citizens without much regulation and in contradiction to existing legal doctrine.

Protecting Society

Another alleged consequence of bail has been to protect society from dangerous offenders. Jurisdictions commonly designate specific offenses as nonbailable in an attempt to protect society, or bail may be set in an amount high enough to ordinarily preclude the release of particular defendants. In practice, the high bail seldom protects society. As we have indicated, bail may actually generate more crime under certain circumstances. In addition, criminals involved with syndicates can meet bail even when it is set high. Again, we see that financial advantage can easily overcome the intent of bail.

The Determination of Bail

What factors should the court consider in setting bail? Historically, the nature of the charge and the defendant's criminal record have been important criteria in setting bail.[7] Some judges recognize that factors extraneous to the offense are also relevant in determining one's probability of appearance. Such factors as residence in the community, employment, and the presence or absence of relatives and friends in the community are now being considered in the administration of bail. This practice stems from an experiment sponsored by the Vera Foundation entitled the "Manhattan Bail Project."[8] The New York City project began in 1961 and involved the use of law students who interviewed defendants to determine present or recent residence at the same address for six months or more, current or recent employment for six months or more, relatives in New York City with whom the defendant was in contact, prior criminal record, and residence in New York City for ten years or more. It was assumed that these factors would be relevant to pretrial release.

After this information was obtained, the staff commenced to determine whether or not to recommend that the defendant be released on recognizance; that is, released without posting bond. If the staff recommended **release on recognizance (ROR)**, the recommendation would be forwarded to the arraignment court. At the arraignment court defendants were randomly assigned to experimental and control groups. Those in the experimental groups had their recommendation given to the judge, prosecutor, and defense attorney; those in the control group did not. The findings were interesting, to say the least: 60 percent of those in the experimental group were granted ROR, while only 14 percent of the control group were released; thus, the presence or absence of the recommendation is of great importance in releasing defendants. In general, those who were released did in fact appear. Those who failed to appear generally did so because of illness, confusion over the legal process, or family emergencies. This project was the forerunner of numerous projects designed to circumvent the often discriminatory nature of bail.[9] Today, the use of ROR is common at all levels and in all jurisdictions.

The use of recognizance bail recognizes that the nature of the charge is not the only factor relevant to a defendant's pretrial release. Factors that tie the accused to the community should also be considered in determining bail. The practice of releasing defendants on their own recognizance has several advantages: (1) it maintains or upholds the principle of no punishment without crime (many defendants can avoid being detained in jail due to lack of money); (2) it limits the negative impact of pretrial detention in terms of costs to the taxpayer; and (3) it makes bail more equitable—those without financial advantage have the same opportunity to be released as the financially advantaged.

The Effects of Monetary Bail

We previously stated that recognizance bails reduce the negative impacts of bail on defendants. In this section we will identify negative impacts that may result from the practice of setting monetary bail.

First, bail may encourage plea bargaining. Some innocent defendants may agree to plead guilty and receive probation or a fine rather than be detained in jail prior to trial. Thus, the principles of justice are subverted. Second, those who cannot make bail may suffer from being detained in jail. It is estimated that over 50 percent of America's jail population is there awaiting trial.[10] Conditions in these jails are bad at best. Inmates are subjected to prolonged boredom, assault, homosexuality, poor physical conditions, substandard medical care, and exposure to convicted criminals. Those who will later be found innocent, as well as those who will be found guilty, are faced with these conditions before a determination of guilt. Third, as a result of being confined, the accused may encounter current or future employment problems. His or her family may be forced to request government assistance and his or her absence alone may be disruptive. Additionally, the stigma of spending time in jail may follow the individual regardless of the outcome of the case. Finally, pretrial confinement may affect the outcome of the case. An accused who undergoes pretrial confinement may lack the ability to assist in his or her own defense. Research by Rankin found significant differences in receiving or not receiving prison sentences between defendants making bail and those being jailed continuously.[11] Inability to make bail may not only induce guilty pleas, but may also increase the likelihood of conviction and a harsher sentence.

In conclusion we have found bail to be a highly discretionary practice with numerous, complex side effects. In its present form, bail cannot assure that defendants will appear, that the public will be protected, or that justice will be done. The use of recognizance bonds may help to alleviate some of the discrimination in setting bail, but the issue of monetary bail remains controversial.

Formal Charging or Accusation

Before an actual criminal trial commences, there must be a formal accusation of the accused. The process of accusation is basically a review of the evidence to insure that the evidence is substantial enough to warrant further processing of the defendant. Here again we see the criminal justice network employing a filter. Those cases that appear to be lacking in evidence are rejected or filtered out, thereby saving the taxpayers money, limiting the stigma facing the accused, and reducing congestion in the courts. The process of formal accusation is usually reserved for felonies and some serious misdemeanor cases. Traffic cases, petty offenses, and minor misdemeanors are usually handled routinely and do not involve a detailed review of the evidence. In many of these cases the defendants answer to charges by pleading guilty at the initial appearance. In the American network of criminal justice there are two basic means of accusation—grand jury indictments and prosecutorial informations. The next section will examine the two procedures and discuss the strengths and weaknesses of each.

The Grand Jury

The Fifth Amendment holds that "No person shall be held to answer for a capital or otherwise infamous crime, unless on a presentment or indictment of a Grand Jury. . . ." The **grand jury** was created in England to insure that arbitrary charges were not brought against the citizenry by the government. We must remember

Table 11.1 Distinctions Between Grand and Petit Juries

	Grand Jury	**Petit Jury**
Purpose	Formal accusation	Determination of guilt or innocence
Size	16–23 members	6–12 members
Level of Proof Required	Probable cause	Beyond reasonable doubt
Secrecy	Secret proceedings	Public proceedings
Rules of Evidence	Can use illegally obtained evidence	Strict rules of evidence
Presiding Authority	Prosecutor	Judge

that, in this era, the judicial and executive branches of government in England were not totally separate. The Crown could, and did, have charges brought against those who spoke out or otherwise opposed the government. In theory, if not in practice, grand jury members were charged with reviewing the facts of a particular case and with the determination of the validity of the charges. Like many other aspects of the English criminal justice system, the concept of the grand jury was adopted as part of the American legal system during the colonial period.

The grand jury is an accusatory jury only and should not be confused with the petit or trial jury (see pages 181–184 and 187–188) which determines innocence or guilt. The two juries differ in size, purpose, level of proof required, and other areas. Still, both give members of the public as one component of the justice network an opportunity for input into the network. Table 11.1 highlights the major differences between grand and petit juries.

Although the Fifth Amendment provides for the use of grand juries, they are not used in all felony cases. Federal courts employ grand juries as mandated by the Fifth Amendment. State courts, not obligated to follow this mandate, vary in their use of grand juries. Some states require grand jury review in all felony cases, while others require it only in cases involving the possibility of a death sentence or life imprisonment, and still other states permit proceedings to commence on a prosecutorial information without grand jury review. It should also be noted that in those jurisdictions requiring grand jury review, the defendant can waive the proceedings.

The grand jury normally has two functions. The first, the presentment, permits the grand jury to act as an investigative unit. The grand jury has the power to investigate possible criminal activity of a general nature. By general nature, we are referring to such activities as police and political corruption, organized crime activities, and offenses against the public at large. It does not investigate specific crimes. The final report and recommendations of the investigation are called the presentment. If the investigation is productive, charges will be sought.

The second and more common function is the accusatory role. In jurisdictions where the grand jury is employed, grand jury members review evidence and determine if it is substantial enough to warrant prosecution. In this role, they represent the community conscience.

It should be remembered that grand juries simply weigh the strength of the evidence. They do not decide guilt or innocence.

Grand jury procedures are nonadversary in nature. Witnesses are called and answer questions from the prosecutor. A grand jury proceeding is an **ex parte proceeding;** that is, it is only for one party, the prosecution. The accused's counsel is not present in the courtroom, nor is the accused unless he or she is testifying. There is no right to cross-examination during grand jury hearings. The only parties present at the technically secret proceeding are the judge, the prosecutor, the grand jury, and the witnesses, who are called individually. If the evidence is sufficient for a *prima facie* case, the jury will issue a *bill of **indictment*** charging the accused with a specific crime. A **prima facie case** is one in which "on the face of it," the evidence without any objections or contradictions is of such a nature that probable cause exists to charge the individual with a crime.

Because the grand jury hearing is nonadversary, it is subject to rules and regulations that differ from those governing the trial process. The grand jury hearing is similar to the trial in that witnesses must take an oath and are subject to charges of perjury if they give false testimony. Witnesses also have the right against self-incrimination. A grand jury may rely upon evidence that would be inadmissible at a trial. The Supreme Court has held that hearsay evidence[12] and evidence obtained illegally[13] can be admitted during grand jury proceedings. The basis for these decisions is that the proceedings are nonadversary in nature. The grand jury is only a fact-finding body, not a determiner of guilt; thus, evidence that cannot be admitted at the trial may still be heard by the grand jury.

Grand juries usually consist of sixteen to twenty-three members with each jurisdiction deciding on the number of members by statute. Selection is usually from those eighteen and over who are residents of the jurisdiction and who possess United States citizenship. Usually grand juries are selected randomly from voting lists or other such means of registration. According to Kalmanoff, grand juries are not proportionately representative by race, age, or income.[14] The grand jury has also been criticized as being costly and subject to easy manipulation by the prosecution.[15] Although such criticisms may be sound, the grand jury remains one of the methods of involving the citizenry in the criminal justice process.

Information and Preliminary Hearings

Most felony cases today proceed on the basis of an information rather than an indictment. An **information** is a written charge issued by the prosecutor rather than the grand jury. When an information is issued, a preliminary hearing will be scheduled. The **preliminary hearing** serves the same purpose as the grand jury—to establish probable cause. If probable cause is established, the accused will stand trial; if not, the charges are dismissed and the accused is given his or her freedom. However, the prosecution is not prohibited from refiling charges later.

Although the functions of the grand jury and the preliminary hearing are similar, the procedures involved differ significantly to insure that only those rightfully accused stand trial. As we noted previously, grand jury proceedings are not open to the public, are conducted *ex parte,* and are not subject to some of the rigid rules of evidence. The preliminary hearing is usually conducted before the judge or magistrate in open court. The accused is represented by counsel and is permitted to cross-examine prosecutorial witnesses as well as to call his or her own. In addition, the defense can challenge the legality of the prosecution's evidence. Even in jurisdictions that require grand jury hearings, many defendants waive the hearing and go forward on an information because they gain the opportunity to challenge the evidence at a preliminary hearing, which they could not do if they were accused by the grand jury. It is often argued that the preliminary hearing is closer to the concept of due process.

In addition to waiving the grand jury, the accused can also waive the preliminary hearing. Reasons for such a waiver may include, but are not limited to, speeding up the process, some compensation in the process of plea bargaining, and avoiding negative publicity that may result from the hearing (e.g., sex crimes and other crimes that invoke strong social response). The advantages of proceeding with the preliminary hearing include the possibility of having the case dismissed and avoiding the stigma of trial, and the opportunity to examine the prosecution's evidence so that the defense can better calculate trial strategy.

As we have seen, there are two distinct methods of formal accusation. Both are designed to determine probable cause; however, they differ in rules, decision makers (prosecutor or judge), and openness of the proceedings. While the information affords the opportunity to confront witnesses and challenge evidence, the grand jury permits the decision to be made by the citizenry. As a practical matter, most cases proceed on the basis of an information and grand juries are not routinely impaneled in many jurisdictions.

Arraignment

The **arraignment** in felony cases usually occurs shortly after the return of an indictment or the issuance of an information. In minor cases, the arraignment occurs at the time of the initial appearance. At the arraignment the judge reads and explains the charges to the defendant in open court. The defendant, who has a right to be represented by counsel, is then asked to plead or answer to the charges. Although jurisdictions vary in the pleas they will accept, the most common are not guilty, guilty, not guilty by reason of insanity, and *nola contendre*. A plea of once in jeopardy is also possible, though it is used infrequently.

If the accused pleads not guilty, the plea will be recorded and a date for trial will be set. If the accused fails to enter a plea, he or she will be considered as *standing mute* and the court will enter a plea of not guilty on the defendant's behalf. Usually any conditions of bail will be continued at this time. It is possible, however, to have the present conditions reconsidered upon request.

The majority of defendants enter a plea of guilty. As previously mentioned, the process of plea bargaining accounts for a substantial majority of guilty pleas. Estimates concerning the frequency of guilty pleas range from 60 to 90 percent of all felony cases. On the surface it may appear that a plea of guilty negates some of the formalities of the proceedings. Obviously, it saves both the court and the defendant time and money, but, because it constitutes a waiver of due process, there is a formal requirement to question the defendant concerning his or her guilty plea. By pleading guilty the accused is relinquishing his or her Fifth Amendment right against self-incrimination and his or her Sixth Amendment rights concerning the rights to trial by jury, to a public trial, and to confront witnesses against himself or herself. The Supreme Court requires judges to question defendants who plead guilty. Through various decisions, the Supreme Court has required the right to counsel during plea negotiations,[16] the need for a public record showing the defendant voluntarily pled guilty,[17] and the necessity that a prosecutor's promise be kept.[18] The judge must ascertain, by questioning the defendant, that the defendant is aware that he or she is waiving his or her constitutional rights and that the plea is being entered voluntarily. In addition, the judge must inform the accused of the statutory provisions for sentencing someone convicted of that particular offense. In many cases, the accused will enter the guilty plea and the prosecutor will recommend a specific sentence in accordance with a bargain they have reached, often with the knowledge of the judge. The judge will then pass sentence. In other cases, a separate sentencing hearing will be set at a later date. This is more likely if the accused pleads guilty without engaging in plea bargaining.

As we have indicated earlier, the plea of not guilty by reason of insanity is one of the most controversial aspects of the criminal justice process. Jurisdictions vary in the labels used and the terms for accepting this plea, which, in essence, holds that the accused did, in fact, engage in the criminal conduct, but lacked the ability to form the necessary mental element of intent and/or is incapable, because of a mental condition, in aiding counsel in his or her defense.

To the public, the finding of not guilty by reason of insanity is tantamount to an acquittal. In reality, those defendants who are so adjudicated may be subjected to longer confinement than if they had pled guilty. In many cases, a defendant found not guilty by reason of insanity is committed to a state mental hospital until he or she is found mentally healthy. Technically this could be a few months, but it could also mean until death. In some jurisdictions defendants are placed in mental hospitals and may be tried if they are later declared sane. The frequency of the not guilty by reason of insanity plea is greatly exaggerated. It usually occurs during the course of murder or serious assault cases, which seems to heighten public attention. Estimates of its successful use range from 2 to 5 percent. The actual decision of sanity is left to the court. In most jurisdictions, once the plea is entered, the accused must undergo psychiatric examination. Evidence resulting from this examination is presented in court, and the jury must then reach a decision.

The insanity plea is fraught with problems. First, the term is strictly a legal one. Psychologists and psychiatrists are concerned with mental disorders that are extremely difficult to define and diagnose, yet we expect them to make pinpoint decisions in court. Second, conflicting psychiatric testimony in court often confuses and baffles jury members who are not familiar with the terminology used or conditions discussed. Finally, it is very time-consuming. Usually both the prosecutor and the defense provide one to three expert witnesses to testify to the accused's mental status. Such testimony consumes valuable time, is often contradictory, and serves to further confuse the jury.[19]

In the early 1980s, a number of politicians called for the abolition of the insanity defense. Although the defense is plagued by serious problems and is in need of reform, to abolish it goes against one of the long-held foundations of law; criminals must have the mental capacity to know they are acting wrongfully. This is the same principle that protects infants and the severely retarded from criminal charges.

The plea of *nola contendre* is essentially a plea of guilty. Its literal translation means "no contest." The consequence of a plea of *nola contendre* is that it cannot be entered into the record of a subsequent civil proceeding. For example, A is driving a vehicle while under the influence of alcohol and runs into B's house. If A enters a plea of *nola contendre* to the criminal charge of driving under the influence, B cannot use the plea as evidence of responsibility in a civil proceeding to hold A responsible for damages to the house. It does not mean that A cannot be held civilly responsible, only that his plea cannot be used in this regard. Other evidence such as a breath or blood test and eyewitness accounts may, of course, be used to find A liable.

Courts vary widely on the acceptance of *nola contendre* pleas. Most limit the plea to specific offenses and require that the judge question the defendant to insure that he or she is aware of the consequences of the plea.[20]

The plea of once in jeopardy is fairly infrequent. The Fifth Amendment holds that ". . . nor shall any person be subject for the same offence to be twice put in jeopardy of life or limb. . . ." By pleading once in jeopardy the defendant is contending that the current charge violates the Fifth Amendment. Usually, through counsel, the defendant will supply evidence contending that the accused has already been held accountable for this act. The court may review such a plea at that time or postpone the arraignment until they have had time to review the evidence.

Pretrial Motions and Hearings

In cases where the defendant pleads not guilty at the arraignment, there are usually several motions and hearings on those motions prior to the actual criminal trial. Most of these motions will be filed by the defense attorney. We must remember that these, in effect, are requests to the court and usually the judge must issue a ruling on such requests. Some of the more common motions follow.

Motion for Change of Venue

Under the principles of due process, the defendant has the right to a trial in the jurisdiction in which the alleged crime occurred. This principle is called venue and means place of trial. The rationale is that local norms, values, and attitudes should be reflected in jury composition.

The motion for a change of venue is usually reserved for the defense. The defense is asking to have the trial moved to another venue—county district or circuit. Usually the motion is based on the contention that the defendant cannot obtain a fair trial in the court of original jurisdiction because of prejudice against him or her. For example, X, who has a prior criminal record, is accused of murdering Y, the only doctor in the county. X was formerly an employee of a local grainery that went bankrupt and left many farmers in the community with heavy financial losses. Factors, such as prior record, occupation, and nature of the crime and victim, may bear heavily on X's right to a fair trial. If X files for a change of venue, he or she must provide evidence or testimony to establish that prejudice and hostility exist. The judge makes the decision and, even if the request is denied initially, it may be honored later, particularly if there is difficulty in selecting and impaneling the jury.[21]

Motion for Continuance

Although the defendant's right to a speedy trial is guaranteed by the Sixth Amendment, it is quite common for trials to take place months and even years after the act for which the accused is being tried. Although there are many reasons for this delay, one of the most common reasons is simply that there has been a request for a continuance.

Either party may ask for a continuance. Usually these motions are made shortly after arraignment, but they can be made at any time. Motions for continuance must be accompanied by an explanation of the reasons why additional time is needed. Some of the more common reasons are illness, unavailability of witnesses, defense counsel's workload is in conflict with the trial date, or defense counsel cannot be prepared.[22] In addition, the court may arrange for a continuance if it finds it is in the interest of justice, usually meaning the docket is overcrowded and space and/or court personnel will not be available on the stated date of trial.

Motions for Suppression and Exclusion of Evidence

In 1961 in *Mapp v. Ohio* (see appendix),[23] the Supreme Court held that evidence obtained or seized illegally was inadmissable in criminal trials at the state level. From that time forward defense attorneys have made motions to exclude evidence on the grounds that it has been obtained in violation of the Fourth Amendment. These motions are usually filed prior to the trial, and the judge conducts a hearing to determine the legality of the search that produced the evidence in question. These hearings are very important because the evidence in question is often the tie between the defendant and the crime, and without this evidence the prosecutor may have only a circumstantial case.[24] In addition, confessions made by the defendant may be subject to suppression motions,[25] if the confessions were made involuntarily, without counsel, or without the defendant being informed of his or her rights pursuant to the Miranda decision (see appendix).[26] Again, even if the judge suppresses the confession, this is not tantamount to an acquittal. Only the confession is suppressed. Other evidence, such as fingerprints, eyewitness identification, and possession of stolen property to name a few types, may still be introduced to increase the likelihood of obtaining a conviction.

Motion for Discovery

In most states, the defense has the right to **discovery;** to examine the prosecutor's evidence prior to trial. The rationale for such a motion is to insure fairness in the trial. Motions to exclude and suppress evidence often occur after the granting of a motion for discovery. States vary in how broadly they apply discovery. Some allow full or complete discovery while others are not as liberal. There is also the possibility of reciprocal discovery where both parties examine their opponent's evidence, but very few jurisdictions have adopted this practice.

Motion for Disclosure

The motion for **disclosure** is usually filed by the defense. If granted, the prosecution must produce a list of witnesses they intend to call with each witness's last known address. This list does not preclude the prosecution from calling additional witnesses if there is good cause for the witnesses not being included on the original list. Like discovery, the purpose of disclosure is to provide the defense with the opportunity to plan a strategy and to investigate the witnesses concerning their credibility. Like many other pretrial procedures, these motions are designed to balance the scales of justice.

Motion for Dismissal

The defense will also frequently make a motion for judicial dismissal of the charges. If previous motions (e.g., exclusion and suppression) have been granted, the case may be weakened to the point that there is insufficient evidence on which to proceed. Motions to dismiss during pretrial stages do not bar prosecution at a later date if new evidence is uncovered.

Summary

In this chapter, we have examined numerous pretrial procedures. As we have seen, the period from arrest to actual trial may be a very active one. Many activities are designed to insure that the defendant will be afforded due process of law. Some of these procedures are brief and relatively uncomplicated, while others are very demanding in both time and energy of the participants. Many of the proceedings, such as bail and the use of grand juries, have been subject to controversy.

Presently there are several proposals in various states to modify pretrial procedures. Most are attempts to "shore up" the insanity defense and to insure that "dangerous" criminals are not released on bail. While pretrial procedures are beset with problems and may require reexamination, we must not lose sight of the fact that they also aid an already overcrowded court docket, save tax dollars by filtering out cases in which evidence is lacking, and afford constitutional protections to the accused.

Key Terms Defined

initial appearance the first appearance of a person taken into custody before a judge (magistrate), at which time a decision is made as to whether probable cause to proceed exists and the person is notified of the charges against him or her and informed of his or her constitutional rights.

probable cause the presence of sufficient facts to convince a reasonable person that some official action (arrest, charging) should be taken.

bail the practice of releasing a defendant prior to trial with the promise that he or she will appear before the court as directed or will forfeit money or property (or some portion of it) accepted by the court as a guarantee of such appearance.

nulla poena sine crimine no punishment without a crime.

bondsman a person who puts up bail money for others for profit.

release on recognizance releasing defendant on his or her promise to appear before the court at the appointed time without requiring that he or she post bail.

grand jury an investigative body whose duty is to determine whether or not to indict an accused.

ex parte **proceeding** a proceeding at which only one party is represented (as in the case of the grand jury where only the prosecution is allowed to present a case).

indictment formal accusation via a grand jury.

prima facie **case** on the face of it, or at first sight.

information a formal accusation made by the prosecutor.

preliminary hearing probable cause hearing in a criminal case.

arraignment a court hearing at which the defendant is formally charged and asked to enter a plea.

nola contendre no contest, essentially a plea of guilty.

motion for discovery a motion to be allowed to examine the evidence of the other side prior to trial.

motion for disclosure a motion to be provided with a list of the witnesses to be called at a trial.

Discussion Questions

1. Why are pretrial procedures sometimes viewed as filtering mechanisms? How do these procedures contribute to due process?

2. What are the functions of bail? What problems plague the bail system?

3. Compare and contrast the two methods of formal accusation.

4. Explain the pleas entered during arraignment. What are the ramifications and legal requirements of each?

5. Explain the concept of venue. Why would the accused ask for a change of venue? List and explain three other pretrial motions or procedures.

Notes

1. For formal definitions, see *Illinois Revised Statutes,* ch. 38, section 110–1.

2. *Illinois Revised Statutes,* ch. 38, section 110f.

3. *Illinois Revised Statutes,* ch. 38, section 110b and 110g.

4. *Illinois Revised Statutes,* ch. 38, section 110–7d.

5. Fredric Suffet, "Bail Setting: A Study of Courtroom Interaction," *Crime and Delinquency* 12 (October 1966).

6. John F. Galliher and James L. McCartney, *Criminology: Power, Crime and Criminal Law* (Homewood, Ill.: Dorsey Press, 1977).

7. Suffet, "Bail Setting"; Charles E. Ares, Ann Rankin, and Herbert Sturz, "The Manhattan Bail Project," *New York University Law Review* 38 (January 1963).

8. Vera Institute of Justice, *1961–1971: Programs in Criminal Justice* (New York: Vera Institute, 1972).

9. Thomas P. O'Rourke and Richard G. Salen, "A Comparative Analysis of Pretrial Procedures," *Crime and Delinquency* 14 (October 1968): 363; Gerald S. Levin, "The San Francisco Bail Project," *American Bar Association Journal* 55 (February 1969): 135.

10. *Sourcebook of Criminal Justice Statistics—1986,* U.S. Department of Justice, (Washington, D.C.: U.S. Government Printing Office, 1987), 395.

11. Anne Rankin, "The Effect of Pretrial Detention," *New York University Law Review* 39 (June 1964): 641.

12. *Castella v. United States,* 350 U.S. 359, 1953.

13. *United States v. Calandra,* 414 U.S. 338, 1974.

14. Alan Kalmanoff, *Criminal Justice Enforcement and Administration* (Boston: Little, Brown, 1976), 276.

15. National Advisory on Criminal Justice Standards and Goals, *Courts* (Washington, D.C.: U.S. Government Printing Office, 1973), 74.

16. *Brady v. United States,* 397 U.S. 742, 1969.

17. *Boykin v. Alabama,* 395 U.S. 238, 1968.

18. *Santabello v. New York,* 404 U.S. 257, 1971.

19. "Questions and Answers with Percy Forman," *Chicago Tribune Magazine* (August 22, 1982): 36.

20. *Illinois Revised Statutes,* ch. 38, section 113–4.1.

21. *Illinois Revised Statutes,* ch. 38, section 114–6, p. 146.

22. *Illinois Revised Statutes,* ch. 38, section 114–4, p. 145.

23. *Mapp v. Ohio,* 367 U.S. 543, 1961.

24. *Illinois Revised Statutes,* ch. 38, section 114–12, p. 147.

25. *Illinois Revised Statutes,* ch. 38, section 114–11.

26. *Miranda v. Arizona,* 384 U.S. 348, 1965.

Suggested Readings

Bureau of Justice Statistics, "Pretrial Release and Detention: The Bail Reform Act of 1984," (Washington, D.C.: U.S. Government Printing Office, 1988).

Clark, Leroy D. *The Grand Jury: The Use and Abuse of Political Power.* New York: Quadrangle/The New York Times, 1975.

Foote, Caleb. "The Coming Constitutional Crisis in Bail." *University of Pennsylvania Law Review* 113, no. 8 (June 1965): 1125–85.

Frankle, Marvin E., and Naftalis, Gary P. *The Grand Jury: An Institution on Trial.* New York: Hill and Wang, 1977.

Galliher, John F., and McCartney, James L. *Criminology: Power, Crime and Criminal Law*. Homewood, Ill.: Dorsey Press, 1977.

Goldfarb, Ronald. *Ransom—A Critique of the American Bail System*. New York: Harper and Row, 1965.

Hans, Valerie P., "An Analysis of Public Attitudes Toward the Insanity Defense," *Criminology*, 24, no. 2 (May 1986), 393–414.

McDonald, William F., "Judicial Supervision of the Guilty Plea Process: A study of Six Jurisdictions," *Judicature* 70, no. 4 (Dec–Jan 1987), 203–215.

Whyte, James P. "Is the Grand Jury Necessary?" *Virginia Law Review* 45 (1959): 461–91.

Criminal Trial   12

In chapters nine and ten, we discussed the organization of the court systems and the roles of the various participants in these systems. In this chapter, we will describe and analyze the actual trial process emphasizing legal requirements, some consequences of these requirements, and societal reaction to them.

The Right to a Speedy Trial

The Sixth Amendment guarantees defendants in federal criminal cases the right to a speedy trial, and the doctrine was extended to the state courts in 1967.[1] In practice, however, many criminal trials still commence months and sometimes years after the filing of formal charges or arrest.

The speedy trial doctrine is often criticized as being vague and ambiguous despite the fact that the Supreme Court has attempted to clarify the meaning of the doctrine through various decisions. In *Klopfer v. Carolina,* the Court applied the speedy trial doctrine to the states, recognizing it as a fundamental right of those accused of crimes.[2] In applying this doctrine, the justices were attempting to protect the defendant from public scorn, protect the defendant's employment status, and to limit the anxiety of those awaiting trial.[3] In short, the Court clearly recognized the numerous hardships the accused may suffer if not afforded the right to a speedy trial.

In contrast, it is not uncommon for a defendant to benefit from judicial delay. The credibility and availability of witnesses diminishes with time. As a result, many defense attorneys waive their clients' rights to a speedy trial as a strategy. Can an accused use the speedy trial doctrine as a defense if his or her attorney's actions have caused or contributed to the delay? In *Barker v. Wingo,*[4] the Court held that such cases must be decided after "balancing" four factors: (1) the length of the delay, (2) the reason for the delay, (3) the defendant's responsibility to assert his or her right to a speedy trial, and (4) the prejudice resulting from the delay.[5] While these tests are far from objective, they do represent attempts to clarify the issue and perhaps make it more difficult for a defendant to ask for continuances, or fail to object to a prosecutor's motion for continuance and still challenge the proceedings on the basis of violation of the right to a speedy trial.

Yet another major legal issue concerning speedy trial involves the determination of when the right commences. For example, Jones burglarizes Smith's house while Smith is vacationing. Five months later, when Smith returns home, he discovers his stereo and some money missing. Smith reports the crime to the police, but the perpetrator is not identified. Four months later, Jones is arrested on another charge and a subsequent search of his premises uncovers Smith's stolen property. Obviously, the time lapse between the offense and the arrest is considerable and it may be another four or five months before the case is brought to trial. Can Jones successfully claim that his right to a speedy trial has been violated? In *United States v. Monroe,* the Court held that the time period involved does not commence until an indictment or information has been issued or the accused has been arrested for a criminal charge.[6] Most jurisdictions employ statutes of limitations that state the maximum allowable time period between the offense and formal accusation (after which time, the offender can no longer be charged with the offense) and this is not to be confused with the time period for a speedy trial. Most jurisdictions also have statutes specifying the time period involved in the speedy trial doctrine. At the federal level, the Speedy Trial Act of 1974 states that a defendant in a federal criminal case must be brought to trial within one-hundred days of arrest.[7] Defendants can still, of course, waive their right to a speedy trial by filing motions for continuances. Only the prosecution is prohibited from prolonging the delay without good cause.

Jury Trials: A Great American Myth

One of the basic elements of the American criminal justice process is the right to a trial by jury. Like the right to a speedy trial, the right to trial by a jury of one's peers is guaranteed by the Sixth Amendment. This right was extended to defendants in state court proceedings through the Supreme Court's decision in *Duncan v. Louisiana*.[8] In a later decision, the Court qualified the doctrine by holding that the right to trial by jury only applies in cases in which the defendant faces the possibility of a prison term of six months or more.[9]

How frequently do jury trials actually occur? The vast majority of cases, about 90 percent, are actually settled by a plea of guilty that may occur at any time between the arraignment and the commencement of trial proceedings. The two major sources of guilty pleas are plea bargains and summary trials.

Plea Bargains

Although we have previously discussed plea bargaining (see chapter 10), a closer look at the way in which it affects criminal trials is in order. You will recall that plea bargaining involves pleading guilty for some consideration. Newman has indicated that the considerations involved fall into four categories: considerations concerning charge; considerations concerning sentence; concurrent sentences; and dropped charges.[10] In bargaining charges, the accused agrees to plead guilty to a charge less serious than the original charge in order to obtain less severe punishment. In bargaining for sentence, the accused pleads guilty to the original charge with the understanding that a lenient sentence will be recommended. In bargaining for concurrent sentences, the accused pleads guilty to more than one charge in return for receiving sentences that run concurrently. For example, a defendant may be arrested for one burglary and, during a legal search of his house, the police may find evidence that he also committed five other burglaries. If burglary is punishable by five years imprisonment, the burglar, if found guilty of all six burglaries, could be sentenced to thirty years in prison. In a bargain for concurrent sentences, the burglar might agree to plead guilty to all six burglaries if the prosecutor agreed to sentence him to six concurrent terms of five years, in which case the defendant would actually serve a maximum of five years. In bargaining to drop charges, the defendant may agree to plead guilty to the most serious charge if all other charges against him are dropped. For example, Green is charged with aggravated battery, disorderly conduct, and resisting arrest. Green might plead guilty to the aggravated battery charge if the prosecutor agreed to drop the disorderly and resisting charges.

On several occasions, the courts have attempted to regulate plea bargaining. In *Boykin v. Alabama,*[11] the Supreme Court held that when a defendant enters a plea of guilty, the judge must question the defendant to insure the plea is being entered voluntarily. The Court noted that the accused is waiving both the Fifth (self-incrimination) and Sixth (trial by jury and right to confront one's accusers) Amendments' protections and, therefore, serious attempts must be made to insure the voluntariness of the plea. Most judges now question the defendant concerning the waiver of his or her rights, inform the defendant of the possible penalties upon conviction, and ask if the plea is being entered voluntarily. In *Brady v. United States,*[12] the Court held that a guilty plea is not invalidated simply because the accused entered negotiations in an attempt to avoid the death penalty. In *Santobello v. New York,*[13] the Court held that the prosecutor must honor promises made during negotiations or the guilty plea may be withdrawn. More recently, the Court has determined that a prosecutor's threat to seek reindictment under an habitual criminal statute if the defendant refuses to plead guilty to a lesser charge does not violate due process.[14]

Plea bargaining is controversial for a variety of reasons. It is largely unobservable and it eliminates citizen participation as jurors. Frequently, victims and witnesses appear at court only to find that their testimony and participation are not required because the case has been bargained. In some cases, plea bargaining makes a mockery of the justice network in that offenders may be convicted of charges quite different from those leading to their arrests and/or may receive punishments that are regarded as extremely lenient by victims and witnesses. Finally, some innocent parties may plead guilty to offenses they did not commit because they fear being convicted on more serious charges if they maintain their innocence to the point of trial. While the actual incidence of such cases is probably very low, all of these criticisms combined have led Alaska to prohibit the practice of plea bargaining with few if any unpleasant side effects.[15] Other proposals to restrict plea bargaining involve increasing court resources and preplea conferences in which the judge, victim, defendant, prosecutor, police, and defense counsel all meet and discuss the issues involved in resolving the case.[16]

Summary Trials

The Sixth Amendment and the Supreme Court's decision in *Duncan v. Louisiana*[17] have defined the right to trial by jury in serious cases. In 1970, the Court went on to define a serious case as one in which the possible penalty is more than six months imprisonment.[18] In *Patton v. United States,*[19] the Supreme Court ruled that a defendant can waive his or her right to trial by jury. In a later decision, the Court upheld a federal statute requiring that the waiver of trial by jury be contingent upon approval of the prosecutor,[20] but why would a defendant waive his or her right to jury trial? Some defendants may feel they will receive some consideration if they save the court's time by not invoking their right to a jury trial. Others may fear a jury because they are charged with an emotion-laden crime such as child molesting. Whatever the reason, some writers estimate that about 40 percent of all major criminal cases involve a waiver of jury trial.[21]

Most criminal defendants are charged with misdemeanors or petty offenses rather than with felonies, and are not guaranteed the right to jury trial. Justice is dispensed for these individuals at **summary trials.** Summary trials are expedient for both the court and the defendant. A large number of cases can be dealt with in a short time period during which charges are read, guilty pleas are accepted, and fines are levied. If we add those dealt with in summary courts to defendants who waive their right to jury trial and those pleading guilty for considerations, it is apparent that only a small number of criminal defendants are tried by a jury of their peers.

The Jury Trial

Jury trials probably occur in somewhere between 2 and 8 percent of all criminal cases. The jury trial, nonetheless, remains important because it is one of the few areas in criminal justice in which members of the public are directly involved (as jurors, witnesses, and victims). Theoretically, the basic advantage of the jury trial is the assurance that the accused will be judged by a fair and impartial group. In order to help insure that this occurs, specific procedures for selecting jurors have been developed.

The pool of citizens from which jurors are selected is called a **venire.** The size of the venire varies according to the population of the jurisdiction. Citizens are randomly selected to serve as members of the venire from voting lists, lists of taxpayers, telephone directories, and lists of those holding driver's licenses in order to obtain a cross-section of the community. Critics argue that all of these lists discriminate against minorities and the poor, who are least likely to be able to afford phones or to register to vote, and most likely to be defendants in criminal cases. Unfortunately, there is no comprehensive list of all adult citizens available and, as a consequence, we cannot insure that every citizen has some chance of being called for jury duty.

A list of citizens is randomly selected to serve as a jury panel for every crime (or for all crimes occurring within a given period). Both the prosecuting attorney and the defense attorney question members of this panel in open court in the process of *voir dire* (literally, "look-speak," or to tell the truth). This process is intended to further the guarantee of a fair trial by allowing interested parties the opportunity to question and discharge jurors who may be biased. For example, thirty people might be directed by the court to appear and be able to serve as jurors on a given date. In court, twelve members of this panel will be summoned to the jury box, where they must take an oath of honesty before answering questions under *voir dire* examination. Both attorneys will question prospective jurors

concerning their knowledge about the case, their relationships with any of the participants, whether they have formed any opinions about the case, and other pertinent issues. In determining the actual jurors, both attorneys may challenge (excuse) potential jurors by using *challenges for cause* and *peremptory challenges*. **Challenges for cause** are unlimited in number. In challenges of this type, the attorney asks the court to excuse a prospective juror because his or her responses to *voir dire* questions show an inability to view the case objectively. The judge actually makes the final decision, based upon evidence heard during *voir dire*. Because challenges for cause are unlimited, most attorneys extensively question potentially hostile jurors in an attempt to prove bias and excuse such jurors.

    Peremptory challenges are usually limited in number by statute. No reason has to be offered for a peremptory challenge, but, because they are limited, most attorneys will try to save them and will challenge jurors for cause if possible. Both the state's and defense attorneys have specific types of people they want to excuse, depending upon the charge, and will often use peremptory challenges to exclude members of these groups. For example, in drunk driving cases prosecutors may want to exclude younger jurors because they are more likely to have recently engaged in similar behavior and will be less likely to return a conviction. In comparison, some defense attorneys will try to exclude females and deeply religious people from serving as jurors in rape cases. If the challenge for cause is not honored, the attorney may utilize one of his or her peremptory challenges to insure that jurors with certain characteristics do not serve on a particular case.

Returning to our example, of the first twelve potential jurors, the prosecutor challenged two jurors and the defense attorney challenged three, which left seven. If both attorneys approve these seven they will not be questioned further and will remain in the jury box until five more jurors have been accepted by the attorneys. Five new prospective jurors will replace those excused, and the *voir dire* examination will continue until twelve members have been chosen. The twelve selected will be sworn in, and the remaining members of the jury panel will be excused but are eligible to be called for future trials.

To many, the process of jury selection is one of the most important stages in the criminal process. Some attorneys attempt to "stack" the jury rather than to obtain a fair jury. It is common for both attorneys to employ investigators to conduct background investigations on prospective jurors so that they can conduct an extensive and complete *voir dire* and select a jury that is more open to their case.

In addition to the trial jury, many jurisdictions also select alternate jurors during *voire dire*. Alternate jurors remain in the courtroom and are able to replace an original juror who has to be excused during the trial. This practice saves the court time and the defendant time and money, since without it, if a juror has to be excused during the trial, a mistrial would be declared and the entire process repeated.

Traditionally, juries have consisted of twelve individuals as in our example above. The Supreme Court, however, has held that juries of six members do not violate constitutional guarantees.[22] In *Williams v. Florida,* the Court upheld a Florida statute permitting six-person juries in noncapital cases. The Court contended that the twelve-person jury was a historical accident and that the right to trial by jury did not specify the number of jurors. This decision does not, of course, require the use of six-person juries, but permits the states to engage in the practice of using fewer than twelve jurors in noncapital cases if they so desire. Most states still employ twelve-member juries, and those permitting juries of fewer than twelve often limit their use to misdemeanor cases.

Another legal issue involved in jury trials centers on the composition of the jury. In *Glasser v. United States,* the Court stated that a jury of one's peers means a random cross-section of the community.[23] Thus, a white female is not entitled to be tried by a jury of all white females, but by a jury that is randomly drawn with all community members having an equal chance of being selected. In *Taylor v. Louisiana,* the Court declared Louisiana's system of excluding females from jury service unconstitutional.[24] Applying the Glasser ruling, we can see that this practice would not provide a cross-section of the community.

While the Court has been explicit in demanding that jury lists not be drawn in a discriminatory manner, the use of peremptory challenges to exclude specific types of jurors remains controversial. In *Swain v. Alabama,* the Court rejected a defendant's claim that Alabama's method of jury selection was discriminatory.[25] In the Swain case, no black had served on a petit (trial) jury in the county of record for fifteen years. The Court acknowledged that the system of drawing the venire was imperfect, but concluded that blacks were excluded by peremptory challenges and not by discriminatory legal procedures. Remembering our discussion of *voir dire,* we can see why the use of peremptory challenges is limited and why attorneys consider their use important in courtroom strategy.

Those who support the practice of trial by jury argue that juries reflect community values, reduce the potential for bias, and are politically free. Those who oppose the jury system argue against the way the principle is applied rather than against the principle, for the most part. One of their arguments focuses on jury composition. In most jurisdictions, citizens in certain professions are systematically excluded from jury duty (e.g., doctors, lawyers, teachers, and other professionals). Other qualified jurors can ask to be excused because jury duty will cause a hardship on them or their families. Who is left to serve? Some critics claim that juries are generally composed of the elderly, the uneducated, and bored homemakers. A further argument against juries centers on the decision-making process. Jurors receive no formal training, and, if the charge that they are educationally unrepresentative is valid, their ability to reach a just decision is questionable. Juries have been accused of relying upon characteristics of the parties involved instead of the evidence presented to determine the outcome of cases. Also, some challenge the ability of jurors to interpret the law, arguing that judges and attorneys who have studied and practiced for years have difficulty in making legal applications.

Once again we are faced with the dilemma of considering the cost of democratic involvement. Given that juries have made mistakes and have decided outcomes on the basis of nonlegal factors, is it worth the sacrifice to exclude the public from court involvement and to relinquish all power to criminal justice officials?

Order of Trial There are well-established procedures in jury trials. As we have discussed, the *voir dire* examination is the first step in the process. Additional steps include opening statements, presentation of evidence, closing arguments, jury instructions, deliberation, return of the verdict, sentencing, and appeal.

Once the jury has been selected, charges will be read in open court and the judge will ask both parties if they wish to make an opening statement. Because the burden of proof rests with the state, the prosecutor makes his or her opening statement first. The defense attorney may make his or her opening remarks immediately after the prosecutor or, in some jurisdictions, may wait until later in the proceedings. Opening statements can be waived, but this is a rarity in major felony trials. There are at least two good reasons for making opening remarks. First, they can provide the jury with a general overview of what the attorney intends to prove and how he or she intends to prove it. Second, the opening statement can help the attorney establish rapport with the jury if he or she maintains good eye contact, talks to the jurors in a personal manner, and explains to the jurors how important their role is in the criminal justice process.

The state has the burden of proving that (1) a crime was committed and (2) the accused was the offender. The prosecutor (state's attorney or district attorney) always presents the state's case first. The prosecutor will rely upon real evidence and testimony to present his or her case. **Real evidence** consists of objects that can be seen by the judge and/or jury. **Testimonial evidence** is simply evidence entered by a witness. When the prosecutor calls and questions a particular witness, he or she is engaging in **direct questioning.** The term is also applied to witnesses called and questioned by the defense attorney. Because the Sixth Amendment guarantees the accused the right to confront his or her accusors, the opposing attorney, in this case the defense attorney, is provided an opportunity to *cross-examine* each witness. During **cross-examination,** attempts may be made to discredit the witness or to lessen the impact of the witness's testimony. For example, a witness testifies under direct examination that he or she saw the accused engaging in criminal activity. Under cross-examination, the defense attorney may ask questions concerning the distances involved, the witness's eyesight, or any other factor that might refute the witness's testimony. Cross-examination is limited in scope. The attorney administering cross-examination can only ask questions to related testimony given under direct examination; questions of "untouched areas" cannot be asked. Once cross-examination is completed, the party calling the witness will be provided the opportunity for *redirect examination,* again being limited to testimony challenged during cross-examination. **Redirect examination** is usually an attempt to clarify points challenged in cross-examination. The opposing party is also provided with a second line of questioning in **recross-examination** and is limited to evidence discussed during redirect examination. As you can see, the rules governing testimony are specific and act as a filter in terms of the quantity of testimony covered.

The prosecutor will proceed by calling all of the witnesses named in disclosure and will provide the defense counsel with the opportunity to cross-examine each witness. When the prosecution has concluded calling all of his or her witnesses, the state will rest its case.

Once the prosecution has rested its case, the defense attorney will usually move to dismiss the charges because the state has failed to reasonably prove that the accused committed the offense. While the motion is generally denied, the judge retains the authority to halt the proceedings if he or she believes the state has failed to prove the charges. By moving to dismiss the charges at this time, the defense attorney is attempting either to have the case dismissed, to lay foundation for possible post-adjudicatory appeals, or both.

Before we continue with our discussion of the stages in the trial process, we need to analyze some of the rules of evidence. Real evidence includes such objects as weapons, fingerprints, shell casings, blood samples, and any physical objects relevant to the proceedings. Before real evidence can be introduced, proper foundation must be provided. For example, in a murder case, the prosecutor must establish that a homicide has occurred and the type of weapon used, before the weapon can be entered into evidence. The process of laying proper foundation may be quite lengthy and involve several witnesses including doctors, victims, witnesses, and laboratory technicians.

Closely related to the rule of laying foundation is the requirement to "certify" expert witnesses. **Expert witnesses** can answer hypothetical questions while lay witnesses can only testify to facts. Certifying an expert witness includes questioning the witness as to his or her education, experience, record of publication, and participation in other cases to prove that the witness possesses a special skill or ability enabling him or her to give an opinion. Qualifying a witness as an expert may provide greater credibility for the witness's testimony and consequently affect the jury's decision. It is this concern that justifies strict controls in qualifying a witness as an expert.

In television and movie trials, one often observes the attorneys objecting to the introduction of direct evidence. Normally, these issues would have been decided during pretrial suppression hearings, but the attorney may enter an objection in order to make that objection a part of the court record and provide greater support for an appeal.

One of the more well-known rules of evidence is the hearsay rule. Generally, **hearsay** evidence is inadmissible. A witness may testify that he or she saw the accused rob a liquor store, but cannot testify that a third party told him or her that they saw the accused commit the robbery. There is a growing list of exceptions to the hearsay rule, and time and space do not permit a detailed analysis of all of these exceptions. Generally, the rule still applies, but we suggest the reader consult his or her jurisdiction's criminal code to learn the exceptions.

The last rule we will cover is that of leading the witness. An attorney is prohibited from asking **leading questions.** From a practical viewpoint, this problem is rare under current practices. Most attorneys meet with their witnesses prior to the trial and "coach" them as to what questions will be asked and how to present their testimony. Because of the familiarity with the questions, the witness can anticipate upcoming questions and the attorney can easily avoid charges of leading the witness.

The rules presented here represent only a portion of the many rules governing the trial and the presentation of evidence, but they are among the most frequently used.

The next stage in the proceedings is the *presentation of the defense's case*. If defense counsel did not make opening statements at the commencement of the proceedings, he or she will make them here. The defense attorney will then present his or her case in much the same manner and by the same rules of evidence as the prosecution presented its case. The defense is not required to present a case, but normally does to refute the state's evidence. Common strategies include, but are not limited to, offering an alibi, casting doubt upon the motive, introducing contradictory testimony, or employing an affirmative defense. Once the defense has called and questioned all of its witnesses, it will rest its case.

The next stage in the proceedings is the *closing arguments*. In some jurisdictions, the order of presentation is reversed at this stage, the defense will present closing arguments first and the prosecution will follow. During **closing arguments,** the parties will summarize their arguments and attempt to conclusively prove their version of the case. Some lawyers also employ dramatic and emotional pleas in an attempt to affect the trial's outcome. The closing arguments are the attorneys' last chance to reach the jury before deliberation, and it is often felt that the impact of closing arguments outweighs the evidence presented.

When closing arguments have concluded, the judge will *charge* the jury to render a true and just verdict and will provide them with legal *instructions*. The instructions stage requires the judge to explain the laws that apply to the case. For example, in homicide cases the judge may have to explain differences between varying degrees of murder or between murder and manslaughter. In many cases the judge also instructs the jury as to what constitutes reasonable doubt. Those who argue against the jury often contend that most jurors are incapable of understanding such instructions, which may vary in length from a few minutes to hours. To alleviate this problem, jurors are sometimes permitted to take sets of written instructions with them into deliberations.

After they have received their instructions, the jury retires to a private area in which they will deliberate the outcome of the case. The bailiff generally serves as a link between the jury and the judge. A first step in most deliberations is the selection of a jury foreman who will preside over the deliberations. The jurors then discuss the case, examine the evidence presented, and may refer to transcripts in order to clear up disagreements or settle disputes. Eventually, the jurors take a vote on the guilt or innocence of the defendant. Traditionally, votes had to be unanimous before a guilty verdict could be returned, but in *Johnson v. Louisiana* and *Apodaca v. Oregon,*[26] the Supreme Court upheld verdicts of nine to three and ten to two respectively. Most jurisdictions still require unanimous decisions, however, and, if the first vote is not unanimous, require that the jury return to deliberation and attempt to produce a unanimous decision concerning guilt. If the jurors cannot reach such a decision, the jury is referred to as a **hung jury** and a decision concerning retrial must be made.

During some trials, publicity concerning the trial becomes an issue. When publicity is extensive, the judge may feel it is difficult to maintain an impartial jury and may choose to **sequester** the jurors, who are then physically isolated from news and other sources of information which might affect their decisions. Since it is a costly operation, sequestering is normally reserved for very highly publicized or sensitive cases.

Once the jurors have reached a decision, the foreman notifies the judge and court is called back into session. The defendant is asked to stand and the verdict is read aloud. The *return of the verdict* is a brief, but obviously important, part of the trial procedure. If the verdict is not guilty, charges are dismissed and the defendant is released. If the verdict is guilty, the judge usually sets a date for sentencing and recesses.

Sentencing

Sentencing in the majority of cases poses no particular problem for the judge. In cases involving plea bargaining, the judge generally accepts the recommendation of the prosecutor as to the sentence. In summary trials, penalties are often standardized by specific fines for specific offenses. In those cases resolved by criminal trial, however, sentencing is often considerably more problematic.

By and large, sentencing is the exclusive province of the judiciary. A few states provide for jury sentencing, but such sentencing is normally limited to cases involving the possibility of the death penalty. The defendant has a right to be represented by counsel at the sentencing hearing. The major complaint against current sentencing practices has to do with sentence disparities. While some disparities are bound to occur, critics argue that sentencing disparities in many cases represent discriminatory practices, generally based upon race, social class, sex, or some combination of these factors. There is little doubt that some judges do engage in discriminatory sentencing, but the judiciary is certainly not the sole body responsible for the overrepresentation of minorities and lower social class males in prison. As we have indicated before, discrimination based upon these factors occurs at all levels of the criminal justice network—in reporting crimes, in making arrests, in decisions to prosecute, and so on. Differential treatment at each of these levels determines the characteristics of those individuals who proceed to the trial and sentencing stages.

Judges have considerable discretion in imposing sentences, as we have previously noted. Several factors appear to affect sentencing decisions, including the judge's view of the defendant (tough or remorseful, for instance), the political ramifications of the case, the nature of the offense, and, more recently, the availability of prison space. Although sentencing is a complex process, few law schools provide much training in sentencing, and few lawyers who become judges have much prior experience with sentencing. As a result of these shortcomings and as a result of the fact that social scientists have very little good information on the effects of various types of sentences, most judges sentence on a trial and error basis. There is, however, a national trend to send judges to sentencing institutes and workshops such as those provided by the National Judicial College at Reno, Nevada. Such workshops are intended to help judges better understand sentencing options and their consequences and, perhaps, reduce sentencing disparities.

Another attempt to reduce the problem of disparate sentencing has been a shift from *indeterminate* to *determinate* sentencing. In indeterminate sentencing, the judge would sentence a convicted party to an indefinite period in prison—for example, two to five years. Prison officials and parole boards actually determine the length of the sentence as a result of their involvement in granting "good time" and early release. In determinate sentencing, the legislature provides a range of possible sentences and the judge must impose a specific sentence within these parameters. For example, the penalty for robbery might be five to twenty-five years and a judge sentencing a guilty party would have to determine the specific number of years to be served—eleven years, for example. At this point, whatever its other positive contributions, determinate sentencing does not appear to have had much impact on sentencing disparity.

One of the decisions made by the judge with respect to sentencing concerns the issue of sentences for multiple offenses. The judge must decide whether such sentences will be concurrent or consecutive sentences, and, in some cases, whether or not to invoke habitual criminal statutes. Suppose, for example, a defendant has been convicted of rape and kidnapping, and is sentenced to concurrent terms of thirty years for rape and ten years for kidnapping. The maximum time that could be served would be thirty years. If the sentences were imposed consecutively, the maximum time to be served would be forty years. Under habitual criminal statutes, persons convicted of committing three or more felonies in a given time period may be sentenced to life imprisonment. Judges' decisions concerning whether or not to sentence under these statutes contributes to the controversy surrounding sentencing.

Prior to passing sentence, the judge will normally require a **presentence investigation.** This investigation is the responsibility of the probation officer and is used to provide the judge with information upon which to base a sentencing decision. The probation officer prepares a report that is made available to the judge, the prosecutor, and defense counsel. Information contained in the report includes prior criminal record, employment, family, military history, length of residence in the community, and, in some cases, a recommendation from the probation officer concerning sentence. When properly conducted, the presentence investigation can be very valuable to the judge. However, two major problems characterize such investigations. First, due to heavy caseloads, some probation officers do not conduct in-depth investigations and/or fail to verify all the information contained in the report. Second, presentence reports are often highly subjective and the biases of the probation officer simply replace those of the judge. Carter and Wilkins found that in California, judges follow the recommendations of probation officers as much as 96 percent of the time.[27] If this is the case nationally, a great deal of sentencing power has been relinquished by judges.

The network approach to criminal justice makes clear the impact of the sentencing decision on various components of the network. To the extent that the judge makes an appropriate sentencing decision, the public is protected for at least some period of time from further crimes by the offender, the police will not be involved with rearrest, the prosecutor with preparing for another trial, and so on. Further, caseloads of probation officers, prison personnel, and parole boards are largely determined by the judges' decisions at sentencing hearings. In some hearings, political ties clearly affect the judge's decision and, for that matter, whether the case is heard on appeal by the higher courts. Inappropriate decisions at this stage also have obvious, and often less desirable, consequences for the various segments of the criminal justice network.

Appeals

Even after the sentence has been imposed, there is no guarantee that a criminal case is over. Convicted parties generally enjoy the right to appeal. Appellate courts review trial transcripts for legal errors such as improper jury instructions or improperly admitted evidence. Such review does not constitute a new trial. Appellate courts reverse about 20 percent of the cases they receive.[28]

Summary

The process of adjudication in criminal cases is complex and often controversial. Most criminal cases are resolved through plea bargaining or summary trials, which involve guilty pleas. In the small percentage of cases decided by a jury, both legal and nonlegal factors play a major role, as can be seen in the selection of jurors, presentation of cases by opposing counsel, and sentencing disparities. During the actual criminal trial, the order of presentation and the types of evidence admitted are governed by a set of procedural regulations. The determination of sentence for those individuals found guilty is one of the most difficult duties of the judge. In order to assist in making sentencing decisions, the judge typically requires a probation officer to conduct a presentence investigation and frequently follows the recommendation of the probation officer in sentencing.

Key Terms Defined

speedy trial trial without unreasonable delay.

plea bargain an agreement between prosecution and defense (sometimes judge also) concerning charges, plea, and often sentence.

summary trials trials in which there is no need to resolve factual issues (as when a defendant pleads guilty to a misdemeanor).

venire the pool of citizens from which jurors are selected.

voir dire look–speak. The process of examining potential jurors to determine whether they are acceptable as actual jurors.

challenge for cause an objection to a prospective juror generally based upon demonstrated (usually during *voir dire*) inability to view a case objectively.

peremptory challenge objection to a prospective juror for which no cause need be stated.

real evidence demonstrative evidence consisting of objects seen by the jury.

testimonial evidence evidence given verbally.

direct questioning the initial questioning of a witness in a trial by the attorney who called the witness.

cross-examination the initial questioning of a witness called by an opposing attorney during a trial.

redirect examination additional questioning of a witness during a trial by the attorney who called the witness.

recross-examination additional questioning of a witness during a trial by an opposing attorney.

expert witness a person possessing special knowledge or skills who (following proper certification) is allowed to testify at a trial concerning both facts and conclusions that may be drawn from those facts.

hearsay second-hand evidence. Information provided to the witness by another party, which has not been substantiated by the personal observations of the witness.

leading questions questions that lead the witness to answer in a particular way.

closing argument a summary of the evidence presented in a trial generally intended to indicate that the evidence presented by the attorney presenting the argument has supported his or her version of the facts in a case.

hung jury a jury that cannot reach a decision as to innocence or guilt.

sequester to isolate (as in isolating a jury from media presentations while the jury is deliberating a case).

presentence investigation an investigation conducted by a probation officer in order to help the judge determine an appropriate sentence.

Discussion Questions

1. Several court decisions have attempted to clarify the meaning of a speedy trial. Discuss the importance of the following cases in this context: *Klopfer v. North Carolina* and *Barker v. Wingo.*

2. Plea bargaining is an important feature of the criminal justice network. Explain the dynamics of plea bargaining and discuss the arguments supporting and opposing plea bargaining.

3. Although relatively few cases are decided through jury trials, these trials are still an important part of our criminal justice network. Why is this the case?

4. The last step in the criminal trial is sentencing. Explain the controversies surrounding sentencing and discuss the roles of the judge and the probation officer in sentencing.

Notes

1. *Klopfer v. North Carolina*, 386 U.S. 213 (1967).
2. *Klopfer v. North Carolina*, 386 U.S. 213 (1967).
3. *Klopfer v. North Carolina*, 386 U.S. 213 (1967).
4. *Barker v. Wingo*, 407 U.S. 514 (1972).
5. *Barker v. Wingo*, 407 U.S. 514 (1972).
6. *United States v. Monroe*, 404 U.S. 307 (1971).
7. Speedy Trial Act, 18 USCA SOS 361 (1974).
8. *Duncan v. Louisiana*, 391 U.S. 145 (1968).
9. *Baldwin v. New York*, 399 U.S. 66 (1970).
10. Donald J. Newman, "Pleading Guilty for Consideration: A Study of Bargain Justice," *Journal of Criminal Law, Criminology, and Police Science* 46 (March/April 1956):780–90.
11. *Boykin v. Alabama*, 395 U.S. 238 (1969).
12. *Brady v. United States*, 397 U.S. 742 (1970).
13. *Santobello v. New York*, 404 U.S. 257 (1971).
14. *Brodenkircher v. Hayes*, 98 S. Ct. 663 (1978).
15. Michael L. Rubinstein and Teresa White, "Alaska's Ban on Plea Bargaining," *Law and Society Review* 13 (1979):367.
16. "Restructuring the Plea Bargain," *Yale Law Review* 82 (1972):300.

17. *Duncan v. Louisiana*, 391 U.S. 145 (1968).
18. *Baldwin v. New York*, 399 U.S. 66 (1970).
19. *Patton v. United States*, 281 U.S. 276 (1930).
20. *Singer v. United States*, 380 U.S. 24 (1965).
21. Harry Kalvan, Jr. and Hans Zeisel, *The American Jury* (Chicago: University of Chicago Press, 1966).
22. *Williams v. Florida*, 399 U.S. 78 (1970).
23. *Glasser v. United States*, 315 U.S. 60 (1942).
24. *Taylor v. Louisiana*, 419 U.S. 522 (1975).
25. *Swain v. Alabama*, 380 U.S. 202 (1965).
26. *Johnson v. Louisiana*, 406 U.S. 356 (1972) and *Apodaca v. Oregon*, 406 U.S. 404 (1972), respectively.
27. Robert M. Carter and Leslie T. Wilkins, "Some Factors in Sentencing Policy," *Journal of Criminal Law, Criminology, and Police Science* 58 (1967):503.
28. Peter W. Lewis and Kenneth D. Peoples, *The Supreme Court and the Criminal Process* (Philadelphia, Pa.: W. B. Saunders, 1978).

Suggested Readings

Alschuler, Albert W. "Plea Bargaining and It's History." *Law and Society* 13, no. 2 (1979):211–45.

Hans, Valerie P., and Vidmar, Neil. *Judging the Jury* (New York: Plenum, 1986).

Hogarth, John. *Sentencing as a Human Process* (Toronto, Ontario: University of Toronto Press, 1971).

Jacob, Herbert. *Justice in America: Courts, Lawyers, and the Judicial Process* (Boston: Little, Brown, 1984).

Lewis, Peter W., and Peoples, Kenneth D. *Constitutional Rights of the Accused: Cases and Comments* (Philadelphia, Pa.: W. B. Saunders, 1979).

Rosset, Arthur, and Cressey, Donald R. *Justice by Consent: Plea Bargains in the American Courthouse* (New York: J. B. Lippincott, 1976).

Rubin, Ted. *The Courts: Fulcrum of the Justice System* (New York: Random House, 1984).

Simon, Rita J. *The Jury System in America: A Critical Review* (Beverly Hills, Calif.: Sage, 1975).

Victims and Witnesses in the Criminal Justice Network

13

Key Terms

victim compensation
victim restitution

subpoena

We have indicated repeatedly that the public plays a crucial role in the criminal justice network. There is, perhaps, no more clear-cut example of the importance of citizen participation than citizen involvement as a victim or witness. The criminal justice network is, to a great extent, dependent upon crime victims and witnesses for information regarding criminal behavior. Without such information, arrests, prosecutions, and convictions are extremely difficult. Lack of trust or confidence in the police, prosecutor, judges, and/or the procedures involved in processing defendants through the criminal justice network may lead to a decision on behalf of victims and witnesses not to cooperate with practitioners in the processing of a given case. Such lack of trust or confidence may arise from the belief that criminal law protects offenders more than victims, from inconveniences and/or unpleasant experiences encountered in prior contacts with criminal justice practitioners, or from general confusion and misunderstanding. Whatever the cause, most prosecutors and most police officers regard the lack of cooperation of victims and witnesses in prosecution of offenders as a very serious problem.[1]

Among the factors that have been associated with lack of cooperation on behalf of victims and witnesses are cold or impersonal treatment by the police or prosecutor, delays in court proceedings, and failure of officials to notify victims concerning their rights to assistance, restitution, or compensation.[2]

Other factors commonly associated with lack of cooperation in reporting and/or prosecuting include the belief that the police, prosecutor, and judge will not be effective in dealing with the offender; personal knowledge of the offender and

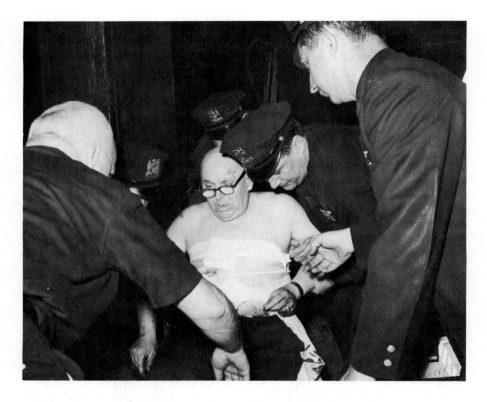

Battered Victim. *The Bettmann Archive*

an attendant lack of desire to see him or her arrested and prosecuted; and fear of retribution. In addition, some citizens clearly believe that the criminal justice network has an almost total preoccupation with the rights of the criminal and largely ignores the rights of crime victims.[3]

The defendant has the right to remain silent and to be furnished with a copy of the charges brought against him or her. On a motion by the defendant, the judge will order the prosecutor to furnish the defendant with a list of prosecution witnesses. The defendant also has the right to a speedy trial before an impartial judge and/or jury. Society ultimately pays for the defense of the indigent defendant, as well as for the room, board, counseling, medical treatment, and rehabilitative training or education of the defendant if he or she is incarcerated. The law, however, does not protect the victim from being legally compelled to give testimony that may be embarrassing or self-demeaning, or that may result in considerable pain and suffering. The rights and privileges of the victim, in short, do not appear to be the same as those of the offender, especially from the perspective of the victim.

It is, of course, quite natural for crime victims to be upset about being victimized. They have been confronted by a deliberate violation of their rights by another. In order to help them deal with these feelings and to improve the chances that they will assist authorities in the apprehension and prosecution of offenders, they need to know what they can expect to receive in the way of assistance and what is expected of them should they decide to cooperate with the police and/or prosecutor. The victim is entitled to an explanation and justice as the person wronged.[4] Each victimization tramples some fundamental personal right of the victim: the right to life, the right to personal security, the right to security of habitation and premises, or the right to retain and enjoy property.[5]

Some authors believe that victims of crime in the United States occupy, as a class, the same position that racial minorities did years ago. To date, few have recognized that these victims do constitute a class that has rights and is entitled to have them enforced.[6] Crime victims are, however, unlike other minorities. They are not a cohesive group unified by religion, race, or language. Crime victims are unified only by fate. Like other minorities, however, crime victims are often misunderstood and ostracized. Just as other minorities are accorded second-class status and are often considered "lazy" or "stupid," crime victims are often blamed for their misfortunes—accused of provoking the criminal, of not resisting strongly enough, or of resisting too strongly.[7]

The ordinary citizen is compelled to depend on the police for protection against bodily harm and loss of property, and must rely on them to effectively insure the safety of street and home against criminal incursion. Police protection is generally viewed as protection of the public—not individuals. The protection of an individual does not generally occur until that individual has been victimized.[8]

Within the framework of an offender-oriented criminal justice network, there is constant pressure for the police to be exclusively concerned with the offender and to view the victim only as an instrument necessary for a successful prosecution.[9]

The decade of the 1960s witnessed a number of U.S. Supreme Court decisions that solidified the rights of alleged offenders. Occasionally dispersed among dissenting opinions are statements noting concern about the impact these decisions might have on future crime victims. In his dissenting opinion in the *Miranda v. Arizona* case in 1966 (as it applied to the ability of law enforcement officials to obtain legally admissable confessions from criminal suspects), U.S. Supreme Court Associate Justice Byron R. White predicted that, "in some unknown number of cases, the Court's ruling will return a killer, a rapist, or other criminal to the streets and to the environment that produced him, to repeat his crime whenever it pleases him."[10] Finally, White stated, with a great deal of irony, that "there is, of course, a saving factor: the next victims are *uncertain, unnamed,* and *unrepresented* in this case."[11]

In an attempt to encourage victims to participate in the arrest and prosecution of offenders, a number of victim-oriented programs based upon the concepts of compensation and restitution have been developed. These concepts are often used interchangeably, but, in fact, they represent two different points of view. **Compensation,** in the criminal–victim relationship, concerns the counterbalancing of a loss suffered by a victim as a result of criminal attack. It is basically payment for the damage or injury caused by the crime. It is an indication of the responsibility of society and it is civil in character; thus, it represents a noncriminal goal in a criminal case. **Restitution** in a criminal–victim relationship involves restoring the victim to his or her position, which was damaged as a result of a criminal attack. It clearly indicates the responsibility of the offender, is penal in character, and represents a correctional goal in a criminal case. Compensation calls for action by the victim in the form of an application and payment by society; restitution calls for a decision by a criminal court and payment by the offender.[12]

There are, generally speaking, four methods of monetary recovery presently available to crime victims. These are (1) civil remedies, (2) restitution, (3) private insurance, and (4) state-subsidized compensation programs.

Civil Remedies

As a result of over two centuries of litigation, our criminal justice network has evolved to a stage where crime is regarded as an offense exclusively against the state. The interests of the crime victim have been eroded to the point where they play little or no part in criminal procedure. Because of this, the victim must seek legal remedy for his or her injury through the civil courts where civil procedures apply. The most obvious limitation to such a system of recovery is the relatively low percentage of offenders ultimately apprehended. For the vast majority of crime victims, a tort recovery is a total impossibility. Even if the offender is apprehended, substantial obstacles to a successful civil action remain. The offender generally has few, if any, reserve funds, and most of these will be expended in the process of defense against criminal charges. If sentenced to prison, the offender has little chance to earn an income that could serve as a basis for a civil award. Finally, the civil court process itself is extremely time-consuming for the victim and may result in substantial expenditures of the victim's own funds.[13] It has been estimated that only 1.8 percent of victims of crime ever collect damages from the perpetrator.[14]

Restitution

In restitution programs, the criminal is perceived as the appropriate source of benefits for the victim of a crime. The criminal court judge has the alternative of deciding the victim's claim and incorporating a monetary settlement into the final decision. An implicit goal of restitution is to once again make whole (as much as possible) the victim, by the direct action of the criminal rather than by a monetary payment by the state. It is sometimes argued that direct repayment by the criminal to the victim has the added benefit of assisting in the rehabilitation of the offender.

As with tort recovery, restitution has proven inadequate for the majority of crime victims mainly because their offender is either unidentified, unapprehended, or unconvicted; or without assets, employment, or skills.

An additional limitation to restitution programs is the cost involved in administering them. MacNamara and Sullivan, for example, claim that "the costs to the state of administrating a system of offender restitution to the victims of his crimes would exceed the sums actually collected to reimburse the victims for their injuries and losses."[15]

The concept of offender restitution has been more popular as a theory than feasible as a practice. As a result, restitution is not used frequently by American judges.

Private Insurance

In the absence of a provision to the contrary, an insurance policy covering accidental injuries also covers victims of unforeseen intentional criminal attacks. However, there are a number of significant problems with respect to private insurance against crime. Many individuals cannot afford premiums to procure coverage for their basic health needs, and it is highly doubtful that they are in a position to afford the luxury of coverage against criminal attacks. Such insurance would be beyond the financial means of a substantial number of families, and making such insurance available and meaningful would require limiting the insurer's option to cancel or refuse to renew policies. Since the highest crime rates are in poverty areas, the insurance premiums would be higher for people living in these areas, even though these citizens are least able and least likely to purchase insurance. Moreover, many insurance companies refuse to issue insurance in high-crime areas. Finally, such coverage is generally inadequate to reimburse the victim for any long-term impairment; rarely is full compensation commensurate with damages attained.[16]

State-Subsidized Compensation Programs

Because of the failure of civil suits, restitution, and private insurance as methods of assisting victims of crime, the concept of compensation by the state has gained favor. Although victim compensation also offers several drawbacks as the principle form of financial aid for victims of crime, it is felt by many to be the most equitable and consistent method of "making the victim whole." Unlike civil suits and restitution schemes, compensation provides a remedy *without* requiring that the assailant either be apprehended and/or convicted, or financially able to repay his/her damages.

Thirty-six states have created victims' compensation programs to repay some of the medical costs and lost income due to victimization. In February 1983, the nine-member President's Task Force on Victims of Crime urged all states to undertake such programs.[17] Although current programs vary in rationale, scope, and methods, they are sufficiently similar to warrant some general comments concerning their standards and practices:

The typical crime victim compensation program serves only as a remedy of last resort to provide reimbursement of certain direct financial costs to certain victims of certain crimes.

Payments are almost universally limited to unreimbursed medical expenses, loss of earnings by the victim, loss of support by the victim's dependents, and funeral and burial expenses occurring as a direct result of the criminal incident.

Specifically excluded is compensation for property loss resulting from theft or vandalism and, in the vast majority of states, compensation for "pain and suffering."

A substantial minority of states forbid their compensation boards from making any award unless the victim would otherwise suffer "financial hardship."

Every jurisdiction with a compensation program has a statutory maximum award that can be made. This ceiling varies from ten thousand to fifty thousand dollars. Similarly, most states require that the victim sustain minimum, out-of-pocket losses before becoming eligible for state compensation.

Generally, the person must have been an innocent victim of a crime and could not have been related to or living with the offender at the time the incident occurred.

After the crime takes place, the victim (or dependent) must report the
crime to the police within a specified period of time (usually two to five
days) and, thereafter, is obligated to fully cooperate with all law
enforcement and judicial officials in the processing of the case.
Additionally, the victim must file a "Notice to Apply" for compensation
within a certain time interval after the occurrence of the crime (normally
within one to two years).

The majority of state programs are funded through general tax revenues;
however, there are some states that subsidize their programs by imposing
an additional fine on all convicted offenders.[18]

Despite the political popularity of providing public assistance to innocent victims of crime, many officials have been reluctant to enact such measures because
of apprehension about potential costs. Other criticisms focus upon the fear that
"the victim, knowing that he will be reimbursed for losses, may become careless
or, conversely, the offender, knowing that the victim will be compensated, may
be less hesitant about inflicting injury."[19] Finally, there are those critics who believe that a victim compensation plan would encourage fraud. They argue that
it will unavoidably result in some citizens using the compensation plan to either
report nonexistent crimes and extract "easy money" from the government—or,
taking this argument to its extreme, fear that people may deliberately injure
themselves in order that they might collect a check from the state.

A Brief Historical Overview of Victim Compensation and Restitution

Historical reference to victim compensation goes back at least as far as the Code
of Hammurabi:

> If a man has committed robbery and is caught, that man shall be put to
> death. If the robber is not caught, the man who has been robbed should
> formally declare what he has lost . . . and the city . . . shall replace
> whatever he has lost for him. If it is the life of the owner that is lost, the city
> or the mayor shall pay one maneh of silver to his kinfolk.[20]

Similarly, the Old Testament indicates that a criminal–victim relationship also
existed among the early Hebrews. If a person was injured, the perpetrator of the
offense was to reimburse him for the time lost from his tasks and to be responsible
for seeing to it that he had the resources to be thoroughly healed, if possible.[21]

These early systems of compensation/restitution were gradually replaced by state-run criminal prosecution that left the victim only civil remedies by which he or she might collect for injuries. One rationale for this new approach was the claim that these fines underwrote expenses incurred by the authorities in apprehending and prosecuting the offender. Schafer traces the demise of public compensation to the Middle Ages:

> It was chiefly owing to the violent greed of the feudal barons and the medieval ecclesiastical powers that the rights of the injured party were gradually infringed upon, and finally, appropriated by these authorities. These authorities exacted a double vengeance upon the offender, first by forfeiting his property to themselves instead of to his victim and then by punishing him by the dungeon, the torture, the stake, or the gibbet. But the original victim of the wrong was ignored.[22]

In the 1760s, Cesare Beccaria took issue with the proposition that the primary function of the criminal justice network was to serve as an aid to private action in obtaining recovery from the offender. Since the system had arisen from a social contract, it must serve the interests of society and not the individual victim. Punishment inflicted by the system should primarily serve to deter the offender from further criminal activity; and, to deter others from committing similar acts. Punishment was not to be imposed to redress private damages. Overall, Beccaria's principles contributed to the already declining role of victims in the criminal justice system.[23]

Lack of consideration for the victim on the part of the state lasted until the twentieth century. This does not mean that there were no advocates of victim rights in the meantime. Nineteenth century writers such as Jeremy Bentham, Enrico Ferri, and Raffaele Garofalo each noted the plight of victims of crime and urged the adoption of public compensation plans. However, the writings of these individuals had little effect on public policy as it applied to reforming the rights of crime victims.

Revival of active interest in compensation from crime victims in contemporary times is attributed to the work of Margaret Fry, an English magistrate and social reformer. Ms. Fry, like many others of her day, was primarily interested in restitution for victims being paid by the offender on the assumption that, "although restitution cannot undo the wrong, it will often mitigate the injury, and it has a real educative value for the offender. Repayment is the best first step toward reformation that a dishonest person can take. It is often the ideal solution."[24]

Ms. Fry felt that the "state which forbids our going armed in self-defense cannot disown all responsibility for its occasional failure to protect."[25] State compensation, she advocated, should not interfere with the possibility of damage awards against the aggressor.

In 1959, Stephen Schafer, an American criminologist, was given a commission by the British Home Office to work on the problem of restitution/compensation. Thus, after an extended period of dormancy, the needs of crime victims once again came to the attention of governmental bodies and have received increasing attention during the last twenty years.

Reiff believes that there should be a "Victim's Bill of Rights" to insure that all citizens who suffer injury or loss as the result of a criminal act have the right to be made "whole again." He believes that all such victims should have the right to immediate emergency aid in the areas of medicine, law, and finances; and that all victims should be protected by the police and the courts from threats or coercion on behalf of the offender or his or her supporters. Further, Reiff contends that victims should be entitled to participate in, or be represented in, any plea bargaining decisions and should be entitled to the immediate return of any recovered stolen property. Victims should be provided with timely information concerning the course of the investigation of their offense and plans for prosecution. In addition, victims should have the right to hold law enforcement officers legally responsible for negligence or poor judgment. Finally, victims should be able to exercise the same rights to silence and legal representation afforded offenders.[26]

Consequences of Dissatisfied Victims and Witnesses

It often occurs that the victim and witnesses in a criminal case are the only participants who have never been in a courtroom before. Frequently, being served with a **subpoena** is the victim's first indication that he or she will be required to testify, and often the victim is poorly prepared to testify because he or she has little or no knowledge of the actual courtroom environment. In many cases, once the victim leaves the courtroom, he or she has little or no further contact with the prosecutor's office. In addition, plea bargaining often allows the accused to plead guilty to some lesser offense in return for dismissal of some or all of the original charges against him or her. Although this procedure speeds up court processes and relieves the court of some scheduling burdens, it essentially neglects the interests of victims and, from the point of view of the victim, it deprives him or her of the opportunity to see "justice" done. Since the victim is seldom apprised that a plea bargain has been arranged, it is not surprising that many victims fail to understand how offenders are found guilty of both different and lesser charges than those originally and accurately filed. Similarly, victims often fail to understand how sentences resulting from relatively serious charges can be so short or how offenders convicted of such charges can be placed on probation. As a consequence, victims may conclude that cooperation with criminal justice authorities is largely a waste of time; thus, they may fail to cooperate in future cases and/or develop a negative image of the criminal justice network. Considering the fact that roughly 30 percent of all U.S. households are touched by crime each year (about twenty-five million households in 1981, for example), the number of citizens involved as victims is quite large and criminal justice practitioners can ill afford to alienate such large numbers of citizens.[27]

Noncooperation of victims and witnesses, when it indicates a failure of criminal justice practitioners to be responsive to the needs of citizens, then, is a serious problem. According to DuBow and Becker, "If the victim is interested in retribution, he may be frustrated by the imposition of a low sentence without explanation of the reasons for leniency or the opportunity to participate meaningfully in the process of reaching a disposition."[28]

Should the victim of a crime be allowed to intervene in criminal prosecution? "The victim should have the right to participate in hearings before the court on dismissals, guilty pleas, and sentences," according to Goldstein.[29] The President's Task Force on Victims of Crime advocated allowing some input at the sentencing hearing for victims of violent crimes,[30] and the state of California has a Victims' Bill of Rights which allows victims of any crime (or next of kin if the victim is deceased) to attend all sentencing proceedings and to express their views concerning the crime at such hearings. Judges are to consider these views when imposing sentence.[31] While most California judges see no need for such legislation, most prosecutors and the vast majority of victims support it.[32]

Available research indicates that most victims want to be kept informed with respect to the disposition of their cases even though they may not be interested in direct participation in the trial/sentencing process.[33] The network perspective would lead us to anticipate a number of undesirable consequences if victims desire to be informed and heard, and are not. The criminal justice process is typically initiated by a victim reporting an offense. In many instances the process is interrupted (by plea bargaining or case dismissal) without the victim's knowledge. When this fact becomes known to the victim, he or she often feels that justice has not been done, or that initiating criminal proceedings (which victims are encouraged to do by other components of the criminal justice network) is a waste of time. Should such individuals be victimized again, they might well decide not to cooperate in arresting or prosecuting the offender, which makes such arrest and prosecution considerably less likely. Further, they might well share their experiences and views with others who might then be less likely to cooperate with the authorities in pursuing criminal cases. At a minimum, keeping victims informed of the progress of their cases would seem a small price to pay for victim cooperation.

Davis summarizes current concerns for victims and witnesses in the criminal justice network when he states, "Clearly, victims/witnesses should not control outcomes in lower criminal courts. But there is a lot of room to institute some sort of role for victim/witnesses in the decision process between the extremes of allowing them to control outcomes and the complete absence of participation that they are now afforded in most cases in most lower criminal courts."[34]

Summary

Cooperation on behalf of the various publics is essential to the effective performance of criminal justice practitioners. One important aspect of this cooperation involves a willingness on behalf of citizens to testify in court as victims/witnesses. Successful apprehension and prosecution of offenders is extremely difficult without such cooperation on the part of victims/witnesses. Cold, impersonal, or discourteous treatment of victims/witnesses by criminal justice practitioners may result in a lack of cooperation among these individuals in future cases. An unwillingness on behalf of criminal justice officials to explain to victims/witnesses their rights to assistance and/or the procedures involved in official processing of offenders decreases the likelihood that future cooperation will be forthcoming. While too much involvement of victims/witnesses in the official processing of offenders is clearly undesirable (for example, allowing them to have direct input into the amount or type of punishment given the convicted offender), too little involvement has serious negative consequences for the criminal justice network.

In an attempt to insure the rights of victims/witnesses and to encourage future cooperation of victims/witnesses, a number of compensation and restitution programs have been developed and implemented. While the concepts of compensation and restitution are not new in criminal justice, increasing emphasis has been placed on programs based on these concepts in recent years, and a majority of states now have such programs. The extent to which these programs will lead to greater cooperation on behalf of victims/witnesses remains to be seen, but it is clear that they will not result in an acceptable level of cooperation unless they are accompanied by attempts on behalf of criminal justice practitioners to insure victims' rights and to explain to victims/witnesses the procedures involved in dealing with offenders.

Key Terms Defined

victim compensation a payment made by the state to the victim of a crime.
victim restitution a payment made by an offender to his or her victim as the result of a court order.
subpoena a court order that directs the recipient to appear in court.

Discussion Questions

1. Why is cooperation on the part of the various publics as victims/witnesses so important to criminal justice practitioners? Why is such cooperation often lacking? What can be done to improve the level of victim/witness cooperation?

2. Discuss some of the alternative strategies for "making the victim of a crime whole again." What are the basic advantages and disadvantages of each of these strategies?

3. What types of victim/witness assistance programs does your state have? To what extent are they used?

4. How much involvement/control should victims have in the processing of offenders?

Notes

1. F. Cannavale, Institute for Law and Social Research, *Witness Cooperation* (Lexington, Mass.: D. C. Heath, 1976).

2. W. McDonald, "Criminal Justice and the Victim: An Introduction," in *Criminal Justice and the Victim,* ed. W. McDonald (Beverly Hills, Calif.: Sage, 1976), 17–55; A. Schneider, J. Burcart, and L. Wilson, "The Role of Attitudes in the Decision to Report Crimes to the Police," in *Criminal Justice and the Victim,* ed. W. McDonald (Beverly Hills, Calif.: Sage, 1976), 89–113; W. Skogan, "Citizen Reporting of Crime: Some National Panel Data," *Criminology,* 13 (1976):535–49; or D. Koenig, "The Effects of Criminal Victimization and Judicial or Police Contacts on Public Attitudes Toward Local Police," *Journal of Criminal Justice* 8 (1980):243–49.

3. Frank G. Carrington, *Victims* (New Rochelle, N.Y.: Arlington House Publishers, 1975), 4.

4. Robert Reiff, *The Invisible Victim: The Criminal Justice System's Forgotten Responsibility* (New York: Basic Books, 1979), 75.

5. Macklin Fleming, *Of Crimes and Rights* (New York: W. W. Norton and Co., 1978), 33.

6. Carrington, *Victims,* 237.

7. J. L. Barkas, *Victims* (New York: Charles Scribner's Sons, 1978), 5.

8. Reiff, *The Invisible Victim,* 83.

9. Reiff, *The Invisible Victim,* 92.

10. Carrington, *Victims,* 3.

11. Carrington, *Victims,* 4.

12. S. Schafer, *Victimology: The Victim and His Criminal* (New York: Random House, 1968), 112.

13. D. M. Carrow, *Crime Victim Compensation: Program Model* (Washington, D.C.: U.S. Government Printing Office, 1980), 8.

14. Carrow, *Crime Victim Compensation,* 8.

15. D. E. MacNamara and J. J. Sullivan, "Making the Crime Victim Whole: Composition, Restitution, Compensation," in *Images of Crime—Offenders and Victims,* ed. T. Thornberry and E. Sagarin (New York: Praeger, 1974), 81.

16. J. Polish, "Rehabilitation of the Victims of Crime: An Overview," *U.C.L.A. Law Review* (October 1973):329–30.

17. Bennett H. Beach, "Getting Status and Getting Even," *Time Magazine* (7 February 1983):40.

18. Raymond J. Kasak, "State Compensation for Victims of Crime: Public Awareness and Support: A Case Study," (M. A. thesis, Western Illinois University, December 1982).

19. B. Galaway and L. Rutman, "Victim Compensation: An Analysis of Substantive Issues," *Social Service Review* (March 1974):71.

20. Reiff, *The Invisible Victim,* 134.

21. H. Edelhertz and G. Geis, *Public Compensation to Victims of Crime* (New York: Praeger, 1974), 8.

22. Stephen Schafer, *Compensation and Restitution to Victims of Crime,* 2d ed. (Montclair, N.J.: Patterson Smith, 1972), 8.

23. W. McDonald, "Towards a Bicentennial Revolution in Criminal Justice: The Return of the Victim," *American Criminal Law Review* (Spring 1976):655.

24. Edelhertz and Geis, *Public Compensation to Victims of Crime,* 110.

25. Edelhertz and Geis, *Public Compensation to Victims of Crime,* 10.

26. Reiff, *The Invisible Victim,* 114.

27. "30% of U.S. Households Hit by Crime Last Year," *Justice Assistance News* 3, no. 8, (Oct. 1982):5.

28. F. L. DuBow and T. M. Becker, "Patterns of Crime Advocacy," in *Criminal Justice and the Victim,* ed. W. McDonald (Beverly Hills, Calif.: Sage, 1976).

29. Abraham S. Goldstein, "Defining the Role of the Victim in Criminal Prosecution," *Mississippi Law Journal* 52, (1982): 515–18.

30. President's Task Force n Victims of Crime, *Report,* (Washington, D.C.: U.S. Government Printing Office, 1982).

31. Edwin Villmoare and Virginia V. Neto, "Victim Appearances at Sentencing Under California's Victims' Bill of Rights," *Research in Brief,* National Institute of Justice (Washington, D.C.: U.S. Government Printing Office, August 1987).
32. Ibid.
33. Ibid.
34. Robert C. Davis, "Victim/Witness Noncooperation: A Second Look at a Persistent Phenomenon," *Journal of Criminal Justice* 11, no. 4 (1983):287–99.

Suggested Readings

Barkas, J. L. *Victims.* (New York: Charles Scribner's Sons, 1978).

Davis, Robert C. "Victim/Witness Noncooperation: A Second Look at a Persistent Phenomenon." *Journal of Criminal Justice* 11, no. 4 (1983):287–99.

Karmen, Andrew. *Crime Victims: An Introduction to Victimology.* (Monterey, Calif.: Brooks/Cole, 1984).

Koenig, Daniel J. "The Effects of Criminal Victimization and Judicial or Police Contacts on Public Attitudes Toward Local Police." *Journal of Criminal Justice* 8 (1980):243–49.

Norton, Lee. "Witness Involvement in the Criminal Justice System and Intention to Cooperate in Future Prosecutions." *Journal of Criminal Justice* 11, no. 2 (1983):143–52.

Corrections

14

Key Terms

early release
banishment
transportation
age of enlightenment
hedonism
Walnut Street Jail
Pennsylvania prisons
Auburn prisons

retribution
specific deterrence
general deterrence
maximum security facilities
medium security facilities
minimum security facilities
recidivism
total institution
warehousing

At the conclusion of the trial process, a number of sentencing alternatives are available to the judge with respect to the guilty party. Among these are probation and incarceration in jail or prison, the topics of this chapter and the next.

In recent years, considerable media, public, and political attention has been devoted to corrections in response to reports of overcrowding and riots in prisons, and in response to early release programs. Here again, the fact that criminal justice is best viewed as a network is apparent. Funds used to build prisons and jails must be appropriated from the public, and prisoners who are released into society must be reintegrated if rehabilitation is one of our goals. Financial support for alternatives to incarceration also comes from the public. Politicians at all levels (local prosecutors to state governors to the president) have used prison conditions as a political football. In Illinois during hard economic times, for example, several cities were involved in competition for new prisons that were to be built. Some of these cities had lost other state facilities (mental hospitals, for instance), and local and state politicians put pressure on the governor to locate the new prisons in these areas. At the same time, local prosecutors successfully challenged the right of the director of the state department of corrections to grant **early release** to prisoners not eligible for early release in order to alleviate prison overcrowding. On several occasions, the media focused on stories of atrocities committed by offenders who had been released early (while conveniently overlooking the much larger number of offenders on early release who did not commit further offenses); thus, the media helped to shape public opinion against such programs. Finally, prison officials in the United States have been traditionally hampered by our inability to decide precisely what it is we want prisons to accomplish. Currently, we ask prison officials to focus on two perhaps incompatible goals—rehabilitation and custody. In the long run, however, the former depends upon our willingness to accept those who have served time in prison back into society. Rehabilitation is, therefore, to some extent beyond the control of prison authorities. Perhaps a look at the historical development of prisons in the United States will help us understand how some of these problems arose.

Historical Development

Although prisons are now characteristic of corrections, this has not always been the case. Early codes, such as the Code of Hammurabi and the Sumerian Code, supported the doctrine of "an eye for an eye and a tooth for a tooth." With this philosophy as a basis for punishment, sanctions were often swift and severe. Torture and execution were commonplace. The situation improved little under Roman and Greek influence, although changes in the rights of defendants were made during these periods. In the Middle Ages, trial by ordeal, exorcism, and other forms of torture continued. Incarceration was simply a way of holding prisoners until corporal punishment could be administered and was not considered a form of punishment.

Forerunners of incarceration as a form of punishment were banishment and transportation. In some cases, **banishment** (exile) was reserved for the more affluent members of society who were convicted of an offense. The person being banished was pronounced civilly dead and was forced to leave the country. Return meant severe corporal punishment or death. **Transportation** emerged during the sixteenth century and was practiced until the latter part of the nineteenth century. England transported between three hundred and two thousand prisoners to America and Australia annually during this period.[1] Banishment and transportation represented alternatives to corporal and capital punishment, and achieved much the same end as incarceration—the isolation of offenders.

Both the English and the Dutch also developed workhouses. In England, cities or counties were required to construct *bridewells* to house the poor and the convicts, and this practice soon spread to other parts of Europe. Conditions in these workhouses were atrocious, and no attempts were made to segregate inmates by age, sex, or type of offense. Inmates were forced to work long hours, corruption

and violence were common among both guards and inmates, and disease was rampant. Nonetheless, workhouses did represent a slight shift in penal philosophy, with society assuming at least minimal responsibility for separating convicts from other citizens.

The Reform Movement

A major turning point in the history of corrections was reached in the late eighteenth and early nineteenth centuries, often referred to as the **"age of enlightenment."** Efforts by Montesquieu, Voltaire, Beccaria, Bentham, and Howard were instrumental in bringing reform to the harsh penal philosophy that had existed prior to this period. These individuals and others were concerned with human rights and limiting the coercive power of the state.

Montesquieu and Voltaire were both concerned with the harsh punishments inflicted upon French citizens. Montesquieu's treatises called for an end to such treatment, and Voltaire was actively involved in defending and appealing cases for alleged offenders. Voltaire was eventually imprisoned for his activities and then banished from France. The efforts of both Montesquieu and Voltaire had considerable impact on Beccaria, who was the person most responsible for bringing about changes in the inhumane conditions to which convicts were subjected.

Stateville Correctional
Center–A Maximum
Security Facility.
*Illinois Department of
Corrections*

Beccaria anonymously published his famous *Essays on Crimes and Punishments* in 1764, and he is remembered as the individual who directed penal philosophy away from punishment and toward corrections. Beccaria argued that man is basically a rational being who is calculating in his behavior and controlled by the principle of **hedonism**—the desire to seek pleasurable experiences and avoid painful ones. He contended that prevention should be the goal of punishment and that the punishment should fit the crime. He abhorred torture and capital punishment, and advocated more extensive use of fines, imprisonment, and banishment. In addition, he was concerned with individual rights and with providing procedural safeguards in the trial process.[2] His principles influenced many of the penologists of his time and remain an important cornerstone of the corrections movement today.

Other contributors to the correctional reform movement include Jerry Bentham and John Howard. Bentham, an Englishman strongly influenced by Beccaria's work, advocated a system of "hedonistic calculus," which would provide graduated penalties based upon the seriousness of the offense. John Howard was a British sheriff in the latter part of the eighteenth century. He was appalled by conditions in English jails, and he attempted to bring about changes in these conditions. Howard travelled throughout Europe to observe confinement facilities and, in his *State of Prisons* (1777), he conveyed his findings on the inhumane conditions he found everywhere. Partly because of Howard's efforts, Parliament

A Minimum Security Facility. *Illinois Department of Corrections*

passed the "Penitentiary Act" of 1779. This act provided for secure and sanitary structures and systematic inspections, among other things.[3] Howard's ideas spread to continental Europe and the United States, and his legacy lives on in a contemporary reform organization bearing his name.

The American Experience

As noted, America's involvement with corrections stems from the early days when prisoners were transported here from England. The early settlers employed corporal punishment much like that in their home countries. One of the earliest attempts to "humanize" treatment of offenders resulted from the efforts of William Penn and his Quaker followers. Penn formulated the "Great Law," which replaced corporal and capital punishment with imprisonment and hard labor. After Penn's death, the law was repealed and treatment of offenders once again became inhumane. However, his philosophy did not die. After the Revolution, it surfaced again to become an important part of American correctional philosophy. In fact, the reform efforts of the Quakers led the Pennsylvania legislature to declare a section of the Walnut Street Jail as a penitentiary to house convicted felons; thus, the **Walnut Street Jail** became known as the first correctional institution in the United States. While housed in this institution, prisoners were permitted to work and receive wages, and were given religious instruction. Corporal punishment was prohibited and the guards were not permitted to carry weapons. According to Menninger, the Walnut Street Jail was the "birthplace of the prison system, in its present meaning. . . ."[4] Other states adopted versions of the Walnut Street philosophy, and before long these institutions became so overcrowded that a new system was developed.

The Pennsylvania and Auburn Systems As a result of the overcrowding mentioned above, the Pennsylvania legislature was forced to establish new and larger institutions to house prisoners. Two new penitentiaries were established in the 1820s. The architecture of the **Pennsylvania prisons** was unique. They were designed with a central hub and numerous wings radiated from this hub. The design reflected the current attitude toward punishment, which was based upon the premise that prison should be a place in which to do penance (thus, the term penitentiary) and that the best way in which to achieve this end was through solitary confinement. So, each wing of the institution consisted of several cells placed back to back in which inmates worked, ate, slept, and received religious instruction. It was assumed that this arrangement would give each inmate time to contemplate his crimes and repent.

At about the same time, the state of New York was also developing a prison system. The architectural design of the **Auburn system** differed substantially from that of the Pennsylvania system. The original Auburn structure was built in the shape of a U and consisted of five tiers with numerous cells on each tier. In contrast to the Pennsylvania system, prisoners in the Auburn system ate and worked with other inmates.[5] A code of silence was enforced, and strict punishment was administered to those who violated regulations. Most prisoners ate and worked with other prisoners, and were placed in their own cells to sleep. Those convicted of the most serious offenses were confined to their cells, and the notion of solitary confinement as a technique for prison discipline emerged from this procedure.

A debate soon ensued over which system was better. Supporters of the Auburn system claimed their choice was more economical and that the congregation of prisoners best suited reform. Advocates of the Pennsylvania system felt their approach was more efficient and orderly. The Pennsylvania system was adopted by several European countries, while the Auburn system became more popular in the United States and remains the model for most of our prisons today.

Contemporary Corrections

In 1870, the National Prison Association (now called the American Correctional Association) met in Cincinnati to discuss prison reform. The group developed a list of thirty-six principles, which led to the establishment of the first reformatory in the United States at Elmira, New York, under the direction of Z. R. Brockway.

Under Brockway's leadership, educational and vocational programs were developed and instituted. Brockway also advocated individual treatment, indeterminate sentencing, and greater use of parole. Although a number of institutions adopted the name *reformatory,* most did not adopt all of Brockway's principles. Nonetheless, the Elmira experiment was to have an impact on future correctional efforts. Brockway's attempts at reformation and rehabilitation of prisoners were forerunners of similar attempts in contemporary prisons. Numerous changes have occurred in corrections since Elmira, including the addition of professional staff members and greater reliance upon social science research, but the emphasis on rehabilitation instead of punishment remains.

Correctional Objectives

It may be said that correctional officials generally pursue two objectives: punishment and rehabilitation. The emphasis shifts from one of the objectives to the other over time with shifts in public opinion and political leadership. In general, as we have indicated above, rehabilitation has received more attention than punishment in recent years.

From a legal viewpoint, the court identified and discussed four objectives of punishment in the case of *Commonwealth vs. Ritter.*[6] These objectives include revenge or retribution, specific deterrence, general deterrence, and rehabilitation or reformation. A brief look at each of these objectives is in order.

Revenge Revenge, or **retribution** as it is commonly called, is one of the oldest known justifications for punishment. It is based on the philosophy that since the victim has suffered, so must the offender (an eye for an eye). While it is easy to understand why revenge is a motive on the part of victims or their loved ones, how do we determine the severity of the punishment to be inflicted upon the offender, and who should make that determination? Suppose Black is the victim of a hit and run accident. Do we adhere to a philosophy of punishment in kind? What if Black dies? Do we then execute the driver of the vehicle? What is appropriate punishment if Black is paralyzed? If we decide not to execute the offender, how do we determine an appropriate prison sentence? It should be apparent that making the punishment fit the crime is not always an easy task. If we add to the questions above the additional factors of plea bargaining and prison overcrowding, the issue becomes even more complex. While revenge may be an ancient and understandable objective, in a practical sense it is difficult to achieve because punishment does not occur in a vacuum.

Specific Deterrence You may recall from our previous discussion that Beccaria felt that punishment should be severe enough to make the potential offender refrain from engaging in crime. However, not all criminals act in a rational manner (many crimes are committed in the "heat of passion," for example), and some who do apparently use a calculus different from that of most people (as may be the case when an angry husband, knowing that he will be apprehended, batters or murders his wife and her lover). In addition, severity of punishment makes a difference to potential offenders only when they believe there is a reasonable chance they will be apprehended for their crimes. Based upon current clearance rates for most crimes except homicide, the likelihood of detection and apprehension is not particularly great; thus, the proposed punishment, no matter how severe, is unlikely to have any great impact on the potential offender. Further, the effects of **specific deterrence** are very difficult to measure. Would an alternative form of punishment have increased or decreased the likelihood of an offense occurring? Research findings on the effects of punishment as a deterrent are contradictory. Chambliss argues that punishment affects some categories of shoplifters and traffic offenders,[7] but Pittman and Gordon contend that punishment has little or no effect on drug addicts and alcoholics.[8] The commonsense appeal of specific deterrence seems to be the basic justification for retaining it as an objective of punishment.

General Deterrence The basic premise of **general deterrence** is that punishing one offender for his or her offenses will help dissuade other potential offenders from engaging in criminal conduct. Again, there is a kind of commonsense appeal to the concept, but the value of general deterrence has also been challenged. Numerous studies have been conducted in attempts to measure the deterrent effect of the death penalty[9] as well as other forms of punishment.[10] Most have failed to demonstrate a significant relationship between type of punishment administered and the likelihood that others will commit a similar offense. Despite this lack of scientific support for general deterrence, substantial numbers of practitioners, politicians, and citizens continue to clamor for a "get tough" approach to punishment. While any given type of punishment may deter certain individuals from engaging in acts that might lead to such punishment, we currently have too little knowledge of the exact nature of this relationship to determine how best to reach those who are most likely to commit offenses.[11]

Rehabilitation The basic assumption underlying rehabilitation as a correctional objective is that behavior can be modified if only we know enough about the prior history of the individual involved (and about the causes of the undesirable criminal behavior). For the most part, programs aimed at rehabilitating offenders concentrate on attempting to discover the causes of the aberrant behavior in order to eliminate or modify the behavior through some form of therapy. Thus, a person identified as committing utilitarian burglary as a result of being a high school dropout and having no vocational skills might be placed in educational and vocational training programs that could provide skills necessary to secure and retain reasonable employment to eliminate the need to commit burglaries. Some segments of the public view rehabilitation programs as catering to criminals and as alternatives that are too lenient. Others have argued that psychological treatment programs reduce inmates to "experimental animals."[12]

Armed man robs prison inmate

POMPANO BEACH, Fla. (AP)— A gunman entered a prison dormitory cell and robbed an inmate serving an armed-robbery sentence, making off with a stereo, radio, TV and other items, officials said Monday.

The inmate and his roommate, who also was robbed, were not injured, prison officials said.

"The whole inmate population is still in shock," said Barry Ahringer, superintendent of the Pompano Beach Community Correctional Center, a minimum-security prison where the holdup occurred.

"If you're not safe in prison from armed robbery, where are you safe?" he said.

Ahringer identified the victims as inmates Roy Whaley, 42, of Columbus, Ohio, who was serving time for armed robbery, and Mark Bukwitz, 22, of Fort Lauderdale, convicted of a weapons charge.

Whaley was sitting on the floor of his room at about 11 p.m. Friday, Ahringer said, when a gunman walked in and announced the robbery while another man stood watch at the door.

The minimum-security facility, which provides a work-release program to its 140 inmates, has no bars, no barbed wire and no armed guards.

Reprinted by permission of Associated Press

One other, perhaps more general, objective of corrections should be mentioned. Traditionally, prisons have been viewed as institutions in which prisoners are isolated or *incapacitated* (prevented from committing further crimes). This is the custodial as opposed to the rehabilitative function of correctional authorities, and the contradiction between these two objectives accounts for many of the problems surrounding imprisonment today. Two major problems with the concept of incapacitation are the failure to consider crimes committed by one inmate against another as "further crimes" (and thousands of these are committed annually) and the fact that incapacitation is temporary, since most inmates will eventually be released whether or not they have been rehabilitated.

Capital Punishment: Timeless Controversy, Ultimate Penalty

No issue in criminal justice has generated as much debate as capital punishment. Capital punishment is the ultimate sanction, the most symbolic reminder of the state's power to punish its citizens. Although the practice is perhaps as old as human life, it has been particularly controversial in the past three hundred years, and the debate has been revived in the past quarter of a century as a result of several heinous and/or spectacular crimes.

When John Hinckley was found not guilty by reason of insanity of attempting to kill President Ronald Reagan, a new wave of concern for criminal justice reform was generated. This concern focuses on "getting tougher" with criminals by limiting or abolishing the insanity defense, imposing longer prison terms, limiting or abolishing parole, and, ultimately, by making criminals "pay" for their crimes with their lives. Heinous crimes, such as the murder of Sharon Tate by the Charles Manson "family" or the killing of eight student nurses by Richard Speck, often lead to a public outcry, which usually includes a call for increased use of the death penalty. While the details of such crimes may invoke an angry reaction in most of us, the question of whether such offenses justify the ultimate penalty is not easy to resolve.

In 1972, the United States Supreme Court, in the case of *Furman v. Georgia,*[13] held that capital punishment, as it was being used, was discriminatory and, therefore, unconstitutional. The court did not rule on the issue of whether capital punishment violated the Eighth Amendment's ban on cruel and unusual punishment. The response to *Furman* was clear-cut. Thirty-eight states passed new legislation concerning the death penalty. Some of this legislation met with the Supreme Court's approval,[14] and about sixty executions have occurred since.

Why has the country with some of the most severe penalties in the civilized world been reluctant to impose the death penalty? If citizens and legislatures approve of capital punishment and the courts accept the practice, why has America averaged fewer than six executions per year in the past eleven years? In order to answer this question, let us examine the history of capital punishment, the argument for retaining or abolishing the death penalty, and the legal guidelines governing its use.

A Brief History of Capital Punishment Capital punishment, an execution in the name of the state, is one of the most ancient forms of punishment. Early legal codes, such as those of Hammurabi, the Greeks, and the Romans, provided for the death penalty upon conviction for a wide range of offenses.[15] In more recent times, the practice of banishment was sometimes equivalent to capital punishment. Convicted offenders were forced into the wilderness with very little chance of survival.

Although records are not totally reliable, it is speculated that Henry VIII had as many as seventy-two thousand people executed during his reign. In the 1500s, the British executed convicted offenders for eight offenses: murder, robbery, rape, burglary, larceny, arson, treason, and petty treason. The popularity of the punishment peaked in the 1600s, subsided in the 1700s, and reemerged in the 1800s. Some historians estimate that the British considered as many as two or three hundred offenses "capital offenses" during this second peak. Offenses such as shoplifting, cutting down trees, and sacrilege were sometimes accorded capital status.[16] While the practice was not common, young children and women were occasionally executed during this period. By the 1840s, England had reduced the number of capital offenses to about twenty; and in 1965, England joined many other European nations (Netherlands, 1886; Sweden, 1921; Italy, 1944; and West Germany, 1949) in abolishing the death penalty.

Early colonial codes provided for execution of those convicted of rape, man-stealing, witchcraft, adultery, and other offenses, but the use of capital punishment was more restricted than in England. It appears that the framers of the Constitution accepted capital punishment as legitimate, and every state permitted the practice at the time the Constitution was ratified.

Beccaria's penal reform philosophy included a stand against the death penalty, and Americans Benjamin Rush and Edward Livingston were influenced by this abolitionist stance. Pennsylvania abolished capital punishment for all crimes except first degree murder in 1794, and in 1834, it became the first state to ban public executions. Michigan was the first state to abolish the death penalty in 1846, and by 1918, eleven other states had followed course. In the 1930s and 1940s, some states reinstated the death penalty. The last public execution occurred in Kentucky in 1936. The number of executions declined in the 1960s (table 14.1) and, in 1967, a moratorium was declared on capital punishment. A decade later, Gary Gilmore was executed by firing squad. He was the first of several offenders to receive the ultimate punishment in the past twelve years. As indicated before, thirty-eight states currently have the death penalty, and there are over twelve hundred prisoners on death rows in the United States. Still, the controversy between those wishing to abolish the death penalty and those wishing to retain it rages on.

Death Penalty Arguments There are basically five issues involved in the controversy surrounding capital punishment:

1. Does capital punishment violate constitutional protections against cruel and unusual punishment?
2. Is capital punishment economical?
3. What is the likelihood that an innocent person will be executed?
4. Does it meet the objectives of punishment previously stated?
5. Is it supported by the public?

The Eighth Amendment to the Constitution prohibits the use of cruel and unusual punishment. Is capital punishment cruel and unusual? In the *Furman* decision, the Court held that the death penalty was being administered in discriminatory fashion, with two of the justices (Marshall and Brennan) indicating that they believe capital punishment is also cruel and unusual. In *Gregg v. Georgia*, the issue of cruel and unusual punishment was addressed directly and the court held that the death penalty does not "invariably violate the constitution."[17]

Table 14.1 Prisoners executed under civil authority by region and jurisdiction, 1930–85 (– represents zero)

Region and jurisdiction	Total	1930 to 1934	1935 to 1939	1940 to 1944	1945 to 1949	1950 to 1954	1955 to 1959	1960 to 1964	1965 to 1969	1970 to 1974	1975	1976	1977	1978	1979	1980	1981	1982	1983	1984	1985
United States	3,909	776	891	645	639	413	304	181	10	–	–	–	1	–	2	–	1	2	5	21	18
Federal	33	1	9	7	6	6	3	1	–	–	–	–	–	–	–	–	–	–	–	–	–
State	3,876	775	882	638	633	407	301	180	10	–	–	–	1	–	2	–	1	2	5	21	18
Northeast	608	155	145	110	74	56	51	17	–	–	–	–	–	–	–	–	–	–	–	–	–
Connecticut	21	2	3	5	5	–	5	1	–	–	–	–	–	–	–	–	–	–	–	–	–
Maine	X	X	X	X	X	X	X	X	X	X	X	X	X	X	X	X	X	X	X	X	X
Massachusetts	27	7	11	6	3	–	–	–	–	–	–	–	–	–	–	–	–	–	–	–	–
New Hampshire	1	–	1	–	–	–	–	–	–	–	–	–	–	–	–	–	–	–	–	–	–
New Jersey	74	24	16	6	8	8	9	3	–	–	–	–	–	–	–	–	–	–	–	–	–
New York	329	80	73	78	36	27	25	10	–	–	X	X	X	X	X	X	X	X	X	X	X
Pennsylvania	152	41	41	15	21	19	12	3	–	–	–	–	–	–	–	–	–	–	–	–	–
Rhode Island	–	–	–	–	–	–	–	–	–	–	–	–	–	–	–	–	–	–	–	–	–
Vermont	4	1	–	–	1	2	–	–	–	–	–	–	–	–	–	–	–	–	–	–	–
Midwest	405	105	113	42	64	42	16	16	5	–	–	–	–	–	–	–	1	–	–	–	–
Illinois	90	34	27	13	5	8	1	2	–	–	–	–	–	–	–	–	–	–	–	–	–
Indiana	43	11	20	2	5	2	–	1	–	–	–	–	–	–	–	–	1	–	–	–	–
Iowa	18	1	7	3	4	1	–	2	X	X	X	X	X	X	X	X	X	X	X	X	X
Kansas	15	X	–	–	2	5	–	1	4	X	X	X	X	X	X	X	X	X	X	X	X
Michigan	X	X	X	X	X	X	X	X	X	X	X	X	X	X	X	X	X	X	X	X	X
Minnesota	X	X	X	X	X	X	X	X	X	X	X	X	X	X	X	X	X	X	X	X	X
Missouri	62	16	20	6	9	5	2	3	1	–	X	X	X	X	X	X	X	X	X	X	X
Nebraska	4	–	–	–	2	1	1	–	–	–	–	–	–	–	–	–	–	–	–	–	–
North Dakota	X	X	X	X	X	X	X	X	X	X	X	X	X	X	X	X	X	X	X	X	X
Ohio	172	43	39	15	36	20	12	7	–	–	–	–	–	–	–	–	–	–	–	–	–
South Dakota	1	X	–	1	–	–	–	–	–	X	X	X	X	X	X	X	X	X	X	X	X
Wisconsin	X	X	X	X	X	X	X	X	X	X	X	X	X	X	X	X	X	X	X	X	X

South	2,351	419	524	413	419	244	183	102	2	—	—	—	—	—	1	—	—	2	5	21	16
Alabama	136	19	41	29	21	14	6	4	1	—	—	—	—	—	—	—	—	—	1	—	—
Arkansas	118	20	33	20	18	11	7	9	—	—	—	—	—	—	—	—	—	—	—	—	—
Delaware	12	2	6	2	2	—	—	—	—	—	—	—	—	—	—	—	—	—	—	—	—
District of Columbia	40	15	5	3	13	3	1	—	—	—	—	—	—	—	—	—	—	—	—	—	—
Florida	183	15	29	38	27	22	27	12	—	X	X	X	X	X	1	X	X	X	1	8	3
Georgia	372	64	73	58	72	51	34	14	—	X	X	X	X	X	—	X	X	X	—	2	3
Kentucky	103	18	34	19	15	8	8	1	—	X	X	X	X	X	—	X	X	X	—	2	—
Louisiana	140	39	19	24	23	14	13	1	—	X	X	X	X	X	—	X	X	X	1	5	1
Maryland	68	6	10	26	19	2	4	1	—	X	—	X	X	X	—	X	X	—	—	—	—
Mississippi	155	26	22	34	26	15	21	10	—	X	X	X	X	X	—	X	X	X	1	—	1
North Carolina	265	51	80	50	62	14	5	1	—	X	X	X	X	X	—	X	X	X	—	2	—
Oklahoma	60	25	9	6	7	4	3	5	1	X	X	X	X	X	—	X	X	X	—	—	—
South Carolina	163	37	30	32	29	16	10	8	—	X	X	X	X	X	—	X	X	X	—	—	1
Tennessee	93	16	31	19	18	1	7	1	—	X	X	X	X	X	—	X	X	X	—	—	—
Texas	307	48	72	38	36	49	25	29	—	X	X	X	X	X	—	X	X	X	1	3	6
Virginia	96	8	20	13	22	15	8	6	—	X	X	X	X	X	1	X	X	X	—	1	2
West Virginia	40	10	10	2	9	5	4	—	X	X	X	X	X	X	X	X	X	X	X	X	X
West	512	96	100	73	76	65	51	45	3	1	X	1	1	1	1	X	X	X	X	X	1
Alaska[a]	X	X	X	X	X	X	X	X	X	X	X	X	X	X	X	X	X	X	X	X	X
Arizona	38	7	10	6	3	2	6	4	—	X	X	X	X	X	—	X	X	X	—	—	—
California	292	51	57	35	45	39	35	29	1	X	X	X	X	X	—	X	X	X	—	—	—
Colorado	47	16	9	6	7	1	2	5	—	X	—	X	X	X	—	X	X	X	—	—	—
Hawaii[a]	X	X	X	X	X	X	X	X	X	X	X	X	X	X	X	X	X	X	X	X	X
Idaho	3	—	—	—	—	2	1	—	—	X	X	X	X	X	1	X	X	X	—	—	—
Montana	6	1	4	1	—	—	—	—	—	—	—	—	—	—	—	—	—	—	—	—	—
Nevada	31	5	3	5	5	9	—	2	—	X	—	X	X	X	1	X	X	X	—	1	—
New Mexico	8	2	—	—	2	2	1	—	—	X	—	X	X	X	—	X	X	X	—	—	—
Oregon	19	1	1	6	6	4	—	—	X	—	X	—	X	X	—	X	X	X	—	—	—
Utah	14	—	2	3	1	2	4	1	—	X	—	1	—	X	—	X	X	X	1	—	—
Washington	47	10	13	9	7	4	2	2	—	X	X	X	X	X	—	X	X	X	—	—	—
Wyoming	7	3	1	2	—	—	—	—	—	—	—	—	—	—	—	—	—	—	—	—	—

Note: In three states, Maine, Minnesota, and Wisconsin, the death penalty was abolished for the entire period covered by the table. Alaska and Hawaii have not had the death penalty since 1960, when they were first included as states. The death penalty was abolished in Michigan in 1963 and in Iowa and West Virginia in 1965. Death penalty legislation expired in 1975 in North Dakota and was not renewed. Death penalty laws were found unconstitutional in Kansas (1973), the District of Columbia (1973), Rhode Island (1979), and New York (1984) and have not been rewritten. In South Dakota, the death penalty was abolished in 1915, restored in 1939, abolished again in 1977, and restored in 1979. Oregon abolished the death penalty in 1914, restored it in 1920, abolished it again in 1964, restored it in 1978, and it was found to be unconstitutional in 1981. Massachusetts abolished the death penalty in 1980, restored it in 1982, and it was found unconstitutional in 1984. In California, the death penalty was found to be partially unconstituional in 1984. In the following states death penalty laws were found unconstitutional but have been revised to meet constitutional standards: Colorado, Delaware, Illinois, Indiana, Kentucky, Maryland, Missouri, New Hampshire, New Jersey, New Mexico, North Carolina, Ohio, Oklahoma, Pennsylvania, Tennessee, and Washington.

[a]As states, Alaska and Hawaii are included in the series beginning Jan. 1, 1960.

Source: Table adapted by SOURCEBOOK staff from table provided by the U.S. Department of Justice, Bureau of Justice Statistics.

Table 14.2 Prisoners executed under civil authority by race and offense, United States, 1930–85 (– represents zero)

Year	Total				White				Black				Other			
	Total	Murder	Rape	Other offenses[a]	Total	Murder	Rape	Other offenses[a]	Total	Murder	Rape	Other offenses[a]	Total	Murder	Rape	Other offenses[a]
1930–85	3,909	3,384	455	70	1,784	1,697	48	39	2,083	1,647	405	31	42	40	2	–
1985	18	18	–	–	11	11	–	–	7	7	–	–	–	–	–	–
1984	21	21	–	–	13	13	–	–	8	8	–	–	–	–	–	–
1983	5	5	–	–	4	4	–	–	1	1	–	–	–	–	–	–
1982	2	2	–	–	1	1	–	–	1	1	–	–	–	–	–	–
1981	1	1	–	–	1	1	–	–	–	–	–	–	–	–	–	–
1980	–	–	–	–	–	–	–	–	–	–	–	–	–	–	–	–
1979	2	2	–	–	2	2	–	–	–	–	–	–	–	–	–	–
1978	–	–	–	–	–	–	–	–	–	–	–	–	–	–	–	–
1977	1	1	–	–	1	1	–	–	–	–	–	–	–	–	–	–
1976	–	–	–	–	–	–	–	–	–	–	–	–	–	–	–	–
1975	–	–	–	–	–	–	–	–	–	–	–	–	–	–	–	–
1974	–	–	–	–	–	–	–	–	–	–	–	–	–	–	–	–
1973	–	–	–	–	–	–	–	–	–	–	–	–	–	–	–	–
1972	–	–	–	–	–	–	–	–	–	–	–	–	–	–	–	–
1971	–	–	–	–	–	–	–	–	–	–	–	–	–	–	–	–
1970	–	–	–	–	–	–	–	–	–	–	–	–	–	–	–	–
1969	–	–	–	–	–	–	–	–	–	–	–	–	–	–	–	–
1968	–	–	–	–	–	–	–	–	–	–	–	–	–	–	–	–
1967	2	2	–	–	1	1	–	–	1	1	–	–	–	–	–	–
1966	1	1	–	–	1	1	–	–	–	–	–	–	–	–	–	–
1965	7	7	–	–	6	6	–	–	1	1	–	–	–	–	–	–
1964	15	9	6	–	8	5	3	–	7	4	3	–	–	–	–	–
1963	21	18	2	1	13	12	–	1	8	6	2	–	–	–	–	–
1962	47	41	4	2	28	26	2	–	19	15	2	2	–	–	–	–
1961	42	33	8	1	20	18	1	1	22	15	7	–	–	–	–	–
1960	56	44	8	4	21	18	–	3	35	26	8	1	–	–	–	–

Year																
1959	49	41	8	—	16	15	1	—	33	26	7	—	—	—	—	—
1958	49	41	7	1	20	20	—	—	28	20	7	1	1	1	—	—
1957	65	54	10	1	34	32	2	—	31	22	8	—	—	—	—	—
1956	65	52	12	1	21	20	—	1	43	31	12	1	1	1	—	—
1955	76	65	7	4	44	41	1	2	32	24	6	—	—	—	—	—
1954	81	71	9	—	38	37	1	—	42	33	8	2	—	1	—	—
1953	62	51	7	4	30	25	1	4	31	25	6	1	—	—	—	—
1952	83	71	12	—	36	35	1	—	47	36	11	—	—	—	—	—
1951	105	87	17	1	57	55	2	—	47	31	15	—	1	1	—	—
1950	82	68	13	1	40	36	4	—	42	32	9	1	—	—	—	—
1949	119	107	10	2	50	49	—	1	67	56	10	1	2	2	—	—
1948	119	95	22	2	35	32	1	2	82	61	21	—	2	2	—	—
1947	153	129	23	1	42	40	2	—	111	89	21	—	—	—	—	—
1946	131	107	22	2	46	45	—	1	84	61	22	1	1	1	—	—
1945	117	90	26	1	41	37	4	—	75	52	22	—	—	—	—	—
1944	120	96	24	—	47	45	2	—	70	48	22	—	3	3	—	2
1943	131	118	13	—	54	54	—	—	74	63	11	—	3	3	—	—
1942	147	115	25	7	67	57	4	6	80	58	21	—	1	1	—	—
1941	123	102	20	1	59	55	4	—	63	46	16	—	1	1	—	—
1940	124	105	15	4	49	44	2	3	75	61	13	1	—	—	—	—
1939	160	145	12	3	80	79	—	1	77	63	12	2	3	3	—	—
1938	190	154	25	11	96	89	1	6	92	63	24	5	2	2	—	—
1937	147	133	13	1	69	67	2	—	74	62	11	—	4	4	—	—
1936	195	181	10	4	92	86	2	4	101	93	8	—	2	2	—	—
1935	199	184	13	2	119	115	2	2	77	66	11	—	3	3	—	—
1934	168	154	14	—	65	64	1	—	102	89	13	—	1	1	—	—
1933	160	151	7	2	77	75	1	—	81	74	6	1	2	2	—	—
1932	140	128	10	2	62	62	—	—	75	63	10	—	3	3	—	—
1931	153	137	15	1	77	76	1	—	72	57	14	2	3	3	—	—
1930	155	147	6	2	90	90	—	—	65	57	6	2	—	—	—	—

aIncludes 25 executed for armed robbery, 20 for kidnaping, 11 for burglary, 6 for sabotage, 6 for aggravated assault, and 2 for espionage.

Source: Table adapted by SOURCEBOOK staff from table provided by the U.S. Department of Justice, Bureau of Justice Statistics.

In discussing the relationship between the Eighth Amendment and the death penalty, we must keep in mind that cruelty and unusualness are two distinct issues. Both of these issues have been brought before the courts on numerous occasions. In *Wilkerson v. Utah*,[18] the court held that mandatory public execution of persons who committed premeditated murder was not cruel. Later, when the electric chair was introduced, the court rejected a claim that it was unusual punishment because it had never been used before. In *Weems v. United States*,[19] the court struck down a sentence to "painful labor" because it was excessive (cruel). Historically, it appears, the courts have interpreted the Eighth Amendment to mean a ban on torture or other clearly inhumane treatment. Currently, there are those who are claiming that capital punishment is unusual in light of the fact that there have been very few executions since 1967. An additional argument contends that capital punishment is administered in a cruel and unusual fashion because most of those executed are black (90 percent between the years 1930 and 1980). Bowers examined the characteristics of those executed as far back as the turn of this century and concluded that blacks have been executed for less serious crimes than whites and that many blacks were executed without appeals.[20]

Given the current cost of incarceration (in the neighborhood of twenty thousand dollars per year) and the fact that a large number of offenders are sentenced to life terms, many contend that capital punishment should be employed to save money if for no other reason.[21] However, capital punishment does not occur immediately following sentencing. Lengthy and costly appeals are involved, and taxpayers bear the burden of these expenses, thereby reducing whatever cost benefits may be related to capital punishment.

Defendants in our criminal justice network are, theoretically at least, innocent until proven guilty. It has been said that we would rather allow one hundred guilty parties to go free than to convict one innocent person. Still, mistakes are possible and occasionally we find that a person who has been incarcerated for a crime did not in fact commit the crime. As might be expected, a major argument against the death penalty is that it is irreversible.

Among the most heated debates concerning the death penalty are those concerning whether or not it achieves the objectives of punishment. Clearly, it precludes the possibility of rehabilitation. Equally clearly, it deters the person executed from further crimes. It also satisfies the revenge motive. But, does it deter other potential offenders? Sellin, reviewing the effects of the death penalty, concludes that its abolition does not significantly jeopardize the lives of police officers, correctional personnel, or prison inmates.[22] Bailey, reviewing numerous studies of the death penalty, found no support for the deterrence hypothesis and, in fact, found that in some states that had abolished the death penalty and later reinstated it, homicides actually increased in numbers.[23] However, Phillips concluded from his recent study of selected, highly publicized executions in London that they lowered the weekly homicide rate.[24] Zeisel, however, criticizes Phillip's conclusions, noting that weekly homicide rates rose again two or three weeks later.[25]

In spite of considerable evidence to the contrary, the American public appears to believe that executions do deter criminals. Public opinion polls have consistently shown that the public favors the death penalty, and recent polls indicate that about 70 percent of the American public supports capital punishment. But, opinion polls are just one measure of the public conscience. Some abolitionists argue that prospective jurors may attempt to avoid jury duty in capital cases. It is quite easy to support the death penalty when one is not directly involved or when one is seeking revenge, but when one must bear the responsibility for assigning the penalty, his or her attitude may be quite different.

Recent Court Decisions and the Death Penalty As we have noted, there have been several important court cases concerning the death penalty. The effect of *Furman* was to invalidate many existing death penalty statutes and to force legislators to develop more objective criteria while eliminating discrimination. The decision mandated that objective criteria and specialized procedures be incorporated into all future death penalty legislation. Of the thirty-eight states that enacted new death penalty measures following *Furman,* Georgia was the first to have the new statutes tested in the courts. Favorable rulings in *Gregg v. Georgia,*[26] *Proffit v. Florida,*[27] and *Jurek v. Texas*[28] facilitated the reinstatement of capital punishment. At the same time, however, the Supreme Court has ruled that mandatory death sentences for rape[29] and murder[30] constitute cruel and unusual punishment. More recently, the court has expedited appeal procedures by allowing death penalty appeals to take precedence on federal dockets,[31] thereby eliminating the lengthy delays death row inmates have traditionally obtained by appealing their sentences to the Supreme Court. Clearly, capital punishment procedures are still being molded by both the states and the courts.

Correctional Organization

Although we commonly use the term "American correctional system," this is a misnomer. Correctional programs in America are actually far more fragmented than unified. There are currently more than five thousand correctional facilities and about twenty-five hundred probation and parole agencies in the United States. There is no central authority controlling these agencies and, to some extent, they pursue different and sometimes conflicting goals.

As is the case with the courts, both the federal government and the states maintain correctional systems. Lack of centralized control is one of the major obstacles to reform, since most jurisdictions provide for autonomy of jails and prisons, which are further segmented by sex, age, and type of offense involved. Similarly, probation, parole, and diversionary programs are also largely autonomous.

The Federal Network Congress established the Bureau of Prisons in 1930. The legislation that established the federal network resulted from serious over-crowding of existing facilities and the associated practice of "leasing" space from local and state facilities. Currently, the federal network has been divided into five regions with headquarters in the following cities: Burlingame, Calif.; Kansas City, Mo.; Dallas, Tx.; Atlanta, Ga.; and Philadelphia, Pa. Heads of thirty-seven institutions and fifteen community facilities report to regional directors who are in turn responsible to the director of the Federal Bureau of Prisons. The Bureau of Prisons has five subdivisions: Correctional Programs, Planning and Development, Medical and Service, Federal Prison Industries, Inc., and the National Institute of Corrections. Each subdivision is responsible for developing and implementing programs that are national in scope, but the daily administration of these programs is left to regional and institutional directors.

Federal institutions vary considerably in size. Those in Atlanta, Georgia, and Leavenworth, Kansas, are quite large, with populations of about two thousand inmates each, and are reserved for more hardened inmates. The facility in Marion, Illinois, is smaller and houses dangerous and violent offenders. The smaller prison in Terre Haute, Indiana, was designed to house inmates thought to have considerable potential for rehabilitation. The present inmate population of the federal prisons is about thirty six thousand, with about nineteen hundred of these being females.

New federal institutions have recently been built in San Diego, New York City, and Chicago. These "metropolitan correctional centers" are designed to house federal offenders serving short sentences and pretrial detainees. Built near federal courts, these new high-rise institutions stand in sharp contrast to older prisons, with unbreakable glass replacing bars, and dormitory or private rooms as opposed to cells.

Through the National Institute of Corrections, the Federal Bureau of Prisons provides assistance to state and local networks through grants, by conducting research, by disseminating research materials, and by conducting training seminars.

State Networks The bulk of the corrections network is located at the state level. There are over seven hundred state correctional facilities for adults, housing over 382,000 inmates.[32] These figures do not include inmates housed in jail and short-term detention facilities. While some states have only one or two correctional facilities, more heavily populated states such as Texas, California, and Illinois have ten or more facilities.

Originally, many prisons were constructed near large urban/industrial areas, and industry made use of the cheap labor available. When this "contract system" was abolished, prison officials were faced with the task of "making work" for inmates. This work often consisted of menial tasks invented solely for the purpose of keeping the inmates occupied.

In rural areas, prison farms were built. The stated intent of these farms was to use prison labor to produce agricultural products; thus, to increase the economic feasibility of the institutions, but abuses occurred and prisoners were leased to farmers as a source of cheap labor. This practice was eventually abolished and, with the advent of mechanized farming, prison officials found it more profitable to lease prison lands to farmers than to force prisoners to tend the land.

A 1973 report by a National Advisory Commission made the following observations with respect to state prison systems:

> All but four states have highly fragmented correctional systems, vesting various correctional responsibilities in either independent boards or noncorrectional agencies. In forty-one states, an assortment of health, welfare, and youth agencies exercise certain correctional responsibilities, though their primary function is not corrections.
>
> In over forty states, neither state nor local governments have full-scale responsibility for comprehensive correctional services. Some corrections services, particularly parole and adult and juvenile institutions, are administered by state agencies, while others, such as probation, local institutions and jails, and juvenile detention are county or city responsibilities.
>
> More than half of the states provide no standard-setting or inspection services to local jails or local adult correctional institutions.[33]

It is not difficult to understand, given the conditions described above, why reform in corrections has been so slow.

Types of Institutions

A major problem with correctional facilities concerns the opportunity they provide for inmates to become more antisocial as a result of their exposure to more hardened offenders. In an attempt to deal with this problem, most jurisdictions have developed classification systems based upon the amount of security required for inmates. Most commonly, prisons are divided into maximum, medium, and minimum security categories.

Maximum Security Facilities

Maximum security prisons most closely reflect the goals of revenge and incapacitation. They are generally characterized by high concrete walls that are typically occupied by armed guards and equipped with floodlights. These institutions are generally reserved for dangerous offenders and those serving long sentences. There are currently one hundred fifty-three maximum security facilities in the United States housing 44 percent of the incarcerated adult offenders. Because of the emphasis on custody, rehabilitation programs are often present in name only in such institutions.

Medium Security Facilities

Medium security facilities have become more popular over the years in the United States. There are now over two hundred twenty-five medium security prisons in existence, and the trend is toward replacing maximum security facilities with medium security institutions. These prisons are usually smaller in size than maximum security and they also house about 44 percent of the nation's prison population. Physically, they often resemble their maximum security counterparts, but they generally provide for more freedom of movement internally. These institutions house younger and less dangerous offenders and place more emphasis on rehabilitation than maximum security facilities.

Minimum Security Facilities

Minimum security facilities house nonviolent and nontraditional offenders, for the most part. They are characterized by dormitory-style living, private rooms, and the absence of armed guards and walls. Most have been built relatively recently in comparison to maximum and medium security facilities, and they generally house fewer inmates than either of the other two types. As a result, the one hundred eighty-two minimum security facilities in the United States house only about 12 percent of the prison population. Work and educational release are integral parts of minimum security programs, and home furlough is also used frequently. These facilities have been criticized as country clubs for white-collar and political offenders, but are thought to provide better opportunities for rehabilitation than other types of prisons because they tend to maximize contact between inmates and the outside world in which they must survive after release from prison.[34]

Jails

In terms of sheer numbers, jails are one of the most important features of the correctional network. There are approximately three thousand three hundred jails in the United States currently housing about 220,000 inmates, about 50 percent of whom have not been convicted of an offense.[35] Jails are usually the first, and sometimes the only, contact offenders have with corrections. Although jails have often been ignored by those interested in corrections, recent criticisms of the deplorable conditions existing in many of these facilities have increased their visibility somewhat.

Man, 96, sent to jail

NEW YORK (AP)—A man who claims to be 96 years old and who has a criminal record dating back to 1929 was sentenced Wednesday to six months in jail after pleading guilty to trying to swindle at least seven women.

State Supreme Court Justice Michael Curci called James Barnes "a flim-flam man" and gave him six months in jail and five years probation.

Barnes pleaded guilty on Feb. 21 to grand larceny, attempted grand larceny and fraudulent accosting.

Probation department caseworkers were unable to verify Barnes' claim that he was born in Chicago in 1887, but they found records that show he has been arrested at least 34 times, the first

in Manhattan on Aug. 19, 1929, for burglary.

He has been in prison numerous times, including a 10–year sentence for murder that he began in 1943 in Pennsylvania.

Barnes was arrested last July after police said he accosted at least seven women on Brooklyn streets and offered them a chance to get rich. He flashed a wad of money, which actually consisted of cut paper with fake currency on top, and offered to split it with them. But first he asked for a deposit to prove their sincerity.

Five of the women gave him a total of $8,000, police said.

Reprinted by permission of Associated Press

History of Jails

Earlier we noted that pretrial detention existed in Europe in the sixteenth century. Flynn describes these early detention facilities as pits, suspended cages, dungeons, and other barbaric forms of incarceration.[36] These facilities were basically holding tanks rather than correctional institutions. As indicated earlier, the Walnut Street Jail was the first institution in America to be used for correctional purposes. Although Fishman documented the poor conditions existing in American jails in 1923, little public attention was devoted to them until 1970, when the first national jail census was conducted.[37]

Control and Organization Jails have been very difficult to reform because they are normally financed and administered at the local or county level. This local autonomy has allowed jails to escape many state and federal reform movements and frequently involves jails in local politics. They have been traditionally low-priority items in county budgets, and they are generally under the direct supervision of the sheriff, an elected official subject to political pressures, which is important because local constituents seldom consider jails the most desirable place to expend funds. In addition, the sheriff is both a law enforcement official and the chief correctional officer in the county, and law enforcement duties have been traditionally considered more important than jail supervision. Jail staffs frequently have little or no correctional training and are generally not well paid. Further, inmate–staff ratios of forty to one are not uncommon in jails. With little supervision, inadequate staff, and high inmate–staff ratios, it is not difficult to see why jails contribute little to correctional efforts.

Jail Problems Beginning with the first jail census, investigations have consistently shown that jail populations are basically male, under thirty years of age, under or unemployed, below the poverty level, and disproportionately from minority groups. Jails are institutions in which the powerless are housed until the time of their trial, until they have served their sentences, or until the charges against them are dropped before going to trial.

In 1975, Goldfarb referred to the jail as "the ultimate ghetto."[38] While this label may sound extreme, many who have studied American jails agree wholeheartedly. Many of these institutions are antiquated, with 25 percent having been constructed more than fifty years ago, and another 6 percent more than one hundred years ago. There are, to be sure, some modern jails, but these are the exception rather than the rule. Because of the bad state of repair, jails have been plagued by fires. In 1982, a jail fire in Biloxi, Mississippi, killed twenty-nine inmates, while another fire in Jersey City, New Jersey, resulted in seven deaths.[39] Many of the older structures are without emergency exits, do not have fire extinguishers that are in working order, and have antiquated locking systems so that inmates are virtually doomed if fire breaks out. Heating, ventilation, and lighting are also problems in many jails, as is outdated or inoperative plumbing.

Despite regulations, convicted offenders are frequently not segregated from pretrial detainees, and juveniles are frequently placed in cellblocks with adults. Many jails also house drunks and vagrants on a short-term basis. As a result of inadequate funding, constant turnover, and the lack of authority to require pretrial detainees (who after all have not been convicted of any offense) to participate, treatment programs are virtually nonexistent in most jails.

Health problems are also common in jail settings. Poor or poorly prepared food characterizes most such institutions. Research conducted by the American Correctional Association found hepatitis, tuberculosis, and syphillis to be far from rare in jails, and fewer than 20 percent of those in charge of jails held daily sick call. Under these conditions, common colds and viruses can become serious health problems.[40]

Some efforts to improve jail conditions have been made. Some states have established new and stricter standards for local jails, but follow-up inspections may or may not be mandated and carried out. Inmates have also sought redress through the courts,[41] and, in at least one instance, a jail was forced to close by federal court decree.[42] However, without proper leadership, funding, and mandated inspections, the jails are likely to remain problematic.

Evaluating Prison Rehabilitation Programs

How do we determine whether or not prison rehabilitation programs are successful? Most commonly, we look at **recidivism** rates, which are based upon the proportion of offenders released from prison who become involved in reported criminal behavior after their release. Many law enforcement officials believe that recidivism rates range from 50–75 percent; that is, that one half to three fourths of all offenders released from prison commit additional offenses. During the past twenty-five years, these estimates have been challenged by a number of researchers. Among the first to challenge traditional conceptions of recidivism was Daniel Glaser, whose research indicated that a figure of 35 percent is more reasonable. Glaser argues that recidivism rates depend upon a number of factors, including the characteristics of offenders sentenced to prison, the manner in which parole is employed, and the type of institution involved. For example, in a jurisdiction that relies heavily on probation, only those offenders considered to be poor risks may be sentenced to prison. Similarly, if parole or early release is used extensively, some inmates may be released prematurely. Finally, when we sentence offenders to maximum instead of medium or minimum security facilities, we are making some assumptions about the likelihood of rehabilitation, and this affects recidivism rates in each of these types of institutions. Glaser makes the additional point that many ex-convicts are returned to prison not because they commit new crimes, but because they commit technical violations of parole requirements that do not necessarily indicate a return to criminal behavior.[43]

The debate concerning recidivism rates continues, with some supporting Glaser's approach and others continuing to believe that recidivism is considerably higher than Glaser would have us believe. The problems of measuring recidivism are complex, but if we are to improve our performance in the area of rehabilitation, accurate measures of recidivism for different types of programs must be developed. What we have learned is that a number of obstacles to rehabilitation exist in the prison setting, and it is to these obstacles that we now turn our attention.

The Prison Society

The potential for successful rehabilitation in prison depends upon a number of factors. Two of the most important factors are the presence of qualified staff members in sufficient numbers and creation of an atmosphere conducive to rehabilitation. Under present conditions in most prisons, neither of these conditions exists. The lack of adequately trained staff in sufficient numbers reflects the fact that prisons have not traditionally received high priority when it comes to allocation of resources. The inability of prison officials to create conditions favorable to rehabilitation results partly from inadequate staff, but equally important is the fact that most of the time spent by inmates is in the company of other inmates. Life inside prison is radically different from the prior experiences of the new inmate. In Goffman's terms, prison is a **total institution.**[44] The inmate's identity is stripped away, and decisions that the inmate previously made concerning eating, sleeping, working, and so forth are now made by the institutional staff. Yet, when we release the offender from prison, we expect him or her to assume full responsibility for these and other decisions in the outside world. Additionally, while the inmate is in prison, he or she is subject to what may be called the "inmates' code." Sykes and Messinger point out that even if the prison administration strongly supports rehabilitation, it is difficult to achieve because peer group pressure forces inmates not to support the goals of the administration.[45] In some prisons, inmate gangs have become so powerful that they actually control the institution and the staff, making rehabilitation unlikely.[46]

Robert Martinson, after studying correctional programs, has argued that very few rehabilitation programs work.[47] Unfortunately, his remarks have been interpreted to mean that nothing can work. This remark has led to the accusation and perhaps rationalization that prisons have simply become warehouses. That is, the manifest goal of corrections has become the incapacitation of the convicted and the protection of the public.

The causes and ramifications of **warehousing** are severe. When warehousing occurs, the administrative agenda, the means of evaluation, and the goals are all redefined. The overcrowding resulting from warehousing leads to tension, limits the opportunity for rehabilitation, and creates a sense of abandonment on the part of the inmate. Prisons which have experienced violent riots are frequently overcrowded and understaffed.

The problem of warehousing can be explained by the network approach. First, the public, and perhaps some criminal justice officials, complain that too many convicted offenders are on the streets or are not receiving appropriate punishment. The legislatures respond by enacting longer sentences and limiting other alternatives. The courts are forced to sentence more defendants to prison and for longer periods of time. Correction officials are often caught: they must accommodate the increase in prison population, but they do not receive concommitant funding to comply with prison regulations. Once the warehousing is revealed through civil suits or a riot, the public is appalled by what has happened. Although they are shocked, do they want to fund a bond issue or increase taxes to provide adequate prison care? There are no easy solutions. The issue of warehousing is extremely complex, and one can see how actions and reactions in one portion of the network affect other components.

Rehabilitation Versus Custody

Another obstacle to rehabilitation is the conflict that often occurs between therapeutic and custodial staff. In many institutions, the staff of one persuasion has little or no respect for those of the other, and inmates sometimes use this lack of trust and respect among staff members to their advantage. Therapeutic staff frequently regard themselves as above custodial staff and are far better paid in most cases. Custodial staff often resent the fact that they take most of the risks in dealing with inmates twenty-four hours a day, but are not regarded as professionals and are not well paid.

Group and some individual therapy occur in most prisons, but costs for this type of treatment are high and success is hampered by insufficient knowledge of the causes of crime, the fact that inmates might see a therapist less than one hour per week (the rest of the time is spent with other inmates under the supervision of custodial staff), and a lack of follow-up after the offender is released from prison. It is also somewhat ironic that we continue to provide psychological therapy to inmates when a great deal of the available evidence suggests that they are no more in need of such therapy than most of the rest of us.

Education and Vocational Training in Prison

As early as the 1830s, education was defined as one means of assisting prisoner rehabilitation,[48] and most prisons currently offer educational programs of one type or another. Many inmates do not have high school educations, and some estimate that as many as 80 percent are illiterate. The quality of educational programs in prisons varies considerably and Nagel, one of the most outspoken critics of prison education, argues that such programs are merely tools to occupy the inmates' time and that, under conditions of confinement, they have little chance to succeed. An additional problem plaguing educational programs in prison is the negative experience that many inmates have had with education in the outside world.

In theory, most prison work programs are designed to provide inmates with job skills that may help them secure employment on the outside. In reality, something quite different often occurs. Many of the skills prisoners are taught are obsolete by the time they are released (and some are obsolete at the time they are taught). Even when the skills learned are current, ex-convicts often find that the stigma of having served time in prison is more important than the skills they possess. In short, no matter how skilled they are, they can't find employment because of their records.

Recent Trends

One of the recent developments in corrections has been the attempts at privatization. A few states (Minnesota, Pennsylvania, and Tennessee) have contracted with private agencies to provide prison care. While this approach may offer some financial advantages, there are many other important considerations. Will the private institutions be subject to legal standards established by court decisions and appropriate regulatory agencies? How will these institutions be monitored, and what guarantees will be made on the quality of care? The privatization of corrections is a new and controversial issue. Many concerns must be addressed before the practice becomes widespread.

Summary

Overcrowding of prisons and jails, the high cost of incarceration, and relatively high recidivism rates indicating the failure of correctional rehabilitation programs have all attracted the attention of the public and politicians in recent years. Nonetheless, jail and prison populations continue to increase and rehabilitation continues to be an elusive goal. Questions concerning the effectiveness of punishment as a deterrent remain basically unanswered, and there has recently been a shift in public opinion toward using incarceration as a means of revenge or retribution, although overall prison and jail conditions are much more humane today than in the past. Inmate codes and lack of adequately trained staff, in addition to staff conflicts, make rehabilitation efforts difficult. Educational and vocational training programs exist in virtually all correctional facilities, but are of varying quality.

Key Terms Defined

early release the release of a prisoner before he or she has served the minimum period of time required for his or her offense.

banishment the process of pronouncing a person civilly dead and forcing him or her to leave the country.

transportation the practice of transporting convicts to a country other than the one in which they are citizens.

age of enlightenment the period during the late eighteenth and early nineteenth centuries when humanitarian reforms occurred with respect to the mentally ill, prisoners, and others.

hedonism the seeking of pleasurable experiences.

Walnut Street Jail the first correctional institution in the United States.

Pennsylvania prisons prisons designed with a central hub and numerous wings radiating from this hub with cells in each wing placed back-to-back for the purpose of isolating prisoners from one another.

Auburn prisons U-shaped prisons with several tiers in which prisoners work and eat together.

retribution exacting repayment (often with a motive of revenge).

specific deterrence refers to the notion that punishment will prevent the criminal from repeating his or her crimes.

general deterrence refers to the notion that punishment will deter others from committing crimes.

maximum security facilities prisons designed to isolate and maintain custody of dangerous offenders and those serving long sentences.

medium security facilities similar to maximum security facilities, but more freedom of movement is generally allowed the inmates.

minimum security facilities prisons without the walls and armed guards characteristic of maximum and medium security facilities, with emphasis on rehabilitation as opposed to custody.

recidivism commission of a new offense by one already convicted.

total institution an institution (such as a prison) in which all decisions concerning working, eating, sleeping, and freedom of movement are made by the staff instead of the inmates.

warehousing placement of offenders in institutions with little regard for treatment or prisoners' rights.

Discussion Questions

1. Trace the historical development of corrections in America. What have been the most significant contributions to reform of American penal institutions?

2. What are the three classifications of prison facilities and what are the characteristics of each?

3. American jails have been called a "national scandal." Why? Suggest reforms that might improve jails. How likely are these reforms to be implemented? Why?

4. Why do rehabilitation programs prove unsuccessful with many, if not most, inmates? What changes would have to occur in order for such programs to be more effective?

Notes

1. Margaret Wilson, *The Crime of Punishment* (New York: Harcourt, Brace and World, 1931), 228.

2. Cesare Beccaria, *Essays on Crimes and Punishments* (Stanford, Calif.: Academic Reprints, 1953).

3. Harry E. Barnes and Negley K. Teeters, *New Horizons in Criminology,* 3d ed. (Englewood Cliffs, N.J.: Prentice-Hall, 1959), 322.

4. Karl Menninger, *The Crime of Punishment* (New York: Viking Press, 1968), 222.

5. This system has often been referred to as the "congregate system."

6. Court of Oyer and Terminer, Philadelphia, 13 DJC 285 (1930).

7. William J. Chambliss, *Crime and the Legal Process* (New York: McGraw-Hill, 1965).

8. David J. Pittman and C. Wayne Gordon, *Revolving Door* (New York: Free Press, 1968).

9. Thorsten Sellin, *The Death Penalty* (Philadelphia, Pa.: American Law Institute, 1959).

10. Jack D. Gibbs, *Crime, Punishment, and Deterrence* (New York: Elsevier, 1975).

11. Johannes Andenaes, "Determination and Criminal Law," *Journal of Criminal Law, Criminology, and Police Science* 47 (Nov.-Dec. 1956):406–13.

12. C. S. Lewis, "The Humanitarian Theory of Punishment," *Res Judicatae* 6 (June 1953).

13. *Furman v. Georgia,* 408 U.S. 238 (1972).

14. *Gregg v. Georgia,* 428 U.S. 153 (1976).

15. Gerhard O. W. Mueller, "Tort, Crime, and the Primitive Law," *Journal of Criminal Law, Criminology, and Police Science* 46 (1955):316–19.

16. Sir William Blackstone, *Commentaries on the Laws of England,* 14th ed. (London: Strahan, 1803).

17. *Gregg v. Georgia,* 428 U.S. 153 (1976).

18. *Wilkerson v. Utah,* 99 U.S. 130 (1878).

19. *Weems v. United States,* 217 U.S. 349 (1910).

20. William J. Bowers, *Executions in America* (Lexington, Mass.: D. C. Heath, 1974).

21. Alfred Blumstein and Joseph B. Kadane, "An Approach to the Allocation of Scarce Imprisonment Resources," *Crime and Delinquency: Special Issue on Prisons and Sentencing Reform* (Oct. 1983):546–60.

22. Thorsten Sellin, ed., *Capital Punishment* (New York: Harper and Row, 1967), 159.

23. William C. Bailey, "Murder and the Death Penalty," *Journal of Criminal Law, Criminology, and Police Science* 65 (Sept. 1974): 416–22.

24. David P. Phillips, "The Deterrent Effect of Capital Punishment: New Evidence on an Old Controversy," *American Journal of Sociology* 86 (July 1981):139–48.

25. Hans Zeisel, "A Comment on the 'Deterrent Effect of Capital Punishment' by Phillips," *American Journal of Sociology* 88 (July 1982):167–69.

26. *Gregg v. Georgia,* 428 U.S. 153 (1976).

27. *Proffit v. Florida,* 428 U.S. 242 (1976).

28. *Jurek v. Texas,* 428 U.S. 262 (1976).

29. *Coker v. Georgia,* 433 U.S. 584 (1972).

30. *Woodson v. North Carolina,* 428 U.S. 280 (1976).

31. *Barefoot v. Estelle,* 77 Led. 2nd 1090 (1983).

32. Sourcebook of Criminal Justice Statistics—1986, U.S. Department of Justice, Bureau of Justice Statistics (Washington, D.C.: U.S. Government Printing Office, 1987).

33. *National Advisory Commission on Criminal Justice Standards and Goals, Corrections* (Washington, D.C.: U.S. Government Printing Office, 1973), 444.

34. Prisoner statistics and percentages taken from U.S. Department of Justice, Bureau of Justice Statistics, *Report to the Nation on Crime and Justice,* 2d ed (Washington, D.C.: U.S. Government Printing Office, March 1988).

35. *Ibid.*

36. Edith E. Flynn, "Jails and Criminal Justice," in *Prisoners in America,* ed. Lloyd E. Ohlin (Englewood Cliffs, N.J.: Prentice-Hall, 1973), 49.

37. Joseph F. Fishman, *Crucibles of Crime: The Shocking Story of the American Jail* (Montclair, N.J.: Patterson Smith, 1969).

38. Ronald Goldfarb, *Jails: The Ultimate Ghetto* (Garden City, N.Y.: Doubleday, 1975).

39. Mary Jo Patterson, "The Price of Neglect is Tragedy," *Corrections Magazine* 9, no. 1 (Feb. 1983):6–21.

40. *Criminal Justice Newsletter* 8, no. 15 (July 1977):5–6.

41. *Brenneman v. Madigan,* 343 F. Supp. 128 (1972).

42. *Inmates of Suffolk County Jail v. Eisenstadt,* 360 F. Supp. 676 (1973).

43. Daniel Glaser, *The Effectiveness of a Prison and Parole System* (Indianapolis, Ind.: Bobbs-Merrill, 1964).

44. Erving Goffman, *Asylums,* (Garden City, N.Y.: Doubleday, 1961).

45. Gresham Sykes and Sheldon Messinger, "The Inmate Social Code," in *The Sociology of Punishment and Corrections,* ed. Norman Johnson et al. (New York: Wiley, 1970), 401–8.

46. Bruce Porter, "California Prison Gangs: The Price of Control," *Corrections Magazine* 8, no. 6 (Dec. 1982):6–19.

47. Robert R. Martinson, "What Works? Questions and Answers About Prison Reform," *The Public Interest* (Spring 1974):22–55.

48. Michael Reagan and Donald Stoughton, eds., *School Behind Bars: A Descriptive Overview of Correctional Education in the American Prison* (Metuchen, N.J.: Scarecrow Press, 1976).

Suggested Readings

Blumstein, Alfred, "Prison Crowding" U.S. Department of Justice (Washington, D.C.: U.S. Government Printing Office, 1987).

"Prisons and Sentencing Reform," *Crime and Delinquency, Special Issue* 29, no. 4 (Oct. 1983).

Fox, Vernon. *Correctional Institutions* (Englewood Cliffs, N.J.: Prentice-Hall, 1983).

Glaser, Daniel. *The Effectiveness of a Prison and Parole System* (Indianapolis, Ind.: Bobbs-Merrill, 1967).

Goldfarb, Ronald. *Jails: The Ultimate Ghetto of the Criminal Justice System* (Garden City, N.Y.: Doubleday, 1975).

Irwin, John. *Prisons in Turmoil* (Boston: Little, Brown, 1980).

Jacobs, James, "Inside Prisons" U.S. Department of Justice (Washington, D.C.: U.S. Government Printing Offices, 1987).

McKelvey, Blake. *American Prisons: A History of Good Intentions* (Montclair, N.J.: Patterson Smith, 1977).

Sykes, Gresham M. *The Society of Captives: A Study of a Maximum Security Prison* (Princeton, N.J.: Princeton University Press, 1958).

Prisoners' Rights and Alternatives to Incarceration

15

Key Terms

civil death
hands-off doctrine
cruel and unusual punishment
good time

community corrections
probation
parole

In the previous chapter, we noted that historically, persons convicted of crime suffered a "civil death." This practice was continued through the development of the penitentiary and reformatory systems, and was recognized by state courts as recently as 1871.[1]

Under the doctrine of **civil death,** convicted offenders were denied the right to vote, hold public office, or enter into contracts. Until the 1960s, the courts would not hear suits from incarcerated offenders, and inmates had no means of challenging the conditions imposed by their keepers. This refusal to hear suits from prison inmates concerning prison officials is commonly referred to as the **"hands-off doctrine."** The basic assumption behind this doctrine was that corrections was not a judicial province and that convicted persons were civilly dead and had relinquished constitutional rights and privileges.

In *Cooper v. Pate,*[2] the Supreme Court ended the hands-off doctrine by ruling that inmates are protected by the Civil Rights Act. The Civil Rights Act states, in part, "Every person who, under color of any statute, ordinance, regulation, custom or usage of any State or Territory subjects, or causes to be subjected, any citizen of the United States or other person within the jurisdiction thereof to the deprivation of any rights, privileges, or immunities secured by the Constitution and laws shall be liable to the party injured in an action at law, suit in equity or other proper proceeding for redress."[3]

Prisoners Learning
Skills. *David S.*
Strickler

The result of this decision was a major change in correctional philosophy commonly referred to as the prisoners' rights movement. The practice of allowing inmates to file actions concerning their confinement has led to numerous suits and has drastically altered some traditional correctional practices. In 1982 alone, almost twenty thousand suits were filed by inmates, an increase of 70 percent over 1977. While very few of the suits filed produce major changes in corrections, some have had dramatic effects. Let us look at some specific changes resulting from suits in the areas of freedom of speech, freedom of religion, freedom from cruel and unusual punishment, and due process.

Freedom of Speech

Historically, prison officials have engaged in practices that denied inmates the use of mail service, censored both incoming and outgoing mail, and denied inmates access to media sources when access might have been embarrassing to such officials. Court decisions have required that such practices be altered. In *Procunier v. Martinez,* the Supreme Court struck down the blanket practice of censoring all incoming and outgoing mail.[4] The Court held that censorship could be practiced, but only if there was a substantial belief that the contents of the mail threatened security. Prior to this decision, the First Circuit Court of Appeals had outlawed a Massachusetts practice that prohibited inmates from sending letters to the news media.[5]

In contrast, in *Saxbe v. Washington Post,* the right of an inmate to grant press interviews was denied on the grounds that it would lead to notoriety, which would undermine the attempts of authorities to provide equal treatment.[6]

Freedom of Religion

Historically, religion has been an important feature of prison life, yet restrictions have been placed on its exercise for economic reasons, for security reasons, and in order for prison officials to maintain authority.[7] Most restrictions have been aimed at religious rituals rather than religious beliefs. Several of the suits filed were in connection with the Black Muslim religion, with the most important being *Cooper v. Pate.*[8] In this decision, the court prohibited prison officials from completely banning religious services, but did permit restricting participation for those who abuse the privilege. In *Walker v. Blackwell,*[9] and *Khan v. Carlson,*[10] federal courts upheld prison officials' refusals to provide special diets for all religious sects.

There have been contrasting decisions concerning what constitutes a religion. In *Theriault v. Carlson,* the Fifth Circuit Court of Appeals ruled that the Church of the New Song and Universal Life did not constitute a religion, but amounted to a mockery and a sham.[11] However, the Eighth Circuit Court of Appeals recognized the same religion and held that its members were protected under the First Amendment.[12]

Cruel and Unusual Punishment

The Eighth Amendment's prohibition of **cruel and unusual punishment** has served as a basis for inmates contesting the legality of prison conditions. Perhaps the most famous of these cases is *Holt v. Sarver,*[13] in which the court ruled that conditions in the Cummings Prison Farm constituted cruel and unusual punishment. More recently, in *Pugh v. Locke,*[14] and *Ruiz v. Estelle,*[15] courts have threatened to close prison systems in Alabama and Texas respectively unless changes were made.

Concerning overcrowding as a form of cruel and unusual punishment, in *Bell v. Wolfish*[16] and in the case of *Rhodes v. Chapman,*[17] the courts have upheld the practice of "double bunking" as long as it doesn't lead to filth, disease, or limit the inmate's participation in prison programs. Additional Eighth Amendment decisions have prohibited the use of corporal punishment and restricted the use of solitary confinement.

Due Process

A number of inmate suits have been concerned with the loss of privileges or **good time.** In *Wolff v. McDonnell*,[18] the Supreme Court held that loss of good time or privileges was important enough to justify some due process requirements. As a result, prison officials must now provide advance notice of charges against inmates, hold a hearing, and allow time for the inmate to call witnesses and obtain assistance in preparing a defense. In a related decision, the court held, however, that inmates have no right to counsel in a disciplinary hearing.[19]

The requirements of due process do not apply to all prison practices. In the companion cases of *Meachum v. Fano*[20] and *Montaye v. Haymes,*[21] the court upheld the practice of not providing due process in the transfer of an inmate from one institution to another.

As you can see, the prisoners' rights movement has had important implications for prison practices. Administrative practices have been altered and prison conditions improved by some of the suits filed by inmates. Keep in mind, however, that court decisions are not always equivalent to action, and if such decisions are to have widespread impact, mandatory inspections are necessary.

Alternatives to Incarceration

In our discussion of prisons, we noted that conditions in these institutions are less than ideal in terms of rehabilitation. Incarceration is also very expensive. Conservative estimates place the annual cost of incarcerating one offender at between twelve and twenty thousand dollars. As an alternative to the expensive, ineffective, and sometimes inhumane practice of incarceration, the concept of corrections in the community has evolved. **Community corrections** programs include probation, parole, work release centers, halfway houses, and other community-based programs. The assumption underlying community corrections is that rehabilitation can best be achieved if contacts are maintained between offenders and the community and family to which he or she must eventually return. While research indicates that community corrections is about as effective as prison in terms of recidivism rates, the former has the advantage of being less expensive.

Probation

Probation is the supervised, conditional, and revokable release of an offender into the community in lieu of incarceration. It is a sentence that is served in the community instead of in prison, and if the conditions of probation are violated, the offender may be sent to prison or jail for the remainder of his or her original sentence.

Probation as we know it began in 1841 when a cobbler named John Augustus requested that judges let him pay fines for and supervise minor offenders. Partly because of his success, Massachusetts passed the first probation law in 1878, and all states now have some form of probation.[22]

Currently, probation may be granted in as many as 80 percent of the cases coming to the attention of the courts. Supporters believe that probation gives offenders a second chance and allows them to avoid the effects of incarceration while maintaining ties in the community to which they would eventually return if incarcerated, while under the supervision of a probation officer. In addition, supporters point out that probation, even if no more effective than incarceration, costs a great deal less. Opponents claim that probation is equivalent to no punishment at all, is too widely granted, and is ineffective because most probation officers provide little or no actual supervision to probationers.

When a judge sentences an offender to probation, she or he specifies the maximum period of time involved, which is established by statute. Probation can be terminated early if the probationer makes satisfactory progress. The probationer is notified by the judge of the conditions of his or her probation, which are, in theory at least, tailored to the specific needs of the probationer. Common conditions of probation include the requirement to refrain from violating any criminal statute, to report or appear in person before a probation officer at certain times, to refrain from possessing a firearm, to make restitution to the injured party, to secure and retain employment, to undergo therapy, and to remain in the county or state of residence unless permitted to leave by the probation officer.[23]

Each probationer is assigned to a probation officer who is responsible for supervising and assisting probationers in activities such as locating employment and housing, managing finances, and dealing with other problems as they arise. Given the fact that many probation officers have caseloads of fifty to one hundred probationers at any given time, the actual amount of supervision provided may be negligible, leading to some of the criticisms mentioned above.

Offenders who violate the conditions of their probation run the risk of having it revoked. The most common ground for revocation is the commission of another offense. The probation officer notifies the judge of the alleged violation and a revocation hearing is held. In 1973, in *Gagnon v. Scarpelli,* the Supreme Court ruled that revocation hearings must be public.[24]

In an earlier decision, the Court held that an accused had the right to counsel during revocation proceedings but had avoided the issue of whether a revocation hearing was mandatory.[25]

Revocation hearings require that the state prove that violations of probation occurred, usually by a preponderance of evidence. Evidence is presented in open court, and the probationer has the right to counsel, to cross-examine witnesses, and to call his or her own witnesses. If the judge finds the allegations unfounded, the probationer is returned to probation under present conditions. If the allegations are substantiated, the court may modify probation conditions or send the offender to prison or jail to serve the remainder of his or her original sentence.

Community Correctional Programs

Community correctional programs are among the most recent attempts at rehabilitation. They are designed to help reintegrate the offender into the community, and they take the form of halfway houses, prerelease guidance centers, and work release programs. While the offender is in residence, he or she is temporarily released to work, attend school, participate in therapy, and visit family. While great hope has been held for such programs, their overall success rate has not been much better (in terms of recidivism) than that achieved by prisons and, compared to probation, they are quite costly. In addition, it is often difficult to find neighborhoods or communities willing to support such programs due to fears that inmates will become involved in further crime and endanger area residents.

Parole

Parole and probation are sometimes confused by the general public. Like probation, **parole** is supervised, revocable release; but unlike probation, it occurs after part of the original sentence has already been served in prison or jail. If the parolee violates the conditions of his or her parole, the parolee can be returned to prison or jail to serve the remainder of the original sentence. Approximately 75 percent of all inmates leave prison on parole, and parole represents an important means of controlling overcrowding in prisons, which leads to frequent criticisms that release on parole depends more upon the number of offenders awaiting incarceration than upon the behavior of the offender released on parole.

The authority to grant parole is usually delegated by statute to some formal body. Some states delegate this authority to prison officials, but in most, a semi-autonomous parole board appointed by the governor is maintained. Qualifications for membership on parole boards vary by jurisdiction. In some areas, board members must have professional experience in corrections, law enforcement, or some other human service. In others, appointment is through patronage and the composition of the board is highly questionable.

In those states with determinate sentencing, the duties of the parole board are minimal. Offenders serve their time minus time off for good behavior and are released automatically. In the remaining states, the parole board has far greater latitude in deciding the release date and conditions of parole.

What factors should be considered in the parole decision? Obviously, the statutory minimum of the sentence must have been completed, but beyond this the criteria to be employed are considerably more difficult to specify. How much weight, for example, should we give to the offender's behavior in prison, the availability of employment, family support, and support services available in the community in which the parolee will reside? Should prison overcrowding be a consideration in granting parole? Should the nature of the offense for which the prisoner was incarcerated be a determining factor? These and other questions make parole decisions difficult. In the final analysis, of course, the reaction of citizens on the outside will determine the success or failure of parole, assuming that the parolee meets the conditions established to successfully complete parole.

The current problem of prison overcrowding has placed greater demands on parole and other forms of community corrections. Some prisons are legally forced to release inmates to avoid exceeding maximum daily population levels. The result is that some inmates may be paroled before the prison staff feel they are prepared to reenter society. This places increased pressure on the parole officer who may already have a heavy caseload. The problem is compounded in some jurisdictions where poor economic conditions have led to layoffs and thus increased caseloads even further. One must question the quantity and quality of supervision the client receives under these conditions.

In conclusion, we would like to emphasize the importance of viewing community corrections from the network perspective. Political decisions, public opinion, the attitudes and practices of criminal justice practitioners, and the behavior of each individual offender all play a part in determining whether alternatives to incarceration will succeed or fail and to what extent. As Solomon notes: "Community treatment programs for released prisoners are still in a relatively early stage of development. Before any firm conclusions can be drawn regarding their effect on reducing recidivism, or other criteria of success, considerably more research will be required."[26]

Summary

In recent years, the prisoners' rights movement and alternatives to incarceration have led to changes in our traditional conceptions of corrections. A number of court decisions have improved conditions in prisons and jails, although many remain substandard. In general, freedom of speech, freedom of religion, immunity from cruel and unusual punishment, and due process guarantees are the areas in which inmate suits have helped define more clearly what constitutes acceptable treatment in institutions. Probation, parole, and other alternatives to incarceration have been tried in the hope that they would prove more successful than imprisonment in reintegrating offenders and in preventing recidivism. Research findings generally fail to indicate the superiority of these alternatives over incarceration, but this may be due in part to the fact that community corrections programs are still relatively new.

Key Terms Defined

civil death denial of the right to vote, the right to hold public office, and the right to enter into contracts.

hands-off doctrine refusal on behalf of the courts to hear suits on behalf of prison inmates.

cruel and unusual punishment punishment administered by the government, which is prohibited by the Constitution.

good time time during which an inmate abides by the rules of the institution, which is then subtracted from his or her sentence.

community corrections correctional programs, such as probation, parole, work release, and halfway houses, in which prisoners are allowed and encouraged to maintain community and family ties.

probation the supervised, conditional, and revocable release of an offender into the community in lieu of incarceration.

parole the supervised, conditional, and revocable release of an offender into the community after he or she has served part of a sentence.

Discussion Questions

1. Explain the hands-off doctrine as it applied to prison inmates. Discuss some of the important changes that have occurred in corrections since this doctrine was dropped by the courts.

2. How are probation and parole similar and different? What role do political decisions play in each? How effective are these two alternatives to incarceration?

3. What is the basic rationale for community corrections programs? Discuss some of the obstacles to developing successful community corrections programs.

4. What kinds of changes do you think we can look forward to in the next few years in prisoners' rights and alternatives to incarceration?

Notes

1. *Ruffin v. Commonwealth,* 62 Va. 780 (1871).
2. *Cooper v. Pate,* 378 U.S. 546 (1964).
3. Civil Rights Act, 42 U.S.C. 1983.
4. *Procunier v. Martinez,* 416 U.S. 396 (1974).

5. *Nolan v. Fitzpatrick,* 451 F.2d 545 (1971).

6. *Saxbe v. Washington Post,* 417 U.S. 843 (1974).

7. John W. Palmer, *Constitutional Rights of Prisoners,* 2d ed. (Cincinnati, Ohio: Anderson, 1977), 64.

8. *Cooper v. Pate,* 378 U.S. 546 (1964).

9. *Walker v. Blackwell,* 411 F.2d 23 (1969).

10. *Khan v. Carlson,* 527 F.2d 492 (1975).

11. *Theriault v. Carlson,* 339 F. Supp 375 (1974).

12. *Reemers v. Brewer,* 494 F.2d 1227 (1974).

13. *Holt v. Sarver,* 300 F. Supp 825 (1970).

14. *Pugh v. Locke,* 406 F. Supp 318 (1976).

15. *Ruiz v. Estelle,* 503 F. Supp 1265 (1982).

16. *Bell v. Wolfish,* 99 S. Ct. 1873 (1979).

17. *Rhodes v. Chapman,* 452 U.S. 337 (1981).

18. *Wolff v. McDonnell,* 418 U.S. 539 (1974).

19. *Baxter v. Palmigiano,* 96 S. Ct 1551 (1976).

20. *Meachum v. Fano* 427 U.S. 215 (1976).

21. *Montaye v. Haymes,* 427 U.S. 236 (1976).

22. Hassim M. Solomon, *Community Corrections* (Boston: Holbrook Press, 1976).

23. Hassim M. Solomon, *Community Corrections* (Boston: Holbrook Press, 1976).

24. *Gagnon v. Scarpelli,* 411 U.S. 471 (1972).

25. *Mempa v. Rhay,* 389 U.S. 128 (1967).

26. Solomon, *Community Corrections,* 390.

Suggested Readings

Abadinsky, Howard. *Probation and Parole: Theory and Practice.* 2d ed. Englewood Cliffs, N.J.: Prentice-Hall, 1982.

Blackmore, John. "Community Corrections." *Corrections Magazine* Vol 6 No 5 (October, 1980) 4–14.

Empey, LaMar T. *Alternatives to Incarceration.* Washington, D.C.: U.S. Government Printing Office, 1967.

Martinson, Robert and Judith Wilks. "Save Parole Supervision." Federal Probation Vol. 41 No. 3 (September 1977) 23–27.

Juvenile Justice   16

Key Terms

age of responsibility
mens rea
parens patriae
in loco parentis
the "era of socialized juvenile justice"
legalists
delinquent act

petition
preliminary conference
status offenders
streetcorner/stationhouse adjustments
adjudicatory hearing
ward of the state
dispositional hearing
diversion programs
waiver of jurisdiction

The juvenile justice network in the United States is distinct from, but not independent of, the criminal justice network. The network approach would lead us to believe that what happens to juveniles as they are processed through the juvenile justice system would have important consequences for other components of the network. For example, if such juveniles are successfully rehabilitated, they will not become problems for the police, courts, and corrections at the adult level, nor will they continue to prey upon other citizens. If our efforts to assist youthful offenders fail, the consequences are equally apparent.

The juvenile justice network in the U.S. is less than one hundred years old. Since its inception, it has been controversial with respect to objectives and procedures. A large gap between theory and practice has characterized the network since 1899, when the first family court was established in Cook County, Illinois. The reasons for the controversy surrounding the juvenile court and the distinction between theory and practice are apparent upon review of the history of the juvenile court.

Juvenile Justice: A Historical Overview

Over four thousand years ago, the Code of Hammurabi contained references to runaway children and youth who disowned their parents. Two thousand years ago, Roman civil law and canon (church) law made distinctions between juveniles and adults based upon the concept of **age of responsibility.** During the eleventh and twelfth centuries, distinctions were made in British common law between youth and adults. For example, children under seven years of age were not subject to criminal sanctions because they were presumed to be incapable of forming criminal intent **mens rea;** and children between the ages of seven and fourteen were exempt from criminal prosecution unless it could be demonstrated that they had formed criminal intent, could distinguish right from wrong, and understood the consequences of their actions.[1] These issues remain important in juvenile court proceedings today. At what age is a child capable of understanding right and wrong? At what age can a child comprehend the consequences of his or her actions?

In the fifteenth century, chancery courts (under the direction of the king's chancellor) were created in England to grant relief and assistance to needy parties including women and children who were left to fend for themselves as the result of the death of the husband/father, abandonment, or divorce. The king, exercising the right of **parens patriae** (parent of his country), permitted these courts to act **in loco parentis** (in the place of parents) in order to provide necessary services to such women and children.

By the sixteenth century, British children could be separated from their pauper parents and apprenticed to others.[2] This practice was based upon the assumption that the state has a primary interest in the welfare of children and has the right to insure such welfare.

At about the same time, attempts were being made in England to settle disputes involving juveniles in a confidential fashion and to segregate youths requiring confinement from adult offenders. The former practice was to help juveniles avoid public shame and stigmatization, the latter to avoid the harmful effects of association with more hardened offenders.[3] Although juveniles continued to be incarcerated in adult institutions throughout most of the 1700s, they were often segregated from adult offenders. In 1788, Robert Young established a separate institution for young offenders that was to "educate and instruct in some useful trade or occupation the children of convicts or other such infant poor as are engaged in a vagrant and criminal course of life."[4]

In the United States during the 1700s, numerous juveniles were imprisoned, but few seemed to benefit from the experience. As a result, several institutions for juveniles were established in the early and mid-1800s. These institutions were oriented toward education and treatment, and away from punishment. By the mid-1800s, these institutions were declared a great success by those who ran them.[5] Others, however, were less enthusiastic about the institutions, and in the second half of the nineteenth century, it was widely recognized that such institutions failed to reform or rehabilitate delinquents. Reform schools became the new means of dealing with delinquents, but they failed to rehabilitate most delinquents, too.

Court decisions in the last half of the nineteenth century were in conflict over the necessity of due process for juveniles, but by the time the first family court appeared in Chicago in 1899, "The delinquent child had ceased to be a criminal and had the status of a child in need of care, protection, and discipline directed toward rehabilitation."[6]

The period between 1899 and 1967 has been called **the era of "socialized juvenile justice."** Emphasis upon obtaining a complete picture of the delinquent in order to determine appropriate care, regardless of legal requirements, became paramount. Informality became the rule and was confirmed by the decision of the Supreme Court not to hear the Holmes case in 1955 on the basis that juvenile courts are not criminal courts and, therefore, the constitutional rights guaranteed to accused adults do not apply to juveniles.[7]

Twelve years later, however, forces opposing the extreme informality and license of the juvenile court won a major victory in the case of Gerald Gault (see appendix). The problems created by extreme informality and lack of concern for constitutional guarantees became abundantly clear in the Gault case. Neither Gault nor his parents were notified properly of the charges against him, of their right to counsel, of their right to cross-examine witnesses, of their right to remain silent, of their right to a transcript of the proceedings, or of their right to appeal.[8] The Supreme Court decision in this case left no doubt that juveniles are protected by these guarantees and brought an end to the era of socialized justice. It did not, however, end the debate between those favoring more formal juvenile court proceedings (the **legalists**) and those favoring a more informal, casework approach (the caseworkers or therapists). That debate rages today with a variety of consequences for juvenile justice practitioners, as we shall see.

Defining and Measuring Delinquency

One of the major problems facing students of delinquency is that of arriving at a suitable definition. Without such a definition, measurement is impossible; and without accurate measurement, prevention and treatment are extremely difficult.

Two different types of definitions of delinquency have emerged over the years—legal and behavioral. Strict legal definitions hold that only those juveniles who have been officially labeled by the courts are delinquents. Such definitions are problematic because, according to self-report studies and victim-survey research, the definitions do not include the vast majority of all juveniles who commit delinquent acts and, therefore, may lead us to seriously underestimate the number of delinquents. In addition, legal definitions vary from state to state and time to time. Behavioral definitions hold that juveniles who have violated delinquency, statutes are delinquent whether or not they are apprehended; thus, the juvenile who engages in acts of vandalism is considered to be delinquent even though he or she has not been officially labeled by the court. Such definitions can provide a more comprehensive picture of the extent and nature of delinquency, provided we are able to collect accurate data from unofficial as well as official sources.

Purpose and Scope of Juvenile Court Acts

Juvenile court acts authorize the creation of juvenile courts with the legal authority to hear certain types of cases, including delinquency, dependency, neglect/abuse, and other cases requiring authoritative intervention (a minor in need of supervision, for example). These acts establish both procedural guidelines and substantive law relative to juveniles, which are to be administered in the interests of juveniles and in the spirit of parental concern. In order to insure that these goals are pursued, a separate nomenclature has been developed for juvenile procedures as indicated in table 16.1.

An examination of the chart shows that juveniles typically have a petition filed in their interests rather than a complaint filed against them. They may be taken into custody instead of arrested, may have a preliminary conference instead of a preliminary hearing, are accused of having committed a delinquent act rather than committing a crime (with some exceptions), go through an adjudicatory hearing rather than a criminal trial, may be found delinquent rather than guilty, and participate in a dispositional hearing instead of a sentencing hearing.

In addition to establishing these guidelines and a distinct language, juvenile court acts specify the age limits within which the juvenile court has jurisdiction and the nature of the acts over which the court has authority. For example, **delinquent acts** are normally defined as acts designated criminal in terms of local, state, or federal law committed by youth under a certain age. Similarly, those considered **status offenders** are typically juveniles who commit acts that are offenses only because of their age—running away from home, being "beyond the control" of parents, or being "incorrigible."

Juvenile Justice Procedures

Court proceedings concerning juveniles officially begin with the filing of a **petition** alleging that the juvenile is delinquent or in need of authoritative intervention of some kind (we will exclude from consideration here children who are dependent or neglected). Prior to the filing of the petition, the youth may have been taken into custody by the police and, in some states, may have been involved

Table 16.1 Comparison of Adult Criminal Justice and Juvenile Justice Systems

Adult	Juvenile
Arrest	Taken into Custody
Preliminary Hearing	Preliminary Conference/Detention Hearing (both optional)
Grand Jury/Information/Indictment	Petition
Arraignment	
Criminal Trial	Adjudicatory Hearing
Sentencing Hearing	Dispositional Hearing
Sentence—Probation, Incarceration, etc.	Disposition—Probation, Incarceration, etc.
Appeal	Appeal

Juveniles. *N. R. Rowan*

in a **preliminary conference** arranged by the juvenile probation officer in an attempt to settle the dispute out of court without filing a petition. Such a conference brings all parties to the dispute together (if they volunteer to attend), and the parties attempt to reach a settlement agreeable to all. If such a settlement cannot be reached or if the victim demands that a petition be filed, the case may be taken into juvenile court.

In any case, it is likely that delinquents who are about to have petitions filed on them will come into contact with the police. This contact may be in the form of an arrest, or may involve taking the juvenile into custody, which does not constitute an arrest (usually for the welfare of the youth involved). Typically, statutes require that the police attempt to contact the parents of any juvenile taken into custody, that the police insure the constitutional rights of the juvenile while he or she is in custody (including the right to counsel), and that the police release the youth from custody as soon as possible unless they intend to detain him or her, which requires a detention hearing involving the juvenile court judge if the detention is to be for more than a few hours. It should be noted here that the vast majority of juvenile cases are settled either at a preliminary conference or through the use of **streetcorner** or **stationhouse adjustments** on behalf of the police. Such adjustments allow the police to process most juveniles unofficially by obtaining agreement on behalf of their parents to see that the victim is compensated in some way for any damages he or she incurred.

When a detention hearing is necessary, the state generally must prove that detention is required to protect the youth, to protect society, or to prevent flight. If the judge agrees that detention is necessary, a specified time period is involved at the end of which the juvenile must be brought before the court or released.

If the case cannot be settled out-of-court, a petition is filed alleging that the youth in question is delinquent or in need of authoritative intervention. A copy of a typical petition is shown in figure 16.1.

Generally speaking, any adult who has knowledge of a delinquent act or has reason to believe a delinquent act has been committed by the youth in question may file a petition. The petition gives the name and age of the juvenile and usually the names and address(es) of the parents. It includes a statement of the facts that bring the youth under the jurisdiction of the juvenile court. The petition is then filed with the prosecutor who decides, often in conjunction with the juvenile probation officer, whether or not to prosecute the case.

If the prosecutor decides to prosecute, proper notice must be given to the juvenile and his or her parents or guardian, as well as to all other concerned parties. The court typically issues a summons specifying the date, place, and time of the adjudicatory hearing and of the right of all parties to counsel. Notification by certified mail or publication are acceptable if the summons cannot be delivered personally.

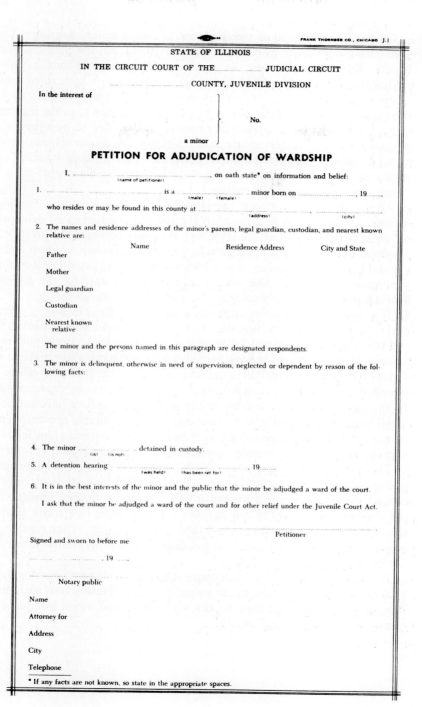

Figure 16.1 Petition for adjudication of wardship.

On the date indicated on the summons, the adjudicatory hearing is held. All parties to the proceedings have the right to attend, but the public is excluded. Unlike adults, juveniles under the jurisdiction of the juvenile court have no right to trial by jury or to a public hearing because the courts have ruled that adjudicatory hearings are not "adversary proceedings." While this may be true in theory, it is often not true in reality, and debate continues as to the legitimacy of these restrictions. Most **adjudicatory hearings** are conducted by a juvenile court judge who decides matters of fact, matters of law, and proper disposition of those found delinquent. The Supreme Court has ruled that the same standard of proof employed in adult criminal trials (guilt beyond reasonable doubt) must be adhered to in delinquency proceedings.[9]

After hearing the evidence, the juvenile court judge makes a decision as to whether the juvenile is delinquent. If the juvenile is adjudicated delinquent, he or she becomes a **ward of the state** and the court becomes the juvenile's legal guardian. At this point, the judge asks the juvenile probation officer to conduct a social background investigation, which will be used to assist in determining an appropriate disposition. The judge may also set the date for the **dispositional hearing,** which is typically separate from the adjudicatory hearing.

The social background investigation focuses on evidence including written and oral reports relating to the juvenile's family, environment, school history, friends, and other material that may be helpful in obtaining an accurate picture of the juvenile's circumstances. In some instances, the probation officer makes a written dispositional recommendation to the judge; in others, the probation officer simply provides the judge with his or her report without making any recommendations. In any case, the juvenile and his or her legal representative have access to the social background investigation, since there is no irrefutable presumption of accuracy attached to the investigation.[10] In fact, such reports often focus on the negative aspects of the juvenile's environment and overlook positive information.

The dispositional alternatives available to the juvenile court judge are specified in each state's juvenile court act. In general, these include placement in a foster home, placement in a private or public detention facility, probation (while the child remains in his or her parent's home or while in a foster home), and commitment to a state correctional facility for juveniles. After reaching a dispositional alternative, the judge issues a dispositional order similar to one of those in figures 16.2, 16.3, and 16.4.

If the juvenile is found to be delinquent at the adjudicatory hearing, he or she becomes a ward of the state, which means legal guardianship rests with the court. The juvenile court judge then decides what disposition would best serve the interests of the juvenile and society.

FRANK THORNBER CO., CHICAGO J-25

STATE OF ILLINOIS

IN THE CIRCUIT COURT OF THE .... JUDICIAL CIRCUIT

.... COUNTY, JUVENILE DIVISION

In the interest of

No.

a minor

DISPOSITIONAL ORDER
(Probation)

The court considered the evidence and finds: it has jurisdiction of the subject matter and the parties; the minor has been adjudged a delinquent; that all statutory prerequisites have been complied with.

It is ordered:

1. Probation is granted to the minor, ..., until ...., 19......., subject to the terms and conditions:

....

....

....

....

....

....

....

....

....

....

....

....

....

2. The minor is released to the custody of ...., and shall not
(parent) (guardian) (legal custodian)
depart from his custody except upon written authorization of the probation officer or order of court.

...., 19.......

....
JUDGE

Figure 16.2
Dispositional order (probation).

Figure 16.3
Dispositional order
(placement).

FRANK THORNBER CO., CHICAGO J-26

STATE OF ILLINOIS

IN THE CIRCUIT COURT OF THE_____ JUDICIAL CIRCUIT

_____ COUNTY, JUVENILE DIVISION

In the interest of

} No.

a minor }

DISPOSITIONAL ORDER
(Placement)

The court considered the evidence and finds: it has jurisdiction of the subject matter and the parties; the minor has been adjudged a delinquent; all statutory prerequisites have been complied with; the parent, guardian, or legal custodian is unfit, unable for some reason other than financial circumstances alone to care for, protect, train or discipline the minor, or is unwilling to do so, it is in the best interest of the minor to take him from such custody.

It is ordered:

1. The minor, _____, is:

    [ ] placed in the custody of _____, a suitable relative or other person,

    [ ] placed under the guardianship of _____, a probation officer,

    [ ] committed to _____, an agency for care or placement,

    [ ] committed to _____, a licensed training or industrial school,

    [ ] placed in the custody and guardianship of _____, Guardianship Administrator, Department of Children and Family Services, or his successor in office,

    [ ] placed _____

2. The clerk of the court deliver a certified copy of this order to the custodian or guardian as proof of his authority. No other process is necessary as authority for the keeping of the minor.

3. This custody shall continue until the minor reaches age 21 unless otherwise ordered by the court.

4. The custodian _____ authorized to consent to any required major medical and
   (is)   (is not)
   dental treatment recommended by a licensed physician.

_____

I certify that the above is a copy of an order entered in this case on _____, 19____

_____, 19____

Clerk of Court
[Seal of Court]

FRANK THORNBER CO., CHICAGO J-24

STATE OF ILLINOIS

IN THE CIRCUIT COURT OF THE .... JUDICIAL CIRCUIT

.... COUNTY, JUVENILE DIVISION

In the interest of

No.

a minor

DISPOSITIONAL ORDER
(Commitment)

The court considered the evidence and finds: it has jurisdiction of the subject matter and the parties; the minor has been adjudged a delinquent; all statutory prerequisites have been complied with; placement under Section 5-7 of the Juvenile Court Act will not serve the best interest of the minor and the public; the parent, guardian, or legal custodian is unfit, unable, or unwilling to care for, protect, train or discipline the minor.

It is ordered:

1. The minor, ..., is committed to the Department of Corrections;
2. The Director, Juvenile Division, Department of Corrections, is appointed legal custodian of the minor;
3. The minor is placed under the guardianship of ....;
4. The .... (appropriate officers) of this county convey the minor forthwith to the appropriate reception depot or other place designated by the Department of Corrections;
5. The clerk of the court deliver a certified copy of this order to the officer.

...., 19........

....
JUDGE

I certify that the above is a copy of an order entered in this case on ...., 19........

...., 19........

....
Clerk of Court
[Seal of Court]

Figure 16.4
Dispositional order (commitment).

Probation is by far the most common disposition in juvenile cases, perhaps accounting for 75 to 85 percent of all such dispositions. As we have indicated previously, probation is a sentence served in the community, under specified conditions, and under the supervision of the probation officer. Conditions commonly imposed upon juvenile probationers require that they must attend school regularly, must not leave the county or state without the approval of the probation officer, must keep regular appointments with the probation officer, must avoid certain places or types of places (pool halls or other game rooms, for example), must find and retain part-time employment, and so forth. If the conditions of probation are violated or if the youth commits another offense while on probation, then probation may be revoked. At the revocation hearing, the judge decides whether such violations occurred and, if they did, whether to revoke probation and send the youth to a private or public detention facility to serve the remainder of his or her time. The length of probation varies, but seldom exceeds two to three years; although in most states it may be continued until the age at which the youth is no longer under the jurisdiction of the juvenile court.

Private and public detention facilities vary tremendously in terms of size, length and type of program, and cost. Some employ behavior modification or peer pressure programs, others concentrate mostly on education and vocational training, and some are basically warehouses with few if any rehabilitation programs. Some allow home visits and some encourage parents to visit and participate in rehabilitation efforts, while others do little along these lines. These institutions are difficult to inspect and control, and some have become infamous because of the brutality and abuse that sometimes occurs under these conditions.

The use of foster home placement as a disposition would appear to hold some promise for delinquents, but a variety of factors combine to limit such placement. First, many parents of teenagers are reluctant to bring a delinquent youth into their homes for fear that their children will pick up the delinquent's habits instead of vice versa. Second, some individuals become foster parents because they mistakenly believe that they can profit financially from the experience. However, for the most part, the subsidy provided by the state or county for each youth placed in a foster home is seldom enough to totally support the youth, let alone supplement the income of the foster parents. Third, foster parents are dealing with "high risk of failure" youth when they agree to work with delinquents and not infrequently become discouraged when their efforts at rehabilitation are less successful than they intended. As a result, they may decide to withdraw from foster home programs.

The least desirable (from the point of view of most juvenile court judges) and the least frequently employed disposition is commitment to a state correctional facility for juveniles. As a rule, only those delinquents regarded as "unsalvageable" are so committed. Such youth include those who commit violent offenses against others, repeatedly appear in juvenile court for relatively serious offenses, and most often have failed to benefit from probation or detention of other types. Many judges believe that sending a delinquent to a state correctional facility virtually guarantees that the youth will pursue a criminal career as an adult.

Regardless of the disposition handed down by the juvenile court judge, juveniles, like adults, have the right to appeal; although in practice, appeals from juvenile courts have been rare.

Current Dilemmas in Juvenile Justice

Among the many dilemmas plaguing the juvenile court network are lack of properly trained and motivated personnel at all levels, failure to protect delinquents from stigmatization and association with other delinquents, and fear on behalf of many adults, which makes reintegration of juveniles who have been found delinquent difficult at best.

Practitioners at all levels of the juvenile justice network are frequently regarded (and often regard themselves) as something less than "real criminal justice officials." Police officers assigned to juvenile bureaus are often regarded as "kiddie cops" by other police officers, even though special dedication and expertise are required of such officers. Prosecutors often dislike handling juvenile cases because they are unlikely to lead to positive publicity even when an adjudication of delinquent is returned, and because preparation of such cases means time away from other cases that may be perceived as more serious or important. Defense attorneys sometimes fail to regard juvenile cases as worthy of the same preparation as adult criminal cases, and we have witnessed juvenile court proceedings in which defense counsel has never met or interviewed his or her juvenile client before the adjudicatory hearing begins. Juvenile court judges are often assigned this duty on a part-time basis and are sometimes unfamiliar with the requirements of the juvenile court act under which they are to operate, and many tend to overlook procedural requirements at the adjudicatory hearing on the grounds that they are interested in the "total picture" of the alleged delinquent. As a result, proper cross-examination of witnesses is sometimes impossible, especially if the witness happens to be an authority figure such as a teacher or a police officer, and hearsay evidence is sometimes considered. It is somewhat ironic that this should be the case when, as we have seen, it is the courts that have decided that the total picture of the delinquent may be considered only if it is obtained using the same legal procedures as are required for adults. As is the case in adult court, few judges are properly trained to decide which of the dispositional alternatives would be most beneficial to the youth in question and so, in spite of good intentions, operate on a trial and error basis with little attempt to do follow-up research to determine the effectiveness of the dispositions they hand down.

Juvenile probation officers face the same dilemmas as their counterparts working with adults. They are officers of the court and must occasionally discipline their charges; but to be effective in helping probationers, they must gain their confidence. As a result, the probation officer must maintain a delicate balance between the roles of counselor/friend and disciplinarian. Recognizing the difficulty of this task, a number of states now require a college degree (some require a graduate degree) for juvenile probation officers, provide mandated annual training for such officers, and subsidize their salaries in the hope of attracting and retaining qualified personnel.

It is true that numerous attempts have been and are being made to insure better-qualified juvenile personnel. A number of states now require specialized training and specific designation for juvenile police officers. Prosecutors and juvenile court judges have their own associations, complete with national and regional meetings which address key issues confronting the juvenile justice system. In addition, specialized training programs and seminars for both judges and prosecutors are available and are frequently well attended.

Attempts to divert youth from the juvenile justice network have also been popular in recent years. **Diversion programs** are of two basic types: those that attempt to divert youth from initial involvement in delinquency and those that attempt to divert youth who have already been involved in delinquent activities from becoming further involved. Although some diversion programs claim considerable success, it is difficult to determine whether such reported success is due to selection procedures or to the programs themselves. In addition, diversion programs have been criticized for keeping youth "under a microscope," that is, monitoring their behavior so closely that they become defined as delinquent for engaging in behaviors similar to those of other youth who are not defined as delinquent simply because no one is monitoring their behavior. It is doubtful that many of us could escape the label "delinquent" if our behaviors were closely monitored all the time. Thus diversion programs sometimes unintentionally create predelinquents who are doomed to become labeled delinquents. It is impossible to know whether they would have been labeled delinquent had they been less closely scrutinized.

The dilemma in juvenile corrections is much the same as in adult corrections—whether to emphasize custody or rehabilitation—and the same staff controversies exist. Further, the inmate subculture is at least as pervasive in juvenile institutions as in adult facilities, and some juvenile correctional facilities are literally run by gangs. There is little doubt that one of the things the delinquent committed to a correctional facility learns is a wide variety of delinquent activities.

Although the language and structure of the juvenile justice network is intended to prevent stigmatization, in practice it occurs routinely. While the public is excluded from juvenile court proceedings, the press may attend and not infrequently the names of delinquents are disclosed through this medium either directly or indirectly. Further, in the case of youth adjudicated delinquent, school officials and other public agency officials are routinely informed of this decision. In many cases, the youth involved publicizes his or her adjudication as a symbol of his or her "toughness." Even in the case of youth who avoid such publicity, weekly visits to or from the probation officer make it difficult to conceal the label.

The public has become increasingly concerned about violent offenses committed by juveniles. We have become, to some extent, afraid of our own children. As a result, the public has called for more severe penalties for youth involved in violent offenses; and it is often possible to automatically transfer youth who commit such offenses to adult court, thereby negating the philosophy of treat, educate, and rehabilitate instead of punish. Violent offenses by juveniles under 18 have actually decreased (about 9 percent in the past ten years), they have increased far less rapidly than similar offenses by adults (about 23 percent in the past ten years).[11]

A current controversy in the juvenile justice network revolves around the issue of transfer of jurisdiction (**waiver of jurisdiction**). Almost all states provide for the transfer of juveniles accused of certain types of offenses to adult court. The basis for transfer is the Supreme Court decision in the *Kent v. United States.* case,[12] which discusses guidelines to be considered in making the transfer decision. In some jurisdictions, the decision to transfer now rests with the prosecutor rather than the judge. While this action may help streamline the transfer process, once such a transfer occurs, the protections offered in juvenile court cease to exist. The juvenile's trial is public, as are records related to the case. Long-term incarceration and loss of civil rights are possibilities, and individualized treatment and rehabilitation become less likely. Opportunities to associate with, and learn from, hardened criminals increase. As a result of such risks, a full hearing before a judge who makes the final waiver decision is probably in the best interests of juveniles. Nonetheless, community pressure supporting the current concept of transfer is considerable because many observers believe that juvenile offenders are "coddled" by the juvenile justice network, even when they commit serious violations.

A number of remedies have been put forth for the problems confronting the juvenile justice network. Many of these remedies are based upon overreaction to the increase in violent juvenile crime discussed above. "Get tough" policies have been adopted in a number of states based on the mistaken belief that the more severe the punishment, the less likely the offender is to commit an offense. There is precious little evidence to indicate that this return to the classical approach (based on assumptions of free will, rational human beings, and a relationship between severity of punishment and likelihood of crime) will produce the desired results. In the meantime, the goals of the juvenile justice network may be set aside or overlooked. It is unlikely that major changes in juvenile delinquency will occur unless there is a shift in demographics leading to a smaller proportion of the population in the twelve- to eighteen-year old age range, or some major changes occur with respect to equal opportunity regardless of race and social class. These changes would provide more and better opportunities for educational and vocational success for minority youth, thus lessening the likelihood of involvement with the delinquent subculture. Frankly, changes of the latter type seem less likely now than a decade ago as the result of the prevailing political and economic climate of the 1980s. Reassessing the basic values and institutions in a society is a difficult undertaking, and "band-aid" solutions are much more attractive to those seeking quick fixes to chronic problems.

Summary

The juvenile justice network in the United States is a separate network less than one hundred years old. The underlying philosophy of juvenile justice in our society is based upon principles *(parens patriae, in loco parentis, chancery/equity)* developed in England and transported to this country.

Since the establishment of the first family court in Illinois in 1899, a debate has raged concerning the nature of official proceedings involving juveniles, and the courts have supported first one and then the other side in this debate. At present, the "legalists" appear to have the advantage as the courts now require a degree of formality in juvenile justice that was absent under the "era of socialized juvenile justice" in which the caseworkers had the upper hand.

Protection of juveniles from stigmatization; recruitment, training, and retention of qualified personnel; and a current wave of public fear of youth are problems confronting juvenile justice practitioners now.

Key Terms Defined

age of responsibility the age at which children are assumed to be responsible (in a legal sense) for their actions.

mens rea a criminal or guilty state of mind.

parens patriae the right of the government to take care of those who cannot legally care for themselves.

in loco parentis in the place of the parents.

the "era of socialized juvenile justice" the period between 1899 and 1967, during which juvenile courts emphasized getting the "total picture" of the juvenile as opposed to adhering only to legal requirements.

legalists those favoring a formal approach to juvenile justice.

delinquent act an act committed by a youth under a specified age, which violates a federal, state, or municipal law.

petition a written request for action directed to the court.

preliminary conference a conference of interested parties at which a juvenile probation officer attempts to adjust juvenile cases without taking official court action.

status offense an act that constitutes an offense only because of the age of the offender.

streetcorner/stationhouse adjustments adjustments in juvenile cases made by a police officer and other interested parties in lieu of taking official action.

adjudicatory hearing a hearing in juvenile cases at which the judge determines whether or not the juvenile in question is delinquent, dependent, abused, or in need of intervention.

ward of the state a juvenile whose guardian is the court.

dispositional hearing a hearing in juvenile cases at which the judge decides on appropriate placement for the juvenile in question.

diversion programs programs intended to divert (redirect) youth from the official juvenile justice network.

waiver of jurisdiction allowing jurisdiction to be transferred.

Discussion Questions

1. Discuss *parens patriae* and *in loco parentis* as they relate to the contemporary juvenile justice work.

2. What are some of the most important court decisions involving juvenile justice? Why?

3. Outline the procedures employed in juvenile court in cases involving delinquents. Compare these procedures to those used for adults.

4. What are some of the current issues in juvenile justice and how might some of these issues be resolved?

Notes

1. William Blackstone, *Commentaries on the Laws of England,* 12th ed. (London: Strahan, 1803), 4:22–24.

2. Douglas R. Rendleman, "Parens Patriae: From Chancery to the Juvenile Court," in *Juvenile Justice Philosophy,* ed. Frederic L. Faust and Paul J. Brantingham (St. Paul, Minn.: West, 1974), 77.

3. Wiley B. Sanders, "Some Early Beginnings of the Children's Court Movement in England," in *Juvenile Justice Philosophy,* ed. Frederic L. Faust and Paul J. Brantingham (St. Paul, Minn.: West, 1974), 46–47.

4. Sanders, "Some Early Beginnings of the Children's Court Movement in England," 48.

5. Clifford E. Simonsen and Marshall S. Gordon III, *Juvenile Justice in America,* 2d ed. (New York: Macmillan, 1982), 23.

6. Ruth Shonle Cavan, *Juvenile Delinquency: Development, Treatment, Control,* 2d ed. (Philadelphia, Pa.: J. B. Lippincott, 1969), 362.

7. *Holmes,* 379 Pa. 599, 109 A. 2d 523 (1954); cert. denied, 348 U.S. 973, 75 S. Ct. 535 (1955).

8. *Gault,* 387 U.S. 1, 49–50, 87 S. Ct. 1428, 1455 (1967).

9. *Winship,* 397 U.S. 358, 90 S. Ct. 1068 (1970).

10. *Kent v. U.S.,* 383 U.S. 541, 86 S. Ct. 1045, 16L. Ed. 2d. 84 (1966).

11. *Sourcebook of Criminal Justice Statistics—1986* (Washington, D.C.: U.S. Government Printing Office, 1987), 294.

12. *Kent v. U.S.,* 383 U.S. 541, 554, 86 S. Ct. 1045, 1053, 16L. Ed. 2d. 84 (1966).

Suggested Readings

Cavan, Ruth Shonle, and Ferdinand, Theodore N. *Juvenile Delinquency,* 4th ed. New York: Harper and Row, 1981.

Cox, Steven M., and Conrad, John J. *Juvenile Justice: A Guide to Theory and Practice,* 2d ed. Dubuque, Ia.: Wm. C. Brown Publishers, 1987.

Cullen, Francis T.; Golden, Kathryn M.; and Cullen, John B. "Is Child Saving Dead? Attitudes Toward Rehabilitation in Illinois," *Journal of Criminal Justice* 11, no. 1 (1983):1–14.

Platt, Anthony. *The Child Savers.* Chicago: University of Chicago Press, 1969.

Yablonsky, Lewis, Haskell, Martin R. *Juvenile Delinquency.* 4th ed. Boston: Houghton Mifflin, 1988.

Career Opportunities in the Criminal Justice Network 17

Career opportunities in criminal justice are both numerous and diverse for individuals who, with appropriate educational backgrounds, are mobile. These opportunities exist in the following areas, which will be discussed individually below: law enforcement, courts, corrections/social services, private security, law/paralegal services, and teaching. Since the duties, requirements, and functions of most criminal justice practitioners have been discussed previously in this book, we will not repeat this discussion below. To refresh your memory concerning the duties and requirements of specific practitioners, you may want to refer back to the appropriate chapter. The employment outlook for most of the positions discussed below appears to be favorable over the next few years.

Careers in Law Enforcement

Career opportunities in public law enforcement exist at the federal, state, county, and municipal levels. At the federal level, career opportunities exist, for example, in the Federal Bureau of Investigation; the Bureau of Alcohol, Tobacco, and Firearms; the Internal Revenue Service; the Department of Immigration and Naturalization Services; Customs; the Postal Department; the Central Intelligence Agency; the National Security Agency; Military Police/Investigations; the Drug Enforcement Agency; the U.S. Park Service; the Department of Health and Human Services; and the Department of Agriculture, to mention just a few.

At the state level, positions are generally available in the state police or highway patrol, and in a variety of state regulatory agencies such as conservation, park services, motor vehicles, university police, drug enforcement, children/family services, and arson investigations.

Employment in law enforcement at the county level is generally with the sheriff's department, although opportunities in other areas involving regulatory functions sometimes exist.

Municipal police departments are constantly seeking new personnel, particularly in rapidly developing areas and in large urban centers.

Mobility and appropriate educational and personal background characteristics are perhaps the most important keys to securing employment in one of the more than 40,000 public law enforcement agencies. Although the majority of positions available are entry-level positions, requirements vary greatly depending upon the type (federal, state, or local) and location (urban/rural and geographic) of agency. As of 1980, the average starting salary for police officers nationwide was over $15,000 per year. Starting salaries for law enforcement officers in urban areas are often considerably higher than the average (in the range of $20,000–$25,000 per year). Working conditions and benefits vary greatly, but are generally considerably better today than they were ten years ago. Employment opportunities in law enforcement are expected to grow about as rapidly as those in other occupational fields over the next ten years.[1] A variety of other positions are also available in law enforcement. These include dispatcher, receptionist/clerk, and computer operator/technician.

Further information on careers in law enforcement may be obtained by writing to one of the following:

International Association of Chiefs of Police
13 First Field Road
Gaithersburg, Md. 20878

National Employment Listing Service (NELS) (information on most of the
    careers discussed in this chapter may be obtained here)
Texas Criminal Justice Center
Sam Houston State University
Huntsville, Tex. 77341

Careers in the Courts

Opportunities for careers in the courts are somewhat more limited than in law enforcement, although they also exist at the federal, state, county, and municipal levels. Generally speaking, court personnel includes court administrators, adult and juvenile probation officers, clerks, members of the prosecutor's staff, members of the public defender's staff, judges, court recorders, and bailiffs. Some of these positions are filled through elections (prosecutor, judge, circuit clerk, for example), some through appointment, and some we will discuss (judge, prosecutor, public defender) later when we discuss careers in law. Careers as probation officers, investigators for the prosecutor or public defender, bailiffs, or court administrators typically depend upon both personal qualifications and political appointment.

The position of court administrator is a relatively recent addition to the ranks of court personnel and many jurisdictions still do not hire court administrators. Statistics on starting salary for this position are not currently available.

Both adult and juvenile probation officer positions may be found at the county level in most states and are sometimes available at the state level. Adult probation officers positions are also found at the federal level. As of 1980, the starting salary for federal probation officers (GS9) was about $17,000 per year.[2] Salaries at the county and state levels vary considerably by region. In the Midwest, for example, current average starting salaries for probation officers appear to be in the area of $13,000–$15,000 per year.

Court recorders are found in almost all courts, and starting salaries for recorders appear to average between $800 and $1,000 per month. Similarly, bailiffs are found in courts at all levels, and the average starting salary in 1980 was about $18,000 per year. Job prospects in these areas appear favorable for the next few years.

Further information on careers in the courts might be obtained from:

NELS

Information Service
The American Bar Association
1155 East 60th Street
Chicago, Ill. 60637

Careers in Corrections/Social Services

Here again, a variety of positions are available at federal, state, county, and local levels. Correctional officer, caseworker, counselor, sociologist, social worker, psychologist, and parole officer are job titles of some of the positions available in the correctional field. Positions are also sometimes available in the administration of correctional facilities. Generally speaking, salaries for correctional employees are not as high as in some other areas in criminal justice. Average starting salary for correctional officers in 1980 was about $13,800 per year, for caseworkers about $12,000 per year, and for parole officers about $13,500.

Caseworker positions may be available with a variety of public and private social service agencies such as Children and Family Services, Catholic Social Services, Public Aid, Youth Service Bureaus, or other diversionary or treatment programs.

Additional sources of information concerning careers in corrections include:

NELS

The American Correctional Association
4321 Hartwick Road
College Park, Md. 20740

Career opportunities in corrections appear to be excellent for the next decade as many states are currently building new correctional facilities to house an ever-increasing number of inmates.

Career Opportunities in Security

Included among the career opportunities in this category are those in industrial and retail security and loss prevention as both line security personnel and security administrators. The security field is a rapidly growing one, and opportunities in this area should continue to grow. Computer security, for example, is an area still in its infancy, antiterrorist security forces are a relatively new concept in the U.S., and prevention and detection of employee theft are now a major concern to many organizations. Some authorities estimate that for every public police officer hired, three people are employed in private security.[3] Security personnel are employed in organizations such as banks, public utilities, hotels, retail stores, insurance companies, oil companies, hospitals, industrial companies, and telecommunications companies. Types of positions include personnel protection, computer security, guard forces, physical security, investigations, plant security, and counterterrorism, to name a few. Salaries in many security positions have become very competitive, and those in security administration are often very good.

For further information about security careers, contact:

NELS

American Society for Industrial Security
2000 K Street N.W., Suite 651
Washington, D.C. 20006

Police Careers—
Records and
Communications.
James L. Shaffer

Career Opportunities in Law and Paralegal Services

Individuals with law degrees or training and education in paralegal services may find employment in a variety of jobs. Most judges are lawyers, as are private attorneys and public prosecutors. Federal agencies such as the F.B.I., the Department of Justice, and the Treasury Department frequently employ lawyers. Some police departments hire lawyers as consultants, and there are over 115,000 private law firms in the U.S., some of which (though not a large number) specialize in criminal defense work. Opportunities for employment also exist for legal secretaries and others qualified to provide paralegal services.

Employment opportunities in criminal justice in the legal profession appear to be best in the urban areas, and with federal and state governments. To qualify for attorney positions, the individual must have graduated from an accredited law school and, in general, must have passed the bar exam of the state in which he or she intends to practice.

Overall, employment opportunities in the criminal justice network for lawyers and paralegal professionals would appear to be somewhat restricted by virtue of the fact that there are a limited number of positions and an abundant supply of applicants. Nonetheless, starting salaries are usually relatively good with government agencies (less so in private practice involving criminal justice).

For additional information concerning careers in the legal profession, contact:

Local or State Bar Associations

Information Service
The American Bar Association
1155 East 60th Street
Chicago, Ill. 60637

Association of American Law Schools
Suite 370, 1 DuPont Circle NW
Washington, D.C. 20036

Careers in Teaching

Teaching opportunities exist in a variety of institutions both in and out of the criminal justice network. There are literally hundreds of criminal justice programs in junior colleges and universities around the country. Employment in these programs generally requires at least a master's degree (junior colleges) and may require a doctorate (most four-year colleges and universities). Those who meet the educational requirements and have some practical experience in criminal justice generally have an advantage when applying for these positions.

Within the criminal justice network, teaching positions may be available in police training institutes and academies; in correctional settings and other types of detention facilities (such as juvenile facilities); in some diversion and alternatives to incarceration programs; and, to a limited extent, in law schools. Salaries vary tremendously with the type of position and the location of the job.

Additional sources of information on teaching positions related to criminal justice include:

NELS

Police Chief Magazine

The Chronicle of Higher Education

Notes

1. U.S. Department of Labor Statistics, *Occupational Outlook Handbook* (Washington, D.C.: U.S. Government Printing Office, March 1980). This figure represents an average of several starting salaries for different types of public law enforcement officers.

2. *National Employment Listing Service for the Criminal Justice System* (Huntsville, Texas: Sam Houston State University, 1980).

3. *Career Opportunities in Security and Loss Prevention* (Washington, D.C.: A.S.I.S. Foundation, 1982).

Appendix: The U.S. Constitution and Selected Landmark Decisions

Constitution of the United States of America*

Preamble

We, the People of the United States, in Order to form a more perfect Union, establish Justice, insure domestic Tranquility, provide for the common defence, promote the general Welfare, and secure the Blessings of Liberty to ourselves and our Posterity, do ordain and establish this Constitution for the United States of America.

Article I

Section 1. All legislative Powers herein granted shall be vested in a Congress of the United States, which shall consist of a Senate and House of Representatives.

Section 2. The House of Representatives shall be composed of Members chosen every second Year by the People of the several States, and the Electors in each State shall have the Qualifications requisite for Electors of the most numerous Branch of the State Legislature.

No Person shall be a Representative who shall not have attained to the Age of twenty-five Years, and been seven Years a Citizen of the United States, and who shall not, when elected, be an Inhabitant of that State in which he shall be chosen.

Representatives and *direct Taxes shall be apportioned* among the several States which may be included within this Union, according to their respective Numbers, *which shall be determined by adding to the whole Number of free Persons, including those bound to Service for a Term of Years,* and excluding Indians not taxed, *three-fifths of all other Persons.* The actual Enumeration shall be made within three Years after the first Meeting of the Congress of the United States, and within every subsequent Term of ten Years, in such Manner as they shall by Law direct. The Number of Representatives shall not exceed one for every thirty Thousand, but each State shall have at Least one Representative; *and until such*

*Effective March 4, 1789

enumeration shall be made, the State of New Hampshire shall be entitled to choose three, Massachusetts eight, Rhode-Island and Providence Plantations one, Connecticut five, New-York six, New Jersey four, Pennsylvania eight, Delaware one, Maryland six, Virginia ten, North Carolina five, South Carolina five, and Georgia three.

When vacancies happen in the Representation from any State, the Executive Authority thereof shall issue Writs of Election to fill such Vacancies.

The House of Representatives shall choose their Speaker and other Officers; and shall have the sole Power of Impeachment.

Section 3. The Senate of the United States shall be composed of two Senators from each State, *chosen by the Legislature thereof,* for six Years; and each Senator shall have one Vote.

Immediately after they shall be assembled in Consequence of the first Election, they shall be divided as equally as may be into three Classes. The Seats of the Senators of the first Class shall be vacated at the Expiration of the second Year, of the second Class at the Expiration of the fourth Year, and of the third Class at the Expiration of the sixth Year, so that one-third may be chosen every second Year; *and if Vacancies happen by Resignation, or otherwise, during the Recess of the Legislature of any State, the Executive thereof may make temporary Appointment until the next Meeting of the Legislature, which shall then fill such Vacancies.*

No Person shall be a Senator who shall not have attained to the Age of thirty Years, and been nine Years a Citizen of the United States, and who shall not, when elected, be an Inhabitant of that State for which he shall be chosen.

The Vice-President of the United States shall be President of the Senate, but shall have no Vote, unless they be equally divided.

The Senate shall choose their other Officers, and also a President pro tempore, in the Absence of the Vice-President, or when he shall exercise the Office of President of the United States.

The Senate shall have the sole Power to try all Impeachments. When sitting for that Purpose, they shall be on Oath or Affirmation. When the President of the United States is tried, the Chief Justice shall preside: And no Person shall be convicted without the Concurrence of two-thirds of the Members present.

Judgment in Cases of Impeachment shall not extend further than to removal from Office, and disqualification to hold and enjoy any Office of honor, Trust or Profit under the United States: but the Party convicted shall nevertheless be liable and subject to Indictment, Trial, Judgment and Punishment, according to Law.

Section 4. The Times, Place and Manner of holding Elections for Senators and Representatives, shall be prescribed in each State by the Legislature thereof; but the Congress may at any time by Law make or alter such Regulations, except as to the Places of choosing Senators.

The Congress shall assemble at least once in every Year, and such Meeting shall be on the first Monday of December, unless they shall by Law appoint a different day.

Section 5. Each House shall be the Judge of the Elections, Returns and Qualifications of its own Members, and a Majority of each shall constitute a Quorum to do Business; but a smaller Number may adjourn from day to day, and may be authorized to compel the Attendance of absent Members, in such Manner, and under such Penalties as each House may provide.

Each House may determine the Rules of its Proceedings, punish its Members for disorderly Behaviour, and, with the Concurrence of two-thirds, expel a Member.

Each House shall keep a Journal of its Proceedings, and from time to time publish the same, excepting such Parts as may in their Judgment require Secrecy; and the Yeas and Nays of the Members of either House on any question shall, at the Desire of one-fifth of those Present, be entered on the Journal.

Neither House, during the Session of Congress, shall, without the Consent of the other, adjourn for more than three days, nor to any other Place than that in which the two Houses shall be sitting.

Section 6. The Senators and Representatives shall receive a Compensation for their Services, to be ascertained by Law, and paid out of the Treasury of the United States. They shall in all Cases, except Treason, Felony and Breach of the Peace, be privileged from Arrest during their Attendance at the Session of their respective Houses, and in going to and returning from the same; and for any Speech or Debate in either House, they shall not be questioned in any other Place.

No Senator or Representative shall, during the Time for which he was elected, be appointed to any civil Office under the Authority of the United States, which shall have been created, or the Emoluments whereof shall have been increased during such time; and no Person holding any Office under the United States, shall be a Member of either House during his Continuance in Office.

Section 7. All Bills for raising Revenue shall originate in the House of Representatives; but the Senate may propose or concur with Amendments as on other Bills.

Every Bill which shall have passed the House of Representatives and the Senate shall, before it becomes a Law, be presented to the President of the United States; if he approve, he shall sign it, but if not, he shall return it, with his Objections, to that House in which it shall have originated, who shall enter the Objections at large on their Journal, and proceed to reconsider it. If after such Reconsideration two-thirds of the House shall agree to pass the Bill, it shall be sent, together with the Objections, to the other House, by which it shall likewise be reconsidered, and if approved by two-thirds of that House, it shall become a Law. But in all such Cases the Votes of both Houses shall be determined by Yeas and Nays, and the Names of the Persons voting for and against the Bill shall be entered on the Journal of each House respectively. If any Bill shall not be returned by the President within ten Days (Sundays excepted) after it shall have been presented to him, the Same shall be a Law, in like Manner as if he had signed it, unless the Congress by their Adjournment prevent its Return, in which Case it shall not be a law.

Every Order, Resolution, or Vote to which the Concurrence of the Senate and House of Representatives may be necessary (except on a question of Adjournment) shall be presented to the President of the United States; and before the Same shall take Effect, shall be approved by him, or being disapproved by him, shall be repassed by two-thirds of the Senate and House of Representatives, according to the Rules and Limitations prescribed in the Case of a Bill.

Section 8. The Congress shall have Power: To lay and collect Taxes, Duties, Imposts and Excises, to pay the Debts and provide for the common Defence and general Welfare of the United States; but all Duties, Imposts and Excises shall be uniform throughout the United States.

> To borrow Money on the credit of the United States;
>
> To regulate Commerce with foreign Nations, and among the several States, and with the Indian Tribes;
>
> To establish a uniform Rule of Naturalization, and uniform Laws on the subject of Bankruptcies throughout the United States;
>
> To coin Money, regulate the Value thereof, and of foreign Coin, and fix the Standard of Weights and Measures;
>
> To provide for the Punishment of counterfeiting the Securities and current Coin of the United States;
>
> To establish Post Offices and post Roads;
>
> To promote the Progress of Science and useful Arts, by securing for limited Times to Authors and Inventors the exclusive Right to their respective Writings and Discoveries;
>
> To constitute Tribunals inferior to the Supreme Court;
>
> To define and punish Piracies and Felonies committed on the high Seas, and Offences against the Law of Nations;
>
> To declare War, grant Letters of Marque and Reprisal, and make Rules concerning Captures on Land and Water;
>
> To raise and support Armies, but no Appropriation of Money to the Use shall be for a longer Term than two Years;
>
> To provide and maintain a Navy;

To make Rules for the Government and Regulation of the land and naval Forces;

To provide for calling forth the Militia to execute the Laws of the Union, suppress Insurrections and repel Invasions;

To provide for organizing, arming, and disciplining the Militia, and for governing such Part of them as may be employed in the Service of the United States, reserving to the States respectively, the Appointment of the Officers, and the Authority of training the Militia according to the Discipline prescribed by Congress;

To exercise exclusive Legislation in all Cases whatsoever, over such District (not exceeding ten Miles square) as may, by Cession of particular States, and the Acceptance of Congress, become the Seat of Government of the United States, and to exercise like Authority over all Places purchased by the Consent of the Legislature of the State in which the Same shall be, for the Erection of Forts, Magazines, Arsenals, dock-Yards, and other needful Buildings;—And

To make all Laws which shall be necessary and proper for carrying into Execution the foregoing Powers, and all other Powers vested by this Constitution in the Government of the United States, or in any Department or Officer thereof.

Section 9. *The Migration or Importation of such Persons as any of the States now existing shall think proper to admit, shall not be prohibited by the Congress prior to the Year one thousand eight hundred and eight, but a Tax or duty may be imposed on such Importation, not exceeding ten dollars for each Person.*

The Privilege of the Writ of Habeas Corpus shall not be suspended, unless when in Cases of Rebellion or Invasion the public Safety may require it.

No Bill of Attainder or ex post facto Law shall be passed.

No Capitation, or other direct, Tax shall be laid, unless in Proportion to the Census or Enumeration herein before directed to be taken.

No Tax on Duty shall be laid on Articles exported from any State.

No Preference shall be given by any Regulation of Commerce or Revenue to the Ports of one State over those of another; nor shall Vessels bound to, or from, one State, be obliged to enter, clear, or pay Duties in another.

No Money shall be drawn from the Treasury, but in Consequence of Appropriations made by Law; and a regular Statement and Account of the Receipts and Expenditures of all public Money shall be published from time to time.

No Title of Nobility shall be granted by the United States; And no Person holding any Office of Profit or Trust under them, shall, without the Consent of the Congress, accept of any present, Emolument, Office, or Title, of any kind whatever, from any King, Prince, or foreign State.

Section 10. No State shall enter into any Treaty, Alliance, or Confederation; grant Letters of Marque and Reprisal; coin Money; emit Bills of Credit; make any Thing but gold and silver Coin a Tender in Payment of Debts; pass any Bill of Attainder, ex post facto Law, or Law impairing the Obligation of Contracts, or grant any Title of Nobility.

No State shall, within the Consent of the Congress, lay any Imposts or Duties on Imports or Exports, except what may be absolutely necessary for executing its inspection Laws; and the net Produce of all Duties and Imposts, laid by any State on Imports or Exports, shall be for the Use of the Treasury of the United States; and all such Laws shall be subject to the Revision and Control of the Congress.

No State shall, without the Consent of Congress, lay any Duty of Tonnage, keep Troops, or Ships of War in Time of Peace, enter into any Agreement or Compact with another State, or with a foreign Power, or engage in War, unless actually invaded, or in such imminent Danger as will not admit of Delay.

Article II

Section 1. *The executive Power shall be vested in a President of the United States of America. He shall hold his Office during the Term of four Years, and, together with the Vice-President, chosen for the same Term, be elected, as follows:*

Each State shall appoint, in such Manner as the Legislature thereof may direct, a Number of Electors, equal to the whole Number of Senators and Representatives to which the State may be entitled in the Congress: but no Senator or Representative, or Person holding an Office of Trust or Profit under the United States, shall be appointed an Elector.

The Electors shall meet in their respective States, and vote by Ballot for two Persons, of whom one at least shall be an Inhabitant of the same State with themselves. And they shall make a List of all the Persons voted for, and of the Number of Votes for each; which List they shall sign and certify, and transmit sealed to the Seat of the Government of the United States, directed to the President of the Senate. The President of the Senate shall, in the Presence of the Senate and House of Representatives, open all the Certificates, and the Votes shall then be counted. The Person having the greatest Number of Votes shall be the President, if such Number be a Majority of the whole Number of Electors appointed; and if there be more than one who have such Majority, and have an equal Number of Votes, then the House of Representatives shall immediately choose by Ballot one of them for President; and if no Person have a Majority, then from the five highest on the List the said House shall in like Manner choose the President. But in choosing the President, the Votes shall be taken by States, the Representation from each State having one Vote. A Quorum for this Purpose shall consist of a Member or Members from two-thirds of the States, and a Majority of all the States shall be necessary to a Choice. In every Case, after the Choice of the President, the Person having the greatest Number of Votes of the Electors shall be the Vice-President. But if there should remain two or more who have equal Votes, the Senate shall choose from them by Ballot the Vice-President.

The Congress may determine the Time of choosing the Electors, and the Day on which they shall give their Votes; which Day shall be the same throughout the United States.

No Person except a natural born Citizen, or a Citizen of the United States, at the time of the Adoption of this Constitution, shall be eligible to the Office of President; neither shall any Person be eligible to that Office who shall not have attained to the Age of thirty-five Years, and been fourteen Years a Resident within the United States.

In Case of the Removal of the President from Office, or of his Death, Resignation, or Inability to discharge the Powers and Duties of the said Office, the Same shall devolve on the Vice-President, and the Congress may by Law provide for the Case of Removal, Death, Resignation or Inability, both of the President and Vice-President, declaring what Officer shall then act as President, and such Officer shall act accordingly, until the Disability be removed, or a President shall be elected.

The President shall, at stated Times, receive for his Services, a Compensation which shall neither be increased nor diminished during the Period for which he shall have been elected, and he shall not receive within that Period any other Emolument from the United States, or any of them.

Before he enter on the Execution of his Office, he shall take the following Oath or Affirmation—"I do solemnly swear (or affirm) that I will faithfully execute the office of the President of the United States, and will, to the best of my Ability, preserve, protect and defend the Constitution of the United States."

Section 2. The President shall be Commander in Chief of the Army and Navy of the United States, and of the Militia of the several States, when called into actual Service of the United States; he may require the Opinion, in writing, of the principal Office in each of the executive Departments, upon any Subject relating to the Duties of their respective Offices, and he shall have Power to grant Reprieves and Pardons for Offences against the United States, except in Cases of Impeachment.

He shall have Power, by and with the Advice and Consent of the Senate, to make Treaties, provided two-thirds of the Senators present concur; and he shall nominate, and by and with the Advice and Consent of the Senate, shall appoint Ambassadors, other public Ministers and Consuls, Judges of the Supreme Court, and all other Officers of the United States, whose Appointments are not herein otherwise provided for, and which shall be established by Law: but the Congress may by Law vest the Appointment of such inferior Officers, as they think proper, in the President alone, in the Courts of Law, or in the Heads of Departments.

The President shall have Power to fill up all Vacancies that may happen during the Recess of the Senate, by granting Commissions which shall expire at the End of their next Session.

Section 3. He shall from time to time give to the Congress Information of the State of the Union, and recommend to their Consideration such Measures as he shall judge necessary and expedient; he may, on extraordinary Occasions, convene both Houses, or either of them, and in Case of Disagreement between them, with Respect to the Time of Adjournment, he may adjourn them to such Time as he shall think proper; he shall receive Ambassadors and other public Ministers; he shall take Care that the Laws be faithfully executed, and shall Commission all the Officers of the United States.

Section 4. The President, Vice-President and all civil Officers of the United States, shall be removed from Office on Impeachment for, and Conviction of, Treason, Bribery, or other high Crimes and Misdemeanors.

Article III

Section 1. The judicial Power of the United States shall be vested in one Supreme Court, and in such inferior Courts as the Congress may from time to time ordain and establish. The Judges, both of the Supreme and inferior Courts, shall hold their Offices during good Behavior, and shall, at stated Times, receive for their Services, a Compensation, which shall not be diminished during their Continuance in Office.

Section 2. The judicial Power shall extend to all Cases, in Law and Equity, arising under this Constitution, the Laws of the United States, and Treaties made, or which shall be made, under their Authority;—to all Cases affecting Ambassadors, other public Ministers and Consuls;—to all Cases of admiralty and maritime Jurisdiction;—to Controversies to which the United States shall be a Party;— to Controversies between two or more States;—*between a State and Citizens of another State;*—between Citizens of different States;—between Citizens of the same State claiming Lands under Grants of different States, *and between a State, or the Citizens thereof, and foreign States, Citizens or Subjects.*

In all Cases affecting Ambassadors, other public Ministers and Consuls, and those in which a State shall be Party, the Supreme Court shall have original Jurisdiction. In all the other Cases before mentioned, the Supreme Court shall have appellate Jurisdiction, both as to Law and Fact, with such Exceptions, and under such Regulations as the Congress shall make.

The Trial of all Crimes, except in Cases of Impeachment, shall be by Jury; and such Trial shall be held in the State where the said Crimes shall have been committed; but when not committed within any State, the Trial shall be at such Place or Places as the Congress may by Law have directed.

Section 3. Treason against the United States, shall consist only in levying War against them, or in adhering to their Enemies, giving them Aid and Comfort. No Person shall be convicted of Treason unless on the Testimony of two Witnesses to the same overt Act, or on Confession in open Court.

The Congress shall have Power to declare the Punishment of Treason, but no Attainder of Treason shall work Corruption of Blood, or Forfeiture except during the Life of the Person attained.

Article IV

Section 1. Full Faith and Credit shall be given in each State to the public Acts, Records and judicial Proceedings of every other State. And the Congress may by general Laws prescribe the Manner in which such Acts, Records and Proceedings shall be proved, and the Effect thereof.

Section 2. The Citizens of each State shall be entitled to all Privileges and Immunities of Citizens in the several States.

A Person charged in any State with Treason, Felony, or other Crime, who shall flee from Justice, and be found in another State, shall on Demand of the executive Authority of the State from which he fled, be delivered up, to be removed to the State having Jurisdiction of the Crime.

No Person held to Service or Labour in one State, under the Laws thereof, escaping into another, shall, in Consequence of any Law or Regulation therein, be discharged from such Service or Labour, but shall be delivered up on Claim of the Party to whom such Service or Labour may be due.

Section 3. New States may be admitted by the Congress into this Union; but no new States shall be formed or erected within the Jurisdiction of any other State; nor any State be formed by the Junction of two or more States, or Parts of States, without the Consent of the Legislatures of the States concerned as well as of the Congress.

The Congress shall have Power to dispose of and make all needful Rules and Regulations respecting the Territory or other Property belonging to the United States; and nothing in this Constitution shall be so construed as to prejudice any Claims of the United States, or of any particular State.

Section 4. The United States shall guarantee to every State in this Union a Republican Form of Government, and shall protect each of them against Invasion; and on Application of the Legislature, or of the Executive (when the Legislature cannot be convened) against domestic Violence.

Article V

The Congress, whenever two-thirds of both Houses shall deem it necessary, shall propose Amendments to this Constitution, or, on the Application of the Legislatures of two-thirds of the several States, shall call a Convention for proposing Amendments, which, in either Case, shall be valid to all Intents and Purposes, as Part of this Constitution, when ratified by the Legislatures of three-fourths of the several States, or by Conventions in three-fourths thereof, as the one or the other Mode of Ratification may be proposed by the Congress; Provided *that no Amendment which may be made prior to the Year One thousand eight hundred and eight shall in any Manner affect the first and fourth Clauses in the Ninth Section of the first Article;* and that no State, without its Consent, shall be deprived of its equal Suffrage in the Senate.

Article VI

All Debts contracted and Engagements entered into, before the Adoption of this Constitution, shall be as valid against the United States under this Constitution, as under the Confederation.

This Constitution, and the Laws of the United States which shall be made in Pursuance thereof and all Treaties made, or which shall be made, under the Authority of the United States, shall be the supreme Law of the Land; and the Judges in every State shall be bound thereby, any Thing in the Constitution or Laws of any State to the Contrary notwithstanding.

The Senators and Representatives before mentioned, and the Members of the several State Legislatures, and all executive and judicial Officers, both of the United States and of the several States, shall be bound by Oath or Affirmation, to support this Constitution; but no religious Test shall ever be required as a Qualification to any Office or public Trust under the United States.

Article VII

The Ratification of the Conventions of nine States, shall be sufficient for the Establishment of this Constitution between the States so ratifying the Same.

DONE in Convention by the Unanimous Consent of the States present the Seventeenth Day of September in the Year of our Lord one thousand seven hundred and Eighty-seven and of the Independence of the United States of America the Twelfth. In witness whereof We have hereunto subscribed our Names, Attest William Jackson
Secretary

G° Washington—
Presidt. and deputy
from Virginia

New Hampshire	John Langdon
	Nicholas Gilman
Massachusetts	Nathaniel Gorham
	Rufus King
Connecticut	Wm. Saml. Johnson
	Roger Sherman
New York	{Alexander Hamilton
New Jersey	Wil: Livingston
	David Brearley.
	Wm. Paterson.
	Jona: Dayton
Pennsylvania	B. Franklin
	Thomas Mifflin
	Robt. Morris
	Geo. Clymer
	Thos. FitzSimons
	Jared Ingersoll
	James Wilson
	Gouv Morris
Delaware	Geo: Read
	Gunning Bedford Jun
	John Dickinson
	Richard Bassett
	Jaco: Broom
Maryland	James McHenry
	Dan of St. Thos Jenifer
	Danl. Carroll
Virginia	John Blair—
	James Madison Jr.
North Carolina	Wm. Blount
	Richd. Dobbs Spaight.
	Hu Williamson
South Carolina	J. Rutledge
	Charles Cotesworth Pinckney
	Charles Pinckney
	Pierce Butler
Georgia	William Few
	Abr Baldwin

Amendments to Constitution of the United States of America

Amendment I

Congress shall make no law respecting an establishment of religion, or prohibiting the free exercise thereof; abridging the freedom of speech, or of the press; or of the right of the people peaceably to assemble and to petition the Government for a redress of grievances.

Amendment II

A well regulated Militia, being necessary to the security of a free State, the right of the people to keep and bear Arms, shall not be infringed.

Amendment III

No Soldier shall, in time of peace be quartered in any house, without the consent of the Owner, nor in time of war, but in a manner to be prescribed by law.

Amendment IV

The right of the people to be secure in their persons, houses, papers, and effects, against unreasonable searches and seizures, shall not be violated, and no Warrants shall issue, but upon probable cause, supported by Oath or affirmation and particularly describing the place to be searched, and the persons or things to be seized.

Amendment V

No person shall be held to answer for a capital, or otherwise infamous crime, unless on a presentment or indictment of a Grand Jury, except in cases arising in the land or naval forces, or in the Militia, when in actual service in time of War or public danger; nor shall any person be subject for the same offence to be twice put in jeopardy of life or limb; nor shall be compelled in any criminal case to be a witness against himself, nor be deprived of life, liberty, or property, without due process of law; nor shall private property be taken for public use, without just compensation.

Amendment VI

In all criminal prosecutions, the accused shall enjoy the right to a speedy and public trial, by an impartial jury of the State and district wherein the crime shall have been committed, which district shall have been previously ascertained by law, and to be informed of the nature and cause of the accusation: to be confronted with the witnesses against him; to have compulsory process for obtaining witnesses in his favor, and to have the Assistance of Counsel for his defence.

Amendment VII

In suits at common law, where the value in controversy shall exceed twenty dollars, the right of trial by jury shall be preserved, and no fact tried by jury, shall be otherwise reexamined in any Court of the United States, than according to the rules of the common law.

Amendment VIII

Excessive bail shall not be required, nor excessive fines imposed, nor cruel and unusual punishments inflicted.

Amendment IX

The enumeration in the Constitution, of certain rights, shall not be construed to deny or disparage others retained by the people.

Amendment X

The powers not delegated to the United States by the Constitution, nor prohibited by it to the States, are reserved to the States respectively, or to the people.
   (Ratification of first ten amendments completed December 15, 1791.)

Amendment XI

The Judicial power of the United States shall not be construed to extend to any suit in law or equity, commenced or prosecuted against one of the United States by Citizens of another State, or by Citizens or Subjects of any Foreign State.
   (Declared ratified January 8, 1798.)

Amendment XII

The electors shall meet in their respective states and vote by ballot for President and Vice-President, one of whom, at least, shall not be an inhabitant of the same state with themselves; they shall name in their ballots the person voted for as President, and in distinct ballots the person voted for as Vice-President, and they shall make distinct lists of all persons voted for as President, and of all persons voted for as Vice-President, and of the number of votes for each, which lists they shall sign and certify, and transmit sealed to the seat of the government of the United States, directed to the President of the Senate;—The President of the Senate shall, in presence of the Senate and House of Representatives, open all the certificates and the votes shall then be counted;—The person having the greatest number of votes for President, shall be the President, if such number be a majority of the whole number of Electors appointed; and if no person have such majority, then from the persons having the highest numbers not exceeding three on the list of those voted for as President, the House of Representatives shall choose immediately, by ballot, the President. But in choosing the President, the votes shall be taken by states, the representation from each state having one vote; a quorum for this purpose shall consist of a member or members from two-thirds of the states, and a majority of all the states shall be necessary to a choice. *[and if the House of Representatives shall not choose a President whenever the right of choice shall devolve upon them, before the fourth day of March next following, then the Vice-President shall act as President, as in the case of the death or other constitutional disability of the President.]—The person having the greatest number of votes as Vice-President, shall be the Vice-President, if such number be a majority of the whole number of Electors appointed, and if no person have a majority, then from the two highest numbers on the list, the Senate shall choose the Vice-President; a quorum for the purpose shall consist of two-thirds of the whole number of Senators, and a majority of the whole number shall be necessary to a choice. But no person constitutionally ineligible to the office of President shall be eligible to that of Vice-President of the United States.

(Declared ratified September 25, 1804.)

Amendment XIII

Section 1. Neither slavery nor involuntary servitude, except as a punishment for crime whereof the party shall have been duly convicted, shall exist within the United States, or any place subject to their jurisdiction.

Section 2. Congress shall have power to enforce this article by appropriate legislation.

(Declared ratified December 18, 1865.)

Amendment XIV

Section 1. All persons born or naturalized in the United States, and subject to the jurisdiction thereof, are citizens of the United States and of the State wherein they reside. No State shall make or enforce any law which shall abridge the privileges or immunities of citizens of the United States; nor shall any State deprive any person of life, liberty, or property, without due process of law; nor deny to any person within its jurisdiction the equal protection of the laws.

Section 2. Representatives shall be apportioned among the several States according to their respective numbers, counting the whole number of persons in each State, excluding Indians not taxed. But when the right to vote at any election for the choice of electors for President and Vice-President of the United States, Representatives in Congress, the Executive and Judicial officers of a State, or the members of the Legislature thereof, is denied to any of the male inhabitants of such State, being twenty-one years of age, and citizens of the United States, or in any way abridged, except for participation in rebellion, or other crime, the basis of representation therein shall be reduced in the proportion which the number of such male citizens shall bear to the whole number of male citizens twenty-one years of age in such State.

Section 3. No person shall be a Senator or Representative in Congress, or elector of President and Vice-President, or hold any office, civil or military, under the United States, or under any State, who, having previously taken an oath, as a member of Congress, or as an officer of the United States, or as a member of any State legislature, or as an executive or judicial officer of any State, to support the Constitution of the United States, shall have engaged in insurrection or rebellion against the same, or given aid or comfort to the enemies thereof. But Congress may by a vote of two-thirds of each House, remove such disability.

Section 4. The validity of the public debt of the United States, authorized by law, including debts incurred for payment of pensions and bounties for services in suppressing insurrection or rebellion, shall not be questioned. But neither the United States nor any State shall assume or pay any debt or obligation incurred in aid of insurrection or rebellion against the United States, or any claim for the loss or emancipation of any slave; but all such debts, obligations and claims shall be held illegal and void.

Section 5. The Congress shall have power to enforce, by appropriate legislation, the provisions of this article.
(Declared ratified July 28, 1868.)

Amendment XV

Section 1. The right of citizens of the United States to vote shall not be denied or abridged by the United States or by any State on account of race, color, or previous condition of servitude—

Section 2. The Congress shall have power to enforce this article by appropriate legislation.
(Declared ratified March 30, 1870.)

Amendment XVI

The Congress shall have power to lay and collect taxes on incomes, from whatever source derived, without apportionment among the several States, and without regard to any census or enumeration.
(Declared ratified February 25, 1913.)

Amendment XVII

The Senate of the United States shall be composed of two Senators from each State, elected by the people thereof, for six years; and each Senator shall have one vote. The electors in each State shall have the qualifications requisite for electors of the most numerous branch of the State legislatures.

When vacancies happen in the representation of any State in the Senate, the executive authority of such State shall issue writs of election to fill such vacancies: *Provided,* That the legislature of any State may empower the executive thereof to make temporary appointments until the people fill the vacancies by election as the legislature may direct.

This amendment shall not be so construed as to affect the election or term of any Senator chosen before it becomes valid as part of the Constitution.

(Declared ratified May 31, 1913.)

Amendment XVIII

[**Section 1.** After one year from the ratification of this article the manufacture, sale, or transportation of intoxicating liquors within, the importation thereof into, or the exportation thereof from the United States and all territory subject to the jurisdiction thereof for beverage purposes is hereby prohibited.

[**Section 2.** The Congress and the several States shall have concurrent power to enforce this article by appropriate legislation.

[**Section 3.** This article shall be inoperative unless it shall have been ratified as an amendment to the Constitution by the legislatures of the several States, as provided in the Constitution, within seven years from the date of submission hereof to the States by the Congress]*

(Declared ratified January 29, 1919.)

Amendment XIX

The right of citizens of the United States to vote shall not be denied or abridged by the United States or by any State on account of sex.

Congress shall have power to enforce this article by appropriate legislation.

(Declared ratified August 26, 1920.)

*Amendment XVIII was repealed by section 1 of amendment XXI.

Amendment XX

Section 1. The terms of the President and Vice-President shall end at noon on the 20th day of January, and the terms of Senators and Representatives at noon on the 3d day of January, of the years in which such terms would have ended if this article had not been ratified; and the terms of their successors shall then begin.

Section 2. The Congress shall assemble at least once in every year, and such meeting shall begin at noon on the 3d day of January, unless they shall by law appoint a different day.

Section 3. If, at the time for the beginning of the term of the President, the President elect shall have died, the Vice-President elect shall become President. If a President shall not have been chosen before the time fixed for the beginning of his term, or if the President elect shall have failed to qualify, then the Vice-President elect shall act as President until a President shall have qualified; and the Congress may by law provide for the case wherein neither a President elect nor a Vice-President elect shall have qualified, declaring who shall then act as President, or the manner in which one who is to act shall be selected, and such person shall act accordingly until a President or Vice-President shall have qualified.

Section 4. The Congress may by law provide for the case of the death of any of the persons from whom the House of Representatives may choose a President whenever the right of choice shall have devolved upon them and for the case of the death of any of the persons from whom the Senate may choose a Vice-President whenever the right of choice shall have devolved upon them.

Section 5. Sections 1 and 2 shall take effect on the 15th day of October following the ratification of this article.

Section 6. This article shall be inoperative unless it shall have been ratified as an amendment to the Constitution by the legislatures of three-fourths of the several States within seven years from the date of its submission.
(Declared ratified February 6, 1933.)

Amendment XXI

Section 1. The eighteenth article of amendment to the Constitution of the United States is hereby repealed.

Section 2. The transportation or importation into any State, Territory, or possession of the United States for delivery or use therein of intoxicating liquors, in violation of the laws thereof, is hereby prohibited.

Section 3. This article shall be inoperative unless it shall have been ratified as an amendment to the Constitution by conventions in the several States, as provided in the Constitution, within seven years from the date of the submission hereof to the States by the Congress.
  (Declared ratified December 5, 1933.)

Amendment XXII

Section 1. No person shall be elected to the office of the President more than twice, and no person who has held the office of President, or acted as President, for more than two years of a term to which some other person was elected President shall be elected to the office of the President more than once. But this article shall not apply to any person holding the office of President when this Article was proposed by the Congress, and shall not prevent any person who may be holding the office of President, or acting as President, during the term within which this Article becomes operative from holding the office of President or acting as President during the remainder of such term.

Section 2. This article shall be inoperative unless it shall have been ratified as an amendment to the Constitution by the legislatures of three-fourths of the several States within seven years from the date of its submission to the States by the Congress.
  (Declared ratified March 1, 1951.)

Amendment XXIII

Section 1. The District constituting the seat of Government of the United States shall appoint in such manner as the Congress may direct:
  A number of electors of President and Vice President equal to the whole number of Senators and Representatives in Congress to which the District would be entitled if it were a State, but in no event more than the least populous State; they shall be in addition to those appointed by the States, but they shall be considered, for the purposes of the election of President and Vice President, to be electors appointed by a State; and they shall meet in the District and perform such duties as provided by the twelfth article of amendment.

Section 2. The Congress shall have power to enforce this article by appropriate legislation.
 (Declared ratified April 3, 1961.)

Amendment XXIV

Section 1. The right of citizens of the United States to vote in any primary or other election for President or Vice President, for electors for President or Vice President, or for Senator or Representative in Congress, shall not be denied or abridged by the United States or any State by reason of failure to pay any poll tax or other tax.

Section 2. The Congress shall have power to enforce this article by appropriate legislation.
 (Declared ratified Feburary 4, 1962.)

Amendment XXV

Section 1. In case of the removal of the President from office or of his death or resignation, the Vice President shall become President.

Section 2. Whenever there is a vacancy in the office of the Vice President, the President shall nominate a Vice President who shall take office upon confirmation by a majority vote of both Houses of Congress.

Section 3. Whenever the President transmits to the President pro tempore of the Senate and the Speaker of the House of Representatives his written declaration that he is unable to discharge the powers and duties of his office, and until he transmits to them a written declaration to the contrary, such powers and duties shall be discharged by the Vice President as Acting President.

Section 4. Whenever the Vice President and a majority of either the principal officers of the executive departments or of such other body as Congress may by law provide, transmit to the President pro tempore of the Senate and the Speaker of the House of Representatives their written declaration that the President is unable to discharge the powers and duties of his office, the Vice President shall immediately assume the powers and the duties of the office as Acting President.
 Thereafter, when the President transmits to the President pro tempore of the Senate and the Speaker of the House of Representatives his written declaration that no inability exists, he shall resume the power and duties of his office unless the Vice President and a majority of either the principal officers of the executive department or of such other body as Congress may by law provide, transmit within four days to the President pro tempore of the Senate and the Speaker of the House of Representatives their written declaration that the President is unable

to discharge the powers and duties of his office. Thereupon Congress shall decide the issue, assembling within forty-eight hours for that purpose if not in session. If the Congress, within twenty-one days after receipt of the latter written declaration, or, if Congress is not in session, within twenty-one days after Congress is required to assemble, determines by two-thirds vote of both Houses that the President is unable to discharge the powers and duties of his office, the Vice President shall continue to discharge the same as Acting President; otherwise, the President shall resume the powers and duties of his office.

(Declared ratified February 10, 1967.)

Amendment XXVI

Section 1. The right of citizens of the United States, who are eighteen years of age or older, to vote shall not be denied or abridged by the United States or by any state on account of age.

Section 2. The Congress shall have the power to enforce this article by appropriate legislation. (Declared Ratified, 1971).

Mapp v. Ohio

Supreme Court of the United States.
367 U.S. 643, 81 S.Ct. 1684, 6 L.Ed.2d 1081 (1961).

Mr. Justice CLARK delivered the opinion of the Court. . . .

On May 23, 1957, three Cleveland police officers arrived at appellant's residence in that city pursuant to information that "a person [was] hiding out in the home, who was wanted for questioning in connection with a recent bombing, and that there was a large amount of police paraphernalia being hidden in the home." . . . Upon their arrival at that house, the officers knocked on the door and demanded entrance but appellant, after telephoning her attorney, refused to admit them without a search warrant. They advised their headquarters of the situation and undertook a surveillance of the house.

The officers again sought entrance three hours later when four or more additional officers arrived on the scene. When Miss Mapp did not come to the door immediately, at least one of the several doors to the house was forcibly opened and the policemen gained admittance. Meanwhile Miss Mapp's attorney arrived, but the officers, having secured their own entry, and continuing in their defiance of the law, would permit him neither to see Miss Mapp nor to enter the house. It appears that Miss Mapp was halfway down the stairs from the upper floor to the front door when the officers, in this high-handed manner, broke into the hall.

She demanded to see the search warrant. A paper, claimed to be a warrant, was held up by one of the officers. She grabbed the "warrant" and placed it in her bosom. A struggle ensued in which the officers recovered the piece of paper and as a result of which they handcuffed appellant because she had been"belligerent" in resisting their official rescue of the "warrant" from her person. Running rough-shod over appellant, a policeman "grabbed" her, "twisted [her] hand," and she "yelled [and] pleaded with him" because "it was hurting." Appellant, in hand-cuffs, was then forcibly taken upstairs to her bedroom where the officers searched a dresser, a chest of drawers, a closet and some suitcases. They also looked into a photo album and through personal papers belonging to the appellant. The search spread to the rest of the second floor including the child's bedroom, the living room, the kitchen and a dinette. The basement of the building and a trunk found therein were also searched. The obscene materials for possession of which she was ultimately convicted were discovered in the course of that widespread search.

At the trial no search warrant was produced by the prosecution, nor was the failure to produce one explained or accounted for. At best, "There is, in the rec-ord, considerable doubt as to whether there ever was any warrant for the search of defendant's home." . . .

. . . [T]his Court in *Weeks v. United States,* 232 U.S. 383, 34 S.Ct. 341, 58 L.Ed. 652 (1914), stated that

> "the Fourth Amendment . . . put the courts of the United States and Federal officials, in the exercise of their power and authority, under limitations and restraints [and] . . . forever secure[d] the people, their persons, houses, papers and effects against all unreasonable searches and seizures under the guise of law . . . and the duty of giving to it force and effect is obligatory upon all entrusted under our Federal system with the enforcement of the laws." At pp. 391–392.

Specifically dealing with the use of the evidence unconstitutionally seized, the Court concluded:

> "If letters and private documents can thus be seized and held and used in evidence against a citizen accused of an offense, the protection of the Fourth Amendment declaring his right to be secure against such searches and seizures is of no value, and, so far as those thus placed are concerned, might as well be stricken from the Constitution. The efforts of the courts and their officials to bring the guilty to punishment, praiseworthy as they are, are not to be aided by the sacrifice of those great principles established by years of endeavor and suffering which have resulted in their embodiment in the fundamental law of the land." At p. 393.

"The striking outcome of the *Weeks* case and those which followed it was the sweeping declaration that the Fourth Amendment, although not referring to or limiting the use of evidence in courts, really forbade its introduction if obtained by government officers through a violation of the Amendment." . . .

In 1949, 35 years after *Weeks* was announced, this Court, in

. . .

Wolf v. Colorado, . . . , again for the first time, discussed the effect of the Fourth Amendment upon the States through the operation of the Due Process Clause of the Fourteenth Amendment. It said:

> "[W]e have no hesitation in saying that were a State affirmatively to sanction such police incursion into privacy it would run counter to the guaranty of the Fourteenth Amendment." . . .

Nevertheless, . . . the Court decided that the *Weeks* exclusionary rule would not then be imposed upon the States as "an essential ingredient of the right." . . . While in 1949, prior to the *Wolf* case, almost two-thirds of the States were opposed to the use of the exclusionary rule, now, despite the *Wolf* case, more than half of those since passing upon it, by their own legislative or judicial decision, have wholly or partly adopted or adhered to the *Weeks* rule. . . . Significantly, among those now following the rule is California, which, according to its highest court, was "compelled to reach that conclusion because other remedies have completely failed to secure compliance with the constitutional provisions. . . ."

. . .

Today we once again examine *Wolf's* constitutional documentation of the right to privacy free from unreasonable state intrusion, and, after its dozen years on our books, are led by it to close the only courtroom door remaining open to evidence secured by official lawlessness in flagrant abuse of that basic right, reserved to all persons as a specific guarantee against that very same unlawful conduct. We hold that all evidence obtained by searches and seizures in violation of the Constitution is, by that same authority, inadmissible in a state court.

Since the Fourth Amendment's right of privacy has been declared enforceable against the States through the Due Process Clause of the Fourteenth, it is enforceable against them by the same sanction of exclusion as is used against the Federal Government. Were it otherwise, then just as without the *Weeks* rule the assurance against unreasonable federal searches and seizures would be "a form of words," valueless and undeserving of mention in a perpetual charter of inestimable human liberties, so too, without that rule the freedom from state invasions of privacy would be so ephemeral and so neatly severed from its conceptual nexus with the freedom from all brutish means of coercing evidence as not to merit this Court's high regard as a freedom "implicit in the concept of ordered liberty." . . . In short, the admission of the new constitutional right by *Wolf* could not consistently tolerate denial of its most important constitutional privilege, namely, the exclusion of the evidence which an accused had been forced to give by reason of the unlawful seizure. To hold otherwise is to grant the right but in reality to withhold its privilege and enjoyment. Only last year the Court itself recognized that the purpose of the exclusionary rule "is to deter—to compel respect for the constitutional guaranty in the only effectively available way—by removing the incentive to disregard it."

. . .

There are those who say, as did Justice (then Judge) Cardozo, that under our constitutional exclusionary doctrine "[t]he criminal is to go free because the constable has blundered." *People v. Defore,* 242 N.Y., at 21, 150 N.E., at 587. In some cases this will undoubtedly be the result. But, as was said in *Elkins,* "there is another consideration—the imperative of judicial integrity." 364 U.S., at 222. The criminal goes free, if he must, but it is the law that sets him free. Nothing can destroy a government more quickly than its failure to observe its own laws, or worse, its disregard of the charter of its own existence. As Mr. Justice Brandeis, dissenting, said in *Olmstead v. United States,* 277 U.S. 438, 485, 48 S.Ct. 564, 72 L.Ed. 944 (1928): "Our Government is the potent, the omnipresent teacher. For good or for ill, it teaches the whole people by its example. . . . If the Government becomes a lawbreaker, it breeds contempt for law; it invites every man to become a law unto himself; it invites anarchy." Nor can it lightly be assumed that, as a practical matter, adoption of the exclusionary rule fetters law enforcement. . . .

The ignoble shortcut to conviction left open to the State tends to destroy the entire system of constitutional restraints on which the liberties of the people rest. Having once recognized that the right to privacy embodied in the Fourth Amendment is enforceable against the States, and that the right to be secure against rude invasions of privacy by state officers, is, therefore, constitutional in origin, we can no longer permit that right to remain an empty promise. Because it is enforceable in the same manner and to like effect as other basic rights secured by the Due Process Clause, we can no longer permit it to be revocable at the whim of any police officer who, in the name of law enforcement itself, chooses to suspend its enjoyment. Our decision, founded on reason and truth, gives to the individual no more than that which the Constitution guarantees him, to the police officer no less than that to which honest law enforcement is entitled, and, to the courts, that judicial integrity so necessary in the true administration of justice.

The judgement of the Supreme Court of Ohio is reversed and the cause remanded for further proceedings not inconsistent with this opinion.

Reversed and remanded.

Miranda v. Arizona

Supreme Court of the United States, 1966.
384 U.S. 436, 86 S.Ct. 1602, 16 L.Ed.2d 694.

MR. CHIEF JUSTICE WARREN delivered the opinion of the Court.

The cases before us raise questions which go to the roots of our concepts of American criminal jurisprudence: the restraints society must observe consistent with the Federal Constitution in prosecuting individuals for crime. More specifically, we deal with the admissibility of statements obtained from an individual who is subjected to custodial police interrogation and the necessity for procedures which assure that the individual is accorded his privilege under the Fifth Amendment to the Constitution not to be compelled to incriminate himself.

We dealt with certain phases of this problem recently in *Escobedo v. State of Illinois,* 378 U.S. 478, 84 S.Ct. 1758, 12 L.Ed.2d 977 (1964). There, as in the four cases before us, law enforcement officials took the defendant into custody and interrogated him in a police station for the purpose of obtaining a confession. The police did not effectively advise him of his right to remain silent or of his right to consult with his attorney. Rather, they confronted him with an alleged accomplice who accused him of having perpetrated a murder. When the defendant denied the accusation and said "I didn't shoot Manuel, you did it," they handcuffed him and took him to an interrogation room. There, while handcuffed and standing, he was questioned for four hours until he confessed. During this interrogation, the police denied his request to speak to his attorney, and they prevented his retained attorney, who had come to the police station, from consulting with him. At his trial, the State, over his objection, introduced the confession against him. We held that the statements thus made were constitutionally inadmissible.

This case has been the subject of judicial interpretation and spirited legal debate since it was decided two years ago. Both state and federal courts, in assessing its implications, have arrived at varying conclusions. A wealth of scholarly material has been written tracing its ramifications and underpinnings. Police and prosecutor have speculated on its range and desirability. We granted certiorari in these cases, 382 U.S. 924, 925, 937, 86 S.Ct. 318, 320, 395, 15 L.Ed.2d 338, 339, 348, in order further to explore some facets of the problems, thus exposed, of applying the privilege against self-incrimination to in-custody interrogation, and to give concrete constitutional guidelines for law enforcement agencies and courts to follow.

. . .

Our holding will be spelled out with some specificity in the pages which follow but briefly stated it is this: the prosecution may not use statements, whether exculpatory or inculpatory, stemming from custodial interrogation of the defendant unless it demonstrates the use of procedural safeguards effective to secure the privilege against self-incrimination. By custodial interrogation, we mean questioning initiated by law enforcement officers after a person has been taken into custody or otherwise deprived of his freedom of action in any significant way. As for the procedural safeguards to be employed, unless other fully effective means are devised to inform accused persons of their right of silence and to assure a continuous opportunity to exercise it, the following measures are required. Prior to any questioning, the person must be warned that he has a right to remain silent, that any statement he does make may be used as evidence against him, and that he has a right to the presence of an attorney, either retained or appointed. The defendant may waive effectuation of these rights, provided the waiver is made voluntarily, knowingly and intelligently. If, however, he indicates in any manner and at any stage of the process that he wishes to consult with an attorney before speaking there can be no questioning. Likewise, if the individual is alone and indicates in any manner that he does not wish to be interrogated, the police may not question him. The mere fact that he may have answered some questions or volunteered some statements on his own does not deprive him of the right to refrain from answering any further inquiries until he has consulted with an attorney and thereafter consents to be questioned.

I. The constitutional issue we decide in each of these cases is the admissibility of statements obtained from a defendant questioned while in custody or otherwise deprived of his freedom of action in any significant way. In each, the defendant was questioned by police officers, detectives, or a prosecuting attorney in a room in which he was cut off from the outside world. In none of these cases was the defendant given a full and effective warning of his rights at the outset of the interrogation process. In all the cases, the questioning elicited oral admissions, and in three of them, signed statements as well which were admitted at their trials. They all thus share salient features—incommunicado interrogation of individuals in a police-dominated atmosphere, resulting in self-incriminating statements without full warnings of constitutional rights.

An understanding of the nature and setting of this in-custody interrogation is essential to our decisions today. The difficulty in depicting what transpires at such interrogations stems from the fact that in this country they have largely taken place incommunicado. From extensive factual studies undertaken in the early 1930's, including the famous Wickersham Report to Congress by a Presidential Commission, it is clear that police violence and the "third degree" flourished at that time. In a series of cases decided by this Court long after these studies, the police resorted to physical brutality—beatings, hanging, whipping—and to sustained and protracted questioning incommunicado in order to extort confessions. The Commission on Civil Rights in 1961 found much evidence to indicate that "some policemen still resort to physical force to obtain confessions," 1961 Comm'n on Civil Rights Rep., Justice, pt. 5, 17. The use of physical brutality and violence is not, unfortunately, relegated to the past or to any part of the country. Only recently in Kings County, New York, the police brutally beat, kicked and placed lighted cigarette butts on the back of a potential witness under interrogation for the purpose of securing a statement incriminating a third party. *People v. Portelli*, 15 N.Y.2d 235, 257 N.Y.S.2d 931, 205 N.E.2d 857 (1965).

The examples given above are undoubtedly the exception now, but they are sufficiently widespread to be the object of concern. Unless a proper limitation upon custodial interrogation is achieved—such as these decisions will advance—there can be no assurance that practices of this nature will be eradicated in the foreseeable future.

. . .

Again we stress that the modern practice of in-custody interrogation is psychologically rather than physically oriented. As we have stated before, "Since *Chambers v. State of Florida,* 309 U.S. 227, 60 S.Ct. 472, 84 L.Ed. 716, this Court has recognized that coercion can be mental as well as physical, and that the blood of the accused is not the only hallmark of an unconstitutional inquisition." *Blackburn v. State of Alabama,* 361 U.S 199, 206, 80 S.Ct. 274, 279, 4 L.Ed.2d 242 (1960). Interrogation still takes place in privacy. Privacy results in secrecy and this in turn results in a gap in our knowledge as to what in fact goes on in the interrogation rooms. A valuable source of information about present police practices, however, may be found in various police manuals and texts which document procedures employed with success in the past, and which recommend various other effective tactics. These texts are used by law enforcement agencies themselves as guides. It should be noted that these texts professedly present the most enlightened and effective means presently used to obtain statements through custodial interrogation. By considering these texts and other data, it is possible to describe procedures observed and noted around the country.

The officers are told by the manuals that the "principal psychological factor contributing to a successful interrogation is privacy—being alone with the person under interrogation." The efficacy of this tactic has been explained as follows:

> "If at all practicable, the interrogation should take place in the investigator's office or at least in a room of his own choice. The subject should be deprived of every psychological advantage. In his own home he may be confident, indigent, or recalcitrant. He is more keenly aware of his rights and more reluctant to tell of his indiscretions or criminal behavior within the walls of his home. Moreover his family and other friends are nearby, their presence lending moral support. In his office, the investigator possesses all the advantages. The atmosphere suggests the invincibility of the forces of the law."

To highlight the isolation and unfamiliar surroundings, the manuals instruct the police to display an air of confidence in the suspect's guilt and from outward appearance to maintain only an interest in confirming certain details. The guilt of the subject is to be posited as a fact. The interrogator should direct his comments toward the reasons why the subject committed the act, rather than court failure by asking the subject whether he did it. Like other men, perhaps the subject has had a bad family life, had an unhappy childhood, had too much to drink, had an unrequited desire for women. The officers are instructed to minimize the moral seriousness of the offense, to cast blame on the victim or on society. These tactics are designed to put the subject in a psychological state where his story is but an elaboration of what the police purport to know already—that he is guilty. Explanations to the contrary are dismissed and discouraged.

The texts thus stress that the major qualities an interrogator should possess are patience and perseverance. One writer describes the efficacy of these characteristics in this manner:

> "In the preceding paragraphs emphasis has been placed on kindness and stratagems. The investigator will, however, encounter many situations where the sheer weight of his personality will be the deciding factor. Where emotional appeals and tricks are employed to no avail, he must rely on an oppressive atmosphere of dogged persistence. He must interrogate steadily and without relent, leaving the subject no prospect of surcease. He must dominate his subject and overwhelm him with his inexorable will to obtain the truth. He should interrogate for a spell of several hours pausing only for the subject's necessities in acknowledgement of the need to avoid a charge of duress that can be technically substantiated. In a serious case, the interrogation may continue for days, with the required intervals for food and sleep, but with no respite from the atmosphere of domination. It is possible in this way to induce the subject to talk without resorting to duress or coercion. The method should be used only when the guilt of the subject appears highly probable."

The manuals suggest that the suspect be offered legal excuses for his actions in order to obtain an initial admission of guilt. Where there is a suspected revenge-killing, for example, the interrogator may say:

> "Joe, you probably didn't go out looking for this fellow with the purpose of shooting him. My guess is, however, that you expected something from him and that's why you carried a gun—for your own protection. You knew him for what he was, no good. Then when you met him he probably started using foul, abusive language and he gave some indication that he was about to pull a gun on you, and that's when you had to act to save your own life. That's about it, isn't it, Joe?"

Having then obtained the admission of shooting, the interrogator is advised to refer to circumstantial evidence which negates the self-defense explanation. This should enable him to secure the entire story. One text notes that "Even if he fails to do so, the inconsistency between the subject's original denial of the shooting and his present admission of at least doing the shooting will serve to deprive him of a self-defense 'out' at the time of trial."

When the techniques described above prove unavailing, the texts recommend they be alternated with a show of some hostility. One ploy often used has been termed the "friendly-unfriendly" or the "Mutt and Jeff" act:

> "In this technique, two agents are employed. Mutt, the relentless investigator, who knows the subject is guilty and is not going to waste any time. He's sent a dozen men away for this crime and he's going to send the subject away for the full term. Jeff, on the other hand, is obviously a kindhearted man. He has a family himself. He has a brother who was involved in a little scrape like this. He disapproves of Mutt and his tactics and will arrange to get him off the case if the subject will cooperate. He can't hold Mutt off for very long. The subject would be wise to make a quick decision. The technique is applied by having both investigators present while Mutt acts out his role. Jeff may stand by quietly and demur at some of Mutt's tactics. When Jeff makes his plea for cooperation, Mutt is not present in the room."

The interrogators sometimes are instructed to induce a confession out of trickery. The technique here is quite effective in crimes which require identification or which run in series. In the identification situation, the interrogator may take a break in his questioning to place the subject among a group of men in a line-up. "The witness or complainant (previously coached, if necessary) studies the line-up and confidently points out the subject as the guilty party." Then the questioning resumes "as though there were now no doubt about the guilt of the subject." A variation on this technique is called the "reverse line-up":

> "The accused is placed in a line-up, but this time he is identified by several fictitious witnesses or victims who associated him with different offenses. It is expected that the subject will become desperate and confess to the offense under investigation in order to escape from the false accusations."

The manuals also contain instructions for police on how to handle the individual who refuses to discuss the matter entirely or who asks for an attorney or relatives. The examiner is to concede him the right to remain silent. "This usually has a very undermining effect. First of all, he is disappointed in his expectation of an unfavorable reaction in the part of the interrogator. Secondly, a concession of this right to remain silent impresses the subject with the apparent fairness of his interrogator." After this psychological conditioning, however, the officer is told to point out the incriminating significance of the suspect's refusal to talk:

> "Joe, you have the right to remain silent. That's your privilege and I'm the last person in the world who'll try to take it away from you. If that's the way you want to leave this, O.K. But let me ask you this. Suppose you were in my

shoes and I were in yours and you called me in to ask me about this and I told you, 'I don't want to answer any of your questions.' You'd think I had something to hide, and you'd probably be right in thinking that. That's exactly what I'll have to think about you, and so will everybody else. So let's sit here and talk this whole thing over."

Few will persist in their initial refusal to talk, it is said, if this monologue is employed correctly.

In the event that the subject wishes to speak to a relative or an attorney, the following advice is tendered:

"[T]he interrogator should respond by suggesting that the subject first tell the truth to the interrogator himself rather than get anyone else involved in the matter. If the request is for an attorney, the interrogator may suggest that the subject save himself or his family the expense of any such professional service, particularly if he is innocent of the offense under investigation. The interrogator may also add, 'Joe, I'm only looking for the truth, and if you're telling the truth, that's it. You can handle this by yourself.' "

From these representative samples of interrogation techniques, the setting prescribed by the manuals and observed in practice becomes clear. In essence, it is this: To be alone with the subject is essential to prevent distraction and to deprive him of any outside support. The aura of confidence in his guilt undermines his will to resist. He merely confirms the preconceived story the police seek to have him describe. Patience and persistence, at times relentless questioning, are employed. To obtain a confession, the interrogator must "patiently maneuver himself or his quarry into a position from which the desired objective may be attained." When normal procedures fail to produce the needed result, the police may resort to deceptive stratagems such as giving false legal advice. It is important to keep the subject off balance, for example, by trading on his insecurity about himself or his surroundings. The police then persuade, trick, or cajole him out of exercising his constitutional rights.

Even without employing brutality, the "third degree" or the specific stratagems described above, the very fact of custodial interrogation exacts a heavy toll on individual liberty and trades on the weakness of individuals. This fact may be illustrated simply by referring to three confession cases decided by this Court in the Term immediately preceding our *Escobedo* decision. In *Townsend v. Sain,* 372 U.S. 293, 83 S.Ct. 745, 9 L.Ed.2d 770 (1963), the defendant was a 19-year-old heroin addict, described as a "near mental defective," id., at 307–310, 83 S.Ct. at 754–755. The defendant in *Lynumn v. State of Illinois,* 372 U.S. 528, 83 S.Ct. 917, 9 L.Ed.2d 922 (1963), was a woman who confessed to the arresting officer after being importuned to "cooperate" in order to prevent her children from being taken by relief authorities. This Court as in those cases reversed the conviction of a defendant in *Haynes v. State of Washington,* 373 U.S. 503, 83

S.Ct. 1336, 10 L.Ed.2d 513 (1963), whose persistent request during his interrogation was to phone his wife or attorney. In other settings, these individuals might have exercised their constitutional rights. In the incommunicado police-dominated atmosphere, they succumbed.

In the cases before us today, given this background, we concern ourselves primarily with this interrogation atmosphere and the evils it can bring. In No. 759, *Miranda v. Arizona,* the police arrested the defendant and took him to a special interrogation room where they secured a confession. In No. 760, *Vignera v. New York,* the defendant made oral admissions to the police after interrogation in the afternoon, and then signed an inculpatory statement upon being questioned by an assistant district attorney later the same evening. In No. 761, *Westover v. United States,* the defendant was handed over to the Federal Bureau of Investigation by local authorities after they had detained and interrogated him for a lengthy period, both at night and the following morning. After some two hours of questioning, the federal officers had obtained signed statements from the defendant. Lastly, in No. 584, *California v. Stewart,* the local police held the defendant five days in the station and interrogated him on nine separate occasions before they secured his inculpatory statement.

In these cases, we might find the defendants' statements to have been involuntary in traditional terms. Our concern for adequate safeguards to protect precious Fifth Amendment rights is, of course, not lessened in the slightest. In each of the cases, the defendant was thrust into an unfamiliar atmosphere and run through menacing police interrogation procedures. The potentiality for compulsion is forcefully apparent, for example, in *Miranda,* where the indigent Mexican defendant was a seriously disturbed individual with pronounced sexual fantasies, and in *Stewart,* in which the defendant was an indigent Los Angeles Negro who had dropped out of school in the sixth grade. To be sure, the records do not evince overt physical coercion or patent psychological ploys. The fact remains that in none of these cases did the officers undertake to afford appropriate safeguards at the outset of the interrogation to insure that the statements were truly the product of free choice.

It is obvious that such an interrogation environment is created for no purpose other than to subjugate the individual to the will of his examiner. This atmosphere carries its own badge of intimidation. To be sure, this is not physical intimidation, but it is equally destructive of human dignity. The current practice of incommunicado interrogation is at odds with one of our Nation's most cherished principles—that the individual may not be compelled to incriminate himself. Unless adequate protective devices are employed to dispel the compulsion inherent in custodial surroundings, no statement obtained from the defendant can truly be the product of his free choice.

. . .

III. Today, then, there can be no doubt that the Fifth Amendment privilege is available outside of criminal court proceedings and serves to protect persons in all settings in which their freedom of action is curtailed in any significant way from being compelled to incriminate themselves. We have concluded that without proper safeguards the process of in-custody interrogation of persons suspected or accused of crime contains inherently compelling pressures which work to undermine the individual's will to resist and to compel him to speak where he would not otherwise do so freely. In order to combat these pressures and to permit a full opportunity to exercise the privilege against self-incrimination, the accused must be adequately and effectively apprised of his rights and the exercise of those rights must be fully honored.

It is impossible for us to foresee the potential alternatives for protecting the privilege which might be devised by Congress or the States in the exercise of their creative rule-making capacities. Therefore we cannot say that the Constitution necessarily requires adherence to any particular solution for the inherent compulsions of the interrogation process as it is presently conducted. Our decision in no way creates a constitutional straitjacket which will handicap sound efforts at reform, nor is it intended to have this effect. We encourage Congress and the States to continue their laudable search for increasingly effective ways of protecting the rights of the individual while promoting efficient enforcement of our criminal laws. However, unless we are shown other procedures which are at least as effective in apprising accused persons of their right of silence and in assuring a continuous opportunity to exercise it, the following safeguards must be observed.

At the outset, if a person in custody is to be subjected to interrogation, he must first be informed in clear and unequivocal terms that he has the right to remain silent. For those unaware of the privilege, the warning is needed simply to make them aware of it—the threshold requirement for an intelligent decision as to its exercise. More important, such a warning is an absolute prerequisite in overcoming the inherent pressures of the interrogation atmosphere. It is not just the subnormal or woefully ignorant who succumb to an interrogator's imprecations, whether implied or expressly stated, that the interrogation will continue until a confession is obtained or that silence in the face of accusation is itself damning and will bode ill when presented to a jury. Further, the warning will show the individual that his interrogators are prepared to recognize his privilege should he choose to exercise it.

The Fifth Amendment privilege is so fundamental to our system of constitutional rule and the expedient of giving an adequate warning as to the availability of the privilege so simple, we will not pause to inquire in individual cases whether the defendant was aware of his rights without a warning being given. Assessments of the knowledge the defendant possessed, based on information as to his age, education, intelligence, or prior contact with authorities, can never be more than speculation; a warning is a clearcut fact. More important, whatever the background of the person interrogated, a warning at the time of the interrogation is indispensable to overcome its pressures and to insure that the individual knows he is free to exercise the privilege at that point in time.

The warning of the right to remain silent must be accompanied by the explanation that anything said can and will be used against the individual in court. This warning is needed in order to make him aware not only of the privilege, but also of the consequences of forgoing it. It is only through an awareness of these consequences that there can be any assurance of real understanding and intelligent exercise of the privilege. Moreover, this warning may serve to make the individual more acutely aware that he is faced with a phase of the adversary system—that he is not in the presence of persons acting solely in his interest.

The circumstances surrounding in-custody interrogation can operate very quickly to overbear the will of one merely made aware of his privilege by his interrogators. Therefore, the right to have counsel present at the interrogation is indispensable to the protection of the Fifth Amendment privilege under the system we delineate today. Our aim is to assure that the individual's right to choose between silence and speech remains unfettered throughout the interrogation process. A once-stated warning, delivered by those who will conduct the interrogation, cannot itself suffice to that end among those who most require knowledge of their rights. A mere warning given by the interrogators is not alone sufficient to accomplish that end. Prosecutors themselves claim that the admonishment of the right to remain silent without more "will benefit only the recidivist and the professional." Brief for the National District Attorneys Association as *amicus curiae,* p. 14. Even preliminary advice given to the accused by his own attorney can be swiftly overcome by the secret interrogation process. Cf. *Escobedo v. State of Illinois,* 378 U.S. 478, 485, n. 5, 84 S.Ct. 1758, 1762. Thus, the need for counsel to protect the Fifth Amendment privilege comprehends not merely a right to consult with counsel prior to questioning, but also to have counsel present during any questioning if the defendant so desires.

The presence of counsel at the interrogation may serve several significant subsidiary functions as well. If the accused decides to talk to his interrogators, the assistance of counsel can mitigate the dangers of untrustworthiness. With a lawyer present the likelihood that the police will practice coercion is reduced, and if coercion is nevertheless exercised the lawyer can testify to it in court. The presence of a lawyer can also help to guarantee that the accused gives a fully accurate statement to the police and that the statement is rightly reported by the prosecution at trial. See *Crooker v. State of California,* 357 U.S. 433, 443–448, 78 S.Ct. 1287, 1293–1296, 2 L.Ed.2d 1448 (1958) (Douglas, J., dissenting).

An individual need not make a pre-interrogation request for a lawyer. While such request affirmatively secures his right to have one, his failure to ask for a lawyer does not constitute a waiver. No effective waiver of the right to counsel during interrogation can be recognized unless specifically made after the warnings we here delineate have been given. The accused who does not know his rights and therefore does not make a request may be the person who most needs counsel. As the California Supreme Court has aptly put it:

> "Finally, we must recognize that the imposition of the requirement for the request would discriminate against the defendant who does not know his rights. The defendant who does not ask for counsel is the very defendant who most needs counsel. We cannot penalize a defendant who, not understanding his constitutional rights, does not make the formal request and by such failure demonstrates his helplessness. To require the request would be to favor the defendant whose sophistication or status had fortuitously prompted him to make it." *People v. Dorado,* 62 Cal.2d 338, 351, 42 Cal.Rptr. 169, 177–178, 398 P.2d 361, 369–370, (1965) (Tobriner, J.).

In *Carnley v. Cochran,* 369 U.S. 506, 513, 82 S.Ct. 884, 889, 8 L.Ed.2d 70 (1962), we stated: "[I]t is settled that where the assistance of counsel is a constitutional requisite, the right to be furnished counsel does not depend on a request." This proposition applies with equal force in the context of providing counsel to protect an accused's Fifth Amendment privilege in the face of interrogation. Although the role of counsel at trial differs from the role during interrogation, the differences are not relevant to the question whether a request is a prerequisite.

Accordingly we hold that an individual held for interrogation must be clearly informed that he has the right to consult with a lawyer and to have the lawyer with him during interrogation under the system for protecting the privilege we delineate today. As with the warnings of the right to remain silent and that anything stated can be used in evidence against him, this warning is an absolute prerequisite to interrogation. No amount of circumstantial evidence that the person may have been aware of this right will suffice to stand in its stead. Only through such a warning is there ascertainable assurance that the accused was aware of this right.

If an individual indicates that he wishes the assistance of counsel before any interrogation occurs, the authorities cannot rationally ignore or deny his request on the basis that the individual does not have or cannot afford a retained attorney. The financial ability of the individual has no relationship to the scope of the rights involved here. The privilege against self-incrimination secured by the Constitution applies to all individuals. The need for counsel in order to protect the privilege exists for the indigent as well as the affluent. In fact, were we to limit these constitutional rights to those who can retain an attorney, our decisions today would be of little significance. The cases before us as well as the vast majority of confession cases with which we have dealt in the past involve those unable to retain counsel. While authorities are not required to relieve the accused of his poverty, they have the obligation not to take advantage of indigence in the administration of justice. Denial of counsel to the indigent at the time of interrogation while allowing an attorney to those who can afford one would be no more supportable by reason or logic than the similar situation at trial and on appeal struck down in *Gideon v. Wainwright,* 372 U.S. 335, 83 S.Ct. 792, 9 L.Ed.2d 799 (1963), and *Douglas v. People of State of California,* 372 U.S. 353, 83 S.Ct. 814, 9 L.Ed.2d 811 (1963).

In order fully to apprise a person interrogated of the extent of his rights under this system then, it is necessary to warn him not only that he has the right to consult with an attorney, but also that if he is indigent a lawyer will be appointed to represent him. Without this additional warning, the admonition of the right to consult with counsel would often be understood as meaning only that he can consult with a lawyer if he has one or has the funds to obtain one. The warning of a right to counsel would be hollow if not couched in terms that would convey to the indigent—the person most often subjected to interrogation—the knowledge that he too has a right to have counsel present. As with the warnings of the right to remain silent and of the general right to counsel, only by effective and express explanation to the indigent of this right can there be assurance that he was truly in a position to exercise it.[5]

Once warnings have been given, the subsequent procedure is clear. If the individual indicates in any manner, at any time prior to or during questioning, that he wishes to remain silent, the interrogation must cease.[6] At this point he has shown that he intends to exercise his Fifth Amendment privilege; any statement taken after the person invokes his privilege cannot be other than the product of compulsion, subtle or otherwise. Without the right to cut off questioning, the setting of in-custody interrogation operates on the individual to overcome free choice in producing a statement after the privilege has been once invoked. If the individual states that he wants an attorney, the interrogation must cease until an attorney is present. At that time, the individual must have an opportunity to confer with the attorney and to have him present during any subsequent questioning. If the individual cannot obtain an attorney and he indicates that he wants one before speaking to police, they must respect his decision to remain silent.

---

5. While a warning that the indigent may have counsel appointed need not be given to the person who is known to have an attorney or is known to have ample funds to secure one, the expedient of giving a warning is too simple and the rights involved too important to engage in *ex post facto* inquiries into financial ability when there is any doubt at all on that score.

6. If an individual indicates his desire to remain silent, but has an attorney present, there may be some circumstances in which further questioning would be permissible. In the absence of evidence of overbearing, statements then made in the presence of counsel might be free of the compelling influence of the interrogation process and might fairly be construed as a waiver of the privilege for purposes of these statements.

This does not mean, as some have suggested, that each police station must have a "station house lawyer" present at all times to advise prisoners. It does mean, however, that if police propose to interrogate a person they must make known to him that he is entitled to a lawyer and that if he cannot afford one, a lawyer will be provided for him prior to any interrogation. If authorities conclude that they will not provide counsel during a reasonable period of time in which investigation in the field is carried out, they may refrain from doing so without violating the person's Fifth Amendment privilege so long as they do not question him during that time.

If the interrogation continues without the presence of an attorney and a statement is taken, a heavy burden rests on the government to demonstrate that the defendant knowingly and intelligently waived his privilege against self-incrimination and his right to retained or appointed counsel. *Escobedo v. State of Illinois,* 378 U.S. 478, 490, n. 14, 84 S.Ct. 1758, 1764, 12 L.Ed.2d 977. This Court has always set high standards of proof for the waiver of constitutional rights, *Johnson v. Zerbst,* 304 U.S. 458, 58 S.Ct. 1019, 82 L.Ed. 1461 (1938), and we reassert these standards as applied to in-custody interrogation. Since the State is responsible for establishing the isolated circumstances under which the interrogation takes place and has the only means of making available corroborated evidence of warnings given during incommunicado interrogation, the burden is rightly on its shoulders.

An express statement that the individual is willing to make a statement and does not want an attorney followed closely by a statement could constitute a waiver. But a valid waiver will not be presumed simply from the silence of the accused after warnings are given or simply from the fact that a confession was in fact eventually obtained. A statement we made in *Carnley v. Cochran,* 369 U.S. 506, 516, 82 S.Ct. 884, 890, 8 L.Ed.2d 70 (1962), is applicable here:

> "Presuming waiver from a silent record is impermissible. The record must show, or there must be an allegation and evidence which show, that an accused was offered counsel but intelligently and understandingly rejected the offer. Anything less is not waiver."

See also *Glasser v. United States,* 315 U.S. 60, 62 S.Ct. 457, 86 L.Ed. 680 (1942). Moreover, where in-custody interrogation is involved, there is no room for the contention that the privilege is waived if the individual answers some questions or gives some information on his own prior to invoking his right to remain silent when interrogated.

Whatever the testimony of the authorities as to waiver of rights by an accused, the fact of lengthy interrogation or incommunicado incarceration before a statement is made is strong evidence that the accused did not validly waive his rights. In these circumstances the fact that the individual eventually made a statement is consistent with the conclusion that the compelling influence of the interrogation finally forced him to do so. It is inconsistent with any notion of a voluntary relinquishment of the privilege. Moreover, any evidence that the accused was threatened, tricked, or cajoled into a waiver will, of course, show that the defendant did not voluntarily waive his privilege. The requirement of warnings and waiver of rights is a fundamental with respect to the Fifth Amendment privilege and not simply a preliminary ritual to existing methods of interrogation.

The warnings required and the waiver necessary in accordance with our opinion today are, in the absence of a fully effective equivalent, prerequisites to the admissibility of any statement made by a defendant. No distinction can be drawn between statements which are direct confessions and statements which amount to "admissions" of part or all of an offense. The privilege against self-incrimination protects the individual from being compelled to incriminate himself in any manner; it does not distinguish degrees of incrimination. Similarly, for precisely the same reason, no distinction may be drawn between inculpatory statements and statements alleged to be merely "exculpatory." If a statement made were in fact truly exculpatory it would, of course, never be used by the prosecution. In fact, statements merely intended to be exculpatory by the defendant are often used to impeach his testimony at trial or to demonstrate untruths in the statement given under interrogation and thus to prove guilt by implication. These statements are incriminating in any meaningful sense of the word and may not be used without the full warnings and effective waiver required for any other statement. In *Escobedo* itself, the defendant fully intended his accusation of another as the slayer to be exculpatory as to himself.

The principles announced today deal with the protection which must be given to the privilege against self-incrimination when the individual is first subjected to police interrogation while in custody at the station or otherwise deprived of his freedom of action in any significant way. It is at this point that our adversary system of criminal proceedings commences, distinguishing itself at the outset from the inquisitorial system recognized in some countries. Under the system of warnings we delineate today or under any other system which may be devised and found effective, the safeguards to be erected about the privilege must come into play at this point.

Our decision is not intended to hamper the traditional function of police officers in investigating crime. See *Escobedo v. State of Illinois,* 378 U.S. 478, 492, 84 S.Ct. 1758, 1765. When an individual is in custody on probable cause, the police may, of course, seek out evidence in the field to be used at trial against him. Such investigation may include inquiry of persons not under restraint. General on-the-scene questioning as to facts surrounding a crime or other general questioning of citizens in the fact-finding process is not affected by our holding. It is an act of responsible citizenship for individuals to give whatever information they may have to aid in law enforcement. In such situations the compelling atmosphere inherent in the process of in-custody interrogation is not necessarily present.

In dealing with statements obtained through interrogation, we do not purport to find all confessions inadmissible. Confessions remain a proper element in law enforcement. Any statement given freely and voluntarily without any compelling influences is, of course, admissible in evidence. The fundamental import of the privilege while an individual is in custody is not whether he is allowed to talk to the police without the benefit of warnings and counsel, but whether he can be interrogated. There is no requirement that police stop a person who enters a police station and states that he wishes to confess to a crime, or a person who calls the police to offer a confession or any other statement he desires to make. Volunteered statements of any kind are not barred by the Fifth Amendment and their admissibility is not affected by our holding today.

To summarize, we hold that when an individual is taken into custody or otherwise deprived of his freedom by the authorities in any significant way and is subjected to questioning, the privilege against self-incrimination is jeopardized. Procedural safeguards must be employed to protect the privilege and unless other fully effective means are adopted to notify the person of his right of silence and to assure that the exercise of the right will be scrupulously honored, the following measures are required. He must be warned prior to any questioning that he has the right to remain silent, that anything he says can be used against him in a court of law, that he has the right to the presence of an attorney, and that if he cannot afford an attorney one will be appointed for him prior to any questioning if he so desires. Opportunity to exercise these rights must be afforded to him throughout the interrogation. After such warnings have been given, and such opportunity afforded him, the individual may knowingly and intelligently waive these rights and agree to answer questions or make a statement. But unless and until such warnings and waiver are demonstrated by the prosecution at trial, no evidence obtained as a result of interrogation can be used against him.

IV. A recurrent argument made in these cases is that society's need for interrogation outweighs the privilege. This argument is not unfamiliar to this Court. See, e.g., *Chambers v. State of Florida,* 309 U.S. 227, 240–241, 60 S.Ct. 472, 478–479, 84 L.Ed. 716 (1940). The whole thrust of our foregoing discussion demonstrates that the Constitution has prescribed the rights of the individual when confronted with the power of government when it provided in the Fifth Amendment that an individual cannot be compelled to be a witness against himself. That right cannot be abridged. As Mr. Justice Brandeis once observed:

> "Decency, security, and liberty alike demand that government officials shall be subjected to the same rules of conduct that are commands to the citizen. In a government of laws, existence of the government will be imperilled if it fails to observe the law scrupulously. Our government is the potent, the omnipresent teacher. For good or for ill, it teaches the whole people by its example. Crime is contagious. If the government becomes a

lawbreaker, it breeds contempt for law; it invites every man to become a law unto himself; it invites anarchy. To declare that in the administration of the criminal law the end justifies the means . . . would bring terrible retribution. Against that pernicious doctrine this court should resolutely set its face." *Olmstead v. United States,* 277 U.S. 438, 485, 48 S.Ct. 564, 575, 72 L.Ed. 944 (1928) (dissenting opinion).[7] In this connection, one of our country's distinguished jurists has pointed out: "The quality of a nation's civilization can be largely measured by the methods it uses in the enforcement of its criminal law."

If the individual desires to exercise his privilege, he has the right to do so. This is not for the authorities to decide. An attorney may advise his client not to talk to police until he has had an opportunity to investigate the case, or he may wish to be present with his client during any police questioning. In doing so an attorney is merely exercising the good professional judgment he has been taught. This is not cause for considering the attorney a menace to law enforcement. He is merely carrying out what he is sworn to do under his oath—to protect to the extent of his ability the rights of his client. In fulfilling this responsibility the attorney plays a vital role in the administration of criminal justice under our Constitution.

In announcing these principles, we are not unmindful of the burdens which law enforcement officials must bear, often under trying circumstances. We also fully recognize the obligation of all citizens to aid in enforcing the criminal laws. This Court, while protecting individual rights, has always given ample latitude to law enforcement agencies in the legitimate exercise of their duties. The limits we have placed on the interrogation process should not constitute an undue interference with a proper system of law enforcement. As we have noted, our decision does not in any way preclude police from carrying out their traditional investigatory functions. Although confessions may play an important role in some convictions, the cases before us present graphic examples of the overstatement of the "need" for confessions. In each case authorities conducted interrogations ranging up to five days in duration despite the presence, through standard investigating practices, of considerable evidence against each defendant.

. . .

It is also urged that an unfettered right to detention for interrogation should be allowed because it will often redound to the benefit of the person questioned. When police inquiry determines that there is no reason to believe that the person has committed any crime, it is said, he will be released without need for further formal procedures. The person who has committed no offense, however, will be better able to clear himself after warnings with counsel present than without. It can be assumed that in such circumstances a lawyer would advise his client to talk freely to police in order to clear himself.

7. In quoting the above from the dissenting opinion of Mr. Justice Brandeis we, of course, do not intend to pass on the constitutional questions involved in the *Olmstead* case.

Custodial interrogation, by contrast, does not necessarily afford the innocent an opportunity to clear themselves. A serious consequence of the present practice of the interrogation alleged to be beneficial for the innocent is that many arrests "for investigation" subject large numbers of innocent persons to detention and interrogation. In one of the cases before us, No. 584, *California v. Stewart,* police held four persons, who were in the defendant's house at the time of the arrest, in jail for five days until defendant confessed. At that time they were finally released. Police stated that there was "no evidence to connect them with any crime." Available statistics on the extent of this practice where it is condoned indicate that these four are far from alone in being subjected to arrest, prolonged detention, and interrogation without the requisite probable cause.

Over the years the Federal Bureau of Investigation has compiled an exemplary record of effective law enforcement while advising any suspect or arrested person, at the outset of an interview, that he is not required to make a statement, that any statement may be used against him in court, that the individual may obtain the services of an attorney of his own choice and, more recently, that he has a right to free counsel if he is unable to pay. A letter received from the Solicitor General in response to a question from the Bench makes it clear that the present pattern of warnings and respect for the rights of the individual followed as a practice by the FBI is consistent with the procedure which we delineate today. It states:

> "At the oral argument of the above cause, Mr. Justice Fortas asked whether I could provide certain information as to the practices followed by the Federal Bureau of Investigation. I have directed these questions to the attention of the Director of the Federal Bureau of Investigation and am submitting herewith a statement of the questions and of the answers which we have received.
>
> " '(1) When an individual is interviewed by agents of the Bureau, what warning is given to him?
>
> " 'The standard warning long given by Special Agents of the FBI to both suspects and persons under arrest is that the person has a right to say nothing and a right to counsel, and that any statement he does make may be used against him in court. Examples of this warning are to be found in the *Westover* case at 342 F.2d 684 (1965), and *Jackson v. United States,* [119 U.S.App.D.C. 100] 337 F.2d 136 (1964), cert. den. 380 U.S.935, 85 S.Ct. 1353,
>
> " 'After passage of the Criminal Justice Act of 1964, which provides free counsel for Federal defendants unable to pay, we added to our instructions to Special Agents the requirement that any person who is under arrest for an offense under FBI jurisdiction, or whose arrest is contemplated following the interview, must also be advised of his right to free counsel if he is unable to pay, and the fact that such counsel will be assigned by the Judge. At the same time, we broadened the right to counsel warning to read counsel of his own choice, or anyone else with whom he might wish to speak.

" '(2) When is the warning given?

" 'The FBI warning is given to a suspect at the very outset of the interview, as shown in the *Westover* case, cited above. The warning may be given to a person arrested as soon as practicable after the arrest, as shown in the *Jackson* case, also cited above, and in *United States v. Konigsberg*, 336 F.2d 844 (1964), cert. den. [*Celso v. United States*] 379 U.S. 933 [85 S.Ct. 327, 13 L.Ed.2d 342] but in any event it must precede the interview with the person for a confession or admission of his own guilt.

" '(3) What is the Bureau's practice in the event that (a) the individual requests counsel and (b) counsel appears?

" 'When the person who has been warned of his right to counsel decides that he wishes to consult with counsel before making a statement, the interview is terminated at that point, *Shultz v. United States*, 351 F.2d 287 ([10 Cir.] 1965). It may be continued, however, as to all matters *other* than the person's own guilt or innocence. If he is indecisive in his request for counsel, there may be some question on whether he did or did not waive counsel. Situations of this kind must necessarily be left to the judgment of the interviewing Agent. For example, in *Hiram v. United States*, 354 F.2d 4 ([9 Cir.] 1965), the Agent's conclusion that the person arrested had waived his right to counsel was upheld by the courts.

" 'A person being interviewed and desiring to consult counsel by telephone must be permitted to do so, as shown in *Caldwell v. United States*, 351 F.2d 459 ([1 Cir.] 1965). When counsel appears in person, he is permitted to confer with his client in private.

" '(4) What is the Bureau's practice if the individual requests counsel, but cannot afford to retain an attorney?

" 'If any person being interviewed after warning of counsel decides that he wishes to consult with counsel before proceeding further the interview is terminated, as shown above. FBI Agents do not pass judgment on the ability of the person to pay for counsel. They do, however, advise those who have been arrested for an offense under FBI jurisdiction, or whose arrest is contemplated following the interview, of a right to free counsel *if* they are unable to pay, and the availability of such counsel from the Judge.' "[8]

The practice of the FBI can readily be emulated by state and local enforcement agencies. The argument that the FBI deals with different crimes than are dealt with by state authorities does not mitigate the significance of the FBI experience.

The experience in some other countries also suggests that the danger to law enforcement in curbs on interrogation is overplayed. The English procedure since 1912 under the Judges' Rules is significant. As recently strengthened, the Rules

8. We agree that the interviewing agent must exercise his judgment in determining whether the individual waives his right to counsel. Because of the constitutional basis of the right, however, the standard for waiver is necessarily high. And, of course, the ultimate responsibility for resolving this constitutional question lies with the courts.

require that a cautionary warning be given an accused by a police officer as soon as he has evidence that affords reasonable grounds for suspicion; they also require that any statement made be given by the accused without questioning by police. The right of the individual to consult with an attorney during this period is expressly recognized.

The safeguards present under Scottish law may be even greater than in England. Scottish judicial decisions bar use in evidence of most confessions obtained through police interrogation. In India, confessions made to police not in the presence of a magistrate have been excluded by rule of evidence since 1872, at a time when it operated under British law. Identical provisions appear in the Evidence Ordinance of Ceylon, enacted in 1895. Similarly, in our country the Uniform Code of Military Justice has long provided that no suspect may be interrogated without first being warned of his right not to make a statement and that any statement he makes may be used against him. Denial of the right to consult counsel during interrogation has also been proscribed by military tribunals. There appears to have been no marked detrimental effect on criminal law enforcement in these jurisdictions as a result of these rules. Conditions of law enforcement in our country are sufficiently similar to permit reference to this experience as assurance that lawlessness will not result from warning an individual of his rights or allowing him to exercise them. Moreover, it is consistent with our legal system that we give at least as much protection to these rights as is given in the jurisdictions described. We deal in our country with rights grounded in a specific requirement of the Fifth Amendment of the Constitution, whereas other jurisdictions arrived at their conclusions on the basis of principles of justice not so specifically defined.

It is also urged upon us that we withhold decision on this issue until state legislative bodies and advisory groups have had an opportunity to deal with these problems by rule making. We have already pointed out that the Constitution does not require any specific code of procedures for protecting the privilege against self-incrimination during custodial interrogation. Congress and the States are free to develop their own safeguards for the privilege, so long as they are fully as effective as those described above in informing accused persons of their right of silence and in affording a continuous opportunity to exercise it. In any event, however, the issues presented are of constitutional dimensions and must be determined by the courts. The admissibility of a statement in the face of a claim that it was obtained in violation of the defendant's constitutional rights is an issue the resolution of which has long since been undertaken by this Court. See *Hopt v. People of Territory of Utah*, 110 U.S. 574, 4 S.Ct. 202, 28 L.Ed. 262 (1884). Judicial solutions to problems of constitutional dimension have evolved decade by decade. As courts have been presented with the need to enforce constitutional rights, they have found means of doing so. That was our responsibility when *Escobedo* was before us and it is our responsibility today. Where rights secured by the Constitution are involved, there can be no rule making or legislation which would abrogate them.

V. Because of the nature of the problem and because of its recurrent significance in numerous cases, we have to this point discussed the relationship of the Fifth Amendment privilege to police interrogation without specific concentration on the facts of the cases before us. We turn now to these facts to consider the application to these cases of the constitutional principles discussed above. In each instance, we have concluded that statements were obtained from the defendant under circumstances that did not meet constitutional standards for protection of the privilege.

No. 759. *Miranda v. Arizona.*

On March 13, 1963, petitioner, Ernesto Miranda, was arrested at his home and taken in custody to a Phoenix police station. He was there identified by the complaining witness. The police then took him to "Interrogation Room No. 2" of the detective bureau. There he was questioned by two police officers. The officers admitted at trial that Miranda was not advised that he had a right to have an attorney present.[9] Two hours later, the officers emerged from the interrogation room with a written confession signed by Miranda. At the top of the statement was a typed paragraph stating that the confession was made voluntarily, without threats or promises of immunity and "with full knowledge of my legal rights, understanding any statement I make may be used against me."[10]

At his trial before a jury, the written confession was admitted into evidence over the objection of defense counsel, and the officers testified to the prior oral confession made by Miranda during the interrogation. Miranda was found guilty of kidnapping and rape. He was sentenced to 20 to 30 years' imprisonment on each count, the sentences to run concurrently. On appeal, the Supreme Court of Arizona held that Miranda's constitutional rights were not violated in obtaining the confession and affirmed the conviction. 98 Ariz. 18, 401 P.2d 721. In reaching its decision, the court emphasized heavily the fact that Miranda did not specifically request counsel.

---

9. Miranda was also convicted in a separate trial on an unrelated robbery charge not presented here for review. A statement introduced at that trial was obtained from Miranda during the same interrogation which resulted in the confession involved here. At the robbery trial, one officer testified that during the interrogation he did not tell Miranda that anything he said would be held against him or that he could consult with an attorney. The other officer stated that they had both told Miranda that anything he said would be used against him and that he was not required by law to tell them anything.

10. One of the officers testified that he read this paragraph to Miranda. Apparently, however, he did not do so until after Miranda had confessed orally.

We reverse. From the testimony of the officers and by the admission of respondent, it is clear that Miranda was not in any way apprised of his right to consult with an attorney and to have one present during the interrogation, nor was his right not to be compelled to incriminate himself effectively protected in any other manner. Without these warnings the statements were inadmissible. The mere fact that he signed a statement which contained a typed-in clause stating that he had "full knowledge" of his "legal rights" does not approach the knowing and intelligent waiver required to relinquish constitutional rights.

. . .

No. 760. *Vignera v. New York.*

Petitioner, Michael Vignera, was picked up by New York police on October 14, 1960, in connection with the robbery three days earlier of a Brooklyn dress shop. They took him to the 17th Detective Squad headquarters in Manhattan. Sometime thereafter he was taken to the 66th Detective Squad. There a detective questioned Vignera with respect to the robbery. Vignera orally admitted the robbery to the detective. The detective was asked on cross-examination at trial by defense counsel whether Vignera was warned of his right to counsel before being interrogated. The prosecution objected to the question and the trial judge sustained the objection. Thus, the defense was precluded from making any showing that warnings had not been given. While at the 66th Detective Squad, Vignera was identified by the store owner and a saleslady as the man who robbed the dress shop. At about 3 P.M. he was formally arrested. The police then transported him to still another station, the 70th Precinct in Brooklyn, "for detention." At 11 P.M. Vignera was questioned by an assistant district attorney in the presence of a hearing reporter who transcribed the questions and Vignera's answers. This verbatim account of these proceedings contains no statement of any warnings given by the assistant district attorney. At Vignera's trial on a charge of first degree robbery, the detective testified as to the oral confession. The transcription of the statement taken was also introduced in evidence. At the conclusion of the testimony, the trial judge charged the jury in part as follows:

> "The law doesn't say that the confession is void or invalidated
> because the police officer didn't advise the defendant as to his rights. Did you
> hear what I said? I am telling you what the law of the State of New York is."

Vignera was found guilty of first degree robbery. He was subsequently adjudged a third-felony offender and sentenced to 30 to 60 years' imprisonment. The conviction was affirmed without opinion by the Appellate Division, Second Department, 21 A.D.2d 752, 252 N.Y. S.2d 19, and by the Court of Appeals, also without opinion, 15 N.Y.2d 970, 259 N.Y.S.2d 857, 207 N.E.2d 527, remittitur amended, 16 N.Y. 2d 614, 261 N.Y.S.2d 65, 209 N.E.2d 110. In argument to the Court of Appeals, the State contended that Vignera had no constitutional right to be advised of his right to counsel or his privilege against self-incrimination.

We reverse. The foregoing indicates that Vignera was not warned of any of his rights before the questioning by the detective and by the assistant district attorney. No other steps were taken to protect these rights. Thus he was not effectively apprised of his Fifth Amendment privilege or of his right to have counsel present and his statements are inadmissible.

No. 761. *Westover v. United States.*

At approximately 9:45 P.M. on March 20, 1963, petitioner, Carl Calvin Westover, was arrested by local police in Kansas City as a suspect in two Kansas City robberies. A report was also received from the FBI that he was wanted on a felony charge in California. The local authorities took him to a police station and placed him in a line-up on the local charges, and at about 11:45 P.M. he was booked. Kansas City police interrogated Westover on the night of his arrest. He denied any knowledge of criminal activities. The next day local officers interrogated him again throughout the morning. Shortly before noon they informed the FBI that they were through interrogating Westover and that the FBI could proceed to interrogate him. There is nothing in the record to indicate that Westover was ever given any warning as to his rights by local police. At noon, three special agents of the FBI continued the interrogation in a private interview room of the Kansas City Police Department, this time with respect to the robbery of a savings and loan association and a bank in Sacramento, California. After two or two and one-half hours, Westover signed separate confessions to each of these two robberies which had been prepared by one of the agents during the interrogation. At trial one of the agents testified, and a paragraph on each of the statements states, that the agents advised Westover that he did not have to make a statement, that any statement he made could be used against him, and that he had the right to see an attorney.

Westover was tried by a jury in federal court and convicted of the California robberies. His statements were introduced at trial. He was sentenced to 15 years' imprisonment on each count, the sentences to run consecutively. On appeal, the conviction was affirmed by the Court of Appeals for the Ninth Circuit. 342 F.2d 684.

We reverse. On the facts of this case we cannot find that Westover knowingly and intelligently waived his rights to remain silent and his right to consult with counsel prior to the time he made the statement. At the time the FBI agents began questioning Westover, he had been in custody for over 14 hours and had been interrogated at length during that period. The FBI interrogation began immediately upon the conclusion of the interrogation by Kansas City police and was conducted in local police headquarters. Although the two law enforcement authorities are legally distinct and the crimes for which they interrogated Westover were different, the impact on him was that of a continuous period of questioning. There is no evidence of any warning given prior to the FBI interrogation nor is there any evidence of an articulated waiver of rights after the FBI commenced its interrogation. The record simply shows that the defendant did in fact confess a short time after being turned over to the FBI following interrogation by local police. Despite the fact that the FBI agents gave warnings at the outset of their interview, from Westover's point of view the warnings came at the end of the interrogation process. In these circumstances an intelligent waiver of constitutional rights cannot be assumed.

We do not suggest that law enforcement authorities are precluded from questioning any individual who has been held for a period of time by other authorities and interrogated by them without appropriate warnings. A different case would be presented if an accused were taken into custody by the second authority removed both in time and place from his original surroundings, and then adequately advised of his rights and given an opportunity to exercise them. But here the FBI interrogation was conducted immediately following the state interrogation in the same police station—in the same compelling surroundings. Thus, in obtaining a confession from Westover the federal authorities were the beneficiaries of the pressure applied by the local in-custody interrogation. In these circumstances the giving of warnings alone was not sufficient to protect the privilege.

No. 584. *California v. Stewart.*

In the course of investigating a series of purse-snatch robberies in which one of the victims had died of injuries inflicted by her assailant, respondent, Roy Allen Stewart, was pointed out to Los Angeles police as the endorser of dividend checks taken in one of the robberies. At about 7:15 P.M., January 31, 1963, police officers went to Stewart's house and arrested him. One of the officers asked Stewart if they could search the house, to which he replied, "Go ahead." The search turned up various items taken from the five robbery victims. At the time of Stewart's arrest, police also arrested Stewart's wife and three other persons who were visiting him. These four were jailed along with Stewart and were interrogated. Stewart was taken to the University Station of the Los Angeles Police Department where he was placed in a cell. During the next five days, police interrogated Stewart on nine different occasions. Except during the first interrogation session, when he was confronted with an accusing witness, Stewart was isolated with his interrogators.

During the ninth interrogation session, Stewart admitted that he had robbed the deceased and stated that he had not meant to hurt her. Police then brought Stewart before a magistrate for the first time. Since there was no evidence to connect them with any crime, the police then released the other four persons arrested with him.

Nothing in the record specifically indicates whether Stewart was or was not advised of his right to remain silent or his right to counsel. In a number of instances, however, the interrogating officers were asked to recount everything that was said during the interrogations. None indicated that Stewart was ever advised of his rights.

Stewart was charged with kidnapping to commit robbery, rape, and murder. At his trial, transcripts of the first interrogation and the confession at the last interrogation were introduced in evidence. The jury found Stewart guilty of robbery and first degree murder and fixed the penalty as death. On appeal, the Supreme Court of California reversed. 62 Cal.2d 571, 43 Cal.Rptr. 201, 400 P.2d 97. It held that under this Court's decision in *Escobedo,* Stewart should have been advised of his right to remain silent and of his right to counsel and that it would not presume in the face of a silent record that the police advised Stewart of his rights.

We affirm. In dealing with custodial interrogation, we will not presume that a defendant has been effectively apprised of his rights and that his privilege against self-incrimination has been adequately safeguarded on a record that does not show that any warnings have been given or that any effective alternative has been employed. Nor can a knowing and intelligent waiver of these rights be assumed on a silent record. Furthermore, Stewart's steadfast denial of the alleged offenses through eight of the nine interrogations over a period of five days is subject to no other construction than that he was compelled by persistent interrogation to forego his Fifth Amendment privilege.

Therefore, in accordance with the foregoing, the judgments of the Supreme Court of Arizona in No. 759, of the New York Court of Appeals in No. 760, and of the Court of Appeals for the Ninth Circuit in No. 761 are reversed. The judgment of the Supreme Court of California in No. 584 is affirmed. It is so ordered.

Judgments of Supreme Court of Arizona in No. 759, of New York Court of Appeals in No. 760, and of the Court of Appeals for the Ninth Circuit in No. 761 reversed.

Judgment of Supreme Court of California in No. 584 affirmed.

Chimel v. California

Supreme Court of the United States, 1969
395 U.S. 752, 89 S. Ct. 2034, 23 L. Ed. 2d 685

Mr. Justice STEWART delivered the opinion of the Court.

. . .

Approval of a warrantless search incident to a lawful arrest seems first to have been articulated by the Court in 1914 as dictum in *Weeks v. United States . . .* in which the Court stated:

> "What then is the present case? Before answering that inquiry specifically it may be well by a process of exclusion to state what it is not. It is not an assertion of the right on the part of the Government, always recognized under English and American law, to search the person of the accused when legally arrested to discover and seize the fruits of evidences of crime." . . .

That statement made no reference to any right to search the *place* where an arrest occurs, but was limited to a right to search the "person." Eleven years later the case of *Carroll v. United States,* 267 U.S. 132 (1925), brought the following embellishment of the Weeks statement:

> "When a man is legally arrested for an offense, whatever is found upon his person *or in his control* which it is unlawful for him to have and which may be used to prove the offense may be seized and held as evidence in the prosecution." (Emphasis added.) . . .

Still, that assertion too was far from a claim that the "place" where one is arrested may be searched so long as the arrest is valid. Without explanation, however, the principle emerged in expanded form a few months later in *Agnello v. United States,* 269 U.S. 20 (1925)—although still by way of dictum:

"The right without a search warrant contemporaneously to search persons lawfully arrested while committing crime and to search the place where the arrest is made in order to find and seize things connected with the crime as its fruits or as the means by which it was committed, as well as weapons and other things to effect an escape from custody, is not to be doubted." And in *Marron v. United States* two years later, the dictum of Agnello appeared to be the foundation of the Court's decision. In that case federal agents had secured a search warrant authorizing the seizure of liquor and certain articles used in its manufacture. When they arrived at the premises to be searched, they say "that the place was used for retailing and drinking intoxicating liquors." They proceeded to arrest the person in charge and to execute the warrant. In searching a closet for the items listed in the warrant they came across an incriminating ledger, concededly not covered by the warrant, which they also seized. The Court upheld the seizure of the ledger by holding that since the agents had made a lawful arrest, "[t]hey had a right without a warrant contemporaneously to search the place in order to find and seize the things used to carry on the criminal enterprise.". . .

That the Marron opinion did not mean all that it seemed to say became evident, however, a few years later in *Go-Bart Importing Company v. United States,* 282 U.S. 344 (1931), and *United States v. Lefkowitz,* 285 U.S. 452 (1932). . . . In *Go-Bart,* agents had searched the office of persons whom they had lawfully arrested and had taken several papers from a desk, a safe, and other parts of the office. The Court noted that no crime had been committed in the agents' presence, and that although the agent in charge "had an abundance of information and time to swear out a valid [search] warrant, he failed to do so.". . . In holding the search and seizure unlawful, the Court stated:

> "Plainly the case before us is essentially different from *Marron v. United States.* . . . There, officers executing a valid search warrant for intoxicating liquors found and arrested one Birdsall who in pursuance of a conspiracy was actually engaged in running a saloon. As an incident to the

arrest they seized a ledger in a closet where the liquor or some of it was kept and some bills beside the cash register. These things were visible and accessible and in the offender's immediate custody. There was no threat of force or general search or rummaging of the place.". . .

This limited characterization of Marron was reiterated in Lefkowitz, a case in which the Court held unlawful a search of desk drawers and cabinet despite the fact that the search had accompanied a lawful arrest. . . .

The limiting views expressed in Go-Bart and Lefkowitz were thrown to the winds, however, in *Harris v. United States,* 331 U.S. 145, decided in 1947. In that case, officers had obtained a warrant for Harris' arrest on the basis of his alleged involvement with the cashing and interstate transportation of a forged check. He was arrested in the living room of his four-room apartment, and in an attempt to recover two canceled checks thought to have been used in effecting the forgery, the officers undertook a thorough search of the entire apartment. Inside a desk drawer they found a sealed envelope marked "George Harris, personal papers." The envelope, which was then torn open, was found to contain altered Selective Service documents, and those documents were used to secure Harris' conviction for violating the Selective Training and Service Act of 1940. The Court rejected Harris' Fourth Amendment claim, sustaining the search as "incident to arrest." . . .

Only a year after Harris, however, the pendulum swung again. In *Trupiano v. United States,* 334 U.S. 699 (1948), agents raided the site of an illicit distillery, saw one of several conspirators operating the still, and arrested him, contemporaneously "seiz[ing] the illicit distillery.". . . The Court held that the arrest and others made subsequently had been valid, but that the unexplained failure of the agents to procure a search warrant—in spite of the fact that they had had more than enough time before the raid to do so—rendered the search unlawful. The opinion stated:

"It is a cardinal rule that, in seizing goods and articles, law enforcement agents must secure and use search warrants wherever reasonably practicable. . . . This rule rests upon the desirability of having magistrates rather than police officers determine when searches and seizures are permissible and what limitations should be placed upon such activities. . . . To provide the necessary security against unreasonable intrusions upon the private lives of individuals, the framers of the Fourth Amendment required adherence to judicial processes wherever possible. And subsequent history has confirmed the wisdom of that requirement.

. . .

"A search or seizure without a warrant as an incident to a lawful arrest had always been considered to be a strictly limited right. It grows out of the inherent necessities of the situation at the time of the arrest. But there must be something more in the way of necessity than merely a lawful arrest.". . .

In 1950, two years after Trupiano, came *United States v. Rabinowitz,* 339 U.S. 56, the decision upon which California primarily relies in the case now before us. In Rabinowitz, federal authorities had been informed that the defendant was dealing in stamps bearing forged overprints. On the basis of that information they secured a warrant for his arrest, which they executed at his one-room business office. At the time of the arrest, the officers "searched the desk, safe, and file cabinets in the office for about an hour and a half". . . and seized 573 stamps with forged overprints. The stamps were admitted into evidence at the defendant's trial, and this Court affirmed his conviction, rejecting the contention that the warrantless search had been unlawful. The Court held that the search in its entirety fell within the principle giving law enforcement authorities "[t]he right 'to search the place where the arrest is made in order to find and seize things connected with the crime. . . .' " . . . Harris was regarded as "ample authority" for that conclusion. . . . The opinion rejected the rule of Trupiano that "in seizing goods and articles, law enforcement agents must secure and use search warrants wherever reasonably practicable." The test, said the Court, "is not whether it is reasonable to procure a search warrant, but whether the search was reasonable.". . .

Rabinowitz has come to stand for the proposition, *inter alia,* that a warrantless search "incident to a lawful arrest" may generally extend to the area that is considered to be in the "possession" or under the "control" of the person arrested. And it was on the basis of that proposition that the California courts upheld the search of the petitioner's entire house in this case. That doctrine, however, at least in the broad sense in which it was applied by the California courts in this case, can withstand neither historical nor rational analysis.

Even limited to its own facts, the Rabinowitz decision was, as we have seen, hardly founded on an unimpeachable line of authority. As Mr. Justice Frankfurter commented in dissent in that case, the "hint" contained in Weeks was, without persuasive justification, "loosely turned into dictum and finally elevated to a decision.". . . And the approach taken in cases such as Go-Bart, Lefkowitz, and Trupiano was essentially disregarded by the Rabinowitz Court.

Nor is the rationale by which the State seeks here to sustain the search of the petitioner's house supported by a reasoned view of the background and purpose of the Fourth Amendment. Mr. Justice Frankfurter wisely pointed out in his Rabinowitz dissent that the Amendment's proscription of "unreasonable searches and seizures" must be read in light of "the history that gave rise to the words"—history of "abuses so deeply felt by the Colonies as to be one of the potent causes of the Revolution. . . ." The Amendment was in large part a reaction to the general warrants and warrantless searches that had so alienated the colonists and had helped speed the movement for independence. In the scheme of the Amendment, therefore, the requirement that "no Warrants shall issue, but upon probable cause," plays a crucial part. As the Court put it in *McDonald v. United States,* 335 U.S. 451 (1948):

> "We are not dealing with formalities. The presence of a search warrant serves a high function. Absent some grave emergency, the Fourth Amendment has interposed a magistrate between the citizen and the police. This was done not to shield criminals nor to make the home a safe haven for illegal activities. It was done so that an objective mind might weigh the need to invade that privacy in order to enforce the law. The right of privacy was deemed too precious to entrust to the discretion of those whose job is the detection of crime and the arrest of criminals. . . . And so the Constitution requires a magistrate to pass on the desires of the police before they violate the privacy of the home. We cannot be true to that constitutional requirement and excuse the absence of a search warrant without a showing by those who seek exemption from the constitutional mandate that the exigencies of the situation made that course imperative.". . . Even in the Agnello case the Court relied upon the rule that "[b]elief, however well founded, that an article sought is concealed in a dwelling house, furnishes no justification for a search of that place without a warrant. And such searches are held unlawful notwithstanding facts unquestionably showing probable cause.". . . Clearly, the general requirement that a search warrant be obtained is not lightly to be dispensed with, and "the burden is on those seeking [an] exemption [from the requirement] to show the need for it. . . ."

. . .

. . . When an arrest is made, it is reasonable for the arresting officer to search the person arrested in order to remove any weapons that the latter might seek to use in order to resist arrest or effect his escape. Otherwise, the officer's safety might well be endangered, and the arrest itself frustrated. In addition, it is entirely reasonable for the arresting officer to search for and seize any evidence on the arrestee's person in order to prevent its concealment or destruction. And the area into which an arrestee might reach in order to grab a weapon or evidentiary items must, of course, be governed by a like rule. A gun on a table or in a drawer in front of one who is arrested can be as dangerous to the arresting officer as one concealed in the clothing of the person arrested. There is ample justification, therefore, for a search of the arrestee's person and the area "within his immediate control"—construing that phrase to mean the area from within which he might gain possession of a weapon or destructible evidence.

There is no comparable justification, however, for routinely searching any room other than that in which an arrest occurs—or, for that matter, for searching through all the desk drawers or other closed or concealed areas in that room itself.

Such searches, in the absence of well-recognized exceptions, may be made only under the authority of a search warrant. The "adherence to judicial processes" mandated by the Fourth Amendment requires no less.

. . .

It is argued in the present case that it is "reasonable" to search a man's house when he is arrested in it. But that argument is founded on little more than a subjective view regarding the acceptability of certain sorts of police conduct, and not on considerations relevant to Fourth Amendment interests. Under such an unconfined analysis, Fourth Amendment protection in this area would approach the evaporation point. It is not easy to explain why, for instance, it is less subjectively "reasonable" to search a man's house when he is arrested on his front lawn—or just down the street—than it is when he happens to be in the house at the time of arrest.

. . .

It would be possible, of course, to draw a line between Rabinowitz and Harris on the one hand, and this case on the other. For Rabinowitz involved a single room, and Harris a four-room apartment, while in the case before us an entire house was searched. But such a distinction would be highly artificial. The rationale that allowed the searches and seizures in Rabinowitz and Harris would allow the searches and seizures in this case. No consideration relevant to the Fourth Amendment suggests any point of rational limitation, once the search is allowed to go beyond the area from which the person arrested might obtain weapons or evidentiary items. The only reasoned distinction is one between a search of the person arrested and the area within his reach on the one hand, and more extensive searches on the other.

The petitioner correctly points out that one result of decisions such as Rabinowitz and Harris is to give law enforcement officials the opportunity to engage in searches not justified by probable cause, by the simple expedient of arranging to arrest suspects at home rather than elsewhere. We do not suggest that the petitioner is necessarily correct in his assertion that such a strategy was utilized here, but the fact remains that had he been arrested earlier in the day, at his place of employment rather than at home, no search of his house could have been made without a search warrant. In any event, even apart from the possibility of such police tactics, the general point so forcefully made by Judge Learned Hand in *United States v. Kirschenblatt* remains:

> "After arresting a man in his house, to rummage at will among his papers in search of whatever will convict him, appears to us to be indistinguishable from what might be done under a general warrant; indeed, the warrant would give more protection, for presumably it must be issued by a magistrate. True, by hypothesis the power would not exist, if the supposed offender were not found on the premises; but it is small consolation to know that one's papers are safe only so long as one is not at home.". . .

Rabinowitz and Harris have been the subject of critical commentary for many years, and have been relied upon less and less in our own decisions. It is time, for the reasons we have stated, to hold that on their own facts, and insofar as the principles they stand for are inconsistent with those that we have endorsed today, they are no longer to be followed.

Application of sound Fourth Amendment principles to the facts of this case produces a clear result. The search here went far beyond the petitioner's person and the area from within which he might have obtained either a weapon or something that could have been used as evidence against him. There was no constitutional justification, in the absence of a search warrant, for extending the search beyond that area. The scope of the search was, therefore, "unreasonable" under the Fourth and Fourteenth Amendments and the petitioner's conviction cannot stand.

Reversed.

[Mr. Justice HARLAN wrote a concurring opinion.]

[Mr. Justice WHITE, with whom Mr. Justice BLACK joined, dissented.]

In Re Gault

Supreme Court of the United States, 1967.
387 U.S. 1, 87 S.Ct. 1428, 18 L.Ed.2d 527.

Mr. Justice Fortas delivered the opinion of the Court.

This is an appeal under 28 U.S.C. § 1257(2) from a judgment of the Supreme Court of Arizona affirming the dismissal of a petition for a writ of habeas corpus. 99 Ariz. 181, 407 P.2d 760 (1965). The petition sought the release of Gerald Francis Gault, appellants' 15-year-old son, who had been committed as a juvenile delinquent to the State Industrial School by the Juvenile Court of Gila County, Arizona. The Supreme Court of Arizona affirmed dismissal of the writ against various arguments which included an attack upon the constitutionality of the Arizona Juvenile Code because of its alleged denial of procedural due process rights to juveniles charged with being "delinquents." The court agreed that the constitutional guarantee of due process of law is applicable in such proceedings. It held that Arizona's Juvenile Code is to be read as "impliedly" implementing the "due process concept." It then proceeded to identify and describe "the particular elements which constitute due process in a juvenile hearing." It concluded that the proceedings ending in commitment of Gerald Gault did not offend those requirements. We do not agree, and we reverse. We begin with a statement of the facts.

I. On Monday, June 8, 1964, at about 10 A.M., Gerald Francis Gault and a friend, Ronald Lewis, were taken into custody by the Sheriff of Gila County. Gerald was then still subject to a six months' probation order which had been entered on February 25, 1964, as a result of his having been in the company of another boy who had stolen a wallet from a lady's purse. The police action on June 8 was taken as the result of a verbal complaint by a neighbor of the boys, Mrs. Cook, about a telephone call made to her in which the caller or callers made lewd or indecent remarks. It will suffice for purposes of this opinion to say that the remarks or questions put to her were of the irritatingly offensive, adolescent, sex variety.

At the time Gerald was picked up, his mother and father were both at work. No notice that Gerald was being taken into custody was left at the home. No other steps were taken to advise them that their son had, in effect, been arrested. Gerald was taken to the Children's Detention Home. When his mother arrived home at about 6 o'clock, Gerald was not there. Gerald's older brother was sent to look for him at the trailer home of the Lewis family. He apparently learned then that Gerald was in custody. He so informed his mother. The two of them went to the Detention Home. The deputy probation officer, Flagg, who was also superintendent of the Detention Home, told Mrs. Gault "why Jerry was there" and said that a hearing would be held in Juvenile Court at 3 o'clock the following day, June 9.

Officer Flagg filed a petition with the court on the hearing day, June 9, 1964. It was not served on the Gaults. Indeed, none of them saw this petition until the habeas corpus hearing on August 17, 1964. The petition was entirely formal. It made no reference to any factual basis for the judicial action which it initiated. It recited only that "said minor is under the age of eighteen years, and is in need of the protection of this Honorable Court; [and that] said minor is a delinquent minor." It prayed for a hearing and an order regarding "the care and custody of said minor." Officer Flagg executed a formal affidavit in support of the petition.

On June 9, Gerald, his mother, his older brother, and Probation Officers Flagg and Henderson appeared before the Juvenile Judge in chambers. Gerald's father was not there. He was at work out of the city. Mrs. Cook, the complainant, was not there. No one was sworn at this hearing. No transcript or recording was made. No memorandum or record of the substance of the proceedings was prepared. Our information about the proceedings and the subsequent hearing on June 15, derives entirely from the testimony of the Juvenile Court Judge, Mr. and Mrs. Gault and Officer Flagg at the habeas corpus proceeding conducted two months later. From this, it appears that at the June 9 hearing Gerald was questioned by the judge about the telephone call. There was conflict as to what he said. His mother recalled that Gerald said he only dialed Mrs. Cook's number and handed the telephone to his friend, Ronald. Officer Flagg recalled that Gerald had admitted making the lewd remarks. Judge McGhee testified that Gerald "admitted making one of these [lewd] statements." At the conclusion of the hearing, the judge said he would "think about it." Gerald was taken back to the Detention Home. He was not sent to his own home with his parents. On June 11 or 12, after having been detained since June 8, Gerald was released and driven home. There is no explanation in the record as to why he was kept in the Detention Home or why he was released. At 5 p. m. on the day of Gerald's release, Mrs. Gault received a note signed by Officer Flagg. It was on plain paper, not letterhead. Its entire text was as follows:

> "Mrs. Gault:
> "Judge McGHEE has set Monday June 15, 1964 at 11:00 A.M. as the date and time for further Hearings on Gerald's delinquency
> "/s/ Flagg"

At the appointed time on Monday, June 15, Gerald, his father and mother, Ronald Lewis and his father, and Officers Flagg and Henderson were present before Judge McGhee. Witnesses at the habeas corpus proceeding differed in their recollections of Gerald's testimony at the June 15 hearing. Mr. and Mrs. Gault recalled that Gerald again testified that he had only dialed the number and that the other boy had made the remarks. Officer Flagg agreed that at this hearing Gerald did not admit making the lewd remarks. But Judge McGhee recalled that "there was some admission again of some of the lewd statements. He—he didn't admit any of the more serious lewd statements." Again, the complainant, Mrs. Cook, was not present. Mrs. Gault asked that Mrs. Cook be present "so she could see which boy that done the talking, the dirty talking over the phone." The Juvenile Judge said "she didn't have to be present at that hearing." The judge did not speak to Mrs. Cook or communicate with her at any time. Probation Officer Flagg had talked to her once—over the telephone on June 9.

At this June 15 hearing a "referral report" made by the probation officers was filed with the court, although not disclosed to Gerald or his parents. This listed the charge as "Lewd Phone Calls." At the conclusion of the hearing, the judge committed Gerald as a juvenile delinquent to the State Industrial School "for the period of his minority [that is, until 21], unless sooner discharged by due process of law." An order to that effect was entered. It recites that "after a full hearing and due deliberation the Court finds that said minor is a delinquent child, and that said minor is of the age of 15 years."

No appeal is permitted by Arizona law in juvenile cases. On August 3, 1964, a petition for a writ of habeas corpus was filed with the Supreme Court of Arizona and referred by it to the Superior Court for hearing.

At the habeas corpus hearing on August 17, Judge McGhee was vigorously cross-examined as to the basis for his actions. He testified that he had taken into account the fact that Gerald was on probation. He was asked "under what section of . . . the code you found the boy delinquent?"

His answer is set forth in the margin.[1] In substance, he concluded that Gerald came within ARS § 8—201, subsec. 6(a), which specifies that a "delinquent child" includes one "who has violated a law of the state or an ordinance or regulation of a political subdivision thereof." The law which Gerald was found to have violated is ARS § 13—377. This section of the Arizona Criminal Code provides that a person who "in the presence or hearing of any woman or child . . . uses vulgar, abusive or obscene language, is guilty of a misdemeanor. . . ." The penalty specified in the Criminal Code, which would apply to an adult, is $5 to $50, or imprisonment for not more than two months. The judge also testified that he acted under ARS § 8—201, subsec. 6(d) which includes in the definition of a "delinquent child" one who, as the judge phrased it, is "habitually involved in immoral matters."[2]

Asked about the basis for his conclusion that Gerald was "habitually involved in immoral matters," the judge testified, somewhat vaguely, that two years earlier, on June 2, 1962, a "referral" was made concerning Gerald, "where the boy had stolen a baseball glove from another boy and lied to the Police Department about it." The judge said there was "no hearing," and "no accusation" relating to this incident, "because of lack of material foundation." But it seems to have remained in his mind as a relevant factor. The judge also testified that Gerald had admitted making other nuisance phone calls in the past which, as the judge recalled the boy's testimony, were "silly calls, or funny calls, or something like that."

The Superior Court dismissed the writ, and appellants sought review in the Arizona Supreme Court. That court stated that it considered appellants' assignments of error as urging (1) that the Juvenile Code, ARS § 8—201 to § 8—239,

---

1. "Q. All right. Now, Judge, would you tell me under what section of the law or tell me under what section of—of the code you found the boy delinquent?
"A. Well, there is a—I think it amounts to disturbing the peace. I can't give you the section, but I can tell you the law, that when one person uses lewd language in the presence of another person, that it can amount to—and I consider that when a person makes it over the phone, that it is considered in the presence, I might be wrong, that is one section. The other section upon which I consider the boy delinquent is Section 8—201, Subsection (d), habitually involved in immoral matters."
2. ARS § 8—201, subsec. 6, the section of the Arizona Juvenile Code which defines a delinquent child, reads:
" 'Delinquent child' includes:
"(a) A child who has violated a law of the state or an ordinance or regulation of a political subdivision thereof.
"(b) A child who, by reason of being incorrigible, wayward or habitually disobedient, is uncontrolled by his parent, guardian or custodian.
"(c) A child who is habitually truant from school or home.
"(d) A child who habitually so deports himself as to injure or endanger the morals or health of himself or others."

is unconstitutional because it does not require that parents and children be apprised of the specific charges, does not require proper notice of a hearing, and does not provide for an appeal; and (2) that the proceedings and order relating to Gerald constituted a denial of due process of law because of the absence of adequate notice of the charge and the hearing; failure to notify appellants of certain constitutional rights including the rights to counsel and to confrontation, and the privilege against self-incrimination; the use of unsworn hearsay testimony; and the failure to make a record of the proceedings. Appellants further asserted that it was [an] error for the Juvenile Court to remove Gerald from the custody of his parents without a showing and finding of their unsuitability, and alleged a miscellany of other errors under state law.

The Supreme Court handed down an elaborate and wide-ranging opinion affirming dismissal of the writ and stating the court's conclusions as to the issues raised by appellants and other aspects of the juvenile process. In their jurisdictional statement and brief in this Court, appellants do not urge upon us all of the points passed upon by the Supreme Court of Arizona. They urge that we hold the Juvenile Code of Arizona invalid on its face or as applied in this case because, contrary to the Due Process Clause of the Fourteenth Amendment, the juvenile is taken from the custody of his parents and committed to a state institution pursuant to proceedings in which the Juvenile Court has virtually unlimited discretion, and in which the following basic rights are denied:

1. Notice of the charges;
2. Right to counsel;
3. Right to confrontation and cross-examination;
4. Privilege against self-incrimination;
5. Right to a transcript of the proceedings; and
6. Right to appellate review.

We shall not consider other issues which were passed upon by the Supreme Court of Arizona. We emphasize that we indicate no opinion as to whether the decision of that court with respect to such other issues does or does not conflict with requirements of the Federal Constitution.

II. The Supreme Court of Arizona held that due process of law is requisite to the constitutional validity of proceedings in which a court reaches the conclusion that a juvenile has been at fault, has engaged in conduct prohibited by law, or has otherwise misbehaved with the consequence that he is committed to an institution in which his freedom is curtailed. This conclusion is in accord with the decisions of a number of courts under both federal and state constitutions.

This Court has not heretofore decided the precise question. In *Kent v. United States*, 383 U.S. 541, 86 S.Ct. 1045, 16 L.Ed.2d 84 (1966), we considered the requirements for a valid waiver of the "exclusive" jurisdiction of the Juvenile Court of the District of Columbia so that a juvenile could be tried in the adult criminal court of the District. Although our decision turned upon the language of the statute, we emphasized the necessity that "the basic requirements of due process and fairness" be satisfied in such proceedings. *Haley v. State of Ohio*, 332 U.S. 596, 68 S.Ct. 302, 92 L.Ed. 224 (1948), involved the admissibility, in a state criminal court of general jurisdiction, of a confession by a 15-year-old boy. The Court held that the Fourteenth Amendment applied to prohibit the use of the coerced confession. Mr. Justice Douglas said, "Neither man nor child can be allowed to stand condemned by methods which flout constitutional requirements of due process of law." To the same effect is *Gallegos v. State of Colorado*, 370 U.S. 49, 82 S.Ct. 1209, 8 L.Ed.2d 325 (1962). Accordingly, while these cases relate only to restricted aspects of the subject, they unmistakably indicate that, whatever may be their precise impact, neither the Fourteenth Amendment nor the Bill of Rights is for adults alone.

We do not in this opinion consider the impact of these constitutional provisions upon the totality of the relationship of the juvenile and the state. We do not even consider the entire process relating to juvenile "delinquents." For example, we are not here concerned with the procedures or constitutional rights applicable to the prejudicial stages of the juvenile process, nor do we direct our attention to the post-adjudicative or dispositional process. We consider only the problems presented to us by this case. These relate to the proceedings by which a determination is made as to whether a juvenile is a "delinquent" as a result of alleged misconduct on his part, with the consequence that he may be committed to a state institution. As to these proceedings, there appears to be little current dissent from the proposition that the Due Process Clause has a role to play. The problem is to ascertain the precise impact of the due process requirement upon such proceedings.

In view of this, it would be extraordinary if our Constitution did not require the procedural regularity and the exercise of care implied in the phrase "due process." Under our Constitution, the condition of being a boy does not justify a kangaroo court. The traditional ideas of Juvenile Court procedure, indeed, contemplated that time would be available and care would be used to establish precisely what the juvenile did and why he did it—was it a prank of adolescence or a brutal act threatening serious consequences to himself or society unless corrected? Under traditional notions, one would assume that in a case like that of Gerald Gault, where the juvenile appears to have a home, a working mother and father, and an older brother, the Juvenile Judge would have made a careful inquiry and judgment as to the possibility that the boy could be disciplined and dealt with at home, despite his previous transgressions.[3] Indeed, so far as appears in the record before us, except for some conversation with Gerald about his school work and his "wanting to go to . . . Grand Canyon with his father," the points to which the judge directed his attention were little different from those that would be involved in determining any charge of violation of a penal statute. The essential difference between Gerald's case and a normal criminal case is that safeguards available to adults were discarded in Gerald's case. The summary procedure as well as the long commitment was possible because Gerald was 15 years of age instead of over 18.

If Gerald had been over 18, he would not have been subject to Juvenile Court proceedings. For the particular offense immediately involved, the maximum punishment would have been a fine of $5 to $50, or imprisonment in jail for not more than two months. Instead, he was committed to custody for a maximum of six years. If he had been over 18 and had committed an offense to which such a sentence might apply, he would have been entitled to substantial rights under the Constitution of the United States as well as under Arizona's laws and constitution. The United States Constitution would guarantee him rights and protections with respect to arrest, search, and seizure, and pretrial interrogation. It would assure him of specific notice of the charges and adequate time to decide his course of action and to prepare his defense. He would be entitled to clear advice that he could be represented by counsel, and, at least if a felony were involved, the State would be required to provide counsel if his parents were unable to afford it. If the court acted on the basis of his confession, careful procedures would be required to assure its voluntariness. If the case went to trial, confrontation and opportunity for cross-examination would be guaranteed. So wide a gulf between the State's treatment of the adult and of the child requires a bridge sturdier than mere verbiage, and reasons more persuasive than cliche can provide. As Wheeler and Cottrell have put it, "The rhetoric of the juvenile court movement has developed without any necessarily close correspondence to the realities of court and institutional routines."

In *Kent v. United States,* supra, we stated that the Juvenile Court Judge's exercise of the power of the state as *parens patriae* was not unlimited. We said that "the admonition to function in a 'parental' relationship is not an invitation

---

3. The Juvenile Judge's testimony at the habeas corpus proceeding is devoid of any meaningful discussion of this. He appears to have centered his attention upon whether Gerald made the phone call and used lewd words. He was impressed by the fact that Gerald was on six months' probation because he was with another boy who allegedly stole a purse—a different sort of offense, sharing the feature that Gerald was "along." And he even referred to a report which he said was not investigated because "there was no accusation" "because of lack of material foundation." With respect to the possible duty of a trial court to explore alternatives to involuntary commitment in a civil proceeding, cf. *Lake v. Cameron,* 124 U.S. App.D.C. 264, 364 F.2d 657 (1966), which arose under statutes relating to treatment of the mentally ill.

to procedural arbitrariness." With respect to the waiver by the Juvenile Court to the adult court of jurisdiction over an offense committed by a youth, we said that "there is no place in our system of law for reaching a result of such tremendous consequences without ceremony—without hearing, without effective assistance of counsel, without a statement of reasons." We announced with respect to such waiver proceedings that while "We do not mean . . . to indicate that the hearing to be held must conform with all of the requirements of a criminal trial or even of the usual administrative hearing; but we do hold that the hearing must measure up to the essentials of due process and fair treatment." We reiterate this view, here in connection with a juvenile court adjudication of "delinquency," as a requirement which is part of the Due Process Clause of the Fourteenth Amendment of our Constitution.[4]

We now turn to the specific issues which are presented to us in the present case.

III. Notice of Charges Appellants allege that the Arizona Juvenile Code is unconstitutional or alternatively that the proceedings before the Juvenile Court were constitutionally defective because of failure to provide adequate notice of the hearings. No notice was given to Gerald's parents when he was taken into custody on Monday, June 8. On that night, when Mrs. Gault went to the Detention Home, she was orally informed that there would be a hearing the next afternoon and was told the reason why Gerald was in custody. The only written notice Gerald's parents received at any time was a note on plain paper from Officer Flagg delivered on Thursday or Friday, June 11 or 12, to the effect that the judge had set Monday, June 15, "for further Hearings on Gerald's delinquency."

A "petition" was filed with the court on June 9 by Officer Flagg, reciting only that he was informed and believed that "said minor is a delinquent minor and that it is necessary that some order be made by the Honorable Court for said minor's welfare." The applicable Arizona statute provides for a petition to be filed in Juvenile Court, alleging in general terms that the child is "neglected, dependent or delinquent." The statute explicitly states that such a general allegation is sufficient, "without alleging the facts." There is no requirement that the petition be served and it was not served upon, given to, or shown to Gerald or his parents.

4. The Nat'l Crime Comm'n Report recommends that "Juvenile courts should make fullest feasible use of preliminary conferences to dispose of cases short of adjudication." Id., at 84. See also D.C. Crime Comm'n Report, pp. 662–665. Since this "consent decree" procedure would involve neither adjudication of delinquency nor institutionalization, nothing we say in this opinion should be construed as expressing any views with respect to such procedure. The problems of preadjudication treatment of juveniles, and of post-adjudication disposition, are unique to the juvenile process; hence what we hold in this opinion with regard to the procedural requirements at the adjudicatory stage has no necessary applicability to other steps of the juvenile process.

The Supreme Court of Arizona rejected appellants' claim that due process was denied because of inadequate notice. It stated that "Mrs. Gault knew the exact nature of the charge against Gerald from the day he was taken to the detention home." The court also pointed out that the Gaults appeared at the two hearings "without objection." The court held that because "the policy of the juvenile law is to hide youthful errors from the full gaze of the public and bury them in the graveyard of the forgotten past," advance notice of the specific charges or basis for taking the juvenile into custody and for the hearing is not necessary. It held that the appropriate rule is that "the infant and his parents or guardian will receive a petition only reciting a conclusion of delinquency. But no later than the initial hearing by the judge, they must be advised of the facts involved in the case. If the charges are denied, they must be given a reasonable period of time to prepare."

We cannot agree with the court's conclusion that adequate notice was given in this case. Notice, to comply with due process requirements, must be given sufficiently in advance of scheduled court proceedings so that reasonable opportunity to prepare will be afforded, and it must "set forth the alleged misconduct with particularity." It is obvious, as we have discussed above, that no purpose of shielding the child from the public stigma of knowledge of his having been taken into custody and scheduled for hearing is served by the procedure approved by the court below. The "initial hearing" in the present case was a hearing on the merits. Notice at that time is not timely; and even if there were a conceivable purpose served by the deferral proposed by the court below, it would have to yield to the requirements that the child and his parents or guardian be notified, in writing, of the specific charge or factual allegations to be considered at the hearing, and that such written notice be given at the earliest practicable time, and in any event sufficiently in advance of the hearing to permit preparation. Due process of law requires notice of the sort we have described—that is, notice which would be deemed constitutionally adequate in a civil or criminal proceeding. It does not allow a hearing to be held in which a youth's freedom and his parents' right to his custody are at stake without giving them timely notice, in advance of the hearing, of the specific issues that they must meet. Nor, in the circumstances of this case, can it reasonably be said that the requirement of notice was waived.

IV. Right to Counsel Appellants charge that the Juvenile Court proceedings were fatally defective because the court did not advise Gerald or his parents of their right to counsel, and proceeded with the hearing, the adjudication of delinquency and the order of commitment in the absence of counsel for the child and his parents or an express waiver of the right thereto. The Supreme Court of Arizona pointed out that "[t]here is disagreement [among the various jurisdictions] as to whether the court must advise the infant that he has a right to counsel." It noted its own decision in *Arizona State Dept. of Public Welfare v. Barlow*, 80 Ariz. 249, 296 P.2d 298 (1956), to the effect "that *the parents* of an infant in a juvenile proceeding cannot be denied representation by counsel of their choosing." (Emphasis added.) It referred to a provision of the Juvenile Code which it characterized as requiring "that the probation officer shall look after the interests of neglected, delinquent and dependent children," including representing their interests in court. The court argued that "The parent and the probation officer may be relied upon to protect the infant's interests." Accordingly it rejected the proposition that "due process requires that an infant have a right to counsel." It said that juvenile courts have the discretion, but not the duty, to allow such representation; it referred specifically to the situation in which the Juvenile Court discerns conflict between the child and his parents as an instance in which this discretion might be exercised. We do not agree. Probation officers, in the Arizona scheme, are also arresting officers. They initiate proceedings and file petitions which they verify, as here, alleging the delinquency of the child; and they testify, as here, against the child. And here the probation officer was also superintendent of the Detention Home. The probation officer cannot act as counsel for the child. His role in the adjudicatory hearing, by statute and in fact, is as arresting officer and witness against the child. Nor can the judge represent the child. There is no material difference in this respect between adult and juvenile proceedings of the sort here involved. In adult proceedings, this contention has been foreclosed by decisions of this Court. A proceeding where the issue is whether the child will be found to be "delinquent" and subjected to the loss of his liberty for years is comparable in seriousness to a felony prosecution. The juvenile needs the assistance of counsel to cope with problems of law, to make skilled inquiry into the facts, to insist upon regularity of the proceedings, and to ascertain whether he has a defense and to prepare and submit it. The child "requires the guiding hand of counsel at every step in the proceedings against him." Just as in *Kent v. United States*, supra, 383 U.S., at 561–562, 86 S.Ct., at 1057–1058, we indicated our agreement with the United States Court of Appeals for the District of Columbia Circuit that the assistance of counsel is essential for purposes of waiver proceedings, so we hold now that it is equally essential for the determination of delinquency, carrying with it the awesome prospect of incarceration in a state institution until the juvenile reaches the age of 21.[5]

During the last decade, court decisions, experts, and legislatures have demonstrated increasing recognition of this view. In at least one-third of the States, statutes now provide for the right of representation by retained counsel in juvenile delinquency proceedings, notice of the right, or assignment of counsel, or a combination of these. In other States, court rules have similar provisions.

The President's Crime Commission has recently recommended that in order to assure "procedural justice for the child," it is necessary that "Counsel . . . be appointed as a matter of course wherever coercive action is a possibility, without

---

5. This means that the commitment, in virtually all cases, is for a minimum of three years since jurisdiction of juvenile courts is usually limited to age 18 and under.

requiring any affirmative choice by child or parent."[6] As stated by the authoritative "Standards for Juvenile and Family Courts," published by the Children's Bureau of the United States Department of Health, Education, and Welfare:

> "As a component part of a fair hearing required by due process guaranteed under the 14th amendment, notice of the right to counsel should be required at all hearings and counsel provided upon request when the family is financially unable to employ counsel." Standards, p. 57.

This statement was "reviewed" by the National Council of Juvenile Court Judges at its 1965 Convention and they "found no fault" with it. The New York Family Court Act contains the following statement:

> "This act declares that minors have a right to the assistance of counsel of their own choosing or of law guardians in neglect proceedings under article three and in proceedings to determine juvenile delinquency and whether a person is in need of supervision under article seven. This declaration is based on a finding that counsel is often indispensable to a practical realization of due process of law and may be helpful in making reasoned determinations of fact and proper orders of disposition."

---

6. Nat'l Crime Comm'n Report, pp. 86–87. The Commission's statement of its position is very forceful:

"The Commission believes that no single action holds more potential for achieving procedural justice for the child in the juvenile court than provision of counsel. The presence of an independent legal representative of the child, or of his parent, is the keystone of the whole structure of guarantees that a minimum system of procedural justice requires. The rights to confront one's accusers, to cross-examine witnesses, to present evidence and testimony of one's own, to be unaffected by prejudicial and unreliable evidence, to participate meaningfully in the dispositional decision, to take an appeal have substantial meaning for the overwhelming majority of persons brought before the juvenile court only if they are provided with competent lawyers who can invoke those rights effectively. The most informal and well-intentioned of judicial proceedings are technical; few adults without legal training can influence or even understand them; certainly children cannot. Papers are drawn and charges expressed in legal language. Events follow one another in a manner that appears arbitrary and confusing to the uninitiated. Decisions, unexplained, appear too official to challenge. But with lawyers come records of proceedings; records make possible appeals which, even if they do not occur, impart by their possibility a healthy atmosphere of accountability.

"Fears have been expressed that lawyers would make juvenile court proceedings adversary. No doubt this is partly true, but it is partly desirable. Informality is often abused. The juvenile courts deal with cases in which facts are disputed and in which, therefore, rules of evidence, confrontation of witnesses, and other adversary procedures are called for. They deal with many cases involving conduct that can lead to incarceration or close supervision for long periods, and therefore juveniles often need the same safeguards that are granted to

The Act provides that "At the commencement of any hearing" under the delinquency article of the statute, the juvenile and his parent shall be advised of the juvenile's "right to be represented by counsel chosen by him or his parent . . . or by a law guardian assigned by the court. . . ." The California Act (1961) also requires appointment of counsel.

We conclude that the Due Process Clause of the Fourteenth Amendment requires that in respect of proceedings to determine delinquency which may result in commitment to an institution in which the juvenile's freedom is curtailed, the child and his parents must be notified of the child's right to be represented by counsel retained by them, or if they are unable to afford counsel, that counsel will be appointed to represent the child.

At the habeas corpus proceeding, Mrs. Gault testified that she knew that she could have appeared with counsel at the juvenile hearing. This knowledge is not a waiver of the right to counsel which she and her juvenile son had, as we have defined it. They had a right expressly to be advised that they might retain counsel and to be confronted with the need for specific consideration of whether they did or did not choose to waive the right. If they were unable to afford to employ

6. *Continued*

adults. And in all cases children need advocates to speak for them and guard their interests, particularly when disposition decisions are made. It is the disposition stage at which the opportunity arises to offer individualized treatment plans and in which the danger inheres that the court's coercive power will be applied without adequate knowledge of the circumstances.

"Fears also have been expressed that the formality lawyers would bring into juvenile court would defeat the therapeutic aims of the court. But informality has no necessary connection with therapy; it is a device that has been used to approach therapy, and it is not the only possible device. It is quite possible that in many instances lawyers, for all their commitment to formality, could do more to further therapy for their clients than can the small, overworked social staffs of the courts.

. . .

"The Commission believes it is essential that counsel be appointed by the juvenile court for those who are unable to provide their own. Experience under the prevailing systems in which children are free to seek counsel of their choice reveals how empty of meaning the right is for those typically the subjects of juvenile court proceedings. Moreover, providing counsel only when the child is sophisticated enough to be aware of his need and to ask for one or when he fails to waive his announced right [is] not enough, as experience in numerous jurisdictions reveals.

The Commission recommends:

"COUNSEL SHOULD BE APPOINTED AS A MATTTER OF COURSE WHEREVER COERCIVE ACTION IS A POSSIBILITY, WITHOUT REQUIRING ANY AFFIRMATIVE CHOICE BY CHILD OR PARENT."

counsel, they were entitled in view of the seriousness of the charge and the potential commitment, to appointed counsel, unless they chose waiver. Mrs. Gault's knowledge that she could employ counsel was not an "intentional relinquishment or abandonment" of a fully known right.[7]

V. Confrontation, Self-Incrimination, Cross-Examination Appellants urge that the writ of habeas corpus should have been granted because of the denial of the rights of confrontation and cross-examination in the Juvenile Court hearings, and because the privilege against self-incrimination was not observed. The Juvenile Court Judge testified at the habeas corpus hearing that he had proceeded on the basis of Gerald's admissions at the two hearings. Appellants attack this on the ground that the admissions were obtained in disregard of the privilege against self-incrimination. If the confession is disregarded, appellants argue that the delinquency conclusion, since it was fundamentally based on a finding that Gerald had made lewd remarks during the phone call to Mrs. Cook, is fatally defective for failure to accord the rights of confrontation and cross-examination which the Due Process Clause of the Fourteenth Amendment of the Federal Constitution guarantees in state proceedings generally.

Our first question, then, is whether Gerald's admission was improperly obtained and relied on as the basis of decision, in conflict with the Federal Constitution. For this purpose, it is necessary briefly to recall the relevant facts.

Mrs. Cook, the complainant, and the recipient of the alleged telephone call, was not called as a witness. Gerald's mother asked the Juvenile Court Judge why Mrs. Cook was not present and the judge replied that "she didn't have to be present." So far as appears, Mrs. Cook was spoken to only once, by Officer Flagg, and this was by telephone. The judge did not speak with her on any occasion. Gerald had been questioned by the probation officer after having been taken into custody. The exact circumstances of this questioning do not appear but any admissions Gerald may have made at this time do not appear in the record. Gerald was also questioned by the Juvenile Court Judge at each of the two hearings. The judge testified in the habeas corpus proceeding that Gerald admitted making "some of the lewd statements . . . [but not] any of the more serious lewd statements." There was conflict and uncertainty among the witnesses at the habeas corpus proceeding—the Juvenile Court Judge, Mr. and Mrs. Gault, and the probation officer—as to what Gerald did or did not admit.

We shall assume that Gerald made admissions of the sort described by the Juvenile Court Judge, as quoted above. Neither Gerald nor his parents were advised that he did not have to testify or make a statement, or that an incriminating statement might result in his commitment as a "delinquent."

7. *Johnson v. Zerbst*, 304 U.S. 458, 464, 58 S.Ct. 1019, 1023, 82 L.Ed. 1461 (1938); *Carnley v. Cochran*, 369 U.S. 506, 82 S. Ct. 884, 8 L.Ed.2d 70 (1962); United States ex rel. *Brown v. Fay*, 242 F. Supp. 273 (D.C.S.D.N.Y. 1965).

The Arizona Supreme Court rejected appellants' contention that Gerald had a right to be advised that he need not incriminate himself. It said: "We think the necessary flexibility for individualized treatment will be enhanced by a rule which does not require the judge to advise the infant of a privilege against self-incrimination."

In reviewing this conclusion of Arizona's Supreme Court, we emphasize again that we are here concerned only with a proceeding to determine whether a minor is a "delinquent" and which may result in commitment to a state institution. Specifically, the question is whether, in such a proceeding, an admission by the juvenile may be used against him in the absence of clear and unequivocal evidence that the admission was made with knowledge that he was not obliged to speak and would not be penalized for remaining silent. In light of *Miranda v. State of Arizona*, 384 U.S. 436, 86 S.Ct. 1602, 16 L.Ed.2d 694 (1966), we must also consider whether, if the privilege against self-incrimination is available, it can effectively be waived unless counsel is present or the right to counsel has been waived.

It has long been recognized that the eliciting and use of confessions or admissions require careful scrutiny. Dean Wigmore states:

> "The ground of distrust of confessions made in certain situations is, in a rough and indefinite way, judicial experience. There has been no careful collection of statistics of untrue confessions, nor has any great number of instances been even loosely reported . . . but enough have been verified to fortify the conclusion, based on ordinary observation of human conduct, that under certain stresses a person, especially one of defective mentality or peculiar temperament, may falsely acknowledge guilt. This possibility arises wherever the innocent person is placed in such a situation that the untrue acknowledgment of guilt is at the time the more promising of two alternatives between which he [is] obliged to choose; that is, he chooses any risk that may be in falsely acknowledging guilt, in preference to some worse alternative associated with silence.
>
> "The principle, then, upon which a confession may be excluded is that it is, under certain conditions, *testimonially untrustworthy*. . . . [T]he essential feature is that the principle of exclusion is a testimonial one, analogous to the other principles which exclude narrations as untrustworthy. . . ."

This Court has emphasized that admissions and confessions of juveniles require special caution. In *Haley v. State of Ohio,* 332 U.S. 596, 68 S.Ct. 302, 92 L.Ed. 224, where this Court reversed the conviction of a 15-year-old boy for murder, Mr. Justice Douglas said:

> "What transpired would make us pause for careful inquiry if a mature man were involved. And when, as here, a mere child—an easy victim of the law—is before us, special care in scrutinizing the record must be used.

Age 15 is a tender and difficult age for a boy of any race. He cannot be judged by the more exacting standards of maturity. That which would leave a man cold and unimpressed can overawe and overwhelm a lad in his early teens. This is the period of great instability which the crisis of adolescence produces. A 15-year-old lad, questioned through the dead of night by relays of police, is a ready victim of the inquisition. Mature men possibly might stand the ordeal from midnight to 5 a.m. But we cannot believe that a lad of tender years is a match for the police in such a contest. He needs counsel and support if he is not to become the victim first of fear, then of panic. He needs someone on whom to lean lest the overpowering presence of the law, as he knows it, crush him. No friend stood at the side of this 15-year-old boy as the police, working in relays, questioned him hour after hour, from midnight until dawn. No lawyer stood guard to make sure that the police went so far and no farther, to see to it that they stopped short of the point where he became the victim of coercion. No counsel or friend was called during the critical hours of questioning."

In *Haley,* as we have discussed, the boy was convicted in an adult court, and not a juvenile court. In notable decisions, the New York Court of Appeals and the Supreme Court of New Jersey have recently considered decisions of Juvenile Courts in which boys have been adjudged "delinquent" on the basis of confessions obtained in circumstances comparable to those in *Haley.* In both instances, the State contended before its highest tribunal that constitutional requirements governing inculpatory statements applicable in adult courts do not apply to juvenile proceedings. In each case, the State's contention was rejected, and the juvenile court's determination of delinquency was set aside on the grounds of inadmissibility of the confession. *In Matters of W. and S.,* 19 N.Y.2d 55, 277 N.Y.S.2d 675, 224 N.E.2d 102 (1966) (opinion by Keating, J.), and *In Interests of Carlo and Stasilowicz,* 48 N.J. 224, 225 A.2d 110 (1966) (opinion by Proctor, J.).

The privilege against self-incrimination is, of course, related to the question of the safeguards necessary to assure that admissions or confessions are reasonably trustworthy, that they are not the mere fruits of fear or coercion, but are reliable expressions of the truth. The roots of the privilege are, however, far deeper. They tap the basic stream of religious and political principle because the privilege reflects the limits of the individual's attornment to the state and—in a philosophical sense—insists upon the equality of the individual and the state. In other words, the privilege has a broader and deeper thrust than the rule which prevents the use of confessions which are the product of coercion because coercion is thought to carry with it the danger of unreliability. One of its purposes is to prevent the state, whether by force or by psychological domination, from overcoming the mind and will of the person under investigation and depriving him of the freedom to decide whether to assist the state in securing his conviction.

It would indeed be surprising if the privilege against self-incrimination were available to hardened criminals but not to children. The language of the Fifth Amendment, applicable to the States by operation of the Fourteenth Amendment, is unequivocal and without exception. And the scope of the privilege is comprehensive. As Mr. Justice White, concurring, stated in *Murphy v. Waterfront Commission,* 378 U.S. 52, 94, 84 S.Ct. 1594, 1611, 12 L.Ed.2d 678 (1964):

> "The privilege can be claimed in *any proceeding,* be it criminal or civil, administrative or judicial, investigatory or adjudicatory. . . . it protects *any disclosures* which the witness may reasonably apprehend *could be used in a criminal prosecution or which could lead to other evidence that might be so used.*" (Emphasis added.)

With respect to juveniles, both common observation and expert opinion emphasize that the "distrust of confessions made in certain situations" to which Dean Wigmore referred in the passage quoted supra, at 1453, is imperative in the case of children from an early age through adolescence. In New York, for example, the recently enacted Family Court Act provides that the juvenile and his parents must be advised at the start of the hearing of his right to remain silent. The New York statute also provides that the police must attempt to communicate with the juvenile's parents before questioning him, and that absent "special circumstances" a confession may not be obtained from the child prior to notifying his parents or relatives and releasing the child either to them or to the Family Court. In *In Matters of W. and S.,* referred to above, the New York Court of Appeals held that the privilege against self-incrimination applies in juvenile delinquency cases and requires the exclusion of involuntary confessions, and that *People v. Lewis,* 260 N.Y. 171, 183 N.E. 353, 86 A.L.R. 1001 (1932), holding the contrary, had been specifically overruled by statute.

The authoritative "Standards for Juvenile and Family Courts" concludes that, "Whether or not transfer to the criminal court is a possibility, certain procedures should always be followed. Before being interviewed [by the police], the child and his parents should be informed of his right to have legal counsel present and to refuse to answer questions or be fingerprinted if he should so decide."

Against the application to juveniles of the right to silence, it is argued that juvenile proceedings are "civil" and not "criminal," and therefore the privilege should not apply. It is true that the statement of the privilege in the Fifth Amendment, which is applicable to the States by reason of the Fourteenth Amendment, is that no person "shall be compelled in any *criminal case* to be a witness against himself." However, it is also clear that the availability of the privilege does not turn upon the type of proceeding in which its protection is invoked, but upon the nature of the statement or admission and the exposure which it invites. The privilege may, for example, be claimed in a civil or administrative proceeding, if the statement is or may be inculpatory.

It would be entirely unrealistic to carve out of the Fifth Amendment all statements by juveniles on the ground that these cannot lead to "criminal" involvement. In the first place, juvenile proceedings to determine "delinquency," which may lead to commitment to a state institution, must be regarded as "criminal" for purposes of the privilege against self-incrimination. To hold otherwise would be to disregard substance because of the feeble enticement of the "civil" label-of-convenience which has been attached to juvenile proceedings. Indeed, in over half of the States, there is not even assurance that the juvenile will be kept in separate institutions, apart from adult "criminals." In those States juveniles may be placed in or transferred to adult penal institutions after having been found "delinquent" by a juvenile court. For this purpose, at least, commitment is a deprivation of liberty. It is incarceration against one's will, whether it is called "criminal" or "civil." And our Constitution guarantees that no person shall be "compelled" to be a witness against himself when he is threatened with deprivation of his liberty—a command which this Court has broadly applied and generously implemented in accordance with the teaching of the history of the privilege and its great office in mankind's battle for freedom.

In addition, apart from the equivalence for this purpose of exposure to commitment as a juvenile delinquent and exposure to imprisonment as an adult offender, the fact of the matter is that there is little or no assurance in Arizona, as in most if not all of the States, that a juvenile apprehended and interrogated by the police or even by the Juvenile Court itself will remain outside of the reach of adult courts as a consequence of the offense for which he has been taken into custody. In Arizona, as in other States, provision is made for Juvenile Courts to relinquish or waive jurisdiction to the ordinary criminal courts. In the present case, when Gerald Gault was interrogated concerning violation of a section of the Arizona Criminal Code, it could not be certain that the Juvenile Court Judge would decide to "suspend" criminal prosecution in court for adults by proceeding to an adjudication in Juvenile Court.

It is also urged, as the Supreme Court of Arizona here asserted, that the juvenile and presumably his parents should not be advised of the juvenile's right to silence because confession is good for the child as the commencement of the assumed therapy of the juvenile court process, and he should be encouraged to assume an attitude of trust and confidence toward the officials of the juvenile process. This proposition has been subjected to widespread challenge on the basis of current reappraisals of the rhetoric and realities of the handling of juvenile offenders.

In fact, evidence is accumulating that confessions by juveniles do not aid in "individualized treatment," as the court below put it, and that compelling the child to answer questions, without warning or advice as to his right to remain silent, does not serve this or any other good purpose. In light of the observations of Wheeler and Cottrell, and others, it seems probable that where children are induced to confess by "paternal" urgings on the part of officials and the confession is then followed by disciplinary action, the child's reaction is likely to be hostile and adverse—the child may well feel that he has been led or tricked into confession and that despite his confession, he is being punished.

Further, authoritative opinion has cast formidable doubt upon the reliability and trustworthiness of "confessions" by children. This Court's observations in *Haley v. State of Ohio* are set forth above. The recent decision of the New York Court of Appeals referred to above, *In Matters of W. and S.* deals with a dramatic and, it is to be hoped, extreme example. Two 12-year-old Negro boys were taken into custody for the brutal assault and rape of two aged domestics, one of whom died as the result of the attack. One of the boys was schizophrenic and had been locked in the security ward of a mental institution at the time of the attacks. By a process that may best be described as bizarre, his confession was obtained by the police. A psychiatrist testified that the boy would admit "whatever he thought was expected so that he could get out of the immediate situation." The other 12-year-old also "confessed." Both confessions were in specific detail, albeit they contained various inconsistencies. The Court of Appeals, in an opinion by Keating, J., concluded that the confessions were products of the will of the police instead of the boys. The confessions were therefore held involuntary and the order of the Appellate Division affirming the order of the Family Court adjudging the defendants to be juvenile delinquents was reversed.

A similar and equally instructive case has recently been decided by the Supreme Court of New Jersey. *In Interests of Carlo and Stasilowicz, supra.* The body of a 10-year-old girl was found. She had been strangled. Neighborhood boys who knew the girl were questioned. The two appellants, aged 13 and 15, confessed to the police, with vivid detail and some inconsistencies. At the Juvenile Court hearing, both denied any complicity in the killing. They testified that their confessions were the product of fear and fatigue due to extensive police grilling. The Juvenile Court Judge found that the confessions were voluntary and admissible. On appeal, in an extensive opinion by Proctor, J., the Supreme Court of New Jersey reversed. It rejected the State's argument that the constitutional safeguard of voluntariness governing the use of confessions does not apply in proceedings before the Juvenile Court. It pointed out that under New Jersey court rules, juveniles under the age of 16 accused of committing a homicide are tried in a proceeding which "has all of the appurtenances of a criminal trial," including participation by the county prosecutor, and requirements that the juvenile be provided with counsel, that a stenographic record be made, etc. It also pointed out that under New Jersey law, the confinement of the boys after reaching age 21 could be extended until they had served the maximum sentence which could have been imposed on an adult for such a homicide, here found to be second-degree murder carrying up to 30 years' imprisonment. The court concluded that the confessions were involuntary, stressing that the boys, contrary to statute, were placed in the police station and there interrogated; that the parents of both boys were not allowed to see them while they were being interrogated; that inconsistencies appeared among the various statements of the boys and with the objective evidence of the crime; and that there were protracted periods of questioning. The court noted the State's contention that both boys were advised of their constitutional rights before they made their statements, but it held that this should not be given "significant weight in our determination of voluntariness." Accordingly, the judgment of the Juvenile Court was reversed.

In a recent case before the Juvenile Court of the District of Columbia, Judge Ketcham rejected the proffer of evidence as to oral statements made at police headquarters by four juveniles who had been taken into custody for alleged involvement in an assault and attempted robbery. *In the Matter of Four Youths,* Nos. 28—776—J, 28—778—J, 28—783—J, 28—859—J, Juvenile Court of the District of Columbia, April 7, 1961. The court explicitly stated that it did not rest its decision on a showing that the statements were involuntary, but because they were untrustworthy. Judge Ketcham said:

> "Simply stated, the Court's decision in this case rests upon the considered opinion—after nearly four busy years on the Juvenile Court bench during which the testimony of thousands of such juveniles has been heard—that the statements of adolescents under 18 years of age who are arrested and charged with violations of law are frequently untrustworthy and often distort the truth."

We conclude that the constitutional privilege against self-incrimination is applicable in the case of juveniles as it is with respect to adults. We appreciate that special problems may arise with respect to waiver of the privilege by or on behalf of children, and that there may well be some differences in technique—but not in principle—depending upon the age of the child and the presence and competence of parents. The participation of counsel will, of course, assist the police, juvenile courts and appellate tribunals in administering the privilege. If counsel was not present for some permissible reason when an admission was obtained, the greatest care must be taken to assure that the admission was voluntary, in the sense not only that it was not coerced or suggested, but also that it was not the product of ignorance of rights or of adolescent fantasy, fright or despair.

The "confession" of Gerald Gault was first obtained by Officer Flagg, out of the presence of Gerald's parents, without counsel and without advising him of his right to silence, as far as appears. The judgment of the Juvenile Court was stated by the judge to be based on Gerald's admissions in court. Neither "admission" was reduced to writing, and, to say the least, the process by which the "admissions," were obtained and received must be characterized as lacking the certainty and order which are required of proceedings of such formidable consequences. Apart from the "admission," there was nothing upon which a judgment or finding might be based. There was no sworn testimony. Mrs. Cook, the complainant, was not present. The Arizona Supreme Court held that "sworn testimony must be required of all witnesses including police officers, probation officers and others who are part of or officially related to the juvenile court structure." We hold that this is not enough. No reason is suggested or appears for a different rule in respect of sworn testimony in juvenile courts than in adult tribunals. Absent a valid confession adequate to support the determination of the Juvenile Court, confrontation and sworn testimony by witnesses available for cross-examination were essential for a finding of "delinquency" and an order committing Gerald to a state institution for a maximum of six years.

The recommendations in the Children's Bureau's "Standards for Juvenile and Family Courts" are in general accord with our conclusions. They state that testimony should be under oath and that only competent, material and relevant evidence under rules applicable to civil cases should be admitted in evidence. The New York Family Court Act contains a similar provision.

As we said in *Kent v. United States,* 383 U.S. 541, 554, 86 S.Ct. 1045, 1053, 16 L.Ed.2d 84 (1966), with respect to waiver proceedings, "there is no place in our system of law for reaching a result of such tremendous consequences without ceremony. . . ." We now hold that, absent a valid confession, a determination of delinquency and an order of commitment to a state institution cannot be sustained in the absence of sworn testimony subjected to the opportunity for cross-examination in accordance with our law and constitutional requirements.

VI. Appellate Review and Transcript of Proceedings Appellants urge that the Arizona statute is unconstitutional under the Due Process Clause because, as construed by its Supreme Court, "there is no right of appeal from a juvenile court order. . . ." The court held that there is no right to a transcript because there is no right to appeal and because the proceedings are confidential and any record must be destroyed after a prescribed period of time. Whether a transcript or other recording is made, it held, is a matter for the discretion of the juvenile court.

This Court has not held that a State is required by the Federal Constitution "to provide appellate courts or a right to appellate review at all." In view of the fact that we must reverse the Supreme Court of Arizona's affirmance of the dismissal of the writ of habeas corpus for other reasons, we need not rule on this question in the present case or upon the failure to provide a transcript or recording of the hearings—or, indeed, the failure of the Juvenile Judge to state the grounds for his conclusion. Cf. *Kent v. United States,* supra, 383 U.S., at 561, 86 S.Ct., at 1057, where we said, in the context of a decision of the juvenile court waiving jurisdiction to the adult court, which by local law, was permissible: ". . . it is incumbent upon the Juvenile Court to accompany its waiver order with a statement of the reasons or considerations therefor." As the present case illustrates, the consequences of failure to provide an appeal, to record the proceedings, or to make findings or state the grounds for the juvenile court's conclusion may be to throw a burden upon the machinery for habeas corpus, to saddle the reviewing process with the burden of attempting to reconstruct a record, and to impose upon the Juvenile Judge the unseemly duty of testifying under cross-examination as to the events that transpired in the hearings before him.

For the reasons stated, the judgment of the Supreme Court of Arizona is reversed and the cause remanded for further proceedings not inconsistent with this opinion. It is so ordered.

Judgment reversed and cause remanded with directions.

Name and Court Case Index

Cohen, A. W., 46
Cohn, A. W., 19
Coker v. Georgia, 237
Cole, G. F., 37, 44–45, 47, 59
Colquhoun, P., 94
Commission Update, 121
Commonwealth v. Ritter, 215
Commonwealth v. Welansky, 80
Conklin, J. E., 154
Conrad, J. J., 75, 266
Cooper v. Pate, 239, 241, 246–47
Cotton, W. L., 46
Cox, S., 154
Cox, S. M., 18, 32, 105, 266
Cressey, D. R., 193
Criminal Justice Newsletter, 46, 238
Critchley, T. A., 104
Cromwell, P. F., 45–46
Cullen, F. T., 266
Cullen, J. B., 266
Cumming, E., 104
Cumming, I., 104
Curran, D. A., 59
Curtis, C. P., 155
Cutshall, C. R., 155

Dabney v. State, 79
Dahrendorf, R., 32
Davis, E. E., 31, 104
Davis, E. M., 96
Davis, F. J., 31, 104
Davis, K. C., 49, 58–60, 105
Davis, R. C., 204, 208
del Carmen, R. V., 33
Dieckman, D., 104, 121
Dienes, C. T., 59
Downie, L., 136
Draper v. United States, 104
DuBow, F. L., 204, 207
Duncan v. Louisiana, 179–80, 192–93
Durkheim, E., 32
Duster, T., 91–92

Edelhertz, H., 91, 207
Edell, L., 104
Ehrlich, E., 24, 32
Ehrmann, H. W., 18, 31–33
Eitzen, D. S., 92
Ekland-Olson, S., 155
Empey, L. T., 247
Ennis, P. H., 18, 46, 59, 79, 105
Escobedo v. Illinois, 18, 105
Eskridge, C. W., 155

Fairchild, E. S., 19
Faust, F. L., 265
Ferdinand, T. N., 266
Ferguson, R. F., 122
Ferri, E., 202
Fishman, J. F., 229, 237
Fitzgerald, J. D., 32, 105
Fleming, M., 206
Flynn, E. E., 229, 237

Foley, L. A., 155
Formby, W. A., 19
Foster, H. H., 31, 104
Fox, V., 40, 45, 238
Fraley, P. K., 122
Frank, J., 137
Frazier, C. E., 148, 155
Fry, M., 202
Furman v. Georgia, 218, 225, 236

Gagnon v. Scarpelli, 243, 247
Galaway, B., 207
Gamage, A. L., 79–80
Gannon, F., 91
Gardiner, J. A., 84, 91
Garofalo, R., 202
Gault, G., 251, 266
Geis, G., 18, 88, 91–92, 207
Gibbs, J. D., 236
Gifis, S., 59
Gilmore, G., 219
Glaser, D., 18, 24, 32, 80, 231, 238
Glasser v. United States, 183, 193
Goffman, E., 232, 238
Golden, K. M., 121, 266
Goldfarb, R., 230, 237–38
Goldstein, A. S., 204, 207
Goldstein, J., 58–59
Gordon, C. W., 216, 236
Gordon, M. S., 266
Gray, T. C., 104–5, 115, 121
Greene, B., 155
Gregg v. Georgia, 219, 225, 236–37
Greylords, 18

Hagan, J., 47
Hans, V. P., 193
Haskell, M. R., 266
Hawkins, G., 104
Hemphill, C. F., 79–80
Herman, R. D., 92
Hoebel, E. A., 31–32
Hogarth, J., 193
Holmes, 251, 266
Holmes, O. W., 24, 32
Holt v. Sarver, 241, 247
Holten, G., 154
Hoover, L. T., 122
Hotchkiss, S., 79
Howard, J., 211–13

Ianni, F., 92
Ianni, F. A. J., 92
Illinois Criminal Procedure for 1980,
  1986, 79
Inbau, F. E., 80
Inmates of Suffolk County Jail v.
  Eisenstadt, 238
Irwin, J., 238
Israel, J. H., 79, 105

Jacob, H., 193
Jacobs, J., 91, 238
Jacoby, J. E., 155
James, H., 60, 136
Johnson v. Louisiana, 187, 193
Jones, J., 59
Jones, M. E., 154
Jones v. State, 33
Jones v. United States, 104
Journal of American Judicial Society,
  154
Jurek v. Texas, 225, 237
Justice Assistance News, 207

Kadane, J. B., 237
Kalvan, H., 193
Kamisar, Y., 105
Karman, A., 208
Kasak, R. J., 207
Kelling, G. L., 104, 121
Kelly, T. V., 120
Kent v. United States, 263, 266
Kerper, H. B., 45–46, 79
Kerstetter, W. A., 60
Khan v. Carlson, 241, 247
Killinger, G. C., 45–46
Kinsie, P. M., 91
Kirkham, G., 105
Klopfer v. Carolina, 177, 192
Koenig, D., 206, 208

L. E. A. A., Newsletter, 121
LaFave, W. R., 80, 105
Laswell, H., 45
Latessa, E. J., 155
Law Enforcement News, 46
Lefstein, N., 46
Lehman, W., 144, 154–55
Lewis, C. S., 236
Lewis, P. W., 193
Livingston, E., 219

McClaren, R. C., 121
McDonald, W., 206–7
McKelvey, B., 238
MacNamara, D. E., 199, 207
Malinowsky, B., 32
Manning, P. K., 120
Mapp v. Ohio, 18
Marbury v. Madison, 132, 136
Martinson, R., 232, 238, 247
Meacham v. Fano, 242, 247
Meier, R. F., 88, 91–92
Mempa v. Rhay, 247
Menninger, K., 236
Messinger, S., 232, 238
Meyer, F. A., 32, 36, 39, 45–47
Milton, C. A., 120
Miranda v. Arizona, 18, 197
Moenssens, A. A., 80
Moll, W. L., 32
Montaye v. Haymes, 242, 247

Subject Index

Prima facie case, 157, 165, 172
Prison education and training, 233
Prison society, 231–32
Prisoners' rights, 235–42
Private prisons, 234
Probable cause, 157–58, 172
Probation, 40, 239, 242–43, 246, 260
Probation officer, 139, 150, 153, 262
Probationary officer, 107, 118, 119
Procedural law, 21, 25, 31
Prosecutor, 37–39, 139–48, 153
Prosecutorial discretion, 53–54, 141–43
Prostitution, 81, 83, 90
Public, 1, 11, 17
Public defender, 139, 143–48, 153
Public discretion, 50

Rape, 61, 67–69, 78
Real evidence, 177, 185, 191
Recidivism, 209, 231, 234
Recross examination, 177, 185, 191
Redirect examination, 177, 185, 191
Rehabilitation, 216, 233
Rehnquist Court, 40
Reformatories, 214–15
Release on recognizance, 157, 162, 172
Research and change in police organizations, 110–13
Retribution, 209, 215, 234
Revenge, 215
Revocation hearing, 243, 260
Robbery, 61, 69–70, 78
Roman law, 29

Sanctions, 21, 23
Second degree murder, 65
Selective enforcement, 49, 51, 57
Self-report studies, 61, 76–77, 78
Sentencing, 188–89
Sequester, 177, 188, 191
Sixth Amendment, 29, 158, 167–68, 177
Social background investigation, 256
Social control, 93, 103
Sodomy, 61, 67–69, 78
Specific deterrence, 209, 215–16, 234
Speedy trial, 12, 14, 30, 123, 132–33, 135, 177–78, 191
Split patrol, 107, 111–12, 119
Stare decisis, 123, 126, 135
State court systems, 127–30
State prisons, 226–27
State's attorney. *See* Prosecutor
Status offenses, 249, 252, 264
Statutory law, 21, 25, 31, 61–62, 77
Statutory rape, 69
Streetcorner/stationhouse adjustments, 249, 254, 264
Subpoena, 195, 203, 205
Substantive law, 21, 25, 30
Suicide, 61, 64, 77
Summary trial, 177, 180–81, 191
Summerian Code, 210
Supreme courts, 123, 129–30, 135

Targeted patrol, 107, 111–12, 119
Team policing. *See* Neighborhood policing
Ten Commandments, 29
Territorial jealousy, 1, 8, 17

Testimonial evidence, 177, 185, 191
Theft, 61, 70–71, 78
Total institution, 209, 232, 234
Transportation, 209–210, 234
Trial courts, 123, 128–29, 135

Uniform Crime Reports, 61, 73–75, 78
United States Supreme Court, 39, 55, 131–32, 166, 168, 170, 183, 251, 256
Unofficial probation, 1, 13, 17

Venire, 177, 181, 191
Venue, 123, 126, 135
Vera Foundation, 161
Victim compensation, 195, 198, 200–203, 205
Victim restitution, 195, 198–203, 205
Victim survey research, 61, 76, 78
Victim's Bill of Rights, 203–4
Voire dire, 177, 181–83, 191
Voluntary manslaughter, 65–66

Waiver of jurisdiction, 249, 263, 264
Walnut Street Jail, 209, 213–14, 234
Ward of the state, 249, 256, 264
Warehousing, 209, 232, 234, 260
Warren Court, 40
White-collar crime, 81, 85–87, 90
Workhouses, 210–11
Writ of certiorari, 123, 131, 135